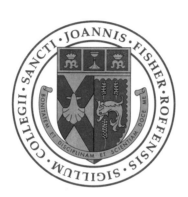

Leading and Managing People in the Dynamic Organization

LEA'S ORGANIZATION AND MANAGEMENT SERIES

Ashforth (Au.): *Role Transitions in Organizational Life: An Identity-Based Perspective*

Bartunek (Au.): *Organizational and Educational Change: The Life and Role of a Change Agent Group*

Beach (Ed.): *Image Theory: Theoretical and Empirical Foundations*

Brett/Drasgow (Eds.): *The Psychology of Work: Theoretically Based Empirical Research*

Darley/Messick/Tyler (Eds.): *Social Influences on Ethical Behavior in Organizations*

Denison (Ed.): *Managing Organizational Change in Transition Economies*

Earley/Gibson (Aus.): *Multinational Work Teams: A New Perspective*

Garud/Karnoe (Eds.): *Path Dependence and Creation*

Lant/Shapira (Eds.): *Organizational Cognition: Computation and Interpretation*

Lord/Brown (Aus.): *Leadership Processes and Follower Self-Identity*

Margolis/Walsh (Aus.): *People and Profits? The Search Between a Company's Social and Financial Performance*

Pearce (Au.): *Organization and Management in the Embrace of the Government*

Peterson/Mannix (Eds.): *Leading and Managing People in the Dynamic Organization*

Riggio/Murphy/Pirozzolo (Eds.): *Multiple Intelligences and Leadership*

Thompson/Levine/Messick (Eds.): *Shared Cognition in Organizations: The Management of Knowledge*

Leading and Managing People in the Dynamic Organization

Edited by

Randall S. Peterson
London Business School

Elizabeth A. Mannix
Cornell University

LEA LAWRENCE ERLBAUM ASSOCIATES, PUBLISHERS
2003 Mahwah, New Jersey
London

Lawrence Erlbaum Associates, Inc., Publishers
10 Industrial Avenue
Mahwah, NJ 07430

Cover design by Kathryn Houghtaling Lacey

Library of Congress Cataloging-in-Publication Data

Leading and managing people in the dynamic organization /
edited by Randall S. Peterson, Elizabeth A. Mannix
    p.   cm.
Includes bibliographical references and index.
ISBN 0-8058-4362-0
    1. Organizational behavior. 2. Management. 3. Supervision of employees.
I. Peterson, Randall S. II. Mannix, Elizabeth A., 1960–
HD58.7 .L397 2003
658.4'092—dc21   2002192700

Books published by Lawrence Erlbaum Associates are printed on acid-free paper,
and their bindings are chosen for strength and durability.

Printed in the United States of America
10 9 8 7 6 5 4 3 2 1

Contents

Series Foreword   vii
Arthur P. Brief and James P. Walsh

Acknowledgments   ix

Part I: Introduction to Leading and Managing People in the Dynamic Organization

1   Introduction: Leading and Managing People in the Dynamic Organization   3
Elizabeth A. Mannix and Randall S. Peterson

2   Dynamic Organizations: Achieving Marketplace and Organizational Agility With People   7
Lee Dyer and Richard Shafer

Part II: Managing the People in the Dynamic Organization

3   Staffing the Dynamic Organization: Rethinking Selection and Motivation in the Context of Continuous Change   41
D. Brent Smith and Marcus W. Dickson

4   Virtual Processes: Implications for Coaching the Virtual Team   65
Ruth Wageman

5   The Role of Subcultures in Agile Organizations   87
Alicia Boisnier and Jennifer A. Chatman

Part III: Managing Information Flow in the Dynamic Organization

6   Managing Teams in the Dynamic Organization: The Effects of Revolving Membership and Changing Task Demands on Expertise and Status in Groups   115
Melissa C. Thomas-Hunt and Katherine W. Phillips

7   Transactive Memory in Dynamic Organizations   135
Richard L. Moreland and Linda Argote

8   Integrative Interests? Building a Bridge Between Negotiation   163
     Research and the Dynamic Organization
     Kathleen M. O'Connor and Wendi L. Adair

Part IV: Leadership in the Dynamic Organization

9   Leadership, Learning, Ambiguity, and Uncertainty   185
     and Their Significance to Dynamic Organizations
     Philip V. Hodgson and Randall P. White

10   Real Options Reasoning and the Dynamic Organization: 201
     Strategic Insights from the Biological Analogy
     Rita Gunther McGrath and Max Boisot

11   Organization Design: A Network View   227
     N. Anand and Brittany C. Jones

Part V: Conclusions

12   Emerging Themes From a New Paradigm   253
     Randall S. Peterson and Ana C. Sancovich

Author Index   263

Subject Index   275

Series Foreword

Arthur P. Brief
Tulane University

James P. Walsh
University of Michigan

Randall Peterson and Elizabeth Mannix are to be commended for putting together a superb collection of essays on dynamic organizations. The book pushes interest in organizations that are in constant flux off the airport bookstand and into the scholar's office. Because our series is about publishing books that will generate research, we could not be more pleased that Peterson and Mannix have joined us. Probably what impressed us most about the book was an observation made in the last chapter that allowed us to make sense out of the previous eleven chapters as a unified body of work. The authors of the last chapter noted that scholars viewing dynamic organizations through quite different lenses (e.g., social psychology, industrial psychology, and strategic management) all reached the same conclusion: "the need to embrace paradox"—to be agile and flexible while maintaining stability and cohesion. What a challenge, for managers to do and for scholars to understand.

Acknowledgments

The chapters in this book were presented at a conference titled "Understanding the Dynamic Organization," held at Cornell's Johnson Graduate School of Management in March of 2001. The conference was designed to bring together a diverse group of scholars and challenge them to think about how to lead and manage in fast-changing and unpredictable environments. We asked them to think about what current research suggests, to theorize about possible relationships, and generally to provide direction for theorists and researchers whose work encompasses the dynamic context. We think they rose to this challenge, and we thank them for excellent scholarly work.

We gratefully acknowledge our sponsors, the Center for Leadership in Dynamic Organizations at the Johnson School, especially including Harvey Benenson for generously providing initial funding for the conference and the Center, and Deans Bob Swieringa and John Elliott for support of the conference. Richard Shafer was instrumental in getting the conference off the ground, and both he and Lee Dyer provided invaluable intellectual advice on conceptualizing the dynamic organization. We also thank Rhonda Velazquez for excellent assistance in coordination of the conference. And finally we thank Ana Sancovich for superb administrative and editorial assistance. We are indebted to Ana for editing all of the manuscripts and organizing the formal submission of the book.

—*Randall S. Peterson*
—*Beta Mannix*

I

INTRODUCTION TO LEADING AND MANAGING PEOPLE IN THE DYNAMIC ORGANIZATION

1

Introduction:
Leading and Managing People
in the Dynamic Organization

Elizabeth A. Mannix
Cornell University

Randall S. Peterson
London Business School

This volume is the result of the first event sponsored by Cornell University's Center for Leadership in Dynamic Organizations (CLDO). The Center's mission is to understand the unique form of leadership found in continuously changing, agile, dynamic organizations. Our goal is to be a catalyst, drawing the parties at the cutting edge of practice and research together. We hope to be a repository for the latest thinking and knowledge, and also work to actively promote organizational action, testing the limits of the new models and facilitating their application.

In March of 2001 we launched the CLDO with an event called *Leadership Week*. For 6 days we drew on the talents and expertise of faculty, corporate executives, and student leaders to examine the challenges of leadership in a rapidly changing and dynamic business environment. The week was divided into three components. The *Corporate Conference* focused on what innovative companies were doing to launch more agile and adaptive business models. The *Graduate Business Conference* brought together more than 150 MBA student leaders from 30 business schools to examine issues of 21st century leadership. Finally, and the focus of this volume, the *Academic Symposium* brought together more than 50 scholars from universities around the world to focus on the attributes and practices required for leaders in dynamic organizations.

From the very beginning the Academic Symposium—aptly titled "Understanding the Dynamic Organization"—was meant to be a learning experience for all involved. We began with a few assumptions to frame the conference. First, most organizations are faced with more external uncertainty than ever before. Ever-expanding global competition, fast-paced technologies, erratic economic fluctuations, unpredictable political instability—these factors have created an increasingly dynamic business environment. This brings us to our second assumption: In order to be successful, individuals within these organizations must be equipped to cope with an unpredictable marketplace and chaotic change. This requires leadership capabilities focused on leading and managing organizations that are in constant flux, facing new challenges that require new solutions virtually every day. As such, today's managers and leaders must be fast and flexible problem solvers, able to mobilize others to diagnose problems, process data, generate effective solutions, and marshal the resources necessary to implement those solutions quickly and efficiently.

Our focus in this volume is primarily on understanding the *people* within the dynamic organization. In researching the background for this conference, however, we found that most of the work on organizational agility has focused either on strategy (e.g., Brown & Eisenhardt, 1998), or on organizational structure and design (e.g., Ashkenas, Ulrich, Jick, & Kerr, 1995). Micro- and mesolevel scholars have not focused on the potential impact of organizational agility for their models of human behavior and interaction. As such, we had to ask several of our contributors to stretch past their current areas of expertise. We asked experts in fields such as motivation, learning, and negotiation to rethink their current models of organizational behavior and to consider a world in which organizations are forced to be dynamic, kinetic, and even without boundaries. If there is no longer a "steady-state" for organizations operating in a dynamic marketplace, what does that mean for our current models of organizational behavior? For example, the current reality of dispersed workgroups makes it impossible to rely on traditional theories of team dynamics. Even classic notions such as Lewin's unfreeze→change→refreeze model of organizational change may no longer be useful when change is constant.

We applaud our contributors for being eager and willing to take on this challenge. Of course, in order to understand people within the dynamic organization, it is necessary to have a contextual framework. In the last decade or so, several scholars (as well as practitioners) have written about the characteristics of a more dynamic organizational form. Senge was perhaps the most celebrated advocate of the "learning organization" (Senge, 1990), whereas others described the kinetic organization (Fradette & Michaud, 1998); the boundaryless organization (Ashkenas et al., 1995); the adaptive organization (Fulmer, 2000; Haeckel, 1999); and the flexible firm (Volberda, 1998). These models vary in their specifics, but all tend to build on concepts from complexity theory (Maguire & McKelvey, 1999) and generally view organizations as organic systems (Burns & Stalker, 1961) capable of holding their own in dynamic or hypercompetitive markets (D'Aveni, 1994; Brown & Eisenhardt, 1998). For this conference we drew on our resident experts on organizational agility, Lee Dyer and Richard Shafer, to guide us (Dyer & Shafer, 1999).

Dyer and Shafer (1999; chapter 2, this volume) have specified a new organizational paradigm for dynamic organizations (also called agile organizations) that views organizational adaptation as a continuous process. Dynamic organizations strive to develop the capability to shift, flex, and adapt "as a matter of course" (Dyer & Shafer, 1999, p. 148). The goal is to keep internal operations at a level of diversity and flexibility that matches the degree of turmoil in the external environment—a principle known as *requisite variety* (Morgan, 1997; see also McGrath & Boisot, chapter 10, this volume).

In Dyer and Shafer's model, organizations are characterized by high levels of direction, stability, and order, while simultaneously exhibiting high amounts of experimentation, discovery, and flexibility. Some firms that exhibit this seemingly contradictory set of attributes include HP, ABB, Nike, and 3M. How do they combine order and chaos in a way that optimizes both? Dyer and Shafer suggest that at least three strategic capabilities might be necessary: (a) the ability to continuously scan the external environment, locate and analyze emerging developments, and quickly turn the resulting information into actionable decisions; (b) the capacity to quickly and easily make decisions and, more important, move resources from where they are to where they need to be to activate these decisions; and (c) the ability to create, adapt, and use information and knowledge to not only improve current operations, but also constantly challenge current ways of thinking and operating.

Clearly, these capabilities have implications for the way in which organizations are designed (e.g., Anand & Jones, chapter 11, this volume), but they also have implications for the skills, abilities, and values that people bring to those organizations (e.g., Thomas-Hunt & Phillips, chapter 6, this volume), as well as how they interact with one another (e.g, Wageman, chapter 4, this volume). Given the relatively new ground on which we are treading, our contributors took some different components of the dynamic organization to emphasize. For example, Smith and Dickson (chapter 3) focus at the intersection of person–organization fit by asking "What kind of person can survive and thrive in a dynamic environment?" Boisnier and Chatman (chapter 5) look at another multiple-level interaction—the impact of subcultures on an organization's ability to adapt and change. By contrast, Hodgson and White (chapter 9) emphasize the demands of the dynamic environment by examining how learning is affected by ambiguity and uncertainty. In addition, some of our contributors focus on the potential benefits of the dynamic organization (e.g., O'Connor & Adair, chapter 8), whereas others emphasize the potential detriments (e.g., Moreland & Argote, chapter 7). These different takes on the dynamic organization reflect the state of this relatively new paradigm. Because we viewed this as a learning experience, and also as a "stretch assignment," we also asked authors to do a fair amount of speculation. They have included many testable ideas, research propositions, agendas, hypotheses, and even full models that might be explored. We believe that scholars urgently need to understand the implications of this new business environment for supporting dynamic and agile organizations. The area is ripe for exploration. Our hope is that this volume is able to stretch readers' minds and fill them with ideas for proceeding with new and stimulating research on this exciting topic.

REFERENCES

Ashkenas, R., Ulrich, D., Jick, T., & Kerr, S. (1995). *The boundaryless organization*. San Francisco: Jossey-Bass.

Brown, S., & Eisenhardt, K. (1998). *Competing on the edge: Strategy as structured chaos*. Boston: Harvard Business School Press.

Burns, T., & Stalker, G. (1961). *The management of innovation*. London: Tavistock.

D'Aveni, R. (1994). *Hyper-competition: Managing the dynamics of strategic maneuvering*. New York: Free Press.

Dyer, L., & Shafer, R.(1999). From human resource strategy to organizational effectiveness: Lessons from research on organizational agility. In P. Wright, L. Dyer, J. B. Boudreau, & G. Milkovich (Eds.), *Strategic human resources management research in the 21st century, research in personnel and human resource management* (pp. 145–174). Stamford, CT: JAI Press.

Fradette, M., & Michaud, S. (1998). *The power of corporate kinetics*. New York: Simon & Schuster.

Fulmer, W. E. (2000). *Shaping the adaptive organization*. New York: AMACOM.

Haeckel, S. (1999). *Adaptive enterprise*. Boston: Harvard Business School Press.

Maguire, S., & McKelvey, B (1999). Complexity and management: Moving from fad to firm foundations. *Emergence, 1*(2), 19–61.

Morgan, G. (1997). *Images of organization* (2nd ed.). Thousand Oaks, CA: Sage.

Senge, P. M. (1990). *The fifth discipline*. New York: Currency Doubleday.

Volberda, H. (1998). *Building the flexible firm*. Oxford, UK: Oxford University Press.

2

Dynamic Organizations: Achieving Marketplace and Organizational Agility With People

Lee Dyer
Richard Shafer
Cornell University

Driven by dynamic competitive conditions, an increasing number of firms are experimenting with new, and what they hope will be more dynamic, organizational forms. This development has opened up exciting theoretical and empirical venues for students of leadership, business strategy, organizational theory, and the like. One domain that has yet to catch the wave, however, is strategic human resource management. In an effort to catch up, we here draw on the dynamic organization and human resource strategy literatures to delineate both a process for uncovering and the key features of a carefully crafted human resources strategy for dynamic organizations. The logic is as follows. Dynamic organizations compete through marketplace agility. Marketplace agility requires that employees at all levels engage in proactive, adaptive, and generative behaviors, bolstered by a supportive mindset. Under the right conditions, the essential mindset and behaviors, although highly dynamic, are fostered by a human resources strategy centered on a relatively small number of dialectical, yet paradoxically stable, guiding principles and anchored in a supportive organizational infrastructure. This line of reasoning, however, rests on a rather modest empirical base and, thus, is offered less as a definitive statement than as a spur for much needed additional research.

Increasingly, firms find themselves, either by design or circumstances, operating in business environments fraught with unprecedented, unparalleled, unrelenting, and largely unpredictable change. For them, competitiveness is a moving target. In this rough and tumble world, many stumble and a few fall, often because the rate of change in their marketplaces outpaces their organizational

7

capacity to keep up (Foster & Kaplan, 2001). Naturally enough, this has led a number of firms to experiment with new, and what they hope will be more dynamic, organizational forms. This, in turn, has opened up exciting new theoretical and empirical venues for students of leadership, business strategy, organizational theory, and the like (Child & McGrath, 2001). One domain that has yet to catch the wave, however, is that of strategic human resources management.

Strategic human resources management is concerned with the contributions that human resource strategies make to organizational effectiveness, and the ways in which these contributions are achieved. A fundamental, although not universally accepted, tenet of the field stems from the resource-based view of the firm (Barney, 1991). As adapted, it postulates that a carefully crafted human resources strategy can be, or at least can result in, a source of sustainable competitive advantage in the marketplace. The phrase carefully crafted here refers to a human resources strategy that successfully engenders a pool of highly motivated and uniquely capable people who individually and collectively use this drive and talent to build and deploy organizational capabilities in ways that competitors cannot easily replicate or obviate (Wright, Dunford, & Snell, 2001). This intuitively appealing and deceptively simple notion raises a number of very thorny conceptual and empirical issues that, as we shall see, have been addressed in a variety of ways.

The resource-based view implies, for example, that a human resources strategy must be tailored to the particulars of the context in which it is embedded (the so-called contingency perspective) because presumably a more generic approach (the so-called universalistic or best practice perspective) would at best produce only parity with other firms. But there is a question as to just how specific, or tailored, this fit needs to be. Here, we take a middle ground by assuming that there is a human resources strategy that is particularly appropriate for dynamic organizations in general, while realizing that any particular dynamic organization would find it necessary to tailor the specifics, or perhaps fine-tune the administration, of this human resources strategy to its own unique circumstances. With this in mind, our purpose here is to draw on the broader dynamic organization and human resources strategy literatures, including some of our own research, to delineate both a process for uncovering, and the key features of, a carefully crafted human resources strategy especially suited to dynamic organizations. Before getting into the heart of the analysis, though, it is necessary, first, to clarify the concept of dynamic organizations that we adopt (as there are many) and, then, to draw selectively from extant human resources strategy theory and research to put this effort in perspective.

A PERSPECTIVE
ON DYNAMIC ORGANIZATIONS

Bureaucratic organizations epitomize continuity. Although they can and do change, they tend to do so reluctantly, incrementally or episodically, and only up to a point. Common responses to new competitive realities have taken the form of programmatic fixes—process reengineering, total quality management, cross-functional teams, employee involvement (or empowerment), and the like (Heckscher, 1994)—as well as seemingly endless rounds of restructuring that move the boxes around without disturbing the underlying structure. These stopgap measures, which are primarily aimed at helping firms improve what they already do, often help—for a while. But they fall short for firms operating in truly dynamic environments because what they need, as Fig. 2.1 suggests, is not so much to get better as it is to get different (Hamel, 2000).

This means exploring alternative organizational paradigms. The options are numerous and expanding. Here we focus on just one of the many possibilities, so-called dynamic organizations. But because this concept, like so many others, lacks definitional specificity, it is necessary to be a bit more precise. For our purposes, we use the term *dynamic organizations* to refer to firms specifically designed to be capable of surfing (Pascale, Millemann, & Gioja, 2000) or competing (Brown & Eisenhardt, 1998) on the "edge of chaos" (see Fig. 2.1). That is, we focus on organizations that deliberately seek to be infinitely innovative and adaptable in the marketplace by adopting loosely coupled organizational forms, referred to by Hock (1999) as "chaordic," that harmoniously blend characteristics of chaos, fluidity, and flexibility on the one hand with a modicum of order, control, and predictability on the other.

It is said that dynamic organizations embody paradox. This is certainly true in the sense that they consciously embrace opposites (chaos and order, change and stability, and so forth). What makes them appear particularly paradoxical, though, is the extent to which their key features are counterintuitive in a world imbued with traditional bureaucratic thinking.

ON STUDYING
HUMAN RESOURCE STRATEGY

As mentioned, strategic human resources management is concerned with both what human resources strategies contribute to organizational success and how they do so. Although theory has focused on both aspects, research has prima-

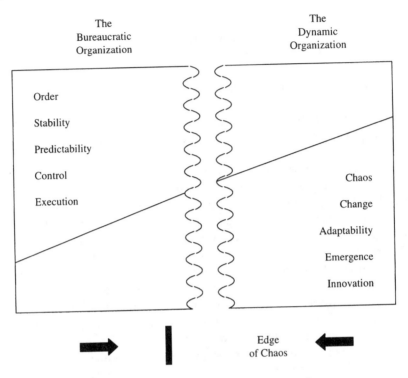

FIG. 2.1.   The dynamic organization: a new paradigm.

rily addressed the former. Most of this research takes the form of large-scale
survey studies in which various measures of firms' human resources strategies
have been statistically related to one or more measures of their financial performance (e.g., return on investment, return on assets, and stock value; for
recent reviews, see Boxall & Purcell, 2000, and Delery & Shaw, 2001). Although plagued by some rather serious theoretical and methodological short-
comings, collectively these studies have produced results credible and positive
enough to keep students of the field intrigued and pushing forward (Wright &
Gardner, in press).

Recently, attention shifted a bit from the what to the how; that is, to trying
to determine what goes on inside the so-called "black box" between human
resources strategy and firm financial performance (see the top of Fig. 2.2).
Many models purport to provide insights here (again, for recent reviews, see
Delery & Shaw, 2001, and Wright & Gardner, in press), as do a small number
of studies (e.g., Wright, McCormick, Sherman, & McMahan, 1999). The
present analysis builds on, and we hope contributes to, these efforts by digging
into dynamic organizations to deepen our understanding of the key variables

and relationships that comprise the "black box" in this particular context (Dyer & Shafer, 1999; Shafer, Dyer, Kilty, Amos, & Ericksen, 2001).

The general model that guides this effort is shown at the bottom of Fig. 2.2. The logic is as follows: (a) dynamic organizations compete, and thus make money, in turbulent marketplaces through marketplace agility; (b) dynamic organizations achieve marketplace agility through organizational agility, one element of which is human resources strategy; and (c) the mindset and behaviors of employees are key mediators between marketplace agility on the one hand and organizational agility on the other. This brings us to the fundamental proposition to be addressed by this line of inquiry:

Proposition 1: For dynamic organizations, the basic task of human resources strategy is to foster, in the context of other features of organizational agility, the employee mindset and behaviors required to achieve marketplace agility.

This logic subsumes positions on what are, in some cases, controversial issues in human resources strategy theory and research. It partially accepts, as

Prevalent

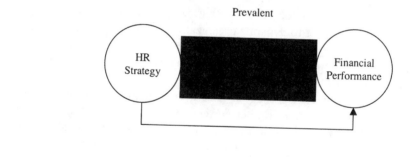

Proposed

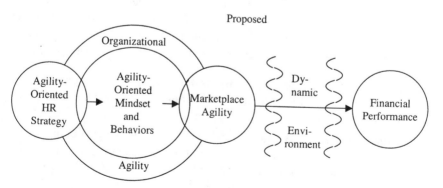

FIG. 2.2. Approaches to studying HR strategy.

indicated earlier, the so-called contingency perspective, which postulates the need to fit human resources strategies to firms' business strategies (here the pursuit of marketplace agility) for best business results; this concept, referred to as *vertical fit*, is one that is, at once, time-honored (Dyer, 1984) but not universally endorsed (e.g., Pfeffer, 1998). Our logic also implies that an agility-oriented human resources strategy consists of a bundle of components and, thus, works best (i.e., is most likely to foster the required employee mindset and behaviors) when these components are consistent with and reinforce one another or, in the lingo, are synergistic; this concept, known as *horizontal fit*, has also been around a long time (Dyer, 1984), but has proven to be an elusive one to pin down (Wright & Sherman, 1999). Furthermore, the model treats employee mindset and behaviors as key mediating variables between human resources strategy and marketplace agility, which again is a persistently popular, although not universally accepted, view among human resources strategy theorists and researchers (Cappelli & Singh, 1992; Schuler & Jackson, 1987; Wright & Gardner, in press). In addition, the model assumes that human resources strategy is but one element of organizational agility and that it is, ultimately, the entire context that fosters the required employee mindset and behaviors, a position not generally found in the human resources strategy literature (Boxall, 1999; Dyer & Shafer, 1999). Finally, and more broadly, our logic infers that, with respect to dynamic organizations, human resources strategy research should be conducted at the business unit level, rather than the more common corporate and plant levels because this is the point at which marketplace agility is manifest (Wright & Gardner, in press).

Obviously, the preceding suggests that it is premature to formulate hypotheses about these matters. Rather, current levels of understanding dictate a focus on exploratory research in the form of carefully selected, qualitatively oriented, intensive case studies to help identify and clarify the nature of the variables and relationships inherent in our general model (and, thus, eventually to guide survey studies as the number of dynamic organizations expands to the point where a decent sample can be identified). Procedurally, the model and logic dictate that these case studies focus on both (Wright & Dyer, 2000):

- Marketplace agility to better grasp its dynamics and imperatives and, especially, the specifics of the employee mindset and behaviors it requires to succeed.
- Organizational agility to ascertain how various components of human resources strategy interact with one another (i.e., achieve horizontal fit) and with other important elements of the organizational agility construct (i.e., a broader notion of horizontal fit) to foster the required employee mindset and behaviors (vertical fit).

In the sections that follow, we illustrate this research approach using data and examples drawn, or inferred, from the dynamic organization and human resources strategy literatures.

FROM MARKETPLACE AGILITY TO THE REQUIRED MINDSET AND BEHAVIORS

Figure 2.3 depicts the first half of our analytical journey, that from marketplace agility to the required mindset and behaviors. The research task here is to "peel the onion," to understand, first, how dynamic organizations compete in the marketplace and the organizational competencies this requires and, second, what it is that employees are required to believe and do if marketplace agility is to be achieved.

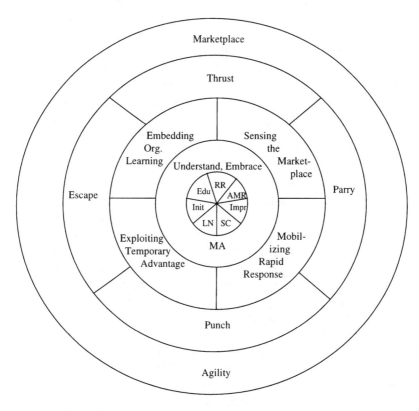

FIG. 2.3. From marketplace agility to the required mindset and behaviors.

Marketplace Agility and Organizational Competencies

Dynamic organizations thrive by being infinitely adaptable in the marketplace —preferably by inducing continuous change, but otherwise by swiftly reacting to disruptions generated by others. They strive to stay ahead of actual and would-be competitors by being consistently better and faster at spotting and exploiting potential opportunities, as well as at discerning and ducking emerging threats. They live, as Fig. 2.3 suggests, in an event-driven world characterized by endless, overlapping rounds of thrust, parry, punch, and escape (Fradette & Michaud, 1998). This involves constant and simultaneous (a) experimentation with ideas not only for new products and services, but also for potentially radical breakthroughs in basic business models (Hamel, 2000); (b) adjustments to often unanticipated curveballs tossed by customers, competitors, purveyors of new technologies, government regulators, and the like; (c) execution to deliver high quality products or services of value to a current customer base; and (d) withdrawals of products and services, and from partnerships and even businesses, when they are no longer delivering above-average returns (to free up resources for potentially more productive uses; Brown & Eisenhardt, 1998; Foster & Kaplan, 2001).

Competing in this manner is a tall order that obviously requires a unique set of organizational capabilities (Barney, 1991). Here the search is for routines or processes that, first, make it possible for dynamic organizations to attain and sustain the agile edge and, second, are primarily "people embodied competencies" (Hamel & Prahalad, 1994) that derive more from the mindset and behaviors of employees than, say, leading-edge technologies. Preliminarily, as shown in Fig. 2.3, we suggest there are four such organizational competencies: sensing the market, mobilizing rapid response, exploiting temporary advantage, and embedding organizational learning (Dyer & Shafer, 1999).

Sensing the market refers to the ability to scan external environments, locate and analyze emerging developments, and quickly turn the resulting information into actionable decisions (Mara & Scott-Morgan, 1996; Teece, Pisano, & Shuen, 1997). *Market* in this context refers not only to current and potential customers, but also to actual and would-be competitors and suppliers, as well as to broad developments and trends in demographics, lifestyles, technology, and public policy. Sensing the market is a people-embodied competency in dynamic organizations because employees at all levels, and not just so-called boundary spanners, are expected to keep their eyes and ears open for potentially useful tidbits of market intelligence and to bring such information in-house for dissemination, processing, and decision making by relevant parties.

Mobilizing rapid response, the second organizational competency, is defined as the capacity to quickly and easily make decisions, translate these decisions into action, and choreograph the essential transitions (Brown & Eisenhardt, 1998). In some cases, this may involve little more than coming up with and making relatively small-scale accommodations to evolving customer needs or competitors' initiatives. More often, though, it involves making major changes: adding, adjusting, or even cannibalizing products or services; scrapping tried and true business models to pursue newer, riskier versions; and totally revamping key business processes (Hamel, 2000). Either way, success depends in large part on the ease and speed with which resources—financial, physical, intangible (e.g., information), and, especially, human—can be moved from less to more promising opportunities.

Dynamic organizations must make money. Thus, amidst the ongoing innovation and adaptation, there is also the need to execute. This brings us to the third organizational competency, exploiting temporary advantage, which refers to the capacity to quickly and easily enter new markets and to deliver competitively priced products or services to these markets as long as, but not longer than, they remain the most attractive options on the horizon. The challenge here is to find ways to infuse dynamic organizations with centers of excellence that are necessarily countercultural in the sense that they must approach the chaos–order paradox from the latter rather than the former direction; to some extent, these centers of excellence serve as a force for relative stability in dynamic organizations. Some dynamic organizations seek to evade the "people embodied" component of this organizational competency (while lowering costs) by outsourcing all or some parts of it. Cisco Systems, for example, serves an ever-changing marketplace with a constantly evolving product line in part by outsourcing most of its manufacturing; orders are routed online directly to contract manufacturers who build and ship the products and process the billing without any involvement by Cisco employees (Serwer, 2000).

The fourth, and final, organizational competency is embedding organizational learning, which is the inherent capacity to constantly create, adapt, distribute, and apply knowledge (Grant, 1996; Levine, 2001; Nonaka, 1991). Learning, in this context, is of two types (Morgan, 1997). The first is so-called adaptive or single-loop, learning that is aimed at making continuous improvements in current operations. The second, referred to as generative or double-loop learning, requires employees at all levels to question all aspects of a business, up to and including its fundamental operating principles, core values, and even strategic direction and vision. Dynamic organizations, in particular, require generative or double-loop learning to avoid the formation of defensive routines, such as obfuscating problems and diluting bad news, that can quickly result in organizational ossification and the loss of marketplace agility (Argyris, 1985; Morgan, 1997).

Taken together, our model suggests that to pursue marketplace agility through these four organizational competencies requires that employees share an agility-oriented mindset and actively engage in agility-oriented behaviors.

Agility-Oriented Mindset and Behaviors

These topics have engaged a great deal of our time and attention. Some insights have emerged from the literature (e.g., Campbell, 2000). But, so far, with one exception (Shafer et al., 2001), we have had only limited success in the field, primarily because, quite surprisingly, firms seem seldom to think about these issues, at least explicitly. So what follows is, perhaps, the most speculative section of our analysis.

Agility-Oriented Mindset. A shared mindset exists when all employees perceive, think about, and value both organizational purposes and processes in a common way (Ulrich & Lake, 1990). In dynamic organizations, as the top of Table 2.1 shows, this means that every employee is required to fully understand and embrace the essentiality and essence of marketplace agility. Top to

TABLE 2.1
Agility-Oriented Mindset and Behaviors

EVERY EMPLOYEE MUST		
Understand and Embrace the Essentiality and Essence of Marketplace Agility		
Be Proactive	*Be Adaptive*	*Be Generative*
Initiate Actively search for opportunities to contribute to organizational success and take the lead in pursuing those that appear promising	*Assume Multiple Roles* Perform in multiple capacities across levels, projects, and organizational boundaries—often simultaneously	*Learn* Continuously pursue the attainment of proficiency in multiple competency areas, eschewing overspecialization and complacency
Improvise Devise and implement new and creative approaches to pursuing opportunities and dealing with threats	*Rapidly Redeploy* Move quickly from role to role *Spontaneously Collaborate* Engage often and easily with others with a singular focus on task accomplishment (and disengage just as easily when contribution is no longer needed)	*Educate* Actively participate in the sharing of information and knowledge through the organization, as well as with its partners and collaborators
Understand and Embrace the Essentiality and Essence of Organizational Agility		

bottom, everyone is expected to be able to credibly articulate: the realities of dynamic environments, approaches to competing successfully in such environments and the consequences thereof, and the nature and necessity of sensing the market, mobilizing rapid response, exploiting temporary advantage, and embedding organizational learning.

Proposition 2: If marketplace agility is to be achieved, all employees must fully understand and embrace its essentiality and essence.

Agility-Oriented Behaviors. Marketplace agility requires that top-level leaders serve as the primary (but not the only) custodians of a firm's broad strategic direction and domain, but not as the only progenitors of these. In Hamel's (2000) words, "top management's job isn't to build strategies. Its job is to build an organization that can continually spawn cool new business concepts, to design context rather than invent content" (p. 244). Then, within this context, the remaining leaders—everyone is a leader, as well as a peer and a follower, at one time or another in dynamic organizations—are, in the broadest terms, required to do whatever it takes to attain marketplace agility.

More specifically, as Table 2.1 shows, fostering marketplace agility requires that employees at all levels be proactive, adaptive, and generative:

• Employees who are proactive **initiate** and **improvise.** They continually and actively search for marketplace opportunities and threats and set in motion whatever actions appear necessary to pursue the former and mitigate the effects of the latter. Furthermore, they generate these ongoing modifications quickly, striving to reduce the time between discovery and execution close to zero (Weick & Quinn, 1999), but also creatively, relying on previously utilized procedures only when they are clearly appropriate (Weick, 1998).

• Adaptive employees **assume multiple roles;** that is, they perform in multiple capacities—leader, major team member, minor team member, and individual contributor—across projects and even external organizational boundaries, sometimes serially, but often simultaneously. Furthermore, they **rapidly redeploy** across these roles with a minimum of wasted time and effort, so that help happens when it needs to happen. And, once in new roles, they **spontaneously collaborate** by actively engaging with colleagues around the task at hand, rather than getting caught up in the peripheral or disruptive activities that so often waste valuable team time.

• Generative employees simultaneously **learn** and **educate.** They continuously pursue the attainment of proficiency in multiple competency domains, while avoiding the temptations of either overspecialization or complacency. To this end, they also take responsibility for each other's learning by openly sharing information and knowledge with colleagues within their own, as well as partner, organizations.

Proposition 3: If marketplace agility is to be achieved, all employees must continuously and proficiently demonstrate the full range of proactive, adaptive, and generative behaviors.

Proposition 4: To achieve marketplace agility requires that all employees both internalize an agility-oriented mindset and manifest agility-oriented behaviors. The former without the latter generates no output; the latter without the former engenders considerable misdirected activity.

If these are the mindset and behaviors required to achieve marketplace agility, how can and do dynamic organizations bring them about?

USING ORGANIZATIONAL AGILITY TO ACHIEVE THE REQUIRED MINDSET AND BEHAVIORS

The second half of our analytical journey is depicted in Fig. 2.4. The starting points, indicated by the two outer rings of the "onion," are the requisite employee mindset and behaviors. The challenge is to delineate a parsimonious set of factors that foster these. One way to go about this is to apply force field analysis (Lewin, 1951); that is, by undertaking a systematic search for conditions or activities that, on the one hand, nurture or, on the other, hinder the development or manifestation of the desired mindset and behaviors. (Hindering factors can be illuminating; in one business unit we studied, for example, the vice president was adamant about the need for employees to take "smart risks" [in our parlance, to improvise] and highly concerned that few were doing so. During interviews with those deeper in the organization, several people cited examples of colleagues who had "stuck their necks out only to have them chopped off," which of course highlighted the agility-hindering effects of the unit's appraisal and reward systems.)

Our model, as Fig. 2.4 suggests, focuses the search for helping and hindering factors on what in the literature is broadly labeled *organizational capability* (Ulrich & Lake, 1990), and what in the current context we call *organizational agility*. Broadly, organizational agility stems from combining two components: an agility-oriented organizational infrastructure and an agility-oriented human resources strategy. The basic premise is that the two must be synergistic.

Proposition 5: Both an agility-oriented organizational infrastructure and an agility-oriented human resources strategy are necessary, and

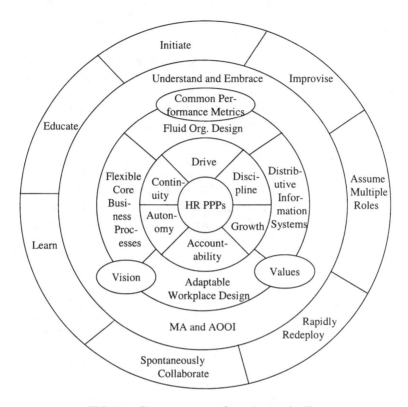

FIG. 2.4. Key components of organizational agility.

together they are sufficient conditions for fostering agility-oriented mindset and behaviors.

This line of reasoning represents a departure from prevailing practice in the strategic human resources management literature, which, to date, has basically ignored organizational infrastructure as a potentially important construct (Wright & Gardner, in press). To support our position, we draw on an example from our own research: When studying a healthcare network that had deliberately set out to become, in the CEO's words, "nimble and change-hardy," we found that salutary behaviors engendered by a very carefully crafted human resources strategy were, to a noticeable degree, hindered by the glacial pace of the information flow coming from an outmoded computer system. A study focusing only on human resources strategy would have missed this unsupportive element of the network's organizational infrastructure (Shafer et al., 2001).

Agility-Oriented Organizational Infrastructure

As Fig. 2.5 shows, an agility-oriented organizational infrastructure consists of two main components that operate much as a gyroscope (a metaphor drawn from Hewlett Packard)—that is, there is a relatively stable inner core surrounded by a constantly reconfiguring frame, or outer ring. Both components, in turn, consist of several elements.

Stable Inner Core.   The role of the stable inner core (assuming, as we shall see, that the human resources strategy is successful in embedding its elements deep into the organization) is to provide some vector for the thrust and, thus, keep organizational agility from degenerating into a metaphor for complete chaos. Our research suggests that in dynamic organizations, the stable inner core consists of some combination of three elements (Dyer & Shafer, 1999; Shafer et al., 2001):

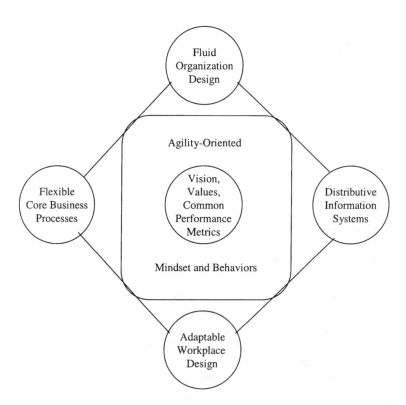

FIG. 2.5.   Agility-oriented organizational infrastructure.

• A clearly articulated vision that is both worthy of pursuit (depicting a cause more than a business, in Hamel's [2000] terms) and, unlike goals, essentially unattainable and thus forever pursuable (Collins & Porras, 1994).

• An equally clearly articulated set of shared values that center on trust, but also often include openness, honesty, prudent risk-taking, mutual respect, and personal accountability (Heckscher, 1994; Shafer et al., 2001).

• A few important common performance metrics that capture the essence of marketplace agility. Rich Fairbank, Chairman and CEO of Capital One, articulates a common metric: "Fifty percent of what we're marketing now did not exist at this company six months ago . . . I'm proud of that fact—until I reflect on its implications. It means that 50% of what we'll be selling six months from now doesn't exist yet." (Fishman, 1999, p. 218).

Reconfigurable Outer Ring. This, as Fig. 2.5 shows, contains four elements each of which, notwithstanding variations in practice, appears to comply with certain common design principles. Necessarily brief descriptions of these elements and principles follow:

• Fluid Organization Design: Dynamic organizations view organization design as a verb, not a noun. Rather than being locked into fixed structures, they adopt designs that foster fluidity both within an organization (e.g., in the form of temporary teams) and across two or more organizations (e.g., in the form of temporary alliances with other firms in their evolving networks). Common organizing principles include: flat (but not without some hierarchy), minimal formal authority; boundarylessness; cellular division into small subunits; and team based (Ashkenas, Ulrich, Jick, & Kerr, 1995; Dove, 2001; Hamel, 2000; Morgan, 1997; Youngblood, 1997).

• Flexible Core Business Processes: As much as possible, dynamic organizations favor soft- over hard-wired business processes, templates over standard operating procedures. Thus, we see, for example: emergent business strategies (vs. formal plans), decisions based on expertise and dialogue (more than formal position or authority), open markets for allocating some resources (mixed with formal procedures for allocating others), and an emphasis on surround communication (as opposed to that based on designated channels; Hamel, 2000; Heckscher, 1994). Here the guiding principle is: routinize only where, when, and as much as absolutely necessary; otherwise have faith in employees' common sense and savvy (Foster & Kaplan, 2001).

• Distributive Information Systems: Dynamic organizations run on real-time, easily accessible information. They favor "broadcast" or consumer models of information technology that facilitate the full and timely flow of information both in and out, while placing responsibility on end-users to establish their own information requirements and, thus, to access only that which is needed when it is needed. The guiding principles: first, systems designed for self- rather than system-control and, second, what one knows all must be able to easily and painlessly access (Dove, 2001).

• Adaptable Workplace Design: Fluid organizations require equally adaptable and nonconfining workplace designs; that is, tensile and modular or mobile buildings, open plan offices, nomadic workstations, plug-and-play technologies, free-standing and movable panels instead of walls, and even remote workplaces (e.g., homes and leased spaces in office "hotels"; Becker & Sims, 2001). The underlying concept is an "integrated portfolio strategy" fashioned to deliver just the right amount and type of space, when and where it is needed, for only as long as it is needed (Becker, 2000; Becker, in press)

For a long time, our research focused on finding prevailing patterns in the elements of organizational infrastructures. The intent was to derive an ideal typology for dynamic organizations. This pursuit has given way to the realities of reconfigurability (and perhaps equifinality). We now believe that it is important to study not only the content of organizational infrastructures, but also the ways in which they are reconfigured in dynamic organizations. Alignment, or synergy, in this context, then, refers more to degree and pattern of reconfigurability than to an immutable pattern of features in the various elements of organizational infrastructure.

The delightfully nonlinear paradox here, however, is that in dynamic organizations, an agility-oriented organizational infrastructure is apparently both a cause and effect of employee mindset and behaviors.

Proposition 6: The right combination of stability (from the inner core) and reconfigurability (in the elements comprising the outer ring) in a dynamic organization's organizational infrastructure constitutes an "edge of chaos" environment that fosters agility-oriented behaviors among employees.

Proposition 7: The cumulative agility-oriented behaviors of employees determine the degree and pattern of reconfiguring that occurs and, thus, the various forms than a dynamic organization's organizational infrastructure assumes over time.

Proposition 8: The process of continuously reconfiguring an organizational infrastructure, if successful, helps employees understand and embrace the essentiality and essence of organizational agility (the second key component of an agility-oriented mindset, as shown at the bottom of Table 2.1)—which in turn enhances the likelihood that employees will continue and, indeed, continuously improve the effectiveness and efficiency of the reconfiguring process.

The research challenge here, in brief, is to improve our understanding of the dynamics of so-called self-organizing or emergent behavior in actual organizations (Dove, 2001; Pascale et al., 2000).

Agility-Oriented Human Resources Strategy

Students of human resources strategy, as noted earlier, are engaged in a lively ongoing debate over the proper conceptualization (and, in quantitatively oriented research, measurement) of the strategy construct. In our research, we focus, in part, on uncovering broad principles that appear to guide the choice of policies, programs, and practices, and it is to these that attention is now turned (Dyer & Shafer, 1999; Shafer et al., 2001; Wright, 1998; Wright & Dyer, 2000). Organizations rarely make principles specific, so the search for them is an extrapolative exercise (Shafer et al., 2001). The challenge is to specify a set of principles—or what Galunic and Eisenhardt (2001) called "simple rules"—that meets the twin tests of necessity and sufficiency; that is, that engender only (or mostly) appropriate policies, programs, and practices in sufficiently synergistic bundles that they foster the required employee mindset and behaviors. At this juncture, we offer a set of six principles that seem to meet these tests, arranged to reflect the paradoxical and dialectical nature of dynamic organizations: drive and discipline; autonomy and accountability; growth and continuity.

Drive and Discipline. To promote a relentless pursuit of marketplace agility among all employees, dynamic organizations require human resources policies, programs, and practices that **(P1) forge a sense of common purpose.** The idea here is to promote dynamic organizations as both causes and businesses (Hamel, 2000) by enhancing employee understanding and internalization of the three elements that comprise the stable inner core of an agility-oriented organizational infrastructure (refer again to Fig. 2.5). To promote the cause, there is a need to embed the organizational vision and core values deep into the bowels of the system. To get down to brass tacks, there is the further need to keep the common performance metrics of choice front and center among all employees. But, alas, fired up employees operating in uncertain environments can easily get off track. So, it is also necessary to **(P2) promote contextual clarity.** This is done by implementing human resources policies, programs, and practices that foster a clear grasp of the dynamics of marketplace agility, as well as of the four elements that comprise the reconfigurable outer ring of an agility-oriented organizational infrastructure (i.e., fluid organization design, flexible core business processes, distributive information systems, and adaptable workplace designs). The assumption here is straightforward: In dynamic organizations, employee actions are more likely to be effective and efficient to the extent they know what it takes to compete successfully in turbulent environments and understand the complexities involved in manipulating various elements of an organizational infrastructure toward desired ends.

Autonomy and Accountability. In dynamic organizations, employees require considerable freedom to pursue agility-oriented behaviors. This freedom emanates from human resources policies, programs, and practices that govern work design and the movement of employees within the organization. Hence **(P3) foster fluid assignments.** But, this, too, can go too far. Fluidity can degenerate to the point where everyone is responsible for everything, and no one is responsible for anything. Thus, dynamic organizations must find ways to help employees coordinate their activities and, more important, take personal accountability for the consequences of the decisions they make and the actions they take. This requires that dynamic organizations have human resources policies, programs, and practices that **(P4) instill ownership of outcomes.**

Growth and Continuity. Continuous learning is a key behavioral expectation in dynamic organizations. Rather than simply getting better and better at what they already know how to do, however, employees are expected to be constantly reaching out to learn new things. An overemphasis on honing current competences tends to inhibit change because employees fear the prospect of obsolescence. More appropriate to dynamic organizations are what Godin (2000) called *serial incompetents,* employees who are relentlessly uncomfortable with the status quo and who willingly and repeatedly run the risk of becoming incompetent—for a while—in the interest of tackling new challenges. To this end, dynamic organizations need human resources policies, programs, and practices that encourage the thirst for, as well as the rapid development of, new competencies: **(P5) facilitate serial incompetence.** Agility-oriented employees gravitate in this direction naturally. The challenge for dynamic organizations is to assure that they do so within their organizations rather than in the open labor market (realizing, of course, that nothing is forever in this increasingly market-mediated world [Cappelli, 1999]). This calls for human resources policies, programs, and practices that enhance dynamic organizations' positions as "employers of choice" for the agility-oriented people they need. Although this is a complex issue (Wright, Dyer, & Takla, 1999), we suggest that, in general, it requires activities that **(P6) encourage continuous employment.**

Proposition 9: Adhering to human resources principles pertaining to drive, autonomy, and growth (P1, P3, and P5) promotes, through motivation, opportunity, and competencies (Boudreau & Ramstad, in press), the innovative behaviors required of employees to achieve marketplace agility.

Proposition 10: Adhering to human resources principles pertaining to discipline, accountability, and continuity (P2, P4, and P6) promotes, through focus, responsibility, and accumulated social capital, the degree of self-control and efficient execution-oriented behaviors required of employees to achieve marketplace agility.

Proposition 11(a): Adhering to human resources principles pertaining both to drive, autonomy, and growth and to discipline, accountability, and continuity is necessary, and also sufficient, to instill an agility-oriented mindset and elicit agility-oriented behaviors among employees.

Proposition 11(b): In dynamic organizations, more emphasis must be put on the human resources principles that promote innovation than on the human resources principles that promote of self-control and efficient execution, otherwise agility-oriented mindset and behaviors will eventually diminish as employees revert to their natural tendencies to seek and, indeed, try to create order, stability, and predictability in their environments (Heckscher, 1994; Pascale et al., 2000).

Do these six human resources principles foster marketplace agility? Or, in more formal theoretical terms, do they collectively demonstrate vertical fit (Wright, 1998; Wright & Sherman, 1999)? Ultimately, of course, this is an empirical question. But, assuming the validity of our first analytical exercise (i.e., that we have correctly identified the mindset and behaviors required to achieve marketplace agility), a modest test of vertical fit involves a simple logic check to see if (a) each aspect of mindset and each behavior is addressed by one, or preferably, more, of the human resources principles, and (b) if each human resources principle addresses one, or preferably more, of the various aspects of mindset and behaviors. Briefly, as Table 2.2 shows, the six human resources principles pass these tests. Each aspect of mindset and/or each behavior is addressed by a minimum of four human resources principles, while each human resources principle addresses at least three aspects of mindset and/or behaviors. Notice that we are not claiming that these six human resources principles are the only possible, let alone the one best, set for enhancing agility-oriented mindset and behaviors and, thus, marketplace agility. Rather, we are making a case that it is, at a minimum, a workable set on which to base a discussion of agility-oriented human resources policies, programs, and practices.

TABLE 2.2
Testing for Vertical Fit*

Agility-Oriented Mindset and Behaviors	Relevant AOHR Principles
Initiate and Improvise	DRIVE reinforces the need for being action-oriented, and creating DISCIPLINE shows how these behaviors contribute to marketplace agility. AUTONOMY nurtures these behaviors, while ACCOUNTABILITY changes them toward marketplace agility. GROWTH provides essential competencies, while CONTINUITY reinforces sensible risk-taking.
Assume Multiple Roles and Rapidly Deploy	DRIVE reinforces the need for internal mobility. DISCIPLINE shows how moving to opportunities contributes to marketplace agility and provides guidance in the "move/don't move" decision. AUTONOMY allows movement. GROWTH provides multiple competencies.
Spontaneously Collaborate	DRIVE reinforces the need for joint effort. DISCIPLINE shows how joint effort contributes to marketplace agility. ACCOUNTABILITY reinforces mutual commitments. CONTINUITY provides a sense of community, familiarity, comfort.
Learn and Educate	DRIVE reinforces the need to nurture collective organizational intelligence. AUTONOMY promotes cross-fertilization of ideas. GROWTH develops dissatisfaction with status quo and mechanisms for individual learning. CONTINUITY supports experimentation and sensible risk-taking and promotes dialogue (real conversation).

Note. *Assumes alignment among essential elements of marketplace agility and agility-oriented mindset and behaviors.

Agility-Oriented Human Resources Policies, Programs, and Practices

The challenge here, remember, is to uncover (or, if in an organization, develop) a synergistic set of human resources policies, programs, and practices that adhere to the preceding human resources principles and, thus, foster agility-oriented mindset and behaviors. The possibilities are many, and space precludes a full discussion. So we focus on human resources policies, programs, and practices that meet one or more of the following conditions: unique to dynamic organizations, particularly important theoretically, supported empirically, or congruent with multiple human resources principles. The discussion, as shown in Table 2.3, is organized around the human resources principles, not human resources policies, programs, and practices, just as we believe human resources strategies should be (Shafer et al., 2001).

Drive/Forge a Sense of Common Purpose.   The human resources policy: Keep the organization's vision, core values, and common performance metrics front and center among all employees at all times. Program and practice options include:

• Involving a cross-section of employees in shaping these three elements of the agility-oriented organizational infrastructure's stable inner core (in newly emerging dynamic organizations where these elements are not already in place).

• "Surround communication" to assure that virtually every piece of formal communication going to and among employees reinforces some aspect of

TABLE 2.3
From AOHR Principles to AOHR Policies, Programs, Practices

AOHR Principles	*Prototypical AOHR Policies, Practices, Programs*
Drive (Common purpose)	• "Surround communication" to promote vision and core values; rewarding (and punishing) those who live (or fail to live) the vision and core values; "breakthrough" objectives focused on core values (Shafer et al., 2001)
Discipline (Contextual clarity)	• "Open book management"—widespread availability of marketplace intelligence; opportunities to learn the inner workings of the AO business model (MA, organizational competencies, AOOI); real time feedback and returns tied to organizational, team, and individual performance (Stack, 1992)
Autonomy (Fluid assignments)	• Discretionary based work design (Dyer & Shafer, 1999) • Open market for talent—bidding and posting (Hamel, 2000)
Accountability (Ownership of outcomes)	• Commitment management protocols to negotiate authentic commitments to outcomes, focus attention on these outcomes, and on-the-spot reinforcement for delivery of the outcomes (Haeckel, 1999)
Growth (Continuous development)	• Egalitarianism in perks and amenities (Pascale et al., 2000) • Commensurate returns, awards, perks, rewards equal to commitment expected (Shafer et al., 2001) • Layoffs as last resort—amply justified and compensated if unavoidable (Fradette & Michaud, 1998)
Continuity (Continuous employment)	• On-the-fly assessments of learning gaps (Shafer et al., 2001) • Zero tolerance of competency obsolescence (Shafer et al., 2001) • Communities of practice to nurture collective intelligence (Dove, 2001)

organizational vision, core values, or common performance metrics. (For an example of how this was carried out at Albert Einstein Healthcare Network, see Shafer et al., 2001).

• Team building efforts, top to bottom, to reinforce core values. Albert Einstein Healthcare Network, for example, in addition to "surround communication," used groups of employees to identify instances where their units' usual behaviors did not live up to the organization's (new) core values. Where gaps were found, these teams formed and implemented action plans to eliminate the lapses. The exercise began with the top executive team, whose members were then used to cascade the process down to the next level, and so forth, until virtually the entire organization was involved (again, see Shafer et al., 2001).

• Forming "breakthrough objectives" around key dimensions of vision, core values, or common performance metrics, and using games and contests as fun ways to pursue these (very serious) objectives (once again, for an example, see Shafer et al., 2001).

Discipline/Promote Conceptual Clarity.   Here the human resources policy imperative is to assure that all employees have all the information they need to thoroughly understand, first, the dynamics of marketplace agility and, second, the functioning and operation of the reconfigurable elements of an agility-oriented organizational infrastructure. Here we cite one tried and true program and one highly speculative one:

• "Surround communication." As previously explained, except that the focus is on the realities of the marketplace and the essence of the dynamic organization business model (again, an example can be found in Shafer et al., 2001).

• "Open book management." This technique was pioneered in a decidedly nonagile manufacturing firm (Stack, 1992). But, presumably it could be adapted to dynamic organizations inasmuch as it is all about promoting conceptual clarity. Core elements include sharing financial and operating information with all employees, facilitating employee understanding of financial statements and of the contribution their work makes to financial results, involving employees in targeting priority areas for improvement and regularly reviewing results, collectively celebrating successes, and (discussed later) providing relevant financial payoffs (Davis, 1997).

Autonomy/Foster Fluid Assignments.   Broadly, the human resources policy is to have all employees positioned as owners of fluid assignments with responsibility for results (and not as occupants of fixed positions with responsibility for completing tasks). On the one hand, this involves discretionary-based work design and, on the other, an open market for talent.

• In dynamic organizations, one instance of TIMJ (that isn't my job; Bridges, 1994) is one too many. So, programmatically dynamic organizations must think of work in terms of assignments, not jobs, and insist that employees frame their assignments in ways that minimize the number of required tasks and maximize zones of discretion in which they are expected to operate as they deem necessary. Discretionary-based work design goes well beyond traditional notions of "empowerment." It relies on employees to define their own assignments (unencumbered by job descriptions) in ways that continuously expand the arenas in which they are expected to function. ("Empowerment," in contrast, is usually a top-down exercise in which managers redesign subordinates' jobs by allowing them to take on a few previously forbidden activities, as, for example, when managers increase the value of returns salespersons can write off without approval). Discretionary-based work design (not to mention organizational learning) is fostered by processes such as the U.S. Army's "after action review," which follows each major exercise or project with a detailed examination of where discretion was used wisely and not so wisely, and a search for ways to improve (Pascale et al., 2000, pp. 252–253).

• A truly open market for talent involves open auctions in which project managers bid for the employees they need and, by deciding when and where to go, employees exercise career control (Hamel, 2000). A modified version involves a more traditional posting system that is more fluid than the typical informal (i.e., old boy or, perhaps, old girl) network, but approaches the fluidity of a truly open market when restrictions on who can be "poached," who can be "protected" from being "poached," and where and how often employees can move are minimized or eliminated. In organizations where projects last a long time, dynamic organizations can institute a practice of periodically reshuffling team memberships, much as occurs at Capital One (Pascale et al., 2000, pp. 260–261).

Accountability/Instill Ownership of Outcomes.   From a human resources policy perspective, all employees must at all times be clear about what outcomes they owe to whom by when. Programmatically, the best approach we have seen thus far is Haeckel's (1999, pp. 148–154) concept of commitment management. This involves a rigorous protocol designed to make it relatively quick and easy for employees to negotiate (and renegotiate) "authentic commitments" with one another and, subsequently, to track the extent to which these commitments were or were not met. Just as discretionary-based work design differs from empowerment, so does commitment management differ from the typical approach to management by objectives. Management by objectives, like empowerment, is a top-down process involving the assignment of (usually annual) goals by managers to subordinates within their units rather than ongoing negotiations of authentic commitments among employees at various levels across multiple units. For an example of the commitment management process at work, warts and all, at a unit of IBM, see Haeckel (1999, pp. 243–247). It should be noted that the commitment management process also helps to promote conceptual clarity as, through negotiations, employees and teams come to clarify the ways in which their efforts mesh to promote marketplace agility.

Growth/Facilitate Serial Incompetence. As a matter of policy, dynamic organizations seek to keep everyone developing in new directions at all times. Careful selection certainly helps, as is discussed in a subsequent section. Other relevant programs and practices include:

• Surround communication, as described earlier, only in this context focused on the message that, in terms of competencies, standing still is tantamount to falling behind (Shafer et al., 2001).

• An open market for talent, also as previously described. In dynamic organizations, constant change means constantly moving competency requirements. Even a moderately open market for talent requires that buyers recognize the need to look for serial incompetents. The corresponding message to employees is one of zero tolerance for complacency or slow learning; those who are overspecialized or unable to learn on the fly soon find fewer and fewer, and eventually no, bidders for their services.

• Training on the fly. Encouraging the need for serial incompetence (in either a positive or negative way) is one thing, helping employees minimize its consequences is quite another. So, dynamic organizations invest heavily in employee development. But because they defy predictability and are by nature very busy places, their heaviest investments are directed toward learning that takes place on assignment and on the spot, often through Web-based or other types of self-study programs, often done on employees' own time (Shafer et al., 2001). Furthermore, dynamic organizations learn to treat well-intentioned mistakes or breakdowns that occur on assignments as learning opportunities, not occasions for recriminations (Pascale et al., 2000, pp. 250–257).

• Communities of practice. Fluid organization design has a way of disrupting natural clusters of those with common occupational identities and baseline competencies. So dynamic organizations develop communities of practice whereby those with common interests and needs can congregate, physically or virtually, to help each other stay up to speed (Cohen & Prusak, 2001, pp. 53–80).

Continuity/Encourage Continuous Employment. Certainly, no dynamic organization can adopt a policy of employment security and probably none of their employees expect them to. But neither can they operate as revolving doors. Employees who thrive at the edge of chaos are (and undoubtedly will continue to be) in short supply. Even more to the point, dynamic organizations have no choice but to invest in human capital, and it makes little sense to keep pouring time, effort, and money into a constantly eroding resource. So dynamic organizations adopt policies, with supporting programs and practices, such as the following:

• Minimize voluntary turnover. Baseline offerings here are, first, the freedom, flexibility, excitement, and opportunities that dynamic organizations inherently offer and, second, competitive pay packages (discussed shortly hereafter). Other approaches involve: careful selection (also discussed later); intensive orientation programs (Shafer et al., 2001); constant communication and storytelling to reinforce the special nature of the place and, especially, the people in it (Cohen & Prusak, 2001, pp. 112–132); and even an array of time-saving, firm-binding, and indeed paternalistic perks and amenities (e.g., day-care centers, take-home meals, concierge services, and the like; Useem, 2000).

• Minimize layoffs or otherwise the effects of layoffs (Lawler, 1996, pp. 190–193). The former involves the first use of standard stopgap measures during temporary downturns. Inevitably, though, dynamic organizations encounter ongoing situations in which these measures are inadequate or inappropriate. Equitable severance and outplacement programs certainly apply here. So do attempts to stay on the radar screens of laid-off employees for the time when things turn around. Charles Schwab, for example, recently offered laid-off employees (through the founder's foundation) up to $20,000 to cover tuition at accredited educational institutions, along with a guaranteed bonus of $7,500 for any laid-off employee who was rehired by the firm within 18 months (Dunham, 2001).

Selection and Rewards. These human resources activities cut across most, if not all, of the human resources principles cited. Dynamic organizations are not for everyone; therefore, it is essential to carefully select new employees who are predisposed to operate in such milieus. One dynamic organization we studied revised its selection process to include situational interviews to assess value congruence between applicants and the organization (Shafer et al., 2001). Kriegel, Inc., a consulting firm in California, has developed "Change-Ready Profile," a copyrighted self-assessment tool that might be adapted by dynamic organizations for selection purposes (Brandt & Kriegel, 1996). Of course, these are obviously only cautious first steps, and much work remains to develop valid selection instruments in the special context of dynamic organizations. Even less progress seems to have been made with respect to rewards systems for dynamic organizations (Shafer et al., 2001). We can speculate about the essential features of an appropriate reward system using the various human resources principles to identify potentially key components: (a) for drive, pay in part for organizational results (profit sharing, stock options), subject to a GE-type practice of no payoffs for those who fail to adhere to the organization's core values; (b) for discipline, a piece that pays for effective team performance; (c) for autonomy, base pay within wide bands based on individual marketability (rather than job evaluation, inasmuch as there are no jobs); (d) for accountability, awards or small bonuses for keeping commitments; (e) for growth, recognition and awards for taking on challenging assignments and for rapid learning, and (f) for continuity, providing commensurate returns (i.e., assuring, as much as possible, that employees' total returns, both financial and nonfinancial, are equal to the substantial contributions they are asked to make to firm success). But how, if at all, these speculations actually come to life in dynamic organizations remains to be seen.

Testing for Horizontal Fit.   Here we are interested in ascertaining whether or not the various human resources policies, programs, and practices are congruent and mutually reinforcing to the point they collectively constitute a synergistic bundle (Wright, 1998; Wright & Sherman, 1999). Obviously, given the piecemeal nature of our presentation, it is premature to attempt any such analysis, although Table 2.4 demonstrates a possible approach. As before, it is a simple logic check to judge whether or not: (a) each human resources principle is addressed by multiple human resources policies, programs, and practices, and (b) each human resources policy, program, and practice addresses multiple human resources principles. An even better approach, once the domain of human resources policies, programs, and practices is more complete, would be to estimate the degree of complementarity among the full set by judging the extent to which doing more (or less) of any one of them would increase (decrease) the returns as opposed to doing the others (Milgrom & Roberts, 1995; for a preliminary application, see Dyer & Shafer, 1999).

BRINGING IT ALL TOGETHER

In a world where real shift happens, even embellished forms of the bureaucratic model, which has served so long and so well, are likely to be inadequate to the task of simultaneously achieving requisite levels of innovation tinged with appropriate levels of discipline (Foster & Kaplan, 2001; Heckscher, 1994;

TABLE 2.4
Testing for Horizontal Fit, Internal Fit, or Synergy

Selected AOHR Policies, Programs, Practices*	Drive	Discipline	Autonomy	Accountability	Personal Growth	Continuity
Staffing						
• Selection based on value congruence	+			+		+
Training						
• Cascading gap analysis	+				+	+
• Survival tactics workshops					+	+
Work Design						
• Flexible assignments			+			
• Project teams			+			+
Performance Management						
• Commitment management protocols		+		+		
Communication						
• Surround sound	+	+				
Returns						
• Recognize, appreciate, celebrate		+		+		

Note. *Adapted from Shafer et al., 2001.

Pascale et al., 2000). So new organizational models are generating interest in practice, as well as among students of leadership, business strategy, organization theory, and the like (Child & McGrath, 2001). The dynamic organization is one such model. It is, as defined here, a "chaordic" form, constantly poised on "the edge of chaos" by attempting to harmoniously blend elements of change, emergence, and innovation on the one hand and stability, coordination, and execution on the other (Brown & Eisenhardt, 1998; Hock, 1999; Pascale et al., 2000).

Thus far, theory and research have generated only a surface understanding of how this delicate balancing act is achieved in practice. From a human resource perspective, it can be said with some certainty that dynamic organizations require of employees a mindset and set of behaviors quite different from those expected of employees in classic bureaucratic organizations (and perhaps in other new organizational forms as well; Proposition 1). Thus, the current interest in probing the "black box" between human resources strategy and firm financial results is well placed (Boxall & Purcell, 2000; Delery & Shaw, 2001; Wright & Gardner, in press). But the efforts need to be conceptualized in broader terms. Specifically, we believe that researchers interested in human resources strategy need to widen their perspectives to include studies of the determinants of required employee attitudes and behaviors (see Propositions 2, 3, and 4), as well as more common studies of the factors that bring these attitudes and behaviors about. And in the latter context, in turn, it would be helpful if researchers would focus their attention on organizational capability (in dynamic organizations on organizational agility) rather than human resources strategy alone (see Proposition 5).

It would also be helpful if at least some of the empirical forays into the "black box" took the form of truly exploratory, intensive, qualitative case studies particularly focused on knowledge-based firms, as most dynamic organizations are, and specifically designed to derive grounded theory (Brown & Eisenhardt, 1998; Shafer et al., 2001). Some thoughts on designing such studies follow.

- Choose research sites, preferably small- to medium-sized business units, on the basis of extant business strategies, and especially on the basis of how the units are trying to compete in the marketplace (price, speed, service, marketplace agility, etc.; Boudreau & Ramstad, in press). Initially lean toward those that provide relatively clear-cut cases of success and (where access can be achieved) a noticeable lack of success.

- Start the analysis by teasing out the mindset and behaviors required of employees; in the dynamic organization context, such studies could be guided by Propositions 2, 3, and 4. This may require segmenting employees into various categories such as core and noncore (Delery & Shaw, 2001; Lepak & Snell, 1999), although probably not in dynamic organizations, where (we believe) all employees are part of the strategic core work force. In most cases, the search for requisite mindset and behaviors is an interpretive exercise. One set of potentially determining factors to consider here are key organizational competencies (capabilities, resources; Barney, 1991), such as sensing the market, mobilizing rapid response, exploiting temporary advantage, and embedding organizational learning.

- Next look for factors that help or hinder the manifestation of the required mindset and behaviors. Here the interest is in what is broadly called organizational capability (Ulrich & Lake, 1990), or what in dynamic organizations we call organizational agility (Proposition 5). Components include organizational factors—again, such as elements of agility-oriented organizational infrastructure (Propositions 6, 7, and 8)—and the principles that guide the choice of human resources policies, programs, and practices (Propositions 9, 10, and 11), as well as the details of the policies, programs, and practices themselves (Wright, 1998). Analyze these components for degree of vertical and horizontal fit, or, more broadly, the synergies of the system (Delery & Shaw, 2001; see Tables 2.2, 2.3, and 2.4).

• Finally, where fit is found, combine these components into a proposed model of organizational capability appropriate to the particular business strategy followed by the firm or unit under investigation. Figure 2.4 depicts the components of organizational agility that we postulate are appropriate for firms and business units attempting to compete on the basis of marketplace agility.

Our analysis rests on two fundamental assumptions: that dynamic organizational competencies (reading the market, mobilizing rapid response, and so forth) required to achieve marketplace agility are stable over time, and that the organizational agility required to develop and sustain these competencies is a synergistic system whose guiding principles can, and indeed must, endure over time (even as the administrative details vary over time and across dynamic organizations). The challenge is to discover and articulate these guiding principles in the interest of advancing both the design and execution of an agility-oriented organizational infrastructure and human resources strategy. Our initial efforts in this direction are, of course, tentative and, we assume, ephemeral. They are offered, therefore, not so much in the hope that they will see the light of day in practice as in the desire that they may spur and influence additional theoretical and empirical work to shed light on the specifics of marketplace and organizational agility, and as a corollary on human resources strategy's infamous "black box."

ACKNOWLEDGMENTS

Financial support for the research that went into this chapter was provided by the Center for Advanced Human Resource Studies (CAHRS), School of Industrial and Labor Relations, Cornell University. The authors would like to thank Randall Peterson, Brent Smith, Randy White, and Pat Wright for helpful comments on an earlier draft of this chapter.

REFERENCES

Argyris, C. (1985). *Strategy, change, and defensive routines.* Boston: Pitman.
Ashkenas, R., Ulrich, D., Jick, T., & Kerr, S. (1995). *The boundaryless organization.* San Francisco: Jossey-Bass.

Barney, J. (1991). Firm resources and sustained competitive advantage. *Journal of Management, 17*(1), 99–120.

Becker, F. (2000). Integrated portfolio strategies for dynamic organizations. *Facilities, 18*(10–12), 411–420.

Becker, F. (in press). Workplace flexibility: Value for money. *Journal of Facility Management.*

Becker, F., & Sims, W. (2001). *Offices that work: Balancing communication, flexibility, and cost.* International Workplace Studies Program, Cornell University, Ithaca, NY.

Boudreau, J., & Ramstad, P. (in press). Strategic I/O psychology and utility analysis. In W. Borman, R. Klimoski, & D. Ilgin (Eds.), *Handbook of industrial and organizational psychology.*

Boxall, P. (1999). Human resource strategy and industry-based competition: A conceptual framework and agenda for theoretical development. In P. Wright, L. Dyer, J. Boudreau, & G. Milkovich (Eds.), *Research in personnel and human resources management (Supplement 4: Strategic human resources management in the 21st century;* pp. 259–282). Stamford, CT: JAI Press.

Boxall, P., & Purcell, J. (2000). Strategic human resource management: Where have we come from and where are we going? *International Journal of Management Reviews, 2,* 183–203.

Brandt, D., & Kriegel, R. (1996). *The change ready profile: A tool for understanding your response to change.* Nevada City, CA: Kriegel.

Bridges, W. (1994). *Job Shift.* Reading, MA: Addison-Wesley.

Brown, S., & Eisenhardt, K. (1998). *Competing on the edge: Strategy as structured chaos.* Boston, MA: Harvard Business School Press.

Campbell, D. (2000). The proactive employee: Managing workplace initiative. *Academy of Management Executive, 14*(3), 52–66.

Cappelli, P. (1999). *The new deal at work.* Boston, MA: Harvard Business School Press.

Cappelli, P., & Singh, H. (1992). Integrating strategic human resources and strategic management. In D. Lewin, O. Mitchell, & P. Scherer (Eds.), *Research frontiers in industrial relations and human resources* (pp. 165–192). Madison, WI: Industrial Relations Research Association.

Child, J., & McGrath, R. G. (2001). Organizations unfettered: Organizational form in an information intensive economy. *Academy of Management Journal, 44*(6), 1135–1148.

Cohen, D., & Prusak, L. (2001). *In good company: How social capital makes organizations work.* Boston, MA: Harvard Business School Press.

Collins, J., & Porras, J. (1994). *Built to last.* New York: Harper-Collins.

Davis, T. (1997). Open book management: Its promise and pitfalls. *Organizational Dynamics, Winter,* 7–19.

Delery, J., & Shaw, J. (2001). The strategic management of people in work organizations: Review, synthesis, and extension. In G. Ferris (Ed.), *Research in personnel and human resources management* (vol. 20, pp. 165–198). Oxford, UK: Elsevier Science.

Dove, R. (2001). *Response ability: The language, structure, and culture of agile enterprise.* New York: Wiley.

Dunham, K. (2001, June 19). Employers seek ways to lure back laid-off workers when times improve. *Wall Street Journal,* B1.

Dyer, L. (1984). Studying human resource strategy: An approach and an agenda. *Industrial Relations, 23*(2), 156–169.

Dyer, L., & Shafer, R. (1999). From human resource strategy to organizational effectiveness: Lessons from research on agile organizations. In P. Wright, L. Dyer, J. Boudreau, & G. Milkovich, (Eds.), *Research in personnel and human resources management (Supplement 4: Strategic Human Resource Management in the 21st century;* pp. 145–174). Stamford, CT: JAI Press.

Fishman, C. (1999, May). This is a marketing revolution. *Fast Company,* 204–218.

Foster, R., & Kaplan, S. (2001). *Creative destruction: Why companies that are built to last underperform the market and how to successfully transform them.* New York: Currency.

Fradette, M., & Michaud, S. (1998). *The power of corporate kinetics.* New York: Simon & Schuster.

Galunic, C., & Eisenhardt, K. (2001). Architectural innovation and modular corporate forms. *Academy of Management Journal, 44*(6), 1229–1250.

Godin, S. (2000, January-February). In the face of change, the competent are helpless. *Fast Company,* 230–234.

Grant, R. (1996). Prospering in dynamically competitive environments: Organizational capability as knowledge integration. *Organizational Science, 7*(4), 375–387.

Haeckel, S. (1999). *Adaptive enterprise: Creating and leading sense-and-respond organizations.* Boston, MA: Harvard Business School Press.

Hamel, G. (2000). *Leading the revolution.* Boston, MA: Harvard Business School Press.

Hamel, G., & Prahalad, C. (1994). *Competing for the future.* Boston, MA: Harvard Business School Press.

Heckscher, C. (1994). Defining the post-bureaucratic type. In C. Heckscher & A. Donnellon (Eds.), *The post-bureaucratic organization: New perspectives on organizational change.* Thousand Oaks, CA: Sage.

Hock, D. (1999). *Birth of the chaortic age.* San Francisco, CA: Barrett-Koehler.

Lawler, E. E., III. (1996). *From the ground up: Six principles for building the new logic corporation.* San Francisco, CA: Jossey-Bass.

Lepak, D., & Snell, S. (1999). The human resource architecture: Toward a theory of human capital allocation and development. *Academy of Management Review, 24*(1), 31–48.

Levine, L. (2001). Integrating knowledge and processes in a learning organization. *Information Systems Management, 18*(1), 21–33.

Lewin, K. (1951). *Field theory in social sciences.* New York: Harper & Row.

Mara, A., & Scott-Morgan, P. (1996). *The accelerating organization.* New York: McGraw-Hill.

Milgrom, P., & Roberts, J. (1995). Complementarities and fit: Strategy, structure and organizational change in manufacturing. *Journal of Accounting and Economics, 19,* 179–208.

Morgan, G. (1997). *Images of organization* (2nd ed.). Thousand Oaks, CA: Sage.

Nonaka, I. (1991, November–December). The knowledge creating company. *Harvard Business Review,* 96–104.

Pascale, R., Millemann, M., & Gioja, L. (2000). *Surfing the edge of chaos.* New York: Crown Business.

Pfeffer, J. (1998). *The human equation: Building profits by putting people first.* Boston, MA: Harvard Business School Press.

Schuler, R., & Jackson, S. (1987). Linking competitive strategies and human resource management practices. *Academy of Management Executive, 1*(3), 207–219.

Serwer, A. (2000, May 15). There's something about Cisco. *Fortune,* 114–138.

Shafer, R., Dyer, L., Kilty, J., Amos, J., & Ericksen, J. (2001). Crafting a human resource strategy to foster organizational agility: A case study. *Human Resource Management, 40*(3), 197–211.

Stack, J. (1992). *The great game of business.* New York: Currency.

Teece, D., Pisano, G., & Shuen, A. (1997). Dynamic capabilities and strategic management. *Strategic Management Journal, 18*(7), 509–533.

Ulrich, D., & Lake, D. (1990). *Organization capability: Competing from the inside out.* New York: Wiley.

Useem, J. (2000, January 10). Welcome to the new company. *Fortune,* 62–70.

Weick, K. (1998). Improvisation as a mindset for organizational analysis. *Organizational Science, 9*(5), 533–555.

Weick, K., & Quinn, R. (1999). Organizational change and development. In J. Spence, J. Darley, & D. Foss (Eds.), *Annual review of psychology, 50*, 361–386.

Wright, P. (1998). Human resources-strategy fit: Does it really matter? *Human Resource Planning, 21*(4), 56–57.

Wright, P., Dunford, B., & Snell, S. (2001). Contributions of the resource based view of the firm to the field of HRM: Convergence of two fields. *Journal of Management, 27,* 701–721.

Wright, P., & Dyer, L. (2000). *People in e-business: New challenges, new solutions.* New York: Human Resource Planning Society.

Wright, P., Dyer, L., & Takla, M. (1999). *Execution: The critical "what's next" in human resource management.* New York: Human Resource Planning Society.

Wright, P., & Gardner, T. (in press). Theoretical and empirical challenges in studying the human resources practice–firm performance relationship. In D. Holman, T. Wall, C. Clegg, P. Sparrow, & A. Howard (Eds.), *The new workplace: People, technology, and organization.* London: Wiley.

Wright, P., McCormick, B., Sherman, W., & McMahan, G. (1999). The role of human resource practices in petro-chemical refinery performance. *The International Journal of Human Resource Management, 10,* 551–571.

Wright, P., & Sherman, S. (1999). The failure to find fit in strategic human resource management: Theoretical and empirical considerations. In P. Wright, L. Dyer, J. Boudreau, & G. Milkovich (Eds.), *Research in personnel and human resources management (Supplement 4: Strategic human resources management in the 21st century;* pp. 53–74). Stamford, CT: JAI Press.

Youngblood, M. (1997). *Life at the edge of chaos: Creating the quantum organization.* Dallas, TX: Perceval Publishing.

II

MANAGING THE PEOPLE IN THE DYNAMIC ORGANIZATION

3

Staffing the Dynamic Organization: Rethinking Selection and Motivation in the Context of Continuous Change

D. Brent Smith
Rice University

Marcus W. Dickson
Wayne State University

Organizations face increasing pressure to become more adaptable, agile, and dynamic. In this chapter, we assume the case of a fully dynamic organization and elaborate on what we consider to be the many human resources implications of dynamic organizations. Specifically, this chapter focuses on the selection and motivation of people in an environment that is inconsistent with human nature's desire for stability. We believe the long-term viability of dynamic organizations rests on reconciling the human need for constancy with the dynamic organization's need for constant change. In this chapter, we suggest that selection and motivation in a dynamic organization requires rethinking the traditional human resources selection model (hiring based on competency) in favor of hiring based on person–organization fit. We explore the limitations in traditional theories of motivation and suggest personality characteristics that may predispose people to be successful in a dynamic organization.

Anyone who has paid any attention to the stock market in the past few years knows that the marketplace has changed dramatically. Organizations merge, acquire other organizations, change their target market, introduce new products and product lines, and drop others, all at a much faster rate than ever before. In short, for many organizations today, there is no longer a cycle of "steady state–change–steady state." Instead, the constant pattern is "change–change again–change yet again."

To be successful in such an environment, organizations must be able to respond quickly to changes in the marketplace (and, indeed, to anticipate those changes and respond preemptively). They rarely have the luxury of establishing clear boundaries and processes, and so must be able to function in a constant state of flux. Many authors have described this pattern (e.g., Ashkenas, Ulrich, Jick, & Kerr, 1995; Dyer & Shafer, 1999; Fulmer, 2000; Haeckel, 1999; Sifonis & Goldberg, 1996; Volberda, 1998), using a variety of terms and definitions, including boundaryless, adaptive, dynamic, agile, and flexible organizations.

Virtually all organizations today face at least some pressure to respond to a rapidly changing environment, and some organizations do so more readily and more successfully than others. In our discussions for this chapter, we reached the conclusion that some organizations at the extreme end of the continuum—those who are engaged in constant change, who readily adopt new technologies and processes and abandon old (or not so old) ones, who change focus, strategy, and market on a routine basis, and who are particularly agile or nimble—fall into a different category from other organizations, and it is these organizations that we consider here and refer to as *dynamic organizations.* In other words, we do not consider the dynamic organization to be something completely unlike—and therefore not comparable with—other types of organizations, but instead see the dynamic organization as a prototypical case of a specific combination of characteristics that many other organizations have in varying degrees.

Taking this approach means first recognizing that all of the demands on more traditional organizations are also present for dynamic organizations, but then focusing on the unique ways in which these demands are manifested in the dynamic organization context, and on the implications of these unique demands for "people issues." For example, all manufacturing organizations need a dependable source of raw materials. Dynamic organizations, however, are unlikely to see long-term contracts as a smart strategy because their needs for materials are likely to change suddenly and unexpectedly. Similarly, although all service organizations need a staff knowledgeable about their offerings, traditional training models may not be suitable in a dynamic organization because the company's offerings are likely to be constantly changing in response to consumer demand and organizational strategy. Thus, we see dynamic organizations not as completely unique in the work world, but as representative of an organizational form in which environmental demands and subsequent responses are magnified dramatically.

With all this talk about systems and environmental demands and strategic responses, it would be easy to lose sight of the basic fact that people—individuals with their own needs, desires, and motives—are the ones who have to actually perform in a dynamic environment. Thus, although all organizations have to wrestle with the question of employee motivation, we believe that the answers to the motivation question are ultimately going to be found by focusing on people. Motivating performance in a dynamic organization, though, might require a unique and altogether different strategy from that found in a traditional organization unencumbered by the constancy of flux experienced by a dynamic organization. Ultimately, we believe that even in the dynamic organization, "the people make the place" (Schneider, 1987).

At the outset, we intended to restrict our discussion of people in dynamic organizations to the question of individual motivation, something of an historical preoccupation for organizational psychologists. However, as we began to contemplate (and in some cases realize) the many, often competing forces at play in a dynamic organization, we quickly realized that we could not be so narrow in our focus and remain true to the complexity of the dynamic organization. Any discussion of individual motivation must be placed in the general context of the factors that create and define a dynamic organization and necessarily include concepts like culture, climate, person–organization ft, and the changing nature of the psychological contract.

In our conversations, we first elaborated some of the critical features of a dynamic organization that we believe necessitate a reconsideration of traditional approaches to motivation. This led us to a focus on staffing and a reconsideration of the traditional staffing model in the postindustrial organization. As you will see, we concluded that in a dynamic organization we likely must reject the traditional selection model in favor of a focus on person–organization fit. Finally, as we began to focus on the issue of selection, we were once again drawn back to the topic of culture—given the population of people who can survive the role conflict, ambiguity, and tension that defines a dynamic organization, what then would be the characteristics of a culture comprising these people and, more importantly, is it sustainable? This chapter follows that general outline. Throughout, we present specific research propositions where we believe such propositions could be supported by the existing research, and identify other avenues for research where there is as yet too little empirical evidence to support specific propositions.

As a final preliminary cautionary note, we remind the reader that we are taking the extreme case for the purposes of exploration of motivation in the dynamic organization. We must admit that we have never "met" a truly dynamic organization—an organization that fits the variety of definitions provided in the chapters in this volume or discussed in the many popular books on the subject (e.g., Fulmer, 2000). We do agree with Murphy (1999) who stated that, "[t]he extent to which the changes suggested . . . have occurred, or are likely to persist beyond the normal life span of other managerial fads, is far from clear (the ratio of hype to evidence in this area is alarming), and it is difficult to distinguish true and lasting changes in the organization of work from mere speculation about the future of organizations. Nevertheless, there does seem to be credible evidence of meaningful changes in the way many organizations approach work, and these changes will have important implications . . ." (p. 296). It is clearly not every industry that feels the pressure of hyperturbulence, nor every organization that needs to be dynamic; however, there do appear to be environmental and marketplace pressures that are forcing organizations to rethink traditional approaches to staffing and motivation.

WHAT CHARACTERIZES
THE DYNAMIC ORGANIZATION?

Our intent here is not to fully elaborate the characteristics of the dynamic organization; others have ably accomplished this in this volume (cf. Dyer & Shafer, chapter 2, this volume). Rather, we wish to highlight a few of the characteristics that cause us to reconsider the issue of motivation, specifically, and staffing, more generally. Many of these characteristics were reported by Ilgen and Pulakos (1999). Dynamic organizations are likely to be characterized by the following:

• Driven by the necessity of adaptability, the concept of a clearly defined job with well-described responsibilities is replaced by loosely defined and constantly changing work roles. Some have argued that work in the future will be organized around specific projects or initiatives rather than stable jobs (Ilgen, 1994).

• Organizations will place a premium on continuous learning as the core competency rather than focusing on specific job knowledge. With rapid changes in work roles and technology dictating continuous reeducation, the ability to learn new skills and to do so quickly and constantly is critical for a dynamic organization's workforce (London & Mone, 1999).

• Organizations will continue to shift toward teams (rather than individuals) as the focal unit (Guzzo & Dickson, 1996; Ilgen, 1994). Furthermore, teams will be constantly reconfigured based on the demands of particular projects or initiatives.

• Performance standards will be dictated primarily by customers rather than by organizations. This change reflects the shift in the U.S. economy away from traditional manufacturing to services organizations. Multiple customers may necessitate multiple performance metrics.

• Control will be significantly more difficult as the nature of leadership and supervision changes. Approaches to supervision in traditional bureaucratic hierarchical organizations must give way to coaching and directing individuals and teams with ambiguous performance standards.

• Lastly, to attain adaptability, contingent workers are likely to become increasingly prevalent in dynamic organizations (Hulin & Glomb, 1999). Contingent workers offer the organization considerable benefits relating to flexibility in staffing and cost of training. However, they, too, bring with them significant difficulties from a motivational perspective. Contingent workers are less likely to be committed to the organization, given the nature of their temporary contract.

Although the implications of these changes in the nature of work and organization are many, we believe the most significant for people will be the inherent role conflict, ambiguity, and stress that are driven by constantly changing demands and expectations (Ilgen & Hollenbeck, 1991; Jackson & Schuler, 1985; Salancik & Pfeffer, 1977). This may be one of the most significant limitations to the long-term viability of dynamic organizations—a topic we attend to later.

WHY SHOULD MOTIVATION BE DIFFERENT IN DYNAMIC ORGANIZATIONS?

The various chapters in this book all focus on different aspects of the world of work and why the dynamic organization context matters for their specific topic. As our focus is fundamentally about motivation, we need to first explain why we believe the dynamic organization environment matters. Once we clarify that issue, we then turn to discussions of what to do about it.

We began our thinking on this topic by considering existing theories of motivation and motivational techniques, and considering whether the dynamic context would change the fundamental motivational processes on which these approaches are built. Mitchell (1997) noted the importance of considering environmental and organizational context when choosing motivational strategies. Time after time, we came to the conclusion that, in fact, the context *would* make these traditional theories and approaches significantly less useful, if not meaningless. To illustrate this, let us consider traditional incentive systems, goal-setting theory and related approaches, and expectancy theory and its analog, the path–goal theory of leadership.

Traditional Reinforcement/Reward Systems

Traditional reinforcement/reward systems in organizations stem from the standard operant psychological assumption that organizations can use rewards to increase specific, desired behaviors of their employees. Employees who are best able to accomplish the desired behaviors (a) receive the most rewards and (b) are the most desirable employees, because they produce the most for the organization. The traditional reinforcement paradigm rests on the assumption that it is possible to identify the specific behaviors to be rewarded and then establish a consistent and coherent process to reward and reinforce those behaviors—an approach that is highly congruent with a traditional task-based job analytic approach.

This approach is untenable, however, when the behaviors that should be rewarded are no longer identifiable or consistent. The constancy of change in a dynamic organization dictates that the behaviors indicative of effective performance today may very well be different tomorrow. As a result, adaptability and flexibility supercede specific prescriptive performance requirements. Thus, traditional reward systems may not apply. Sanchez and Levine's (1999) provocatively titled chapter "Is Job Analysis Dead, Misunderstood, or Both? New Forms of Work Analysis and Design" addresses this topic, highlighting the trend away from analysis of "jobs" and toward the analysis of "work" in contemporary organizations. They point out, however, that even if work analysis is rapidly becoming more appropriate for the nature of the workplace today, the American legal system as it relates to workplace issues is highly invested in a job analytic approach. This could stymie efforts to establish viable dynamic organizations over the long run, at least in the United States. The legality of selection systems based on "work" analysis is yet to be entertained by the courts, which by virtue of precedent have focused on traditional task-based job analysis as the foundation of a legally defensible selection system.

Murphy and Jackson (1999) identified several major challenges for reward systems in contemporary organizations, and many of these are clearly present in the dynamic context. Specifically, they point out that:

• There is tension between short-term and long-term reward perspectives. For dynamic organizations, employees may demand short-term rewards, as they come to recognize that the organization's foci change rapidly and that what is rewarded today may not be rewarded tomorrow. Additionally, employees may want to be rewarded for developing competencies that may (or may not) be useful in the future, rather than for specific achievements, as the usefulness of any particular training program could change quickly. Hesketh's (1997) argument that training in contemporary organizations is often focused on short-term needs rather than long-term performance, and that organizations should invest in training in managing change, is also supportive of this argument.

• It is often unclear whether the organization should be rewarding behaviors or outcomes. For dynamic organizations, there may not be a prescribed order of behaviors, or indeed anyone able to monitor whether specific behaviors occurred. Thus, the reward system may focus instead on achievement of outcomes rather than the process by which those outcomes were achieved. One danger here is that an organizational outcomes focus may well lead to a de facto climate regarding ethics that does not support the organization's de jure ethical standards (Dickson, Smith, Grojean, & Ehrhart, 2001).

• There is tension between offering individual-based, team-based, or organization-based rewards. In dynamic organizations, teams are not likely to be long lasting, and organizational performance is unlikely to reflect the efforts of specific individuals. As Murphy and Jackson (1999) noted, however, "The research literature has yet to provide evidence that can be used with reasonable confidence to design an effective approach to linking formal rewards to the accomplishments of unstable teams and loosely structured and shifting work groups" (p. 352). In short, the very characteristics of the dynamic organization are those for which there is as yet no accepted strategy for assigning rewards.

• Issues of control of reward systems can affect the outcomes of those systems. This is discussed in more detail later, in relation to Expectancy Theory.

Additional concerns arise over the question of organizational justice. Murphy and Jackson (1999) noted that "Employee motivation through the effective management of justice concerns will be an increasingly challenging leader responsibility given greater workforce diversity, variation among jobs, temporary work, frequent job changes, and compensation policies such as pay for skills" (p. 351). Many of these concerns are again magnified in the dynamic organization, and consequently it seems likely that there would be even greater opportunity for perceptions of injustice when using a traditional reward/reinforcement system in the dynamic organization than in more traditional settings.

Based on these concerns, we saw several areas where further research is clearly needed. Two in particular we here present as research propositions:

Proposition 1: The importance and efficacy of change management training are greater in dynamic organizations. Training in change management will be more effective in dynamic organizations than in other, less dynamic, types of organizations.

Propostion 2: The strength (Schneider, Salvaggio, & Subirats, 2002) of the organizational climate regarding ethics (Dickson et al., 2001) will be weaker in dynamic organizations than in other, less dynamic, types of organizations.

Climate strength is the degree to which group members agree about the policies, practices, and procedures of the organization, and this proposition builds on the premise that there is likely to be dissonance between organizational emphases on process versus achievement in dynamic organizations.

Given all of these concerns about reward systems in contemporary organizations, and the degree to which those concerns are significantly magnified in dynamic organizations, we were left wondering whether traditional incentive approaches to motivation are tenable in a dynamic context. So we turned to an old standby in motivation—goal-setting theory.

Goal-Setting

Locke and Latham's (1990) goal-setting theory is well established as an approach to increasing motivation and increasing performance in both work and nonwork settings. There are some specific boundary conditions related to goal setting, however, that seem to make goal setting less applicable in the context of the dynamic organization. Specifically, the goal-setting approach requires difficult, specific, and achievable goals in order for the goal-setting process to be effective. Goals that are vague consistently have been shown to lead to lower than maximal performance, as have "do your best" goals. Additionally, most successful goal-setting programs in organizations have some level of formality to them—the goals for specific individuals and units are based on the goals adopted by the organization, rather than having each supervisor–subordinate dyad setting goals in a free-lance or ad hoc fashion.

In the context of the dynamic organization, however, the entire setting is inherently vague. When there is constantly a sense that the organization's goals (and thus individual goals) can change frequently, when performance standards are not well established (because the jobs themselves may change readily and frequently), and when the strategies used to achieve long-term goals change in fairly rapid time, it becomes difficult to establish the required "difficult but specific" goals for the individuals in the organization. In fact, "do your best" goals may be the only type of goals that can be set in such a dynamic and turbulent environment. Thus, goal-setting strategies may not prove the most useful or most practical strategies in the setting of the dynamic organization. Furthermore, given the heavy reliance of Management by Objectives (MBO) programs on systemic and wide-spread goal setting, at individual, group, and unit levels, along with the emphasis on clear job definition and longer-term planning (cf. Szilagyi & Wallace, 1983), we see MBO programs as suffering from many of the same deficiencies in the dynamic organization as would other forms of goal-setting programs.

It is possible that the situation is not as dire as we have painted it to be, however. Certainly, organizational goals in dynamic organizations do not change moment to moment, and perhaps they change no more often than quarter to quarter (or even less often), as financial data on current performance is processed and reviewed. Our focus has also been on the extreme end of the dynamic organization continuum, and perhaps less dynamic organizations would have less difficulty in this arena. If this is the case, then goal-setting approaches may be more useful than we have argued. We thus suggest that research is needed to address some specific propositions arising in this area.

Proposition 3: Goal-setting approaches to employee motivation become less useful as organizations become more dynamic.

To recap, we argue that the more dynamic the organization is, the more difficult it will be to have an effective system of organizational and individual goal-setting in place, meaning that "do your best" goals will be more common in more dynamic organizations, whereas more specific goals may be possible in less dynamic organizations.

Proposition 4: Goal commitment decreases as organizations become more dynamic.

Here, our proposition is based on the premise that even if organizational (and thus individual) goals do not change as often as possible, employees in highly dynamic organizations are aware that goals *could* change at almost any time. Goals themselves need not change rapidly for motivation to be decreased—as long as people have the belief that goals are *likely* to change, the motivation to pursue those goals is likely to be diminished.

Expectancy Approaches

The traditional expectancy theory model (Porter & Lawler, 1968; Vroom, 1964) is based on the argument that three components must all be high for there to be high levels of motivation: *expectancy,* or the belief that with sufficient effort goals can be attained; *instrumentality,* or the belief that if goals can be attained rewards will follow; and *valence,* or the value placed on the available rewards. This model has been demonstrated to be a reasonably useful predictor of level of effort expended toward the achievement of work goals (van Eerde & Thierry, 1996). Furthermore, a core assumption of the model is that the model is multiplicative—if any of the three components are low, then motivation will be low. (This is a matter of some debate in the literature, as some researchers find that an additive model is as good a predictor of performance as a multiplicative model; see Ambrose & Kulik, 1999, for a good summation of these issues).

Furthermore, in traditional work organizations, it is possible to establish work routines that allow employees to gain sufficient experience and expertise to ensure that expectancy is high, and to allow sufficient history with the organization to ensure that instrumentality is high, and to use rewards that ensure that valence is high. It is this set of conditions that gave rise to the Path–Goal Theory of leadership (House, 1971), in which leaders define the path for employees to follow to acquire desired outcomes.

However, in the dynamic organization, jobs are much less clearly defined, and consequently the tasks are much less clearly defined, as are the goals. Even the process for the assessment of performance is not clear (Murphy, 1999). Thus, by their very nature, dynamic organizations are likely to lead to decreased levels of both expectancy (because when employees are not sure what the tasks and goals are, they cannot be confident of their abilities to reach them) and instrumentality (because employees cannot be confident of receiving pay-offs for goal attainment, if the organization no longer embraces those goals). Murphy and Jackson (1999) listed these threats to instrumentality and expectancy as one of the critical issues "plaguing" reward systems in contemporary organizations, and it seems clear that this issue would only be magnified in dynamic organizations. We thus propose:

> Proposition 5: Instrumentality and expectancy are both likely to be lower in dynamic organizations than in other, less dynamic, types of organizations.

Motivation from Group Cohesion

Some authors (e.g., Guzzo & Dickson, 1996; Guzzo, Yost, Campbell, & Shea, 1993) have suggested that individuals working in team-based settings, doing work that could clearly not be accomplished by any single individual, may have high group instrumentality (or group "potency"). To date, this remains a relatively unexplored topic, and the patterns of interactions of group-level instrumentality with individual-level valence and expectancy are unknown. However, recent research has shown that group potency moderates the relationship between time pressure and group performance, such that groups with high potency perform better under time pressure than do low-potency groups (Gevers, van Eerde, & Rutte, 2001).

Given that dynamic organizations are likely to be more team oriented than individual oriented, and that dynamic organizations are likely to be high-pressure environments in many ways, the development of group potency could provide a buffer against some of the other motivation–performance concerns we have identified. In short, this could prove an interesting and important component of motivational processes in the dynamic organization, although to date that is purely speculative. Conversely, it is possible that these two factors (high pressure, group orientation) could *reduce* potency and motivation—a significant amount of social psychological research has shown that people under pressure do prefer company (building on the work of Schachter, 1959), but that they prefer company that is *not* under pressure (e.g., Firestone, Kaplan, & Russell, 1973). Thus, it is unclear whether this combination of factors would lead to the possibility of enhanced or reduced motivation in the dynamic organization context. We thus do not present a specific research proposition in this case, but encourage research on this question.

We encountered similar problems over and over—in one way or another, the boundary conditions for a wide variety of motivational theories, techniques, and facilitators are pushed (if not violated) when they are applied in the context of a dynamic organization. In hindsight, this is not surprising; if the dynamic organization is truly a new form of organization, or at least is at a new frontier on the continuum of organizational dynamism, then prior theorizing about motivation has occurred in the context of more traditional organizations, and the characteristics of those more traditional settings are embedded in the theories. In a new context, the theories and techniques seem less applicable. So what, then, might we do to address the question of motivation in the dynamic organization?

It seems clear that the motivation construct takes on a different meaning in the dynamic organization, and that a different set of assumptions about organizational functioning—and therefore organizational staffing—is required. In short, we conclude that for dynamic organizations, operating through the traditional assumptions of personnel psychology and human resources management (i.e., to hire based on ability and to create motivation through incentives or rewards or goals or other motivational systems) is unlikely to be successful. Instead, a more appropriate approach in this setting is to hire based on motivation (assuming that there is adequate general ability and general intelligence). In other words, we are led to the conclusion that in this context, we must treat motivation as something that is generated internally through the interaction of the employee with his or her environment, rather than something whose roots are external, as in traditional reward systems. Based on these arguments, it might seem that we should focus on Deci and Ryan's (1985) Cognitive Evaluation Theory, which is the dominant theory of intrinsic motivation. However, that theory and others focused on intrinsic motivation have been consistently criticized for lacking construct clarity and being inapplicable to work organizations. For space considerations, we chose to not consider these theories further here.

Our assumption is that in the dynamic organization, the organization would need to create the requisite workforce characteristics (competencies) through what would essentially be a "just-in-time training" approach, a training system that would constantly change and adapt with the dynamic marketplace. Alternatively, the organization could rely primarily on contingent workers, keeping only a small core of regular employees. Thus, rather than hiring people who are capable of performing the set of tasks that are known to be required, we conclude that the dynamic organization needs to hire people who have the ability to learn new tasks and skills quickly and who have both the motivation to perform in ambiguous settings and the tolerance of ambiguity that the environment will require. We turn now to this issue.

HOW DOES STAFFING CHANGE IN THE DYNAMIC ORGANIZATION?

As noted earlier, we find ourselves drawn to the conclusion that, in the dynamic organization, the traditional staffing model simply may not apply. Rather than hiring people based on skill sets and competencies, the dynamic nature of the organization and its concomitant characteristics may, in fact, suggest the need to hire for survival rather than specific competencies. Ultimately, we concluded that, given the inability to specifically prescribe the characteristics of a "job" in a dynamic organization, an appropriate staffing model would focus on fit—"hiring for the organization, not the job" (Bowen, Ledford, & Nathan, 1991), and if not specific competencies, then probably broader personal characteristics—personality traits, values, and motives (Hogan, 1992). If we are unable to create motivation, can we then select for motivation?

Prior meta-analyses have supported the limited utility of personality as a predictor of work performance (Barrick & Mount, 1991; Tett, Jackson, & Rothstein, 1991; Salgado, 1997); however, we believe that dynamic organizations provide a context in which personality is fundamental to both individual and organizational success. Our thinking about personality in the context of dynamic organizations was guided by two basic questions. First, what kind of person will be satisfied (happy) in a dynamic organization or, more bluntly, can survive a dynamic organization? For instance, what kind of person can tolerate (and thrive on) the ambiguity, instability, and complexity of dynamic organizations? Second, what personality characteristics play a role in the behaviors (abilities or competencies) described by others as critical for a dynamic organization's workforce (e.g., Dyer & Schafer, this volume)? Given the limited research in this area, we primarily extrapolated from the more general literature on personality and, where possible, we worked backwards from these competencies to derive a profile of traits, values, and motives on which fit to a dynamic organization could be assessed.

By survival, we suggest that the dynamic organization is most certainly not for everyone (Dyer & Shafer, this volume); in fact, we conclude that the dynamic organization may "be" for very few people—people with an unlikely mix of characteristics that predispose them to thrive in a dynamic organization. In what follows, we outline what we believe to be some of the necessary characteristics of people who can not only survive but thrive in a dynamic organization. In many places, we have to rely on supposition and conjecture. We use the five-factor model (FFM) of personality to organize our thoughts and discussion (Costa & McCrae, 1995; Goldberg, 1993; John, 1990). Generally speaking, the FFM represents the current orthodoxy in personality measurement and the consensus of hundreds if not thousands of studies of the structure of normal personality based on both theoretical models of personality and empirical examinations of natural language personality descriptors. The FFM was intended to represent a common language for people to discuss personality characteristics, and it is our intent to use it that way here. Although there remain disagreements regarding the labeling of the five factors and their respective content, they are commonly referred to as:

- Neuroticism (or emotional stability): reflects the tendency to be moody, irritable, lacking in self-esteem and self-confidence, self-pitying, emotional, and intolerant of stress, rather than calm, even-tempered, having high self-esteem and self-confidence, stress-tolerant, and independent.

- Extroversion: reflects being outgoing, dominant, assertive, gregarious, sociable, and energetic, rather than passive, submissive, introverted, quiet, reserved, shy, and withdrawn.

- Openness to experience: reflects the tendency to be broadminded, creative, imaginative, and inquiring versus being conventionally or practically minded, unoriginal, shallow, and narrow in interests.

- Agreeableness: reflects the tendency to be warm, friendly, trusting, and empathetic versus being cold, aloof, quarrelsome, distrustful and cynical.

- Conscientiousness: reflects the tendency to be prudent, organized, precise, planful, dependable, achievement-oriented, and persistent versus being undependable, impulsive, careless, and inattentive to detail.

For us, the essential tension in the dynamic organization is between the need to constantly adapt and change as the external marketplace dictates and the need to maintain the internal stability needed for people to function in any organization, including dynamic organizations. Dynamic organizations must be both stable (internally) and flexible (externally) to have longevity. As we read various authors discussing the dynamic organization, we noted a tendency to assume what we refer to as the "myth of infinite human adaptability."

Simply, this myth assumes that those who populate a dynamic organization are infinitely capable of adapting with the changing organization, regardless of what those changes may be or how frequently they occur. In fact, humans are predisposed to reduce uncertainty and ambiguity, seek constancy, and maintain stability and predictability (Eibl-Eibesfeldt, 1989; Hogan, 1982). Constant change is quite opposed to the very fabric of human nature.

Earlier, we noted that the inherently high levels of role conflict, ambiguity, and stress were, to us, the most significant limitations of the dynamic organization. Murphy and Jackson (1999) argued cogently that as we shift from the bureaucratic model of organizations to the dynamic organization, role ambiguity and conflict necessarily result. This seems intuitive, and ambiguity is inbuilt in the definition of the dynamic organization. However, most research on role ambiguity and conflict suggests substantial negative consequences for both individuals and organizations. Particularly, there is a large and well-replicated literature demonstrating that role conflict and ambiguity lead to dissatisfaction, lower levels of organizational commitment, and turnover (Fisher & Gitelson, 1983; Gupta & Beehr, 1979; Jackson & Schuler, 1985; Schaubroeck, Cotton, & Jennings, 1989). All else being equal, we would expect an organization attempting to adopt "agile" characteristics to experience a substantial increase in turnover. In fact, turnover may simply be an intrinsic characteristic of dynamic organizations. To manage turnover, dynamic organizations would need to select people who prefer change, and subsequently to retain those with the ability to readily adapt to environmental flux.

Research does suggest, however, that there is a dispositional propensity toward tolerance of ambiguity. Budner (1962) conducted the pioneering research on tolerance of ambiguity as a stable personality characteristic (actually, Budner focused primarily on intolerance). Regarding the FFM, tolerance for ambiguity is positively related to openness to experience and negatively related to both conscientiousness and neuroticism. Judge, Thoreson, Pucik, and Welbourne (1999) examined managerial coping with organizational change and demonstrated that tolerance for ambiguity moderated many of the negative consequences of organizational change. Their research suggested that tolerance for ambiguity was related to indicators of neuroticism (self-esteem, generalized self-efficacy, and locus of control), openness to experience, risk aversion, and positive affectivity (occasionally considered a component of extroversion). It is clear, however, that the level of change described in the research by Judge et al. did not reach the magnitude expected in a dynamic organization. It remains unclear if tolerance for ambiguity can mollify the effects of extreme change. Interestingly, the kind of extreme tolerance for ambiguity that may be necessary for survival in a dynamic organization has been investigated as a manifestation of clinically maladaptive behavior (Meek, 1968).

In a related study, Venkatachalam (1995) examined the moderating effect of organizational support mechanisms and personal hardiness on the role-stress–outcome relationship. Personal hardiness (primarily stress tolerance and ego strength, both of which are components of neuroticism) moderated the negative impact of role stress. So, in answer to our first question, it seems that those capable of surviving in a dynamic organization would be low in neuroticism, high in openness to experience, and low in conscientiousness. Such individuals seem to prefer less restrictive and novel environments and are resistant to some of the negative consequences of continuous change.

With regard to our second question (what personality characteristics play a role in the competencies identified as critical for a dynamic organization), to paraphrase Dyer and Shafer (this volume), dynamic organizations need workers who have:

• A sense of urgency regarding the need to adapt to a changing marketplace (this implies higher scores on neuroticism—stress-intolerant people are quick to sense the urgency of a situation).

• Willingness to take initiative (this implies lower scores on neuroticism-self-confidence, higher scores on extroversion-ambition and dominance, and higher scores on conscientiousness-achievement orientation).

• A willingness to assume multiple roles and to change roles quickly (as we have noted, this implies someone who is tolerant of ambiguity—low neuroticism, high openness to experience, and low conscientiousness).

• A willingness to spontaneously collaborate and work in multiple teams (this implies high scores on agreeableness).

• The ability to be innovative, constantly creating new and better products or services (this suggests high openness to experience—the only personality characteristic that is demonstrably related to creativity and perhaps, lower scores on conscientiousness; Judge, Bono, Illies, & Gerhart, 2002).

• A willingness to continuously learn (low neuroticism and high openness to experience).

As noted, some of the competencies imply people who are simultaneously high and low on certain personality characteristics (e.g., high on neuroticism—sense of urgency and low on neuroticism—initiative, learning, and assuming multiple roles, or high on conscientiousness—willing to take initiative and low on conscientiousness—tolerant of ambiguity). Subsequently, selecting people for particular competencies may be difficult in the dynamic organization.

We, therefore, propose the following propositions:

Proposition 6: Over the long term, turnover will be higher in a dynamic organization than in a traditional organization.

Proposition 7: Organizations attempting to shift from a bureaucratic model to a dynamic organization model will experience substantial turnover as those uncomfortable with ambiguity and change leave.

Proposition 8: Neuroticism will be the best predictor of turnover in a dynamic organization.

The first to leave a dynamic organization will be those who are intolerant of ambiguity.

Proposition 9: Openness to experience will be a better predictor of performance and conscientiousness a worse predictor of performance in a dynamic organization.

Current meta-analyses suggest that conscientiousness is the only generalizable predictor of job performance in organizational settings. However, in a dynamic organization, we believe openness to experience would likely be more critical given its relation to continuous learning and the need for novelty. Conscientiousness may, in fact, be negatively related to performance.

Given our concerns, should we address survival or should we select for competencies?

CULTURAL FIT

Values are at the core of many definitions of organizational cultures (Schneider, 1992). Examining the fit between people and dynamic organizations implies examining the alignment of organizational and individual values (O'Reilly, Chatman, & Caldwell, 1991). If, for the moment, we take seriously the notion of selecting people for their fit to a dynamic organization (rather than focusing solely on specific abilities), then to what personal values should we attend? Although there is a substantial literature on the various effects of person–organization fit (suggesting primarily positive consequences of fit and negative consequences of misfit; Kristof, 1996), there is a paucity of research on fit with dynamic organizations. We therefore must rely primarily on conjecture. Our review of the personal values literature suggests several values characteristics that could create a substantial misfit between a person and a dynamic organization. Consider the following core values as examples:

• Security: People who value security have a high need for stability and predictability. Given the lack of constancy in a dynamic organization, security values represent a key dimension of misalignment.

• Tradition: People who value tradition have a dedication to ritual and history. It is unlikely that a dynamic organization would be focused on entrenched rituals and institutional history (it would be constantly rewritten). Consequently, a person who values ritual and history is unlikely to fit a dynamic organization.

• Recognition: People who value recognition desire attention, approval, praise, and public signs of status. However, in a dynamic organization, given changing job and project assignments and loose reporting relationships, status boundaries are unlikely to be clearly visible, and recognition is likely to be difficult to achieve. Further, rewarding individual performance and achievement would be counter to the reconfigurable, ad hoc team structure of the dynamic organization.

• Power: People who focus on power enjoy success and control over others. However, a dynamic organization requires individuals who are simultaneously comfortable being a leader and a follower (in other words, a team player). People with high power motives have difficulty in subordinate positions and are unlikely to function effectively in a dynamic organization.

As is probably obvious, these values typify a pattern that is quite common in traditional bureaucracies, particularly among successful managers. Conversely, a person with this pattern of values seems to us to be highly unlikely to be successful in a dynamic organization. We suggest the following research propositions:

Proposition 10: Personal values will be a better predictor of success (both longevity and performance) in a dynamic organization.

Proposition 11: The typical value pattern for a team leader (high power, tradition, and recognition/status values) will be different in a dynamic organization.

STRATEGIC ATTRITION?

The move from being a traditional organization to one with a dynamic structure is clearly a change in culture, as well as a change in structure. As noted elsewhere (Schneider, 1987), the people make the place, and if the people in place no longer fit the new model of the organization, then they may well find themselves uncomfortable and unhappy in the new environment, and they may thus choose to leave the organization in search of a different place where they would again have the comfort of good fit. However, if they do not leave, and refuse to embrace the new structure and form of the organization (e.g., through insisting on adherence to job descriptions, resisting change in procedures, insisting on hierarchical communications patterns, etc.), then it may be necessary to move them out involuntarily. Of course, this is never a preferred solution, but when specific individuals raise significant barriers to the successful implementation of the new dynamic culture, selective termination of employment may prove to be quite beneficial.

QUESTIONS AND FINAL RESEARCH PROPOSITIONS

There are a great many questions that remain about staffing and motivation in the dynamic organization, even if one accepts the model we presented here. Partly this is because the dynamic organization remains rare and difficult to study, and the newness of the form prevents making many statements with certainty. Where there is sufficient research to justify research propositions, we present some final ones. However, given that there is little existing research on many of these issues, we present some of these as questions, rather than as specific research propositions:

- Does dynamic organization effectiveness require that all employees have high G? High EI?

- If so, would this mean dynamic organizations will always be rare and idiosyncratic?

Dynamic organizations, as we and others throughout this book have noted, are turbulent environments, and they require employees who are able to make decisions in the absence of all desirable information, and in quick succession. This suggests that successful dynamic organization employees would be people with high levels of generalized intelligence, or G (to make good decisions rapidly and under pressure), and perhaps high levels of emotional intelligence (Goleman, 1997) or EI (to understand how to respond to and thrive in the inherently stressful environment, and to recognize the responses of others).

Although both G and high EI have been shown by others to be important in a variety of jobs, they have also been shown to be relatively uncommon, and the combination of the two is surely rarer still. If this is the case, then dynamic organizations will have a very limited pool of potentially successful employees on which to draw. Thus, successful dynamic organizations (i.e., those surviving for the long term) may prove to be quite rare, anasmuch as there is simply not a sufficient population of qualified employees to staff more than a few dynamic organizations. Indeed, a variety of authors (cf. Rothstein, 1999) have noted that there is an increasing demand for a broader array of skills and characteristics in even entry-level employees across the employment spectrum leading to an undersupply of sufficiently capable potential employees. This would certainly hold true for dynamic organizations. In fact, the shortage of employees likely to be successful in dynamic organizations may well be even more intense than for more traditional organizations, given the more specific requirements for specific personality characteristics, intelligence, values, and motives, etc.

As further evidence, the *1997 Survey of Human Resource Trends* (Society for Human Resource Management, 1997), for example, shows that over 60% of managers responding to the survey believe that there are significant deficiencies in critical skills among those applying for jobs in their organizations. Some might argue that this is a result of decreased focus on these skills in the educational system, but we believe it is more likely a result of the increase in the range of skills required in many modern workplaces.

- ♦ If societal values (e.g., uncertainty avoidance) are reflected in personal values, will culture cause dynamic organizations to flourish in some societies and wither in others?

A variety of researchers (e.g., Hofstede, 1980, 2000; House et al., in press) have demonstrated that there are dimensions that can be used to differentiate between societies. One of those dimensions is uncertainty avoidance, or the tendency to prefer certainty in life and to avoid ambiguity. Some societies are quite high on this dimension (e.g., Switzerland, Germany, China), whereas others are quite low (e.g., Russia, Guatemala, Greece).[1]

The fundamental nature of the dynamic organization is high uncertainty. The problems already mentioned, of finding sufficient qualified employees to staff a dynamic organization, are quite likely magnified in societies where the cultural tendency is away from uncertainty. Certainly there is variation within any society in the degree to which specific individuals exemplify widely shared cultural characteristics, but when an organization is trying to staff itself with people who are significant distances from the societal mean on a value, the population to draw from is going to be quite small. Conversely, in societies that embrace uncertainty, it may be significantly easier to staff the dynamic organization with people who will thrive in the environment. This likelihood is made stronger by the recent findings by von Oudenhoven (2001) showing that there is congruence between the characteristics of organizations and the characteristics of the societies in which those organizations exist.

The implication of this is that this novel form of organization may thrive in some societies and wither in others. In fact, dynamic organizations may prove to be much less rare in societies low on uncertainty avoidance than we have presented them as likely to be in the United States. We thus propose:

---

[1] These data are from House et al., in press.

Proposition 12: Dynamic organizations will be less common in societies high on uncertainty avoidance.

Proposition 13: Dynamic organizations will be less successful in societies high on uncertainty avoidance.

What About Contingent Workers?

Hulin and Glomb (1999) noted the increased use of contingent workers as a strategy employed by many organizations to maintain flexibility given the changing demands of the marketplace. Contingent workers minimize the risk of a new hire for organizations, yet they bring with them significant concerns from a commitment/motivation perspective. Murphy and Jackson (1999) and others noted the motivational difficulties associated with contingent workers who, as temporary employees, do not identify with and are less committed to the organization. It remains unclear to what extent contingent employees represent an effective staffing strategy for dynamic organizations. They do offer flexibility—however, without the associated commitment that would seem to be necessary to maintain a dynamic organization. To follow this idea further, it seems possible that if turnover in the dynamic organization is as high as many authors posit, employees not at the very core of the organization may come to think of themselves as essentially contingent employees, with many or all of the negative consequences associated with that perception.

CONCLUSIONS

As we reflect on this chapter, it appears as though we are less than optimistic about the success of the dynamic organization as an entity. In fact, we fundamentally question the longevity of an organization that embodies the many "dynamic" characteristics described by authors in this volume (e.g., Dyer & Shafer). What we do want to point out is that the issue of selection and motivation in a dynamic organization is complex. Likely, the tried and true models that are the focus of much theory and research are of limited utility in a dynamic organization. This leaves us with a substantial amount of work to do. Essentially, we have proposed that the broad issue of motivation is far too complex in a dynamic organization to expect easy solutions. Rather, the more basic question is who can survive the extremes of role conflict, stress, and ambiguity that will accompany a shift to dynamic organizational practices. Even here, though, we have limited footing with which to propose a selection system for a dynamic organization.

As a final note, we have largely neglected the issue of culture change. It remains unclear to us if it is viable for an organization to adopt a "dynamic" model. That is, the transition from a traditional organization to a dynamic organization will likely entail necessary attrition. Schneider (1987), Schein (1992), and many others noted the consonance between organizational culture and the people who populate an organization. Such a radical change in culture will likely require a radical change in people.

REFERENCES

Ambrose, M. L., & Kulik, C. T. (1999). Old friends, new faces: Motivation research in the 1990s. *Journal of Management, 25*(3), 231–292.

Ashkenas, R., Ulrich, D., Jick, T., & Kerr, S. (1995). *The boundaryless organization.* San Francisco: Jossey-Bass.

Barrick, M. R., & Mount, M. K. (1991). The Big Five in personality dimensions and job performance: A meta-analysis. *Personnel Psychology, 44,* 1–26.

Bowen, D. E., Ledford, G. E., Jr., & Nathan, B. R. (1991). Hiring for the organization, not the job. *Academy of Management Executive, 5,* 35–51.

Budner, S. (1962). Intolerance of ambiguity as a personality variable. *Journal of Personality, 30,* 29–50.

Costa, P. T., & McCrae, R. R. (1995). Solid ground in the wetlands of personality: A reply to Block. *Psychological Bulletin, 117,* 216–220.

Deci, E. L., & Ryan, R. M. (1985). *Intrinsic motivation and self-determination in human behavior.* New York: Plenum Press.

Dickson, M. W., Smith, D. B., Grojean, M. W., & Ehrhart, M. (2001). An organizational climate regarding ethics: The outcome of leader values and the practices that reflect them. *Leadership Quarterly, 12,* 197–217.

Dyer, L., & Shafer, R. A. (1999). From human resource strategy to organizational effectiveness: Lessons from research on organizational agility. In P. M. Wright, L. Dyer, J. B. Boudreau, & G. T. Milkovich (Eds.), *Strategic human resources management research in the 21st century, research in personnel and human resource management* (Supplement 4, pp. 145–174). Stamford, CT: JAI Press.

Eibl-Eibesfeldt, E. (1989). *Human ethology.* New York: Aldine de Gruyter.

Firestone, I. J., Kaplan, K. J., & Russell, J. C. (1973). Anxiety, fear, and affiliation with similar-state versus dissimilar-state others: Misery sometimes loves nonmiserable company. *Journal of Personality & Social Psychology, 26*(3), 409–414.

Fisher, C. D., & Gitelson, R. (1983). A meta-analysis of the correlates of role conflict and ambiguity. *Journal of Applied Psychology, 68,* 320–333.

Fulmer, W. E. (2000). *Shaping the adaptive organization.* New York: AMACOM.

Gevers, J. M. P., van Eerde, W., & Rutte, C. G. (2001). Time pressure, potency, and progress in project groups. *European Journal of Work & Organizational Psychology, 10*(2), 205–221.

Goldberg, L. (1993). The structure of phenotypic personality traits. *American Psychologist, 48,* 26–34.

Goleman, D. (1997). *Emotional intelligence: Why it can matter more than IQ.* New York: Bantam Books.

Gupta, N., & Beehr, T. A. (1979). Job stress and employee behaviors. *Organizational Behavior and Human Decision Processes, 23,* 373–387.

Guzzo, R. A., & Dickson, M. W. (1996). Teams in organizations: Recent research on performance and effectiveness. *Annual Review of Psychology, 47,* 307–338.

Guzzo, R. A., Yost, P. R., Campbell, R. J., & Shea, G. P. (1993). Potency in groups: Articulating a construct. *British Journal of Social Psychology, 32*(1), 87–106.

Haeckel, S. H. (1999). *Adaptive enterprise.* Boston: Harvard Business School Press.

Hesketh, B. (1997). Dilemmas in training for transfer and retention. *Applied Psychology: An International Review, 46*(4), 317–339.

Hofstede, G. (1980). *Culture's consequences: International differences in work-related values.* Thousand Oaks, CA: Sage.

Hofstede, G. (2000). *Culture's consequences: International differences in work-related values* (2nd ed.). Thousand Oaks, CA: Sage.

Hogan, R. T. (1982). *A socioanalytic theory of personality.* Nebraska Symposium on Motivation. University of Nebraska Press.

Hogan, R. T. (1992). Personality and personality measurement. In M. D. Dunnette & L. M. Hough (Eds.), *Handbook of industrial and organizational psychology* (Vol. 2, 2nd ed., pp. 873–919). Palo Alto, CA: Consulting Psychologist Press.

House, R. J. (1971). A path-goal theory of leadership. *Administrative Science Quarterly, 16,* 321–338.

House, R. J., Hanges, P. J., Javidan, M., Dorfman, P. W., Gupta, V., and GLOBE Associates. (in press). *Cultures, Leadership, and Organizations: GLOBE, A 62 Nation Study* (Vol. 1). Thousand Oaks, CA: Sage.

Hulin, C. E., & Glomb, T. M. (1999). Contingent employees: Individual and organizational considerations. In D. R. Ilgen & E. D. Pulakos (Eds.), *The changing nature of performance: Implications for staffing, motivation, and development* (pp. 87–118). San Francisco, CA: Jossey-Bass.

Ilgen, D. R. (1994). Jobs and roles: Accepting and coping with the changing structure of organizations. In M. G. Rumsey, C. B. Walker, & J. H. Harris (Eds.), *Personnel selection and classification* (pp. 13–22). Hillsdale, NJ: Lawrence Erlbaum Associates.

Ilgen, D. R., & Hollenbeck, J. R. (1991). The structure of work: Job design and roles. In M. D. Dunnette & L. M. Hough (Eds.), *Handbook of industrial and organizational psychology* (Vol. 2, 2nd ed., pp. 165–207). Palo Alto, CA: Consulting Psychologist Press.

Ilgen, D., & Pulakos, E. (1999). Introduction: Employee performance in today's organization. In D. R. Ilgen & E. D. Pulakos (Eds.), *The changing nature of performance: Implications for staffing, motivation, and development* (pp. 87–118). San Francisco, CA: Jossey-Bass.

Jackson, S. E., & Schuler, R. S. (1985). A meta-analysis and conceptual critique of research on role ambiguity and role conflict in work settings. *Organizational Behavior and Human Decision Processes, 36,* 16–78.

John, O. P. (1990). The "Big Five" factor taxonomy: Dimensions of personality in the natural language and in questionnaires. In L. Pervin (Ed.), *Handbook of personality: Theory and research* (pp. 66–100). New York: Guilford.

Judge, T. A., Bono, J., Illies, R., & Gerhart, M. (2002). Personality and leadership: A qualitative and quantitative review. *Journal of Applied Psychology, 87,* 765–780.

Judge, T. A., Thoreson, C. J., Pucik, V., & Welbourne, T. M. (1999). Managerial coping with organizational change: A dispositional perspective. *Journal of Applied Psychology, 84,* 107–122.

Kristof, A. L. (1996). Person–organization fit: An integrative review of its conceptualizations, measurement, and implications. *Personnel Psychology, 49*(1), 1–49.

Locke, E. A., & Latham, G. P. (1990). *A theory of goal setting and task performance.* Englewood Cliffs, NJ: Prentice Hall.

London, M., & Mone, E. M. (1999). Continuous learning. In D. R. Ilgen & E. D. Pulakos (Eds.), *The changing nature of performance: Implications for staffing, motivation, and development* (pp. 119–153). San Francisco, CA: Jossey-Bass.

Meek, P. M. (1968). *Extreme tolerance of ambiguity: A manifestation of maladaptive behavior.* Unpublished doctoral dissertation, University of Florida, Gainesville, FL.

Mitchell, T. R. (1997). Matching motivational strategies with organizational contexts. *Research in Organizational Behavior, 19,* 57–149.

Murphy, K. E. (1999). The challenges of staffing the post industrial workplace. In D. R. Ilgen & E. D. Pulakos (Eds.), *The changing nature of performance: Implications for staffing, motivation, and development* (pp. 295–324). San Francisco, CA: Jossey-Bass.

Murphy, P. R., & Jackson, S. E. (1999). Managing work role performance: Challenges for twenty-first-century organizations and their employees. In D. R. Ilgen & E. D. Pulakos (Eds.), *The changing nature of performance: Implications for staffing, motivation, and development* (pp. 325–365). San Francisco, CA: Jossey-Bass.

O'Reilly, C. A., Chatman, J., & Caldwell, D. F. (1991). People and organizational culture: A profile comparison approach to assessing person–organization fit. *Academy of Management Journal, 34,* 487–516.

Porter, L. W., & Lawler, E. E. (1968). *Managerial attitudes and performance.* Homewood, IL: Irwin.

Rothstein, H. (1999). Recruitment and selection: Benchmarking at the millenium. In A. Kraut & A. Korman (Eds.), *Evolving practices in human resource management* (pp. 69–89). San Francisco: Jossey-Bass.

Salancik, G., & Pfeffer, J. (1977). An examination of need-satisfaction models of job attitudes. *Administrative Science Quarterly, 22,* 427–456.

Salgado, J. F. (1997). The five factor model of personality and job performance in the European community. *Journal of Applied Psychology, 82,* 30–43.

Sanchez, J. I., & Levine, E. L. (1999). Is job analysis dead, misunderstood, or both? New forms of work analysis and design. In A. Kraut & A. Korman (Eds.), *Evolving practices in human resource management* (pp. 43–68). San Francisco: Jossey-Bass.

Schachter, S. (1959). *The psychology of affiliation: Experimental studies of the sources of gregariousness.* Stanford, CA: Stanford University Press.

Schaubroeck, J., Cotton, J. L., & Jennings, K. R. (1989). Antecedents and consequences of role stress: A covariance structure analysis. *Journal of Organizational Behavior, 10,* 35–58.

Schein, E. (1992). *Organizational culture and leadership* (2nd ed.). San Francisco: Jossey-Bass.

Schneider, B. (1987). The people make the place. *Personnel Psychology, 40,* 437–453.

Schneider, B. (1992). *Organizational climate and culture.* San Francisco, CA: Jossey-Bass.

Schneider, B., Salvaggio, A. N., & Subirats, M. (2002). Climate strength: A new direction for climate research. *Journal of Applied Psychology, 87*(2), 220–229.

Sifonis, J. G., & Goldberg, B. (1996). *Corporation on a tightrope: Balancing leadership, governance, and technology in an age of complexity.* New York: Oxford University Press.

Society for Human Resource Management. (1997). *1997 survey of human resource trends.* Alexandria, VA: Author.

Szilagyi, A. D., Jr., & Wallace, M. J., Jr. (1983). *Organizational behavior and performance* (3rd ed.). Glenview, IL: Scott Foresman.

Tett, R. P., Jackson, D. N., & Rothstein, M. (1991). Personality measures as predictors of job performance: A meta-analytic review. *Personnel Psychology, 44,* 703–742.

von Oudenhoven, J. P. (2001). Do organizations reflect national cultures?: A 10-nation study. *International Journal of Intercultural Relations, 25*(1), 89–107.

van Eerde, W., & Thierry, H. (1996). Vroom's expectancy models and work-related criteria: A meta-analysis. *Journal of Applied Psychology, 81*, 575–586.

Venkatachalam, M. (1995). *Personal hardiness and perceived organizational support as links in the role stress–outcome relationship: A person–environment fit model.* Unpublished doctoral dissertation, University of Alabama, Birmingham, AL.

Volberda, H. W. (1998). *Building the flexible firm.* Oxford, UK: Oxford University Press.

Vroom, V. H. (1964). *Work and motivation.* New York: Wiley.

4

Virtual Processes: Implications for Coaching the Virtual Team

Ruth Wageman
Dartmouth College

This chapter examines the work processes that typically occur in an increasingly common structure in dynamic organizations: virtual teams. The chapter explores the existing research on virtual teams to show that process losses are highly likely in such teams, while the opportunities for synergistic process gains is relatively low. It presents a model of effective team coaching, and shows how such coaching might help defend virtual teams against threats to their ultimate effectiveness.

The "dynamic organization" is a phenomenon often characterized as arising out of external pressures such as market complexity, rapid technological change, and the globalization of markets. In this new context, organizations are creating novel partnerships with other organizations and individuals. Many of these relationships vary in significant ways from more traditional alliances. Frequently, such relationships are project-based, temporary, and idiosyncratic. And they often are relationships among individuals, groups, or organizations that are not located in the same building, organization, or even continent (Dess, Rasheed, McLaughlin, & Priem, 1995; Grenier & Metes, 1995). Virtual teams are a new type of task-performing group that is emerging in the time of the dynamic organization.

Virtual teams—teams composed of individuals who are located in different places, different time zones, and sometimes, different organizations—originate for the explicit purpose of bringing together people who might not otherwise be able to collaborate. Virtual teams can, of course, vary in the degree to which they are "virtual." That is, some subset of members may be collocated, or all may be physically dispersed. Some virtual teams may operate electronically by choice, whereas others may rely on technology of necessity because of physical distance among members. Some virtual teams may be composed of members who have worked together on previous occasions: others may be composed of strangers. In this chapter, I address the most extreme forms of virtual teams: teams in which physically dispersed members who have not previously worked together are assigned responsibility for one particular project.

The growing interest in such teams, and in popular-press books about how to manage them, suggests that they are at least viewed as offering significant competitive advantage to the organizations that create them. Claims for their great benefits as task-performing units are as enthusiastic as those about most management fads (Abrahamson, 1996). Here are some of them:

• Virtual teams have more talent than traditional, collocated teams. The logic behind this argument is that creating virtual teams allows organizations to form teams of experts regardless of where those experts are, thus producing better products and services than a similar, collocated team.

• Virtual teams allow better use of human resources. Part of the emerging ethos of virtual teams is that memberships in such teams are temporary; therefore, human resources can enter the team when needed, and then move on to other projects where they are needed, while the remaining members complete the work.

• Virtual teams can respond to opportunities, wherever they arise, faster than more localized units. Because the work virtual teams do can arise from an opportunity identified locally, and then draw on experts wherever they sit, using virtual teams allows organizations to deploy resources to take advantage of a discovered opportunity with little delay.

• Virtual teams offer a level of "empowerment" that more traditional collocated teams do not achieve. As with any individual or team that operates far from headquarters, virtual teams, by mere function of the fact that no manager can observe, monitor, and direct all their daily actions, have the chance for real control over what they do (Dess et al., 1995; Duarte & Snyder, 1999; Townsend, DeMarie, & Hendrickson, 1998).

Such are the promises of virtual teams. Will virtual teams live up to the claims for their potential, or become yet another management fad that dies off after the initial enthusiasm fades in the face of failures? The jury is still out on this question, and research on real, organizational teams that operate virtually is still very rare indeed. Nevertheless, it is certainly possible to reflect on what we have learned in research about teams more generally to identify and explore some of the potential barriers to the effectiveness of virtual teams. In some ways, virtual teams are just teams—and as such, need the basic design and support structures that any team needs (Hackman, 2002). In other ways, virtual teams are different—primarily in their operating practices—and may need different kinds of hands-on support than more traditional teams. The purpose of this chapter is to draw on existing theory and research about team design, team process, and team coaching to make some predictions about the likely outcomes of virtual teams and their requirements, and to raise additional researchable questions about the functioning of such units.

I begin by elaborating a theoretical perspective on team process that is useful for thinking about the challenges and opportunities facing virtual teams. I then identify two major threats to the likely effectiveness of such teams, drawing on research about both traditional and virtual teams. I then play out the practical implications of those threats for those who lead and operate in virtual teams, ending with several researchable questions relevant to the hands-on coaching of virtual teams.

TEAM PROCESS AND PERFORMANCE

Following Hackman and Morris (1975), I posit that team performance effectiveness is a joint function of three key performance processes: (a) the level of effort group members collectively expend carrying out their work, (b) the appropriateness to the task of the performance strategies the group uses in its work, and (c) the amount of knowledge and skill (talent) members bring to bear on the team task. Any group that brings high levels of effort to its work, develops and uses a task-appropriate performance strategy, and brings high levels of talent to bear on the task is quite likely to achieve a high standing on outcome criteria of effectiveness: the standards of quality, quantity, timeliness, and the like, that one would apply to their work product.

These three key processes are not the ultimate test of how well a group has performed, but they are useful both for assessing how a group is doing as it proceeds with its work and for identifying the nature of the problem if things are not going well. One can readily ask, for example, whether a group is having difficulties because of an effort problem, a talent problem, or a strategy problem, and then target remedial interventions to those processes.

Associated with each of the three performance processes are both characteristic "process losses" (Steiner, 1972) and opportunities for positive synergy, referred to here as *process gains* (Hackman & Wageman, 2002). That is, members may interact in ways that undermine the team's effort, the appropriateness of its strategy, and/or the utilization of member talent; alternatively, their interaction may enhance collective effort, generate uniquely appropriate strategies, and/or actively develop members' knowledge and skills (Hackman & Wageman, 2002). For example, the most typical process loss around talent in traditional, collocated teams is the misweighting of member knowledge and skill. That is, the ideas and other inputs of team members are treated with seriousness based on gender, status, or other personal characteristics not related to actual talent. Such misweighting of member capabilities prevents the group from making use of its full complement of knowledge and skill. Groups can also attain positive synergies, or process gains, around talent as well. When members actively engage in mutual teaching and learning in the course of their work, they actually build the complement of resources that the group can draw on in completing its task. Similar characteristic process losses and gains can and do occur in traditional, face-to-face teams for effort and for task performance strategy.

Task processes have been heavily studied in traditional face-to-face teams, but our purpose here is not to summarize those findings per se; rather, it is to apply these ideas to the virtual team and make some predictions about such patterns in teams that do not operate face-to-face. Interaction processes of virtual teams is one arena in which some existing research does help us examine virtual teams. Although field studies of such teams are rare, a number of laboratory studies of teams whose members communicate exclusively via computers do exist, and most offer direct comparisons to face-to-face teams. I draw here on some of these studies, as well as a few descriptive characterizations of virtual teams in the practitioner-oriented literature, to explore patterns of process losses and of process gains in virtual teams.

THREATS TO EFFECTIVE PROCESSES IN VIRTUAL TEAMS

Process Losses in Virtual Teams

Here I describe the ways in which process losses—particularly around the effort and use of talent of team members—may take different behavioral forms for virtual teams than for traditional teams. Note that I conclude (tentatively) in this discussion that process losses are equally relevant and equally likely for virtual as for traditional teams. It is their causes and behavioral manifestations that differ from their more traditional cousins.

Effort.   First, process losses having to do with member effort may be especially common in virtual teams. Two structural aspects of virtual teams may contribute to motivation losses: physical distance between members and asynchronous communication.

Virtual team members, by definition, work in locations remote from their fellow team members. They often take part in virtual teamwork as only part of their job requirements (Duarte & Snyder, 1999; Haywood, 1998). Although members of such teams may have many other organization members around them with whom they are interdependent for other tasks, these individuals are not their virtual team members. Traditional teams, by contrast, may share similar characteristics—but their team members also are nearby. This structural difference from traditional face-to-face teams may contribute to effort-related process losses in virtual teams, as follows.

Team members who are collocated have at least as much chance as other organization members of gaining the attention and cooperation of their fellow team members. By contrast, members of virtual teams may be frequently pulled by local coworkers into tasks unrelated to the team's work (Haywood, 1998; Lipnack & Stamps, 1997). This withdrawal of effort by one member, however unintentional, may well lead to the withdrawal of effort by other members, for several reasons.

First, team members may make untested attributions about the level of commitment to the team of a member whose responsiveness to team needs is less than swift. That is, other members may assume that a member's low effort levels reflect low motivation to contribute to the team—without explicitly testing this assumption. This tendency to make assumptions about others' commitment levels without discussing them is a common problem for any kind of team (Argyris, 1982). It engenders process losses around effort when other members respond by reducing their own commitment levels in the interests of equity of contribution (Schwarz, 1994).

But even in teams in which equity concerns are secondary, the tendency of a member or two to assign even temporary low priority to the group's work can spread to other members. Groups often tacitly develop norms of appropriate effort by observing and imitating the behavior of other members (Bettenhausen & Murnighan, 1985). That is, they may assume that a slow pace of responsiveness to others or delays in accomplishing the team's work is acceptable and typical of this group. Without explicit discussion of effort expectations among team members, effort norms may fall to the lowest common denominator via a process of observation and imitation.

These tacit processes—untested attributions about commitment, and the emergence of implicit effort norms—may thus lead to a downward spiral of effort among team members, triggered by any member's responsiveness to more local work demands.

To be sure, other, unrelated work demands can cause a pattern of effort withdrawal in collocated teams as well. But such teams face conflicting demands from equally present parties. By contrast, virtual teams face choices between the demands of a person standing in the office doorway, as it were, and one sending increasingly urgent e-mails. Which of these two demands is likely to be met first is fairly characteristic—the more immediate and salient demand is likely to be given priority. Indeed, some observers of virtual teams note that a consistent process problem identified by members of virtual teams is the inability to claim the attention of other team members away from other, more local demands (e.g., Haywood, 1998). Such behaviors may well lead virtual team members to conclude that their team is low priority, leading to a downward spiral of decreasing effort.

Asynchronous communication also may contribute to this pattern. Asynchronous communication refers to communication in which time lags exist between the sending, receiving, and response to messages (McGrath & Hollingshead, 1994). Members of virtual teams, which rely heavily on electronic mail and other forms of asynchronous communication, are more dependent on the receiver for the timing of needed responses to work-related messages. In descriptive studies of virtual teams, team members report considerable difficulty in getting other team members to respond swiftly to electronic communications (Grenier & Metes, 1995; Haywood, 1998; Mantovani, 1994). Such a pattern may equally contribute to shared perceptions that the team's work is of relatively low priority—and the downward spiral of social loafing. I address later what kinds of interventions might usefully prevent such a pattern from arising; for now, I merely note the high risk of effort-related process losses in virtual teams, driven by the conflicting demands of present versus absent colleagues and by the signals about the importance of the team's work that can occur when members communicate asynchronously.

Knowledge and Skill. Process losses around member knowledge and skill also may arise out of the physical dispersal of members and electronic communications media. Virtual teams often are touted in the popular press as a means by which organizations can create groups of people with more task-relevant skills than traditional teams, because team member selection is not limited to the set of people in the same place or even the same organization (e.g., Duarte & Snyder, 1999). Whether the net skill level of virtual teams is, on average, greater than that of traditional teams remains to be seen. What may be problematic for virtual teams is using the special knowledge and skills that members do have, by the task-appropriate weighting of ideas and other inputs from individual members.

Misweighting of member talents in traditional teams, as described earlier, often takes the form of nonskill-related member characteristics, such as status or gender, determining how much weight is given to the inputs of team members. Research suggests that this form of misweighting is actually less likely in virtual teams than in face-to-face teams because such demographic cues are considerably less salient in teams that operate through computer-mediated communication (McGuire, Kiesler, & Siegel, 1987; McLeod, Baron, Marti, & Yoon, 1997). As a consequence, inputs from team members that differ in their demographic characteristics are treated equally and are equally likely to influence a group decision. Moreover, participation in virtual-group discussions is generally more inclusive than in face-to-face groups (Jessup, Connolly & Galegher, 1990; Siegel, Dubrovsky, Kiesler, & Mc Guire, 1986). That is, such teams are relatively unlikely to contain members that are shut out of the conversation entirely, and the number of comments coming from each member tends to be more evenly distributed than in traditional teams. These are hopeful signs of the ultimate performance effectiveness of virtual teams. These constructive patterns, however, do not necessarily mean that virtual teams make better decisions about subtask assignments, relative expertise, which members' views bear the weight of real knowledge behind them, and the like. Virtual teams may have considerably less knowledge about members' key task-relevant knowledge and skill than do traditional teams.

Researchers note in virtual teams a tendency toward deindividuation—that is, a pattern of treating all members as if they were indistinguishable. This tendency may be caused both by the narrow content of interaction in computer-mediated groups and by the, on average, lower level of knowledge about group members from relatively distant locations (Kiesler & Sproull, 1992). As a consequence, virtual teams may well have the same tendency as traditional teams to misweight the inputs of members, but for different reasons and in different ways. That is, inputs may be treated equally, without regard to source, for lack of differentiating information about the players' task-relevant knowledge and skill (Dubrovsky, Kiesler, & Sethna, 1991). Treating all inputs on a given subject equally, without regard to underlying knowledge and skill, is no better in theory than differentiating them on the basis of some individual characteristic uncorrelated with talent. As a consequence, virtual teams are no more likely to use their full complement of knowledge and skill than are collocated teams.

Again, interventions into virtual teams may be possible that build members' knowledge of other team members' capabilities; for now, I note that the natural process of virtual teams around the use of talent are vulnerable to a particular pattern of misweighting that can undermine their effectiveness.

Task Strategy. I put task strategy last in this section because little descriptive data exist that allow us to characterize virtual team processes in this arena. I suggest, however, that the most typical process loss around strategy in collocated teams—the automatic adoption of habitual routines—may be at least temporarily unlikely in virtual teams while they are still, for many individuals, a novel means of working collaboratively.

A habitual routine exists when "a group repeatedly exhibits a functionally similar pattern of behavior in a given situation without explicitly selecting over alternative ways of behaving" (Gersick & Hackman, 1990). That is, a team may mindlessly enact a particular approach to completing their work without explicitly testing its appropriateness or considering potentially more suitable alternatives. Habitual task strategy routines generally require time and experience to arise, as a team encounters repeated exposure to the same or similar situations. They can be adaptive, in the sense that the development of routines saves time and energy, and allows easy coordination as all members enact expected patterns of behavior. Their dysfunctions arise when groups enact a routine without recognizing the novelties of the current situation that can make that routine inappropriate (Gersick & Hackman, 1990).

A virtual team such as the kind addressed here—one whose members have not met and who are working together for the first time—will not have had the opportunity to develop their own group-specific habitual routines. On the other hand, groups of all kinds import routines—for better or for worse—from other groups, and the importation of task routines from face-to-face teams into virtual teams may be especially inappropriate, as so many features of the performance context are unlike those for which such routines were developed. Moreover, one common habitual routine—the tendency to divide all group work into subtasks performed by individuals working independently—may be especially likely in virtual teams because of the technical challenges of conducting tasks interactively. Teams that so subdivide their work can lose the integration and coordination of parts that teams working interdependently can achieve (Wageman & Gordon, 2002). But the task strategies typically adopted by virtual teams, and their ultimate effects on virtual team performance, remain an area that calls for much more extensive descriptive research than currently exists.

Thus far I have argued that process losses around effort, strategy, and talent are as likely in virtual as in collocated teams, although different in their causes and behavioral manifestations. I turn next to the potential for process gains in such teams.

Process Gains in Virtual Teams

For all the popular-press excitement about the performance potential of virtual teams, it may be that the limited communication forms used by most virtual teams directly prevent the kinds of synergies possible with traditional teams. Virtual teams rely predominantly on electronic mail, the electronic transfer of documents, computer-mediated "conferencing," and, to a lesser extent, teleconferencing. These forms of communication limit the contextual richness of interpersonal communications in ways that prevent synergies from developing through the interactions of team members.

Process gains around team effort, strategy, and talent happen through contagion of enthusiasm, debate and assessment of alternatives, and mutual teaching and learning, respectively. These behaviors are promoted by intensive interaction among team members—interaction that provides affective information, the opportunity to elaborate, test, argue, and iterate ideas, and the latitude to share knowledge and experience that other members may not have. It is precisely these kinds of intensive interactions that do not occur in virtual teams because they are the kinds of interaction that are most limited by computer-mediated communications (Daft, Lengerl, & Trevino, 1987; Jarvenpaa, Knoll, & Leidner, 1998).

Effort. Research has shown that virtual teams communicating via e-mail or the exchange of documents engage in less frequent interaction, and that when interaction occurs, members communicate significantly less content than do collocated teams (Kiesler & Sproull, 1992). These limited interactions may simply be a function of the relative inefficiency of typing versus speaking. But teams also using voice or teleconferencing do not tend to fare much better in the coverage and depth of idea exchange or the richness of communication (Fussel & Benimoff, 1995). Moreover, the relatively high levels of effort that managing electronic communications demands may detract from the effort members are able to expend in the content of their communications. Thus, even virtual teams expending high overall levels of effort on their work may be sharing less information—and less complex information—than an equally talented and motivated collocated team. This attenuation of content can exact a high cost from the potential for process gains in virtual teams.

Knowledge and Skill. Process gains around knowledge and skill occur when members take the time in the course of their work interactions to teach and learn from each other. Again, the high levels of effort demanded in simply using electronic media preclude engaging in information exchange that has no obvious short-term task relevance. Moreover, learning new knowledge happens for individuals much more readily under conditions in which the learner can receive the information multimodally and process it interactively (Duarte & Snyder, 1999)—conditions that seldom exist for teams operating virtually. Taken together, these patterns suggest that process gains around knowledge and skill are quite unlikely to arise naturally in virtual teams.

Strategy. Furthermore, consider characteristic process gains around task performance strategy. Groups invent uniquely suited task strategies well into the course of their work. They do so by first spending time engaged in doing the task (Hackman, Brousseau, & Weiss, 1976), then revisiting their approach. It is in this revisiting—group interaction aimed at examining the risks and benefits of a given approach relative to other approaches, and revising it based on collective debate and learning—that synergies around task strategies arise. But collective debate is generally of poorer quality in virtual teams. Research has shown that when virtual team members do engage in debate, they have a stronger tendency to assert positions and avoid giving reasons for those positions (Kiesler & Sproull, 1992). As a consequence, team members have little of the underlying logic of different approaches available to them and little information on which to base their strategic choices and to adapt well-suited strategies to their work.

To be sure, process gains are by no means guaranteed even in well designed and well led traditional teams. It takes specific, focused effort aimed at reexamining task strategies and focusing on cross-training members, for example, for such gains to be likely. Such synergies may be more prevalent in ongoing teams in which such efforts are seen as investment in future performances—and most virtual teams are not intended to be ongoing, multitask teams. But the effort involved in strategic reflection as a group and in mutual teaching and learning, via electronic media, is substantial, time consuming, and costly. And the lack of opportunity for process gains in virtual teams is especially troublesome given their vulnerability to process losses that undermine their effectiveness.

Thus far I have argued that process losses are more likely, and process gains less likely, for virtual teams than for traditional face-to-face teams. I turn now to addressing how coaching a team well can affect such processes, then suggest some means by which good coaching might help defend virtual teams against these threats to their ultimate effectiveness.

TEAM COACHING

I summarize here a perspective on team coaching that specifies the kinds of coaching and the timing of coaching interventions that may be most helpful to task-performing teams of all kinds. I then apply this perspective to intervening in virtual teams to help them develop high-quality task processes.

Teams, even when well designed and well launched, benefit from skilled coaching. Team coaching refers to direct interaction with a team that is intended to help members develop and use effective processes in accomplishing the team's work (Hackman & Wageman, 2002). Coaching is a form of team leadership distinct from other forms of leadership such as composing the team, designing its reward system and task, and similar actions aimed at creating a helpful team structure and context. I refer to those forms of team leadership as *design work*. Note that I assume that design characteristics are every bit as relevant for virtual teams as collocated teams (Hackman, 2002). I do not examine here the ways in which virtual teams are less likely to be well designed than are traditional, collocated teams, although some recent research (Hertel, Konradt, & Orlikowski, 2002) suggested they do often lack some very basic design elements. For purposes of this chapter, I focus not on design issues, but rather on team process—and hands-on coaching.

The role of the coach is to help members learn how to minimize the process losses that occur in groups and to help them learn to work together to increase the chances of process gains. Regardless of whether the coach is the team leader, a team member, or someone outside the team, effective coaching can serve three different functions, paralleling the three key task processes.

Coaching that addresses *effort* is motivational in character; its functions are to minimize social loafing and to build shared commitment to the group and its work. Coaching that addresses *performance strategy* is consultative in character; its functions are to minimize the mindless adoption or execution of task performance routines and to foster the invention of ways of proceeding with the work that are especially well suited to the task. Coaching that addresses *knowledge and skill* is educational in character; its functions are to minimize inappropriate weighting of members' contributions and to foster the development of members' knowledge and skill.

How helpful a coaching intervention is depends not just on its focus, but also on the time in the group's life cycle when it is made. The issues that a group faces when it is first formed, for example, are quite different from those that compel their attention while they are engaged in doing the work. Effective coaching interventions address issues that are naturally alive for the group at the particular time they are made. Scholars of hands-on coaching of teams (e.g., Kozlowski, Gully, Salas, & Cannon-Bowers, 1996; Schein, 1988) argued that even competently executed coaching interventions are unhelpful if they are offered at a time when the team is not ready for them. In fact, ill-timed interventions may actually do more harm than good, in that they can distract or divert a team from other issues that do require members' attention at the time they are made.

When is coaching particularly helpful to task-performing teams? Some suggestions for when interventions into team process are and are not likely to help a team arise from the scholarly work on time in work teams. Regularities in group life cycles have been empirically explored for quite some time. A number of conceptual frameworks have sought to summarize research findings about group development, the most prominent being the "forming–storming–norming–performing" model proposed by Tuckman (1965). Most of these frameworks viewed group development as following a fixed set of stages, with each successive stage being contingent on successful completion of the previous one (although the possibility of returning to an earlier stage to complete unfinished developmental work is allowed by some models).

In recent years, research on temporal issues in group development and performance have raised doubt about the generality and validity of stage models (Ancona & Chong, 1999; Gersick, 1988; Ginnett, 1993; McGrath & Kelly, 1986; Moreland & Levine, 1988). Of special relevance for present purposes are the findings of Gersick, which point to the types of coaching intervention that may be especially helpful at different times in the group life cycle. In a field study of the life histories of a number of task-performing teams, Gersick (1988) found that each of the groups she tracked developed a distinctive approach toward its task as soon as it commenced work, and stayed with that approach until precisely half way between its first meeting and its project deadline. At the midpoint of their lives, almost all teams underwent a major transition. In a concentrated burst of changes, they dropped old patterns of behavior, reengaged with outside supervisors, and adopted new perspectives on their work. Following the midpoint transition, groups entered period of focused task execution that persisted until very near the project deadline, at which time a new set of issues having to do with termination processes arose and captured members' attention.

It appears, therefore, that there may be three times in the life of a task-performing team when members are especially open to coaching interventions: (a) at the beginning, when a group is just starting its work, (b) at the midpoint, when half the work has been done and/or half the allotted time has passed, and (c) at the end, when a piece of work has been finished. Moreover, each of the three coaching functions discussed in the previous section may be uniquely appropriate at one of those three times: motivational coaching at beginnings, consultative coaching at midpoints, and educational coaching at ends (Hackman & Wageman, 2002).

IMPLICATIONS FOR COACHING
THE VIRTUAL TEAM

What will it take to coach a virtual team effectively? If most virtual team process happens through electronic media, and most interaction between the coach and the team also happens electronically, can coaching functions be accomplished at all? There does seem to be some doubt about that question among practitioners of virtual team management. In exploring the existing literature on virtual teams, I noticed an interesting pattern. Although books in the practitioner-oriented press about coaching and facilitating collocated teams abound, even the most thorough treatments of managing virtual teams have little or nothing to say about intervening to improve virtual team process. Indeed, although I encountered extensive commentary on process problems that arise in virtual teams, the advice about how to intervene in virtual team process tended to take three forms only: (a) detecting signs that the leader should take over the team and start issuing directives, because the team process is not working; (b) times when one should intervene to change a particular team member's behavior (or remove him from the team); and (c) descriptions of behavioral norms that the team must establish right from the very beginning of its work (in one treatment, I counted 32 distinct norms) in order to keep group process constructive (Duarte & Synder, 1999; Grenier & Metes, 1995; Haywood, 1998). Of the three, only the last would fall into the domain of coaching the team, and the establishment of that many norms at a first meeting strikes this reader, at least, as highly unlikely.

Nevertheless, I am not ready to concede that virtual teams are uncoachable. Ultimately, the successful coaching of virtual teams depends on taking action that helps decrease the likelihood of process losses and increases the chances of process gains. To do so effectively, I argue, coaching a virtual team demands occasional face-to-face contact by the team as a whole.

Consider the implications of the previous discussion of group processes in virtual teams for the kinds of interventions that would be especially helpful to them. An effective virtual-team coach should help the team develop: (a) sufficient motivation to place the virtual teams' work as high priority, even in the face of local demands; (b) a means of exploring and identifying the particular task-relevant knowledge and skill that make a member especially well suited to take on a particular aspect of the team's work; (c) agreed-upon methods and standards for signaling other members that a particular communication or request for help is urgent; (d) processes that invite and allow the team to reflect on its task-strategy choices; and (e) processes that allow members to teach and learn from each other.

How might a virtual team coach intervene to help create such conditions? Drawing on the previous discussion of effective team coaching, I suggest two particular coaching activities that offer real promise for enhancing the processes of virtual teams: paying particular attention to team launch, and using several natural breakpoints in the team's life cycle to induce active reflection. Both these actions are best done face-to-face.

Team Launch

Beginnings are of critical importance to the performance effectiveness of any task-performing team (Gersick, 1988; Ginett, 1993, Hackman, 2002). Indeed, what work is done to design and launch a team well from its beginnings is a primary driver of the magnitude of subsequent process losses and gains. For example, to the degree that team purposes are articulated in a way that is clear and challenging, that the task itself is engaging, and that members know right from the beginning that there are valued rewards available contingent on ex-cellent team performance, process losses around effort become less likely and less severe, and process gains around effort become more possible (Hackman, Wageman, Ruddy, & Ray, 2000). What happens at group launch establishes for the team a trajectory that will continue long into the working life of the group (Ginett, 1993). The likelihood of a team deploying adequate effort, choosing appropriate performance strategies, and bringing to bear their full complement of talent to the work is thus greatly increased by the quality of the basic platform that is established for the group from its beginning.

Two essential conditions, in particular, can establish that positive trajectory and protect a virtual team against typical process losses if the group is launched face-to-face. First is a clear and motivating purpose—a prime determinant of collective motivation.

Clear, shared purpose arises when the person or persons who commissioned the team articulate its basic direction, and allow the team to respond, to seek clarification, and to put its own "spin" on the work (Hackman, 2002). Teams launched virtually have little such opportunity. More often, the direction state-ment of a virtual team is a list of measurable objectives for a project, sent to individual members via e-mail. This kind of complex interchange about mean-ing is undermined by the limits of electronic communication described earlier. Such a process undermines the team's ability to clarify and make their own a genuinely engaging purpose. Observers of virtual teams note the difficulty of developing a sense of the team as an interdependent entity when individuals have not met each other, heard a clear statement of purpose in direct interac-tion with the authority who commissioned the team, or engaged in their own rich discussions of what the team task means to them (Whitworth, Gallupe, & McQueen, 2000). Scholars studying the effects of computer-mediated com-munication confirm this observation when they note the lack of rich inter-change of personal and contextual information (e.g., Walther, 1992) that is essential to allowing the team to develop its own shared understanding of its direction. The communication requirements of establishing shared purpose are one aspect of team launch that calls for the richness allowed by face-to-face interaction. And doing so will create a motivational platform that at least increases the chances that collective commitment to the virtual team's work will remain high.

The second key function of team launch is the establishment of team boundaries. Team boundaries—shared understanding of who is in the team and why, including knowledge of task-related skills of other members—are also unlikely to be achieved when teams are launched virtually. The mutual explorations of skills and knowledge bases, of past experiences and present goals, also are too time-consuming and content-rich for computer media. Indeed, many practitioner accounts of how to deal with this lack in members' knowledge of each other place the burden of assigning roles and identifying key information sources firmly on the team's leader, and not on members (e.g., Duarte & Snyder, 1999). Although this piece of advice might help with the misweighting process loss, it undermines the authority of the team to manage its own processes and helps not at all with the potential for process gains. The establishment of deep knowledge of member talents at launch through rich interaction greatly improves a virtual team's changes of using their knowledge and skill well, and avoiding their characteristic process losses around talent.

I am by no means the first to suggest the implication that virtual teams may best be launched face-to-face (Grenier & Metes, 1999; Haywood, 1998; Lipnack & Stamps, 2000). As yet, no research has directly addressed this question. For the moment, I offer as a proposition the idea that the launch of the group is best performed in the same manner for (eventually) virtual teams as it is for face-to-face teams. Once a good basic trajectory is established for the team at launch, small corrections delivered by a competent coach can make a big difference in the quality of task processes (Wageman, 1997). Once past the team launch, interventions such as engaging the team in a quick assessment of its processes via questionnaire or by establishing additional behavior norms via individual idea-generation processes such as the Nominal Group Technique —interventions that electronic media are good for—are likelier to make a constructive difference in the level of process losses occurring in the team.

Natural Breakpoints

The establishment of high quality processes around effort, strategy, and talent are unlikely to occur from one face-to-face meeting and minor process interventions thereafter. The opportunity for process gains, in particular, also begs for the kinds of rich interaction that can only occur face-to-face. It may well behoove the coach of a virtual team to bring the team together not just at the beginning of its life, but also in the middle—for purposes of evaluating and altering task strategies—and toward the end of its task—for purposes of harvesting lessons from the team's experience.

Consider process gains around task strategy—the development of creative, innovative ways of approaching the work that are superior to what any one individual in the team might generate independently. Coaching interventions that encourage members to reflect on their work thus far and on the challenges they will face next can be helpful to them in revising and improving their task performance strategies (Woolley, 1998). As noted earlier, the kind of high-quality debate and assessment of assumptions and approaches needed to achieve positive synergies around strategy are severely truncated by electronic communications. Choosing a natural breakpoint in the work of the virtual team—once they have logged significant experience with the task—and bringing them together once again to reflect on their strategy increases the chances for innovation that is often the underlying reason for having created such teams in the first place.

A third important opportunity for coaching occurs at the end of a perform-ance period, when the work is finished or a significant subtask has been accomplished. The postperformance period is an especially good time for edu-cational interventions that help members assess and internalize the lessons that were learned from their work together. Such interventions not only build the team's reservoir of talent, which increases its performance capabilities for subsequent tasks, but also contribute directly to the personal learning of indi-vidual team members. Without coaching interventions, virtual team members are unlikely to take initiatives at the end of their work on a task to those lessons that can be learned from that work. Once the work is finished, virtual team members may be more motivated to move their attention and effort to the next such project, thereby losing the opportunity for learning that is so essential to the organizations that rely on them.

My prediction is that the value of face-to-face interaction for virtual teams will not decline as the level of experience collaborating virtually rises. Process gains, in particular, will always depend on a depth of human interplay that does not arise otherwise.

CONCLUSION

I close by raising, briefly, two researchable issues about the future effectiveness of virtual teams and their role in dynamic, adaptive organizations. The first issue is about habitual routines in groups: What is their role in the effective functioning of virtual teams in dynamic organizations? The second is about the kinds of skills that coaching a virtual team demands in the context of dynamic organizations: Does effectively coaching a virtual team demand a broader set of skills that experienced coaches of traditional, face-to-face teams may need to acquire? I address each of these two issues in turn, identifying their importance to dynamic organizations more broadly.

Habitual Routines in Virtual Teams

I noted earlier that working virtually may be novel enough for most individuals that few virtual teams have yet developed the kinds of uninspected and mindless patterns of behavior that are habitual routines in teams. Habitual routines develop when an intact group is exposed to repeated stimulus situations that vary little over time. Especially for teams composed of relative strangers working on a single project, such repetition is highly unlikely to arise. The paucity of habitual routines for virtual teams may have both functional and dysfunctional consequences both for the group and for the organization.

On the positive side, virtual teams and the organizations they serve are in essence forced to innovate in the absence of routines. Each time a virtual team is formed for a new task, it must create ways of operating that suit the team and the situation. The very temporariness and novelty of such teams increases the chances that they will do for dynamic organizations exactly that for which they are often formed: create new ways of working.

On the negative side, members of such teams also pay a high price for the constant novelty they face with each new team, new purpose, or new task. Habitual routines save time and energy. They require no thought or coordination to enact. Without the low-demand "shortcut" of a routine, the interpersonal processes, task strategies, and coordination practices of virtual teams require very high effort levels. Might certain kinds of habits be established for virtual teams that offer both some energy savings that come with automatic processes and the flexibility to change and adapt? Some scholars have identified precisely this issue for dynamic organizations as well. Even the most adaptive organizations, they argue, need some structure in order to maintain a degree of coordination and efficiency of operations (e.g., Brown & Eisenhardt, 1995a).

One researchable possibility is that effective virtual teams tend to develop two kinds of high-level routines: routines that allow swift startup, and routines that trigger reflection. These two kinds of routines together may offer the possibility of both efficient coordination and protection from reduced innovation. The sooner that groups are able to develop simple, habitual processes of making quick assessments of who should do what, and how, and in what order, the more swiftly and efficiently they can get down to work (Haywood, 1998)— thus shortcutting constant effortful decision making about task processes. But such quick decisions run the risk of inappropriateness to the context, especially if that context changes. Developing simple routines that call for team members to reflect—to periodically ask what has changed, what processes need changing in response, what is working, and what is not—can help maintain the innovativeness and creativity for which such teams often are created.

Of course, for such routines to be established in a virtual team of strangers brought together for a one-time task, individual members must import them from prior experience in other teams and situations. They must then share them with the group and get them established. To the degree that members have worked together before or on similar tasks, such routines are likely to be more readily established and adopted. The process via which and the degree to which virtual teams are able to develop time- and energy-saving routines remains a significant area for descriptive as well as predictive research.

Skills for Coaching Virtual Teams

It has been suggested by many of those who reflect on dynamic organizations that successful virtual team members need a set of skills that members of more traditional teams often can manage without: for example, tolerance of ambiguity, initiative, willingness to be only temporarily a member of a team, and others (Haywood, 1998; Lipnack & Stamps, 1997). These predictions about team member skills may or may not turn out to be true. But clearly, effective coaches of virtual teams face a different set of challenges from those who coach collocated teams. And those challenges do suggest some differences in their needed skills—skills that may be broadly relevant in dynamic organizations, and not just for those who coach virtual teams.

Let us examine what skills it would take to coach a virtual team effectively. Drawing on the previously described model of team coaching, I conclude that to coach any team effectively, one needs two key resources: (a) ability to observe a team and extrapolate from their behavior what process losses and gains are occurring, and (b) a behavioral repertoire of coaching interventions that allow the coach to take effective action. Both of these skills may be more demanding for the coaches of virtual teams than for those who coach traditional teams.

First, the prior discussion of process losses and gains in virtual teams suggests that coaches of such teams might need to be aware of different kinds of process problems: What they look for in virtual team process may need to expand beyond what they are used to seeing in collocated teams. Coaches of virtual teams need to look for signs that, for example, the group is not doing a sufficiently good job deindividuating members and working to identify the individuals in the team with the most appropriate knowledge and skill to address a particular problem. Similarly, they need to be aware of excessive delays in communication that may indicate that a downward spiral of collective effort is beginning. Ultimately, this aspect of coaching a team is a function of having a good conceptual understanding of the three key task processes and an ability to interpret particular behavioral signs in terms of effects on effort, strategy, and talent.

But the very limitations of electronic media in providing richly nuanced social information affects anyone in the coaching role just as much as it does members. Whereas observing a face-to-face team in action can provide good data about the quality of effort, strategy, and use of talent in such teams, those very processes may be more difficult to observe solely by reading textual interactions among team members. Coaches of virtual teams must therefore be adept at using more than just monitoring of already occurring electronic team member interactions. Astute observers of teams can rely on more than just what team members say. Perhaps good virtual team coaches must rely on questionnaires, one-on-one interviews, collective process discussions, and other, more active data-collection techniques to provide rich data about team processes (Schein, 1988; Schwarz, 1994). A repertoire of additional observation tools that engage members themselves in diagnosing their own processes also seems especially useful for those who coach virtual teams.

This set of skills—developing novel data-collection practices, generating hypotheses from imperfect data, engaging others in analysis—may be skills desirable for members of dynamic organizations in general. Managing at a distance, monitoring a changing environment, remaining alert for novel opportunities—all these actions essential to the functioning of a dynamic organization require the same high-level data-gathering and analysis skills as does coaching a virtual team.

The second resource—a repertoire of interventions—also may demand a different key skill than does coaching a collocated team. Good coaches of traditional teams can rely primarily on what they do and say in direct interaction with a team to influence and improve team processes. By contrast, those who coach virtual teams cannot rely solely on interaction with the team itself. The need to periodically bring the team together face-to-face suggests that coaches also need upward and lateral influence skills. They must be able to identify and garner the resources and authority needed to bring them together at key points in the team life cycle. To coach a virtual team well, then, such individuals need as much influence external to the team as internal to it (Brown & Eisenhardt, 1995b). Moreover, garnering such resources can be a significant challenge indeed in those organizations for which part of the logic of keeping teams virtual is avoiding the expense of travel for face-to-face interaction. Indeed, dynamic organizations may need to rely on line managers with real authority for the coaching role, rather than on the staff facilitators or consultants who can play that role well in traditional organizations. Or perhaps a truly dynamic organization that relies on well-coached virtual teams must place special focus on attracting, retaining, and offering real authority to those individuals who possess high-level informal influence skills.

REFERENCES

Abrahamson, E. (1996). Management fashion. *Academy of Management Review, 21,* 254–285.

Ancona, D., & Chong, C. L. (1999). Cycles and synchrony: The temporal role of context in team behavior. In E. Mannix, M. Neale, & R. Wageman (Eds.), *Groups in context* (pp. 33–48). Stamford, CT: JAI Press.

Argyris, C. (1982). *Reasoning, learning, and action.* San Francisco: Jossey-Bass.

Bettenhausen, K., & Murnighan, J. K. (1985). The emergence of norms in competitive decision-making groups. *Administrative Science Quarterly, 30,* 350–372.

Brown, S. L., & Eisenhardt, K. M. (1995a). *Core competence in product innovation: The art of managing in time.* Working paper, Department of Industrial Engineering and Engineering Management, Stanford University, Stanford, CA.

Brown, S. L., & Eisenhardt, K. M. (1995b). Product development: Past research, present findings, and future directions. *Academy of Management Review, 20,* 343–379.

Daft, R. L., Lengerl, R. H., & Trevino, L. K. (1987). Message equivocality, media selection, and performance: Implications for information systems. *MIS Quarterly, 11,* 355–368.

Dess, G. G., Rasheed, A. M. A., McLaughlin, K. J., & Priem, R. L. (1995, August). The new corporate architecture. *Academy of Management Executive,* 1–11.

Duarte, D. L., & Snyder, N. T. (1999). *Mastering virtual teams.* San Francisco: Jossey-Bass.

Dubrovsky, V. J., Kiesler, S., & Sethna, B. N. (1991). The equalization phenomenon: Status effects in computer mediated and face-to-face decision-making groups. *Human–Computer Interaction, 6,* 119–146.

Fussel, S., & Benimoff, N. (1995, June). Social and cognitive processes in interpersonal communications: Implications for advanced telecommunications technology. *Journal of Human Factors and Ergonomics,* 229–242.

Gersick, C. J. G. (1988). Time and transition in work teams. *Academy of Management Journal, 31,* 9–41.

Gersick, C. J. G., & Hackman, J. R. (1990). Habitual routines in task-performing teams. *Organizational Behavior and Human Decision Processes, 47,* 65–97.

Ginnett, R. C. (1993). Crews as groups: Their formation and leadership. In E. L. Wiener, B. G. Kanki, & R. L. Helmreich (Eds.), *Cockpit resource management* (pp. 71–98). Orlando, FL: Academic Press.

Grenier, R., & Metes, M. (1995). *Going virtual.* Upper Saddle River, NJ: Prentice Hall.

Hackman, J. R. (2002). *Leading teams: Setting the stage for great performances.* Boston, MA: Harvard Business School Press.

Hackman, J. R., Brousseau, K. R., & Weiss, J. A. (1976). The interaction of task design and group performance strategies in determining group effectiveness. *Organizational Behavior and Human Performance, 16,* 350–365.

Hackman, J. R., & Morris, C. G. (1975). Group tasks, group interaction process, and group performance effectiveness: A review and proposed integration. In L. Berkowitz (Ed.), *Advances in experimental social psychology* (Vol. 8, pp. 45–99). New York: Academic Press.

Hackman, J. R., & Wageman, R. (2002). *Toward a theory of team coaching.* Manuscript under editorial review.

Hackman, J. R., Wageman, R., Ruddy, T. M., & Ray, C. R. (2000). Team effectiveness in theory and practice. In C. Cooper & E. A. Locke (Eds.), *Industrial and organizational psychology: Theory and practice* (pp. 109–129). Oxford, England: Blackwell.

Haywood, M. (1998). *Managing virtual teams.* Boston, MA: Artech House.

Hertel, G., Konradt, U., & Orlikowski, B. (2002). *Managing distance by interdependence: Goal-setting, task interdependence, and team-based rewards in virtual teams.* Manuscript submitted for publication.

Jarvenpaa, S. L., Knoll, K., & Leidner, D. E. (1998). Is anybody out there? The antecedents of trust in global virtual teams. *Journal of Management Information Systems, 14,* 29–64.

Jessup, L. M., Connolly, T., & Galegher, J. (1990, September). The effects of anonymity on GDSS group process with an idea-generating task. *MIS Quarterly,* 313–321.

Kozlowski, S. W. J., Gully, S. M., Salas, E., & Cannon-Bowers, J. A. (1996). Team leadership and development: Theory, principles, and guidelines for training leaders and teams. In M. Beyerlein, D. Johnson, & S. Beyerlein (Eds.), *Advances in interdisciplinary studies of work teams: Team leadership* (Vol. 3, pp. 251–289). Greenwich, CT: JAI Press.

Kiesler, S., & Sproull, L. (1992). Group decision-making and communication technology. *Organizational Behavior and Human Decision Processes, 52,* 96–123.

Lipnack, J., & Stamps, J. (1997). *Virtual teams.* New York: John Wiley & Sons.

Mantovani, G. (1994). Is computer-mediated communication intrinsically apt to enhance democracy in organizations? *Human Relations,* 47, 45–56.

McGrath, J. E., & Hollingshead, A. B. (1994). *Groups interacting with technology.* Thousand Oaks, CA: Sage.

McGrath, J. E., & Kelly, J. R. (1986). *Time and human interaction: Toward a social psychology of time.* New York: Guilford Press.

McGuire, T., Kiesler, S., & Siegel, J. (1987). Group and computer-mediated discussion effects in risk decision-making. *Journal of Personality and Social Psychology, 52,* 917–930.

McLeod, P. L., Baron, R. S., Marti, M. W., & Yoon, K. (1997). The eyes have it: Minority influence in face-to-face and computer mediated communication. *Journal of Applied Psychology, 82,* 706–718.

Moreland, R. L., & Levine, J. M. (1988). Group dynamics over time: Development and socialization in small groups. In J. E. McGrath (Ed.), *The social psychology of time: New perspectives* (pp. 151–181). Newbury Park, CA: Sage.

Schein, E. H. (1988). *Process consultation* (Vol. 1). Reading, MA: Addison-Wesley.

Schwarz, R. M. (1994). *The skilled facilitator.* San Francisco: Jossey-Bass.

Siegel, J., Dubrovsky, V., Kiesler, S., & Mc Guire, T. (1986). Group processes in computer-mediated communication. *Organizational Behavior and Human Decision Processes, 37,* 157–187.

Steiner, I. D. (1972). *Group process and productivity.* New York: Academic Press.

Townsend, A. M., DeMarie, S. M., & Hendrickson, A. R. (1998). Virtual teams: Technology and the workplace of the future. *Academy of Management Executive, 12,* 17–29.

Tuckman, B. W. (1965). Developmental sequence in small groups. *Psychological Bulletin, 63,* 384–399.

Wageman, R. (1997, Summer). Critical success factors for creating superb self-managing teams. *Organization Dynamics,* 49–61.

Wageman, R., & Gordon, F. (2002). As the twig is bent: How group values shape emergent task interdependence in groups. Under editorial review.

Walther, J. B. (1992). Interpersonal effects in computer-mediated interaction. *Communication research, 19,* 52–90.

Whitworth, B., Gallupe, B., & McQueen, R. (2000). A cognitive three-process model of computer-mediated group interaction. *Group Decision and Negotiation, 9,* 431–456.

Wooley, A. W. (1998). Effects of intervention content and timing on group task performance. *Journal of Applied Behavioral Science, 34,* 30–49.

5

The Role of Subcultures in Agile Organizations

Alicia Boisnier
Jennifer A. Chatman
University of California, Berkeley

Our goal in this chapter is to develop a framework for understanding how subcultures influence strong culture organizations' agility. We begin with the proposition that organizations benefit from simultaneously managing strong, stable cultures while maintaining the flexibility and adaptability necessary to survive the ebbs and flows of turbulent environments (e.g., Tushman & O'Reilly, 1996). We then distinguish among various types of values to consider how subcultures can co-exist and evolve within strong organizational cultures. We also investigate the conditions that stimulate subcultures to emerge from individual, group, and organizational levels of analysis. Finally, we describe how subcultures can increase organizational agility by providing a source of creativity and flexibility.

Organizations face increasingly dynamic environments characterized by substantial and often unpredictable technological, political, and economic change. How can organizations respond rapidly to such changes or become more agile? Organizational agility, according to Dyer (2001), "requires a judicious mix of stability and reconfigurability" (p. 4). We consider an unlikely source of agility: organizational culture. This may seem like an odd juxtaposition because strong unitary cultures exert a stabilizing force on organizations by encouraging cohesion, organizational commitment, and desirable work behaviors among members (e.g., Deal & Kennedy, 1982; Nemeth & Staw, 1989; O'Reilly & Chatman, 1986). This stability generates cultural clarity and consistency among members, forces that, if the culture is strategically aligned, enhance organizational performance (e.g., Kotter & Heskett, 1992; O'Reilly, 1989). But, such stability may also constrain strong culture organizations from initiating or reacting to environmental change (e.g., Benner & Tushman, 2002, in press), a necessary capability for optimizing performance (Child, 1972;

Lawrence & Lorsch, 1967). Thus, strong cultures can provide organizations with significant advantages, but when the basis for survival rests on an organization's ability to change and adapt, a strong culture can be a liability.

We propose that one way that strong culture organizations can become agile without losing their basis of strength is by allowing certain types of subcultures to emerge. We explore how organizations can simultaneously reap the benefits of building and maintaining a strong culture while remaining responsive to dynamic environments. Subcultures can permit an organization to generate varied responses to the environment without necessarily destroying its internal coherence. Subcultures may provide the flexibility and responsiveness that a unitary culture may limit.

Interestingly, the very existence of a strong organizational culture, one whose members agree and care about their organization's values, seems to preclude subcultures (O'Reilly, 1989; Saffold, 1988). Indeed, researchers have depicted subcultures as detracting from a strong organizational culture (Martin, 1992). We suggest, instead, that subcultures have certain properties that can even strengthen an organization's overall organizational culture. First, subcultures vary in the extent to which they disrupt the overarching culture. Second, subcultures often emerge in response to changing demands and can serve as an outlet for members to express conflict and dissent arising during turbulent times. Thus, subcultures may provide a mechanism for changing less central values. Indeed, that subcultures are potentially important with respect to affecting core values may further substantiate how difficult it is to change an organization's culture (e.g., Trice & Beyer, 1984). Reducing change-induced disruption can be particularly advantageous if the overarching culture is strategically aligned and effective.[1]

Our goal in this chapter is to understand how subcultures, or relatively small clusters of members that share a set of norms, values, and beliefs, influence strong culture organizations' agility. We begin with the proposition that organizations benefit from simultaneously managing strong, stable cultures while maintaining the flexibility and adaptability necessary to survive the ebbs and flows of turbulent environments (e.g., Tushman & O'Reilly, 1996; Tushman & Smith, 2002). We then distinguish among various types of values to consider how subcultures can coexist and evolve within strong organizational

---

[1] It is possible that an organization's overarching culture is ineffective and *misaligned* with its competitive realities. In this case, disrupting the overarching culture may be desired, and subcultures may well be a useful tool to initiate more radical cultural change. We restrict our discussion to cases in which the overarching culture is reasonably effective and relatively aligned with an organization's competitive position, rather than focusing on cases in which the overarching culture requires wholesale change.

cultures. We also investigate the individual, group, and organizational conditions that stimulate subculture emergence. Finally, we describe how subcultures can increase organizational agility by providing a source of creativity and flexibility.

HOW STRONG CULTURES
CREATE STABILITY

We define *organizational culture* as shared values that inform organizational members about how to behave appropriately (e.g., O'Reilly & Chatman, 1996). Organizations with a strong culture create clear and coherent values (Chatman & Cha, in press; Saffold, 1988) and expect that members agree with and care intensely about those values (Jackson, 1966; O'Reilly, 1989), even if core values emphasize dissent and creativity (e.g., Flynn & Chatman, 2001; Sutton & Hargadon, 1996). Agreement refers to the level of consensus (or crystallization, cohesion, consistency, or dispersion) among members about organizational values and associated behavioral norms, whereas intensity refers to members' demonstrated commitment to those values.

Academics and practitioners have touted the virtues of strong organizational cultures that emphasize strategically relevant values. By increasing members' understanding of organizational objectives, ties to one another, and commitment, organizations with strong cultures increase the chances that members can execute those objectives and, as a collective, increase organizational performance (Deal & Kennedy, 1982; Pottruck & Pearce, 2001; Tushman & O'Reilly, 1997). Although some researchers have questioned how well strong cultures improve bottom-line performance (Saffold, 1988), a growing body of research and a host of salient examples demonstrate how organizations attain strategic advantages through strong cultures (Collins & Porras, 1994; Gordon & DiTomaso, 1992; O'Reilly & Pfeffer, 2000b). For example, Southwest Airlines' ability to perform better than industry competitors over a sustained period of time has been attributed to its strong culture focusing on keeping costs low and customers happy (e.g., Friedberg & Friedberg, 1996; O'Reilly & Pfeffer, 2000a).

Strong cultures may, however, impose a level of stability on organizations, and such stability has mixed implications for performance. Denison and Mishra (1995) found that "stability traits" such as a firm's mission, consistency, and normative integration, were related to its profitability. Specifically, organizations with strong cultures had greater returns on investments, but only in the short run; after 3 years the relationship between cultural consistency and performance became negative (Denison, 1990). Strong cultures may enhance short-term success but inhibit long-term organizational performance; they may even contribute to long-term failure by preventing organizations from adapting to changing contingencies.

Sorensen (2002) found that organizations with stronger cultures were most effective when their environments favored exploiting, or fully executing existing objectives using existing organizational knowledge and approaches, rather than exploring, or discovering and developing new objectives using new approaches. He reasoned that incremental adjustments to organizational routines were easier in strong culture firms because participants have an agreed-upon framework for interpreting environmental feedback and a common set of routines for responding to different signals from the environment (Sorensen, 2002, p. 70). Using the same reasoning, however, an agreed-upon framework and set of routines may inhibit an organization's ability to embark on more radical strategic shifts. Reanalyzing Kotter and Heskett's (1992) data set of 200 firms and their cultures, Sorensen (2002) found that strong culture organizations were more financially successful in stable environments and less successful in dynamic environments. Thus, although cultural strength and stability may enhance organizational performance in the short run and in stable environments, they may also inhibit an organization's ability to change, adapt, or innovate.

Gagliardi (1986) suggested that organizations with strong cultures are capable of only limited change because members are especially resistant to changing those strongly held and widely shared values. This resistance limits the range of permissible value changes to those that are compatible with existing core values. Thus, even when strong culture organizations could benefit from changes that require modifying their core values, resistant members may prevent such change from occurring. Wilkins and Ouchi (1983) suggested that strong cultures can be adaptive, but cannot withstand radical changes that directly challenge their basic assumptions. For example, such resistance threatened Westinghouse's survival by preventing it from reaping any benefits from acquiring a factory automation business. The head of Westinghouse's advanced technology group concluded after this significant failure that, "It was a classic case of trying to merge an entrepreneurial organization into a relatively slow-moving, large American corporation" (Nohria, Dwyer, & Dalzell, 2002, p. 11). Taken together, these perspectives suggest that firms with stronger cultures are better at staying the course but that innovation poses a major challenge (e.g., Nemeth & Staw, 1989; Staw, Sandelands, & Dutton, 1981). Despite this evidence, we propose that the claims of the incompatibility between strong cultures and organizational agility have been overstated; instead, we propose that organizations with strong cultures can use subcultures to become more agile and to drive innovation.

CAN SUBCULTURES EMERGE IN STRONG CULTURE ORGANIZATIONS?

Although there is no single definition of an *organizational subculture,* most approaches to subcultures have common distinctions and features. For example, although many researchers have discussed the role of subgroups in organizations (Lawrence & Lorsch, 1967; Van de Ven & Ferry, 1980), not all subgroups can be considered subcultures. Subcultures are groups whose common characteristic is a set of shared norms and beliefs. In contrast to subgroups, subcultures need not form around existing subdivisions, such as departmental or functional groups (although they often do), nor do they need to be consciously or intentionally formed, as we discuss later (Trice & Beyer, 1993). The range and variety of subcultures is as diverse as the range and variety of existing organizational cultures. Although subcultures' ubiquitous presence in organizations has been well documented (Bloor & Dawson, 1994; Hofstede, 1998; Jermier, Slocum, Fry, & Gaines, 1991; Martin & Siehl, 1983; Van Maanen & Barley, 1984; Trice, 1993), few have proposed that subcultures may instigate the sort of adaptation that also does not threaten an organization's coherence (see Tushman & O'Reilly, 1996, for an exception).

Martin (1992) distinguished between conceptualizations of organizational cultures that were cohesive and unitary, or *integrated,* and those characterized as collections of subcultures, or *differentiated.* A *fragmented* culture is ambiguous and open to members' multiple interpretations. These distinctions imply that an integrated culture precludes differentiated subcultures and vice versa, or that an organization may have either a single culture with no subcultures, or subcultures with no overarching organizational culture. But this typology does not consider the possibility that subcultures might coexist within an overarching culture. Perhaps this reflects a conceptual division among organizational culture scholars; those focusing on the advantages of strong cultures tend to highlight overarching cultures and rarely consider subcultures (e.g., Kotter & Heskett, 1992; O'Reilly, 1989), whereas those focusing on organizations as collections of subcultures rarely consider that they could be united by a strong, overarching organizational culture (e.g., Rose, 1988; Sackmann, 1992; Trice & Beyer, 1993). By considering culture content and strength, we propose that subcultures can develop within strong integrated cultures without weakening the overarching culture.

Culture Content and Strength and the Coexistence of Subcultures: Distinguishing Between Pivotal and Peripheral Values

Culture content refers to the specific emphases or activities to which the values and derived behavioral norms are directed, or *which* values and norms emerge within an organization (Flynn & Chatman, 2001). Despite their importance, we understand relatively little about how and why specific values and norms emerge. Why, for example, do some work groups emphasize norms that regulate dress (e.g., Pratt & Rafaeli, 1997), whereas others adopt norms that regulate where people should sit in meetings (e.g., Puffer, 1999) or when they should arrive (e.g., Sutton & Hargadon, 1996)? Flynn and Chatman (in press) suggested that values and norms arise from a group or organization's demographic composition. Visible differences create social categories influencing whether a group values, for example, cooperative versus individualistic approaches to work (e.g., Chatman & Flynn, 2001). *Culture strength* refers to members' level of agreement with and approval of those norms and values (e.g., O'Reilly, 1989). In stronger cultures, members are more likely to be rewarded for adhering to, or sanctioned for violating, core values (O'Reilly & Chatman, 1996).

Schein (1988) observed that values varied across organizations and that members' cared more intensely about some values than others, distinguishing between *pivotal* and *peripheral* values. Pivotal values are central to an organization's functioning; members are required to adopt and adhere to the behavioral norms derived from these values and are typically rejected from the organization if they do not (e.g., Chatman, 1991; O'Reilly & Chatman, 1996). Peripheral values are desirable, but are not believed by members to be essential to an organization's functioning. Members are encouraged to accept peripheral values, but can reject them and still function fully as members. Thus, members' degree of conformity to peripheral norms can vary considerably.

The strongest culture organizations, total institutions such as cults and prisons, could embrace pivotal values that are so widely adopted and enforced that they preclude the emergence of peripheral values, and, by implication, subcultures (e.g., O'Reilly & Chatman, 1996; Schein, 1961; Van Maanen & Barley, 1984). Most business organizations, however, do not operate with only one culture (Trice & Beyer, 1993). A more likely profile is a strong culture firm that emphasizes both a set of pivotal values important to its functioning and identity and a set of peripheral values that are less relevant to each member's or unit's functioning. Although Schein discussed the role of pivotal values for organizations, he did not consider their potential role in subcultures. We propose that pivotal and peripheral values may be more relevant to some parts of the organization than to others. Specifically, peripheral values may be important to subcultures within an organization while being less essential to the identity and functioning of members of the dominant organizational culture.

At strong culture Johnson & Johnson, for example, widely shared, intensely held core values were pervasive across the organization; however, individual operating units were given the autonomy to determine how to operate on a daily basis. Although the company's credo emphasized customer and employee satisfaction, the operating culture in a new medical products division was distinctly less conservative and more innovative than a more mature product division. In this way, subunits were able to act on the values that were important to them but peripheral to the functioning of the organization, leaving the core pivotal values of the organization intact (Tushman & O'Reilly, 1997, pp. 26–27).

Similarly, in a home health care service organization, Bloor and Dawson (1994) observed that pivotal values included high professional standards and a commitment to client rehabilitation. Social workers within the organization simultaneously embraced core values but also focused on ethical behavior and client advocacy. Because they agreed that the pivotal values were important and the peripheral values they adopted did not interfere with the organization's pivotal values, social workers' beliefs did not detract from the strength of the dominant organizational culture. We, therefore, suggest the following proposition regarding the coexistence of strong pivotal and varying peripheral cultural values:

Proposition 1: Organizations with strong pivotal values (high agreement and intensity among members) can also sustain peripheral values on which members' agreement and intensity varies.

Types of Subcultures and Their Likely Emergence in Strong Culture Firms

The conceptual dichotomy between unitary cultures and those characterized by subcultures may be rooted in the misconception that subcultures always consist of people who oppose the dominant culture (e.g., Cohen, 1955; Hebdige, 1979; Webster, 1993; Willis, 1993; Yinger, 1970). From its origin in sociology and anthropology, the term *subculture* has been associated with images of deviants, delinquents, gangs, and other nonconformists such as hippies, British punk teenagers, or cult members. Organizational ethnographers have found a variety of types of organizational subcultures, not all of which are based on expressing opposing views (Bloor & Dawson, 1994; Jermier et al., 1991; Martin & Siehl, 1983; Sackmann, 1992).

Using a parent–child metaphor, Wolfgang and Ferracuti (1970) suggested that a subculture, like a child, could never be entirely different from its "parent," the larger culture. Instead, because the subculture emerges from the dominant culture's values, some subcultural values may conflict with the dominant cultures' while others may not. Researchers have distinguished between subcultures and countercultures (e.g., Wolfgang & Ferracuti, 1970; Zellner,

1995). Subcultures represent tolerated deviations that do not disrupt the normative solidarity of the larger culture's values. In contrast, members of countercultures hold discordant values and, by virtue of their membership, explicitly oppose certain aspects of the larger culture. Countercultures are, therefore, unacceptable to members of the larger organization.

Recognizing that not all subcultures are countercultures, therefore, it is useful to distinguish among subculture types. Martin and Siehl (1983) developed a typology of organizational subcultures, including enhancing, orthogonal, and countercultures, in which each type exemplified a different level of congruence with the dominant culture's values. Incorporating the notions of pivotal and peripheral values with this subculture typology makes it possible to consider how subcultures can exist in an organization without detracting from the strength of the overall culture. Members of *enhancing* subcultures adhere to dominant organizational culture values even more enthusiastically than do members of the rest of the organization. They agree with and care about both pivotal and peripheral values, consistent with the larger organization's core values. Their intense commitment to particular peripheral values, that are consistent with those of the overarching culture, distinguishes them as a subculture.

Members of *orthogonal* subcultures both embrace the dominant cultures' values but also hold their own set of distinct, but not conflicting, values. They embrace the pivotal organizational values but, simultaneously, hold values that are peripheral to those of the overarching culture. Because the values that differ between orthogonal subculture members and members of the dominant culture are less important to the functioning and identity of the organization than are the pivotal values, the existence of an orthogonal subculture does not threaten the cohesiveness of the overarching culture. Finally, members of a *counterculture* disagree with the core values of the dominant culture and hold values that directly conflict with core organizational values. Counterculture members hold values that conflict with pivotal organizational values and can, therefore, threaten the strength of the overarching culture.

Peripheral and pivotal values vary in terms of their likely adoption in overall cultures versus subcultures, and they may also vary independently of one another because the two kinds of values have distinct qualities and function differently in organizations. One key difference is that peripheral values, contained within subcultures, are more likely to change than pivotal core organizational values. Further, the relative ease with which peripheral values within subcultures can change may provide organizations with the capacity to respond to dynamic environments. First, because core values are tied to an organization's and its members' identities, they are quite difficult to change without substantial resistance (e.g., Ashforth & Mael, 1989; Dutton & Dukerich, 1991; Gagliardi, 1986). Furthermore, internal mobility patterns in organizations, in which people are likely to move across jobs and divisions, make it likely that people ultimately become more committed to their organization over time than to specific subgroups in which they are members for shorter periods of time (Chatman & Cha, in press). Providing that the majority of subculture members are more deeply committed to the core values of the organization than to the peripheral values of their subgroup (an assumption that may not hold up in all cases, and that we consider later), peripheral values, on which orthogonal subcultures primarily differ from the larger organization, may be easier to change than pivotal values.

Finally, that subcultures are typically smaller makes them more malleable and responsive than an entire organization. Smaller groups are more likely to be given a degree of autonomy that is less viable in large, centralized organizations. In some cases, smaller groups are associated with being strategically weak and, therefore, not threatening (e.g., Galunic & Eisenhardt, 2001). Indeed, some organizations intentionally keep subunits small in order to stimulate innovation (Tushman & O'Reilly, 1996). The capacity to change and adapt at the subculture level has important implications for organizations that have to respond to the evolving demands of a dynamic environment. We, therefore, propose that:

Proposition 2: Peripheral values associated with orthogonal subculture membership are more likely to change over time than are pivotal organizational values.

The Paradox of Strong Cultures and Countercultures

We suggested that enhancing and orthogonal subcultures need not detract from strong organizational cultures and that countercultures, by definition, *do* conflict with the dominant culture. Therefore, countercultures may fail to emerge in strong cultures because the opposition they introduce would weaken a strong culture and would likely stimulate members of the larger organization to defend overarching values. We suggest, instead, that countercultures may well emerge, perhaps for relatively short periods of time, in strong cultures. First, strong cultures can be oppressive. When values are strong, dissent forms in reaction to the imposed values (Bourdieu, 1990; Hebdige, 1979). Brehm's (1966) theory of psychological reactance suggests that when peoples' sense of behavioral freedom is threatened, they may attempt to reassert it through direct or indirect (e.g., vicarious) oppositional behavior. In particular, threatened individuals may develop a greater liking for the behavior that has been restricted.

Second, strong cultures can produce countercultures because, in promoting conformity, small variations in behavior and attitudes become exaggerated

(O'Reilly & Chatman, 1996). Even the slightest variation in behavioral norms may encourage in-group distinctions to form (Brewer, 1979). Therefore, those who are at all different may choose to separate themselves from the rest of the organization in order to maintain their beliefs. Those who disagree with the strong culture values may be able to find a pocket of dissent within the organization, that is, a counterculture (Martin & Siehl, 1983). In weaker cultures, dissent is not necessary because there is enough freedom for varied values to emerge without being constrained by a dominant overarching value framework. Thus, we propose that:

> Proposition 3: Countercultures are more likely to emerge in organizations with strong overarching cultures than in organizations with weak overarching cultures.

We suggest that strong organizational cultures can produce countercultures, but paradoxically, countercultures may strengthen organizational cultures. Just as values are more salient when they are violated (Kahneman & Miller, 1986), a counterculture's opposition increases the salience of dominant cultural values. Through a process of reflection and comparison with the values of the counterculture, formerly implicit values become explicitly considered and openly debated. This may be likened to the comparison process that is evoked when organizational members are considering whom to hire and how to socialize them (e.g., Sutton & Louis, 1987), and the salience of value differences between merging firms (e.g., Marks & Mirvis, 2001). For example, the recent Hewlett-Packard merger with Compaq focused H-P employees on how consensus-driven H-P was and led them to resist the "cowboy" culture at Texas-based Compaq, where "process is for wimps" (Quinn, 2002, p. 3).

The presence of a contrary point of view, or, in this case, a contrary set of values, can then strengthen one's commitment to a previously held set of beliefs or course of action (Lord, Ross, & Lepper, 1979). Thus, the salient challenges posed by a counterculture may result in increased resistance by the dominant culture (Staw et al., 1981). This value-reinforcing response is more likely to occur under some conditions than others. Countercultures may be more disruptive, for example, when the organizational environment is unstable and an organization's strategic direction is less clear.

> Proposition 4: Countercultures may increase noncounterculture members' commitment to the existing overarching organizational culture.

This proposition may be most relevant early on in the life of a new counterculture's existence. If, over time, a counterculture proves that its norms and values are superior to those of the overarching culture, the counterculture may gain support and grow in membership. In such cases, the counterculture's norms and values may eventually usurp those of the dominant culture. For example, Martin and Siehl (1983) described how John DeLorean created a counterculture that focused on dissent and independence because he was dissatisfied with General Motors' overarching organizational culture that valued loyalty and conformity. Through charismatic leadership and vivid storytelling practices, DeLorean was able to convince others that his cultural orientation was superior to GM's. His counterculture movement gained such tremendous momentum that the counterculture's values were eventually integrated into the dominant culture.

The previous discussion suggests that culture strength may contribute to counterculture emergence. Next we consider a fuller array of factors leading to the emergence of specific types of subcultures, as well as their likely consequences in strong culture organizations.

HOW SUBCULTURES EMERGE AND CHANGE IN ORGANIZATIONS

Most discussions of organizational subcultures assume that organizations operate in stable environments; they place less emphasis on how subculture formation patterns may differ when environments are uncertain or unstable (Rose, 1988; Trice, 1993; Van Maanen & Barley, 1985). We, therefore, consider how a dynamic organizational environment may affect whether subcultures are likely to emerge and change.

Subcultures can form based on a variety of societal, organizational, and individual characteristics. Large, complex organizations are likely to resemble the larger society in which they are situated (Gregory, 1983) and may, therefore, contain many of the same subcultures, or groupings of values, as would be found outside an organization. Although the subgroups found in society may also appear in organizations, a variety of organization-specific subcultures may also emerge. Organizational subcultures may be based on membership in various groups such as departments, work groups, and teams; levels of hierarchies, such as management versus support staff; professional and occupational affiliations; physical location in the organization; sociodemographic categories such as sex, ethnicity, age, or nationality; informal groups like those formed by friendships; and performance-related variables such as organizational commitment and work performance (Jermier et al., 1991; Rose, 1988; Trice & Beyer, 1993; Van Maanen & Barley, 1984, 1985).

Various organizational, group, and individual characteristics contribute to subculture formation and, given the tradeoffs to individuals of forming subcultures, including the time investment or the risk involved in looking less loyal to the overarching organization, they are unlikely to join or form subcultures without support from others. We suggest that subculture formation is contingent on (a) structural properties that make organizations conducive to subculture formation, (b) group processes that cause individuals to come together to form subcultures, and (c) individual members' propensity to form and join subcultures. We explore each of these factors next.

Structural Bases for Subculture Formation

Certain characteristics, such as organizational size, task differentiation, power centrality, and demographic composition, make some organizations more susceptible to subculture divisions than others. Subcultures are more likely to develop in larger, more complex, or bureaucratic organizations because these organizations are more likely to encompass a variety of functions and technologies (Rose, 1988; Trice & Beyer, 1993; Van Maanen & Barley, 1985). Employees have less contact with one another as organizations grow in size, as distinctions among their tasks increase, and as task interdependence decreases (Koene, Boone, & Soeters, 1997). Similarly, task differentiation is typically associated with different occupational and professional orientations. The existence of distinct professional groups within an organization may encourage subculture formation as professionals in organizations tend to hold values that cut across organizational boundaries but may differ from the values of the nonprofessionals within an organization (Bloor & Dawson, 1994; Trice, 1993; Van Maanen & Barley, 1984). Thus, subcultures are more likely to form around differentiated tasks, ultimately leading to lower cohesion among organizational members not working on the same tasks.

Subcultures may also emerge in organizations in which power is decentralized. Martin and Siehl (1983) attributed the emergence of DeLorean's counterculture to General Motors' decentralized power structure; Hage and Aiken (1967) found that more decentralized power was associated with more professional activity and hierarchical differentiation. Similarly, Tushman and O'Reilly (1996) identified decentralized decision making as important to the autonomy and functioning of organizational subcultures in innovating firms because it enabled members to obtain the resources and autonomy necessary to construct and maintain a subculture. We, therefore, propose that:

> Proposition 5: Subcultures are more likely to emerge in larger organizations with greater task differentiation, more divisions (functional or product), more groups of professionals, and more decentralized power and decision making than in smaller organizations with less task differentiation, fewer divisions or professional groups, and more centralized power and decision making.

Changes in environmental conditions may lead to structural changes that drive subculture formation. As employees within an organization become more diverse or tasks become more differentiated, subcultures will be more likely to form. Structural changes resulting from environmental uncertainty, such as decentralization (e.g., Burns & Stalker, 1961), are likely to lead to an increase in subculture emergence. For example, professional groups may be more likely to assert their distinct values when they perceive the organizational environment to be unsettled (Bloor & Dawson, 1994). Although a professional subculture may exist relatively undetected for some time, the degree to which the subculture's values become articulated is somewhat dependent on the stability of the organizational context. We, therefore, propose that:

Proposition 6: Subcultures are more likely to emerge in organizations operating in more dynamic than static environments.

Group Processes Affecting Subculture Formation

Subcultures are likely to form among members who interact often and who face similar problems, providing them with opportunities to exchange concerns about the existing culture (Cohen, 1955). Thus, existing organizational groupings, such as work groups, are particularly likely to evolve into subcultures. Subcultures are more likely to form when individuals work together on a task because values may become specific to the task on which the group is focused (Koene et al., 1997; Trice & Beyer, 1993; Van Maanen & Barley, 1985). A preexisting work group transforms into a subculture when members develop and adopt task-specific norms and values. For example, a peripheral overall cultural value that favors individualism may be dysfunctional for a team that requires close, interdependent teamwork to complete their tasks (e.g., Chatman & Spataro, 2002). Therefore, the team may adopt a different set of more collectivistic values, forming an orthogonal subculture.

Alternatively, a critical mass of similar-thinking individuals could join together to form a subculture. For example, Rose (1988) proposed that when individuals disagree about, or are dissatisfied with, an organization's values, they will form smaller groups comprised of members who agree with one another. In his study of youth gang culture, Cohen (1955) described how dissatisfied youths "shopped around" for kindred souls. A process of mutual conversion occurred gradually as members began subtly expressing their oppositional views to one another. If others supported those views, the conversations between them became more explicit and intense until actors had identified themselves as a group with a subculture, that is, a shared frame of reference that members preferred to the existing cultural frame.

Like-minded individuals are attracted to subcultures in each of these cases for the same reasons: The well-supported similarity-attraction paradigm suggests that individuals prefer to be around others with similar attitudes, including perceptions of the organization and their jobs (Berscheid, 1985). Therefore, when members of an organization are particularly satisfied or dissatisfied about their organization's values, they may seek the camaraderie of others who share their views. In sum, shared values combine with frequent interpersonal interaction to create subcultures (Braver & Wilson, 1986; Cohen, 1955).

Like structural forces, group forces also change when the environment changes. Task groups, or groups that have a high level of task interdependence and regular face-to-face contact, may be particularly likely to become subcultures during times of organizational uncertainty. First, such groups may find that their values begin to diverge from those held by members of the dominant culture as they respond to the specific changing demands of their task environment. For example, if a group that initially focused on discovering new technology actually identified one that was, subsequently, widely adopted in the market, they might then be asked to make that technology as efficient as possible rather than to continue to discover other new technologies (e.g., Benner & Tushman, 2002). This shift from exploration to exploitation would clearly require a shift in cultural values (Sorensen, 2002). Thus, as a work group's performance expectations and goals change, their values change as well.

A critical mass of like-minded individuals may also develop in response to unpredictable events as a way for members to maintain a sense of stability. For example, the changing environment that is produced by mergers or acquisitions may result in subculture formation as members of the consolidated firm attempt to cling to their previous firm's values (Nahavandi & Malekzadeh, 1988). We, therefore, propose that:

Proposition 7: Work groups operating in more dynamic environments are more likely to transform into subcultures.

Individual Bases for Subculture Formation

People must be willing to join in order for subcultures to form. However, this should not imply that people necessarily consciously or intentionally choose to belong to a subculture. Instead, people may find themselves part of a subculture without making the conscious decision to join. In the previous section on group processes, we described ways that individuals may gradually, and even unintentionally, come together to form subcultures. In this section we discuss the dimensions that are relevant to people's propensity to join subcultures. Three dimensions are likely to be associated with an individual's propensity to join a subculture: psychological reactance; satisfaction with dominant culture values; and commitment to the organization. Each of these has a dispositional and situational component, and we, therefore, treat each factor as an existing psychological state emerging from individual differences or contextual cues.

When people believe that their behavioral freedom has been threatened, they may experience reactance and are likely to behave in oppositional ways (Brehm, 1966). Reactance can be induced by situations that are perceived to be behaviorally restrictive. This might include a situation in which an authority figure, such as a manager, makes demands on behavior, or in which the normative demands of the situation require high levels of behavioral conformity (e.g., O'Reilly & Chatman, 1996). Thus, strong culture firms are likely to induce more behavioral reactance among members than are weaker cultures, consistent with Proposition 3.

Furthermore, regardless of contextual factors, some people may be more prone to oppositional behavior and attitudes than are others (Dowd, Milne, & Wise, 1991). Characteristics associated with reactance include a person's tendency to be argumentative, uncooperative, behaviorally deviant, and unwilling to take others' advice or to do as others ask. A person's tendency to behave oppositionally has implications for his or her propensity to join a subculture. People who are predisposed to nonconformity are more likely to reject strong culture values regardless of their content. Whether situationally or dispositionally based, individuals higher in reactance are more likely to deviate from an organization's values than are those lower in reactance, and those who are higher in reactance are more likely to join a subculture.

A person's propensity to join a subculture may also be determined by his or her level of satisfaction with dominant cultural values (Martin & Siehl, 1983; Rose, 1988). An extensive literature on the dispositional nature of work satisfaction has accumulated (see Judge & Larsen, 2001, for a review). Researchers have demonstrated that a person's tendency to be satisfied at work is stable over time and across situations; it is positively associated with positive affectivity, self-esteem, and self-efficacy, and negatively associated with negative affectivity and neuroticism (e.g., Staw, Bell, & Clausen, 1986; Staw & Ross, 1985).

A person's satisfaction can also be influenced by the organizational context (e.g., Arvey, Bouchard, Segal, & Abraham, 1989). Through a process of reflecting on and interpreting organizational culture, organization members may perceive contradictions that result in dissatisfaction (Cha & Edmondson, 2001). People are primarily motivated to form subcultures to solve the problems they perceive with the dominant culture (Cohen, 1955). Subcultures allow members to resolve the discrepancies between actual and desired cultural norms by providing a different, more personally satisfying, frame of reference. Thus, being dissatisfied with one's job or organization is likely to increase one's propensity to join a subculture (Rose, 1988). This is consistent with the view that subcultures develop in response to ideological conflict or even intentional countercultural movements (Trice & Beyer, 1993; Van Maanen & Barley, 1985).

Similarly, employees who believe that the values held by members of their organization are inappropriate to accomplish their goals or drive their organization's success, more generally, may attempt to modify those values (Graham, 1986). Theories of self-justification suggest that disagreeing with an organization's values while continuing to work for that organization is an unstable state; people are motivated to reduce this dissonance (e.g., Aronson, 1968; Staw, 1977). Joining a subculture comprised of people who share one's values may be one way to resolve such dissonance by providing means to exercise voice, as depicted in Hirschman's (1970) well-known exit–voice–loyalty model.

Levels of individual organizational commitment, or a loyalty toward and identification with one's employer (Meyer & Allen, 1991; O'Reilly & Chatman, 1986), may also influence subculture formation. Like work satisfaction, commitment may be partially determined by dispositional traits such as positive and negative affectivity (e.g., Cropanzano, James, & Konovsky, 1993). More commonly, however, commitment has been examined in terms of the organizational context, and members of strong culture firms are more likely to be committed to their organization (Caldwell, Chatman, & O'Reilly, 1990; Chatman, 1991; O'Reilly, 1989; O'Reilly & Chatman, 1996). This is particularly true for normative commitment, which stems from a psychological attachment to an organization and involves identifying with and internalizing an organization's values (O'Reilly & Chatman, 1986). As the organization's identity becomes integrated into a person's self-view, he or she becomes more committed to promoting the organization's well-being, leading strong cultures to grow stronger over time. The link between strong culture firms and compliance-based commitment, or commitment based on instrumental or extrinsic rewards, is less clear (e.g., Meyer & Allen, 1991; O'Reilly & Chatman, 1986).

In sum, we suggest that an individual's propensity to join a subculture increases with higher levels of psychological reactance and lower levels of satisfaction with pivotal norms and normative commitment to the organization. Essentially, each of these states produces a negative response to the overarching organizational culture, leading to the desire to belong to a subculture. However, we expect individuals experiencing these negative responses to be more likely to join some types of subcultures than others. Specifically, those who are high in reactance and low in satisfaction and commitment would be more likely to join either an orthogonal subculture or counterculture, rather than an enhancing subculture, because orthogonal subcultures deviate somewhat from the organization's peripheral values and countercultures deviate completely from the organization's pivotal values. People who experience lower levels of reactance and higher levels of satisfaction and commitment may actually be more likely to join an enhancing subculture, which is comprised of individuals who embrace cultural values even more strongly than the rest of the organization. Therefore, we propose that:

> Proposition 8: People who experience higher levels of reactance and lower levels of satisfaction and normative commitment are more likely to join orthogonal subcultures or countercultures than enhancing subcultures compared to people who experience lower levels of reactance and higher levels of satisfaction and normative commitment.

Because levels of psychological reactance, satisfaction, and commitment may be partially situationally determined, they may be susceptible to change along with the organizational and normative environment. Changing situational dynamics could moderate one's dispositional tendency toward reactance and make one behave more or less oppositionally. One of the main reasons that people resist change is that they anticipate losing power (e.g., Frost & Egri, 1991). However, people can view change as a threat or an opportunity. A person's dispositional level of reactance may determine how positively he or she views organizational change in response to a dynamic environment. Those members of organizations facing more dynamic environments who are prone to reactance may be more likely to perceive that previously held freedoms are threatened. In contrast, those who are less prone to reactance may view changes as opportunities that actually liberate them to take certain desired risks. We, therefore, propose that one's tendency toward reactance will moderate one's reaction to dynamic environments, and, specifically, one's propensity to join a subculture.

Like reactance, satisfaction levels are susceptible to change along with the organizational and normative environment. Values are more likely to shift among organizations facing dynamic environments. These shifts are likely to influence members' satisfaction with organizational values. In a longitudinal study of research and development firms, Hall and Mansfield (1971) found that environmental change and satisfaction were related. Members' job satisfaction and job identification decreased in response to cutbacks in available financial resources provided by U.S. government funding. In another longitudinal study, organizational change *increased* nursing educators' satisfaction with their jobs (Bojean, Brown, Grandjean, & Macken, 1982). People's perceptions of whether changes are positive or negative will influence whether they join subcultures in response to dynamic environments.

A person's commitment may be as susceptible to change from outside forces as is his or her reactance and satisfaction. Inasmuch as normative commitment is highly dependent on one's identification with and attachment to the values of one's subculture and the organization, the level of commitment may change if organizational values change in response to external contingencies driven by a dynamic environment. For example, Jones (2000) described how changes in the task environment stimulated subculture emergence in a domestic appliance factory. When a new managing director eliminated the use of scientific management practices in favor of more modern human resource management techniques, a group of former engineers, who continued to be personally committed to the old way of doing things, formed their own subculture. As a result of the organization's attempt to adapt to a new environment, these members relocated their commitment from the organization to their subculture.

People's experiences with changes in the organizational environment may moderate their preexisting levels of reactance, satisfaction, and commitment to produce changes in their tendencies to join subcultures. When people perceive changes as negative, they may be more likely to join orthogonal subcultures and countercultures and less likely to join enhancing subcultures (and vice versa for positive changes). Whether or not changes are perceived as positive or negative is partially determined by preexisting levels of psychological reactance, satisfaction, and commitment. Therefore, we propose that:

> Proposition 9:   Peoples' levels of dispositional reactance, satisfaction with changes, and commitment to the organization will moderate the relationship between environmental dynamism and their propensity to join a subculture. Those high in reactance, those who perceive changes as dissatisfying, and those who are highly normatively committed will be more likely to join an orthogonal subculture or counterculture when their organization experiences a more dynamic environment, whereas those whose dispositional reactance is low, those who perceive changes as satisfying, and those who are less normatively committed will be less likely to join these subcultures regardless of the level of environmental dynamism their organization faces.

CONSEQUENCES OF SUBCULTURES
FOR STRONG CULTURE ORGANIZATIONS

Having identified various types and features of subcultures, the conditions under which they are likely to emerge, and the individual characteristics that might compel a person to join a specific type of subculture, we are now in a position to consider the impact subcultures may have on the organizations in which they exist. Researchers have speculated about whether subcultures are beneficial or detrimental to organizations (e.g., Galunic & Eisenhardt, 2001; Meyer, 1982; Tushman & O'Reilly, 1996). For example, Van Maanen and Barley (1985) characterized subcultures as containing seeds of conflict; this conflict may emerge when members of differing cultures are forced to confront one another. Similarly, Gregory (1983) noted that ethnocentrism operated in multicultural organizations; members of subcultures perceived things only from their cultural perspective, also perpetuating conflict. Hofstede (1998) did not specify whether subcultures were inherently good or bad for organizations, but suggested that managers' lack of awareness of existing or potential subcultures can be damaging inasmuch as subculture formation provides information about employees' perceptions about the organization.

We suggest that subcultures can both weaken an organization's culture or provide important benefits to strong culture organizations, particularly those operating in dynamic environments. Organizations facing dynamic environments are breeding grounds for subculture emergence. Members of strong cultures may more vehemently resist change, and change within strong culture organizations induces major conflict and dissent. Subcultures can absorb this conflict and dissent while leaving the overarching values of the organizational culture intact. Subcultures may, therefore, serve as mechanisms to contain conflicting priorities that may otherwise be widespread and potentially more difficult to manage at the organizational level (Meyer, 1982). Strong culture organizations can consider the benefits of alternative values and approaches that the subculture presents without destabilizing the entire organization.

In this way, subcultures may offer a way for strong culture organizations to remain flexible enough to change and adapt to external contingencies. This is an enormous benefit considering how difficult it is for strong culture organizations to innovate, as some say, squelching creativity by encouraging conformity of thought and behavior (e.g., Nemeth & Staw, 1989). We suggest that strong cultures can also foster innovation by stimulating subcultures of creativity, or subcultures in which creativity is the central value. That is, subcultures can develop in response to constraints imposed by the strong values of the larger organizational culture. At the same time, subcultures can serve as containers of creativity in which ideas can formulate relatively independently of the constraints or influences of the strong culture (Martin & Siehl, 1983). The idea that creativity flourishes only in isolation of strong organizational pressures is not new (e.g., Galbraith, 1982). But subcultures provide an additional advantage to managing innovation because, although they are separate enough to allow creativity to flourish, they are also still part of an organization. If successful innovation requires both coming up with creative ideas and getting them implemented (Caldwell & O'Reilly, 1995; O'Reilly & Flatt, 1986), subcultures may provide a place for creativity to grow as well as a way to coordinate with members of the dominant culture to implement the ideas (Kanter, 1988). Subcultures can make this seemingly contradictory pair of requirements possible because they are both somewhat removed from strong culture norms and, at the same time, connected to the larger resources and coordination capabilities of an organization.

Tushman and O'Reilly (1996) observed ambidextrous organizations containing multiple cultures and characterized them as being simultaneously tight and loose; they had strong, consistent cultures across the entire organization, but allowed for "appropriate variations to occur across units" (p. 27). These organizations were successful because of their normative structure in which the strong overarching cultures allowed for trust and predictability and promoted information and resource sharing, while their subcultures provided flexibility by allowing each business unit to determine how best to innovate. Although the subunits had enough autonomy to innovate in their own way, they were still part of a larger organization that was unified and capable of implementing their new ideas. Thus, we propose that:

Proposition 10: Strong culture firms that allow subcultures to emerge will be more innovative than strong culture firms that prevent subcultures from emerging.

IMPLICATIONS AND CONCLUSIONS

We explored the relationship between strong organizational cultures and subcultures in dynamic organizations. We suggested that, although strong culture organizations and their associated stability generally enjoy better performance than do weaker culture organizations, strong culture organizations are not as adaptive as may be necessary for their long-term survival, particularly those facing dynamic environments. We suggested that strong culture firms might become more agile by allowing subcultures to emerge. In some ways, our theory of subcultures can be compared to Ashby's (1956) law of requisite variety in the organizational strategy domain. He proposed that organizations with more variety are better equipped to respond to a complex environment. We propose that norm variation, generated by subcultures characterized by creativity, can similarly foster innovation and adaptation to dynamic environments. In addition to generating norm variation, our view of subcultures focuses on the relationship between subcultures and strong culture organizations for making an organization more agile.

We suggested that, in contrast to the popular notion that strong organizational cultures may preclude subcultures from emerging, strong cultures may actually sow the seeds of subculture emergence. Following Martin and Siehl (1983), we distinguished between different types of subcultures that vary in terms of the extent to which members agree with overarching cultural values. Extending Schein's (1988) ideas about organizations having pivotal values that are critical to the organization, as well as peripheral values that are desired but not essential, we suggested that peripheral values can vary at the subcultural level without negatively affecting the organization's pivotal values.

We then turned to the causes for subculture emergence and considered various individual, group-level, and structural bases for subculture formation. In addition, we speculated about how these factors may change in dynamic environments. We proposed that subculture emergence, as well as changes in subculture membership and prominence, would be more frequent in organizations facing dynamic environments. Finally, we depicted subcultures in strong culture organizations facing dynamic environments as receptacles for dissent and potential sources of creativity and flexibility. More specifically, agile organizations may contain subcultures that generate creativity within a strong overarching culture and foster the innovation that is critical for them to survive in dynamic environments.

Although we have only provided one perspective on the role of subcultures in agile, strong-culture organizations, many more perspectives and issues might be considered in future research. For example, specific values or norms are likely to be associated with the emergence of certain types of subcultures. Specific bases for subculture formation (functional departments, demographic differences, friendships, etc.) may, likewise, influence the type or content of subculture formation. For example, orthogonal subcultures may be more likely to form around departments or other functional work divisions as these emphasize specific work-related values, whereas countercultures may form around union affiliation as it has historically been associated with animosity toward management.

Researchers might also distinguish organizations that allow subcultures to emerge from those that prevent subcultures from emerging. Particular organizational forms or stages of organizational growth may be associated with subculture emergence. Are subcultures more common in start-ups or well-established firms? Furthermore, characteristics of the task environment may influence the ways subcultures form and interact with the organizational culture, such as the degree to which tasks are aligned with the goals of the organization or the types of tasks being performed. Finally, industry or market-level factors should be considered. For example, subculture formation may be affected by labor market conditions. Dissatisfied people may leave a firm rather than form or join a subculture when exit options are plentiful, and, likewise, they may form or join countercultures when exit options are more constrained.

Orthogonal cultures may form when countercultures are too risky for individual members. Finally, researchers might consider the temporal nature or typical life cyle of subcultures, including when a subculture is likely to form, thrive, decline, and dissipate, particularly in relation to an organization's life cyle.

Our objective in this chapter was to develop an agenda for subculture research. As such, we may have raised more questions than we answered, but we hope that we have contributed to mapping the relevant terrain in order to better understand the role of subcultures in strong culture organizations.

ACKNOWLEDGMENTS

The second author wrote this chapter while a Marvin Bower Fellow at the Harvard Business School and is grateful for their support. We also thank Elizabeth Mannix, Rita McGrath, and an anonymous reviewer for their insightful suggestions.

REFERENCES

Aronson, E. (1968). Dissonancy theory: Progress and problems. In R. P. Abelson, E. Aronson, W. J. McGuire, T. M. Newcomb, M. J. Rosenberg, & P. H. Tannenbaum (Eds.), *Theories of cognitive consistency: A sourcebook* (pp. 5–17). Chicago: Rand McNally.

Arvey, R., Bouchard, T., Segal, N., & Abraham, L. (1989). Job satisfaction: Environmental and genetic components. *Journal of Applied Psychology, 74,* 187–192.

Ashby, W. R. (1956). *An introduction to cybernetics.* London: Chapman & Hall.

Ashforth, B., & Mael, F. (1989). Social identity theory and the organization. *Academy of Management Review, 14,* 20–39.

Benner, M. J., & Tushman, M. L. (2002). *Process management and technological innovation: A longitudinal study of the paint and photography industries.* Working paper, The Wharton School, University of Pennsylvania.

Benner, M. J., & Tushman, M. L. (in press). Exploitation, exploration, and process management: The productivity dilemma revisited. *Academy of Management Review.*

Berscheid, E. (1985). Interpersonal attraction. In G. Lindzey & E. Aronson (Eds.), *Handbook of social psychology* (pp. 413–484). New York: Random House.

Bloor, G., & Dawson, P. (1994). Understanding professional culture in organizational context. *Organization Studies, 15,* 275–295.

Bojean, C. M., Brown, B. J., Grandjean, B. D., & Macken, P. O. (1982). Increasing work satisfaction through organizational change: A longitudinal study of nursing educators. *Journal of Applied Behavioral Science, 18,* 357–369.

Bourdieu, P. (1990). *The logic of practice.* Stanford, CA: Stanford University Press.

Braver, S., & Wilson, L. (1986). Choices in social dilemmas: Effects of communication within subgroups. *Journal of Conflict Resolution, 30,* 51–62.

Brehm, J. W. (1966). *A theory of psychological reactance.* New York: Academic Press.

Brewer, M. B. (1979). In-group bias in the minimal intergroup situation: A cognitive-motivational analysis. *Psychological Bulletin, 86,* 307–324.

Burns, T., & Stalker, G. M. (1961). *The management of innovation.* London: Tavistock Publications.

Caldwell, D., Chatman, J., & O'Reilly, C. (1990). Building organizational commitment: A multi-firm study. *Journal of Occupational Psychology, 63,* 245–261.

Caldwell, D., & O'Reilly, C. (1995, August). *Promoting team-based innovation in organizations: The role of normative influence.* Paper presented at the fifty-fourth annual meeting of the Academy of Management, Vancouver, British Columbia.

Cha, S. E., & Edmondson, A. (2001). *How promoting shared values can backfire: Leader action and employee attribution in a young, idealistic organization.* Working paper, Harvard University, Cambridge, MA.

Chatman, J. A. (1991). Matching people and organizations: Selection and socialization in public accounting firms. *Administrative Science Quarterly, 36,* 459–484.

Chatman, J. A., & Cha, S. A. (in press). Leading through organizational culture. In S. Chowdhury (Ed.), *Next generation business series: Leadership.* Upper Saddle River, NJ: Financial Times–Prentice Hall Publishers.

Chatman, J. A., & Flynn, F. J. (2001). The influence of demographic heterogeneity on the emergence and consequences of cooperative norms in work teams. *Academy of Management Journal, 44,* 956–974.

Chatman, J. A., & Spataro, S. A. (2002). *Getting people to cooperate: Understanding personality and relational demography based variations in people's responsiveness to organizational inducements.* Harvard Business School Working Paper Series (#02–087), Boston, MA.

Child, J. (1972). Organizational structure, environment and performance: The role of strategic choice. *Sociology, 6,* 1–22.

Cohen, A. K. (1955). A general theory of subcultures. *Delinquent boys: The culture of the gang.* New York: The Free Press.

Collins, J. C., & Porras, J. I. (1994). *Built to last: Successful habits of visionary companies.* New York: Harper Business.

Cropanzano, R., James, K., & Konovsky, M. A. (1993). Dispositional affectivity as a predictor of work attitudes and job performance. *Journal of Organizational Behavior, 14,* 595–606.

Deal, T., & Kennedy, A. (1982). *Corporate cultures.* Reading, MA: Addison-Wesley.

Denison, D. R. (1990). *Corporate culture and organizational effectiveness.* New York: Wiley.

Denison, D. R., & Mishra, A. K. (1995). Toward a theory of organizational culture and effectiveness. *Organization Science, 6,* 204–223.

Dowd, T. E., Milne, C. R., & Wise, S. L. (1991). The therapeutic reactance scale: A measure of psychological reactance. *Journal of Counseling and Development, 69,* 541–545.

Dutton, J., & Dukerich, J. M. (1991). Keep an eye on the mirror: Image and identity in organizational adaptation. *Academy of Management Journal, 34,* 517–554.

Dyer, L. (2001). *Some thoughts on dynamic organizations: Lots of stuff we need to know.* Paper presented at the Conference on Dynamic Organizations, Cornell University.

Flynn, F., & Chatman, J. A. (2001). Strong cultures and innovation: Oxymoron or opportunity? In S. Cartwright, C. Cooper, C. Earley, J. Chatman, T. Cummings, N. Holden, P. Sparrow, & W. Starbuck (Eds.), *International handbook of organizational culture and climate* (pp. 263–287). Sussex: John Wiley & Sons.

Flynn, F., & Chatman, J. A. (in press). What's the norm here? Social categorization as a basis for group norm development. In J. Polzer, E. Mannix, & M. Neale (Eds.), *Research in groups and teams.* Greenwich, CT: JAI Press.

Friedberg, K., & Friedberg, J. (1996). *Nuts! Southwest Airlines' crazy recipe for business and personal success.* Austin, TX: Bard Press.

Frost, P., & Egri, C. (1991). The political process of innovation. In B. Staw & L. Cummings (Eds.), *Research in organizational behavior* (Vol. 13, pp. 229–296). Greenwich, CT: JAI Press.

Gagliardi, P. (1986). The creation and change of organizational cultures: A conceptual framework. *Organization Studies, 72,* 117–134.

Galbraith, J. (1982). Designing the innovating organization. *Organizational Dynamics, 103,* 5–25.

Galunic, D. C., & Eisenhardt, K. M. (2001). Architectural innovation and modular corporate forms. *Academy of Management Journal, 44,* 1229–1249.

Gordon, G. G., & DiTomaso, N. (1992). Predicting corporate performance from organizational culture. *Journal of Management Studies, 29,* 783–798.

Graham, J. W. (1986). Principled organizational dissent: A theoretical essay. In B. M. Staw & L. L. Cummings (Eds.), *Research in Organizational Behavior* (Vol. 8, pp. 1–52). Greenwich, CT: JAI Press.

Gregory, K. L. (1983). Native-view paradigms: Multiple cultures and culture conflicts in organizations. *Administrative Science Quarterly, 28,* 359–376.

Hage, J., & Aiken, M. (1967). Relationship of centralization to other structural properties. *Administrative Science Quarterly, 12,* 72–91.

Hall, D. T., & Mansfield, R. (1971). Organizational and individual response to external stress. *Administrative Science Quarterly, 16,* 533–547.

Hebdige, R. (1979). *Subculture, the meaning of style.* London: Routledge.

Hirschman, A. O. (1970). *Exit, voice, and loyalty: Responses to decline in firms, organizations, and states.* Cambridge: Harvard University Press.

Hofstede, G. (1998). Identifying organizational subcultures: An empirical approach. *Journal of Management Studies, 35,* 1–12.

Jackson, J. (1966). A conceptual and measurement model for norms and roles. *Pacific Sociological Review, 9,* 35–47.

Jermier, J. M., Slocum, J. W., Fry, L. W., & Gaines, J. (1991). Organizational subcultures in a soft bureaucracy: Resistance behind the myth and facade of an official culture. *Organization Science, 2,* 170–194.

Jones, O. (2000). Scientific management, culture and control: A first-hand account of Taylorism in practice. *Human Relations, 53,* 631–653.

Judge, T. A., & Larsen, R. J. (2001). Dispositional affect and job satisfaction: A review and theoretical extension. *Organizational Behavior & Human Decision Processes, 86,* 67–98.

Kahneman, D., & Miller, D. (1986). Norm theory: Comparing reality to its alternatives. *Psychological Review, 93,* 136–153.

Kanter, R. M. (1988). When a thousand flowers bloom: Structural, collective and social conditions for innovation in organization. In L. Cummings & B. Staw (Eds.), *Research in Organizational Behavior* (Vol. 10, pp. 169–211). Stamford, CT: JAI Press.

Koene, B., Boone, C., & Soeters, J. (1997). Organizational factors influencing homogeneity and heterogeneity of organizational cultures. In S. Sackmann (Ed.), *Cultural complexity in organizations* (pp. 273–294). Thousand Oaks, CA: Sage.

Kotter, J. P., & Heskett, J. L. (1992). *Corporate culture and performance.* New York: Free Press.

Lawrence, P. R., & Lorsch, J. W. (1967). *Organization and environment.* Cambridge, MA: Harvard University Press.

Lord, C., Ross, L., & Lepper, M. (1979). Biased assimilation and attitude polarization: The effects of prior theories on subsequently considered evidence. *Journal of Personality and Social Psychology, 37,* 2098–2109.

Marks, M. L., & Mirvis, P. H. (2001). Making mergers and acquisitions work: Strategic and psychological preparation. *Academy of Management Executive, 15*(2), 80–92.

Martin, J. (1992). *Cultures in organizations: Three perspectives.* New York: Oxford University Press.

Martin, J., & Siehl, C. (1983). Organizational culture and counterculture: An uneasy symbiosis. *Organizational Dynamics, 122,* 52–65.

Meyer, A. D. (1982). How ideologies supplant formal structures and shape responses to environments. *Journal of Management Studies, 19,* 45–61.

Meyer, J., & Allen, N. (1991). A three-component conceptualization of organizational commitment. *Human Resource Management Review, 1,* 61–89.

Nahavandi, A., & Malekzadeh, A. R. (1988). Acculturation in mergers and acquisitions *Academy of Management Review, 13,* 79–90.

Nemeth, C. J., & Staw, B. M. (1989). The tradeoffs of social control and innovation in groups and organizations. In L. Berkowitz (Ed.), *Advances in experimental social psychology* (Vol. 22, pp. 175–210). San Diego, CA: Academic Press.

Nohria, N., Dwyer, D., & Dalzell, F., Jr. (2002). *Changing fortunes: The rise and fall of the industrial corporation.* New York: Wiley.

O'Reilly, C. A. (1989). Corporations, culture, and commitment: Motivation and social control in organizations. *California Management Review, 314,* 9–25.

O'Reilly, C. A., & Chatman, J. A. (1986). Organizational commitment and psychological attachment: The effects of compliance, identification and internalization on prosocial behavior. *Journal of Applied Psychology, 71,* 492–499.

O'Reilly, C. A., & Chatman, J. A. (1996). Culture as social control: Corporations, cults, and commitment. In B. M. Staw & L. Cummings (Eds.), *Research in Organizational Behavior* (Vol. 18, pp. 287–365). Stamford, CT: JAI Press.

O'Reilly, C. A., & Flatt, A. (1986). *Executive team demography, organizational innovation and firm performance.* Organizational Behavior & Industrial Relations Working Paper; no. OBIR-9, University of California, Berkeley, CA.

O'Reilly, C. A., & Pfeffer, J. (2000a). Cisco Systems: Acquiring and retaining talent in hypercompetitive markets. *Human Resource Planning, 23,* 38–52.

O'Reilly, C. A., & Pfeffer, J. (2000b). *Hidden value: How great companies achieve extraordinary results with ordinary people.* Boston: Harvard Business School Press.

Pottruck, D. S., & Pearce, T. (2001). *Clicks and mortar: Passion-driven growth in an Internet-driven world.* San Francisco: Jossey-Bass.

Pratt, M. G., & Rafaeli, A. (1997). Organizational dress as a symbol of multilayered social identities. *Academy of Management Journal, 40,* 862–898

Puffer, S. M. (1999). CompUSA's CEO James Halpin on technology, rewards, and commitment. *Academy of Management Executive, 13,* 29–36.

Quinn, M. (2002, February 10). Collision of cultures: The HP–Compaq battle. *San Jose Mercury News,* 1.

Rose, R. A. (1988). Organizations as multiple cultures: A rules theory analysis. *Human Relations, 412,* 139–170.

Sackmann, S. (1992). Culture and subcultures: An analysis of organizational knowledge. *Administrative Science Quarterly, 37,* 140–161.

Saffold, G. S. (1988). Culture traits, strength, and organizational performance: Moving beyond "strong" culture. *Academy of Management Review, 13,* 546–558.

Schein, E. (1961). *Coercive persuasion.* New York: Norton.

Schein, E. (1988). Organizational socialization and the profession of management. *Sloan Management Review, 30,* 53–65.

Sorensen, J. B. (2002). The strength of corporate culture and the reliability of firm performance. *Administrative Science Quarterly, 47*, 70–91.

Staw, B. M. (1977). Knee-deep in the big muddy: A study of escalating commitment to a chosen course of action. *Organizational Behavior and Human Performance, 16*, 27–44.

Staw, B. M., Bell, N. E., & Clausen, J. A. (1986). The dispositional approach to job attitudes: A lifetime longitudinal test. *Administrative Science Quarterly, 31*, 56–77.

Staw, B. M., & Ross, J. (1985). Stability in the midst of change: A dispositional approach to job attitudes. *Journal of Applied Psychology, 70*, 469–480.

Staw, B. M., Sandelands, L. E., & Dutton, J. E. (1981). Threat-rigidity effects in organizational behavior: A multilevel analysis. *Administrative Science Quarterly, 26*, 501–524.

Sutton, R. I., & Hargadon, A. (1996). Brainstorming groups in context: Effectiveness in a product design firm. *Administrative Science Quarterly, 41*, 685–718.

Sutton, R. I., & Louis, M. R. (1987). How selecting and socializing newcomers influences insiders. *Human Resource Management, 26*(3), 347–361.

Trice, H. (1993). *Occupational subcultures in the workplace.* Ithaca, NY: ILR Press.

Trice, H., & Beyer, J. M. (1993). *The culture of work organizations.* Englewood Cliffs, NJ: Prentice-Hall.

Trice, H. M., & Beyer, J. M. (1984). Studying organizational cultures through rites and ceremonials. *Academy of Management Review, 9*, 653–669.

Tushman, M. L., & O'Reilly, C. A. (1996). Ambidextrous organizations: Managing evolutionary and revolutionary change. *California Management Review, 384*, 8–30.

Tushman, M. L., & O'Reilly, C. A. (1997). *Winning through innovation: A practical guide to leading organizational change and renewal.* Boston: Harvard Business School Press.

Tushman, M. L., & Smith, W. (2002). Organizational technology. In J. A. Baum (Ed.), *The Blackwell companion to organizations* (pp. 386–414). Oxford, UK: Blackwell.

Van de Ven, A. H., & Ferry, D. L. (1980). *Measuring and assessing organizations.* New York: Wiley-Interscience.

Van Maanen, J., & Barley, S. R. (1984). Occupational communities: Culture and control in organizations. In B. M. Staw & L. Cummings (Eds.), *Research in organizational behavior* (Vol. 6, pp. 287–365). Stamford, CT: JAI Press.

Van Maanen, J., & Barley, S. R. (1985). Cultural organization: Fragments of a theory. In P. M. Frost, L. F. Moore, M. R. Louis, C. C. Lundberg, & J. Martin (Eds.), *Organizational culture,* (pp. 31–53). Beverly Hills, CA: Sage.

Webster, C. (1993). Communes. In S. Hall & T. Jefferson (Eds.), *Resistance through rituals: Youth subcultures in post-war Britain* (pp. 126–134). London: Routledge.

Wilkins, A. L., & Ouchi, W. G. (1983). Efficient cultures: Exploring the relationship between culture and organizational performance. *Administrative Science Quarterly, 28*, 468–481.

Willis, P. E. (1993). The cultural meaning of drug use. In S. Hall & T. Jefferson (Eds.), *Resistance through rituals: Youth subcultures in post-war Britain* (pp. 106–118). London: Routledge.

Wolfgang, M. E., & Ferracuti, F. (1970). Subculture of violence: An integrated conceptualization. In D. O. Arnold (Ed.), *The sociology of subcultures* (pp. 135–149). Berkeley, CA: The Glendessary Press.

Yinger, J. M. (1970). Contraculture and subculture. In D. O. Arnold (Ed.), *The sociology of subcultures* (pp. 121–134). Berkeley, CA: The Glendessary Press.

Zellner, W. W. (1995). *Countercultures: A sociological analysis.* New York: St. Martin's Press.

III

MANAGING INFORMATION FLOW IN THE DYNAMIC ORGANIZATION

6

Managing Teams in the Dynamic Organization: The Effects of Revolving Membership and Changing Task Demands on Expertise and Status in Groups

Melissa C. Thomas-Hunt
Cornell University

Katherine W. Phillips
Northwestern University

In this chapter we discuss the role of teams in dynamic organizations and the particular challenges that they face in a dynamic environment. We focus on the constant membership and task changes that teams must accommodate in dynamic organizations. We further discuss how these changes might obscure information about who has expertise in the group. We suggest that these problems are, in large part, due to the increased use of inappropriate status cues. We offer several propositions that might help management scholars who are concerned about the process and performance of work teams.

Dynamic organizations are defined by their ability to reinvent the rules of business by creating and exploiting new opportunities and rapidly adapting to the evolving environments in which they find themselves (Dyer, 2001). Such organizations must continually update by gathering new information, seeking new markets, and redefining the way in which work is conceptualized and configured. Consequently, dynamic organizations must introduce systems that support the instantaneous accumulation and distribution of information. The proliferation of organizational work teams throughout dynamic organizations may provide a mechanism through which organizations can access and exploit individuals' efforts and knowledge as needed.

In an attempt to foster the cross-pollenization of ideas, many organizations have already begun to rely on cross-functional and new-product development teams, task forces, and other groups whose purpose is to learn through interaction (Sundstrom, 1999). Dynamic organizations necessitate that their teams mimic task forces—groups designed to address a particular project or purpose (Arrow & McGrath, 1993, 1995). Such teams can be assembled to accomplish particular goals or tasks and then be quickly dissolved or reconfigured as circumstances change. They can be used to develop innovations to new problems or improve on the technologies already in place in dynamic organizations. These teams may even incorporate individuals from outside the traditional bounds of the organization, providing the opportunity for exposure to different pools of knowledge, paradigms, and ideologies. This boundary-spanning capacity of teams contributes to the radical reconceptualization of organizational work that characterizes dynamic organizations.

The success of teams in dynamic organizations, in large part, relies on the liberal exchange and open discussion of member knowledge, especially expert knowledge not previously known by all group members (see Argote, Gruenfeld, & Naquin, 2000 for review). By utilizing these teams, organizations hope to increase access to task-relevant skills and knowledge, strengthen ties between individuals within the organization, increase motivation, and enhance buy-in into the final outcome. Although work teams may make dynamic organizations more agile, the challenges faced by work teams are likely to be exaggerated when continuous changes in task demands and membership become the status quo. Such changes virtually ensure that the composition of teams will mutate and the relative status of individuals within teams will evolve. In this chapter we are concerned with understanding the factors that dynamic organizations must consider as they enlist organizational work teams. In particular, we consider how existing theory on expertise and status in work teams can inform our understanding of the problems dynamic organizations may face as their teams try to exploit the expert knowledge that their organizational members possess.

We start the chapter by first characterizing the membership and task challenges that teams in dynamic organizations face. We then discuss the factors that contribute to the failure of groups to accurately assess and access members' expertise. Next, consideration is given to how the dynamic environment may further obscure group members' expertise. Additionally, we discuss research that focuses on the effects of three types of status differences on the recognition and consideration of expertise within groups. We continue with a discussion of how membership changes and shifting task demands may exacerbate group members' reliance on potentially illegitimate status hierarchies. Throughout the chapter, we contemplate what new theoretical questions may arise from a more systematic construal of teams within the dynamic organization.

TEAM CHALLENGES
WITHIN DYNAMIC ORGANIZATIONS

Revolving Membership

Within dynamic organizations, the pursuit of new initiatives, projects, and markets, and the necessity to combine organizational resources in novel ways, requires the constant formation of new teams and the reconfiguration of old teams. Consequently, teams within dynamic organizations may resemble a hybrid form of team and task force. Team researchers in more static examinations of groups distinguished between teams and task forces by characterizing the relative importance of the purpose and people on the constitution and functioning of the group (Arrow & McGrath, 1995). Task forces are created to address a particular purpose or project and are then staffed with people who have the requisite skills and knowledge. Once the project has been completed, the task force is disbanded and its members return to their ongoing organizational responsibilities. In contrast, people define teams. The people may possess or need to acquire the necessary skills. The team is usually assigned to projects as they arise. Once a project is completed, the people continue and another assignment is given to the team. Within dynamic organizations, the distinctions between team and task force may become blurred; teams become more project focused and the required rapid pace necessitates that team members have less time to acquire skills and knowledge and are therefore more likely to be chosen for the task-relevant expertise that they possess. Consequently, teams within dynamic environments must consider the impact of routine membership changes on their ability to acquire, recognize, and integrate member expertise.

Membership changes may result from member subtraction, addition, or replacement (Ziller, Behringer, & Goodchilds, 1960). Within dynamic organizations, team members may be added to provide previously unrepresented skill sets, moved to another team in greater need of that person's skills, or redeployed from another team to replace a departing member. The loss or gain of a member may be complete or partial. Often, dynamic organizations necessitate that team members maintain membership in one team while acquiring membership in another. In instances in which individuals maintain membership in multiple teams, they must distribute their efforts and knowledge across the teams in which they hold membership (Thomas-Hunt & Gruenfeld, 1998). Whether a team possesses exclusive rights to a member or shares rights with another team is likely to have a profound effect on the team's functioning.

First, when members are completely lost from a team, a resource deficit may occur. Current members may take on the lost member's responsibilities or replacements may be added; however, there is a possibility that the team will not be able to recoup all of the resources that it previously possessed. To the extent that member expertise was well specified and roles were clear, teams will have a better chance of replenishing the lost resources. Nevertheless, the loss of resources is often accompanied by the disruption of team cohesion (Arrow & McGrath, 1993) and the depletion of transactive memory systems (Moreland, Argote, & Krishnan, 1998).

As a result of the constant flux in membership associated with teams in dynamic organizations, it may be difficult to establish rules and norms unless some core of members remains constant (cf. Arrow & McGrath, 1995). The maintenance of an established core may create a status hierarchy that results from having permanent and transient members on the team. Core members function as oldtimers and transient members as perpetual newcomers. The addition of a new member or replacement of an old member creates a situation in which newcomers must be socialized into the group (Moreland & Levine, 1989). Researchers have determined that there are numerous newcomer characteristics that influence their socialization. In particular, possessing task-relevant competence (Bartell, 1971; Davis, 1968; Fromkin & Klimoski, 1972; Mendenhall & Oddou, 1985) and high social status (Dodge, Schlundt, Schocken, & Delugach, 1983; Zander & Cohen, 1955; Ziller et al., 1960) have been shown to facilitate newcomer socialization. These factors are likely to have an impact on newcomers' willingness and ability to contribute expert knowledge and influence their teams. Because of the continual movement of team members in dynamic organizations, the possibility exists that the socialization process will be abbreviated. This will require the partial assimilation of newcomers and partial accommodation by oldtimers. To the extent that the arrival and departure of members becomes routine, teams in dynamic organizations may come to construe their membership as open (Ziller, 1965) and may more readily make the necessary adjustments in their rapidly shifting structures (Gersick & Hackman, 1990).

Second, whether a team must share members is likely to depend on the expected duration of participation on a newly formed team, the demands of team involvement, and the constraints of human capital within the organization. Multiple commitments may produce role conflict (Katz & Kahn, 1978) and cause members of multiple groups to lose credibility (Adams, 1976) and become less influential than when membership is not shared (Gruenfeld & Fan, 1999). For instance, individuals who distribute their efforts across teams may be viewed as defectors, siphoning resources from one group for the benefit of another. In contrast, they may be viewed as a source of ideas and information not previously accessible to a team. It is not clear what factors contribute to the motivational attributions that group members make about their boundary-spanning members. Recent research by Gruenfeld, Martorana, and Fan (2000), examining groups that experienced turnover in membership, begins to address these issues. They found that groups were less appreciative of the knowledge and ideas provided by a group member who left to work with another group and then came back to the original group (i.e., itinerant group members) than they were of temporary visitors to the group. This suggests that individuals who possess multiple group memberships may be more influential in their new groups than they are in the original groups in which they held membership. This matter is a complicated one and deserves more attention both in static and more dynamic environments.

We have considered that groups within dynamic environments may experience continuous membership changes in much the same way that the configuration of people within task forces changes. Alternatively, such groups may maintain their membership, but the demands of their task environment may shift frequently and, in doing so, alter the task-related competencies needed within the group. This is consistent with how the task demands of work teams change over time. However, teams in dynamic organizations must often deal with both membership and task changes simultaneously. The speed of change in dynamic environments necessitates that teams continuously assess the match between members' skills and task demands. Unless groups remain vigilant, it may be difficult for them to continuously assess the skills most needed (Kim, 1997).

Task Demands

In a dynamic organization, the uncertainty created by the constant search for new ideas and possibilities may diminish an individual's ability to comprehend the true nature of the task with which he or she is faced: Will success depend on speed of delivery, sophistication of product features, quality of the services provided, or the ability to create a demand where none previously existed? The process of charting new territory may require teams to undertake complex tasks with which they have minimal familiarity.

Task familiarity improves team performance by increasing the task ability of group members (Littlepage, Robison, & Reddington, 1997). This suggests that teams within dynamic organizations may experience performance decrements because they are less familiar with their work than teams within static contexts. Furthermore, members of newly constituted teams are most effective at sharing expert knowledge when they possess task experience (Kim, 1997). In dynamic organizations, individuals may not only be unfamiliar with the tasks with which they are presented, but the novelty of the situation may preclude teams from having a clear sense of the appropriate process and key evaluation criteria for any given project.

In rapidly evolving environments, teams may not detect that the factors critical for success have mutated. In such instances, teams may adhere to previous performance goals or expectations despite the shift required by the environment. In groups where individuals have the opportunity to establish and maintain roles and responsibilities, team members are more likely to have well-defined boundary spanners, responsible for managing the external boundary of the group (Ancona & Caldwell, 1992). As part of the boundary maintenance function, teams often enlist *scouts* to continually search the environment for cues about expectations held for the team. When members are rapidly redeployed, team roles become less well defined and the boundary management function may be sacrificed, leaving teams without an effective mechanism for detecting changing task demands. Challenged by an obscured understanding of their task demands, the difficulty of expertise recognition may be complicated by teams' inability to comprehend what expertise is most relevant to their task.

THE IMPORTANCE OF EXPERTISE

We have conceptualized teams within dynamic organizations as reservoirs in which individual repositories of member knowledge are integrated and directed toward achieving a collective outcome. The variation in member knowledge may be derived from differences in functional area, training, experiences, or assigned role. For example, one may imagine a client team at an e-commerce consulting firm consisting of a marketer, a salesperson, a web designer, a project manager, and an industry specialist. Each of the team members possesses a set of skills that reflects his or her training, functional background, and previous client, product, or team experience. Although there may be some overlap in possessed competencies, each individual is an expert in the domain in which his or her skill set surpasses those of other members. The ability of group members to recognize others' and communicate their own expertise is critical to the success of groups in both static and dynamic environments. The changing group membership and task demands already discussed may further affect expertise recognition and communication in dynamic organizations. Next we discuss how what we know about expertise in static environments might be affected by the characteristics of dynamic organizations.

Recognition of Expertise

Research in static environments has shown that the amount of task-relevant expertise contained within a group has a positive impact on group performance (Laughlin & Adamopoulos, 1980; Littlepage et al., 1997). However, merely possessing task-relevant knowledge is not sufficient. If the members of our e-commerce client team are unaware that the industry expert possesses strategic knowledge about the direction of the client's industry, they will be less able to make informed decisions about how to design or best promote the client's Web site, and in what time frame the project must be completed to maintain the client's competitive edge. Consequently, successful functioning necessitates that the group not only possesses, but also is able to assess, access, and appropriately incorporate member expertise (Bottger & Yetton, 1988; Einhorn, Hogarth, & Klempner, 1977; Henry, 1995; Libby, Trotman, & Zimmer, 1987; Littlepage, Schmidt, Whisler, & Frost, 1995). Research on transactive memory (Wegner, 1986) indicates that groups in which members have a shared knowledge of both their own and other members' competencies perform better than those in which members do not possess such shared knowledge (Liang, Moreland, & Argote, 1995; Moreland, 1999; Moreland & Myaskowsky, 2000).

Although groups are often able to recognize and exploit member expertise when tasks are simple (Henry, 1995), research on groups embedded in more complex task environments indicates that groups have some (Libby et al., 1987; Yetton & Bottger, 1982), if not considerable, difficulty identifying and harnessing member expertise (Littlepage et al., 1997; Littlepage et al., 1995; Trotman, Yetton, & Zimmer, 1983). One reason for this difficulty is groups' tendency to focus on shared information at the expense of discussing unique information (Gigone & Hastie, 1993; Stasser & Titus, 1985). Even when expert knowledge is shared, group members tend to focus a disproportionate amount of attention on shared versus unique or expert knowledge (Larson, Christenson, Abbott, & Franz, 1996; Stasser, Taylor, & Hanna, 1989). Such biased emphasis on shared information may lead groups to arrive at suboptimal decisions (Gruenfeld, Mannix, Williams, & Neale, 1996; Stasser & Stewart, 1992; Stasser, Stewart, & Wittenbaum, 1995). Recent research has begun to focus on why expertise is often underutilized (Thomas-Hunt, Ogden, & Neale, 1999; Wittenbaum, Hubbell, & Zuckerman, 1999). For example, Wittenbaum et al. (1999) argued that group members have a need to validate one another's task knowledge and this contributes to members' emphasis on shared knowledge at the expense of unshared knowledge. They termed this phenomenon *mutual enhancement*.

Communication of Expertise

Researchers have also attributed groups' difficulty identifying expertise to group members' inability to communicate the level of confidence that they have in their unique task-related judgments (Sniezek & Henry, 1989). If individuals are not confident about their opinions, they are less likely to be influential (Phillips, 2002) and people will be less likely to assess their knowledge as expertise. In the absence of other information, group members may rely on confidence cues to assess the validity of member competence (Dovidio & Ellyson, 1982). Consequently, in groups where members are able to clearly communicate their level of confidence, performance is better than in those where communications of confidence are ambiguous (Bloomfield, Libby, & Nelson, 1996).

Individuals displaying higher levels of confidence are often perceived to have expertise (Horai, Naccari, & Fatoullah, 1974; Hovland, Janis, & Kelley, 1953; Trafimow & Sniezek, 1994). Therefore, groups may mistakenly identify experts on the basis of the amount of displayed confidence, despite the fact that displayed confidence may not be closely related with true expertise. Furthermore, individuals with expertise may withhold accurate communications of their confidence to other group members, especially when such communications contradict those of higher status and may heighten group tensions (Bloomfield et al., 1996). Such self-censorship may further obscure the expertise within groups.

Alternatively, members may attempt to contribute their knowledge by confidently asserting their expertise. However, others in the group may reject expertise assertions, foregoing the opportunity to capitalize on such knowledge. Such inaccurate assessments of expertise may arise in situations where expert members' accurate construal of their confidence is ignored or discounted because of low preconceived expectations of performance held for that member (Berger, Fisek, Norman, & Zelditch, 1977). These preconceived expectations may be a result of in-group/out-group biases, past experiences, or reputation.

Expertise in Dynamic Organizations

Within dynamic organizations, the frequent membership changes within teams may further diminish individuals' opportunities to acquire firsthand knowledge of one another's competencies. Further still, shifting task demands will make it more difficult for team members to determine the relevance of member expertise once it is communicated. Thus there will be an increased reliance on the communicated confidence of team members and other individuals' impressions (i.e., reputation) to make these assessments. The already difficult and flawed process of recognizing and communicating ones' expertise may become even more difficult in dynamic organizations.

Proposition 1: Within dynamic organizations, the more rapidly membership changes, the more communicated confidence will have a positive effect on the recognition and consideration of member contributions.

Proposition 2: Within dynamic organizations, the more rapidly membership changes, the more members' reputations will determine the recognition and consideration of member contributions.

Proposition 3: Within dynamic organizations, the greater the shift in task demands, the greater difficulty teams will have recognizing and considering member contributions.

In many instances, misattribution of expertise may be linked to the status hierarchy in groups. Research indicates that status within groups affects both individuals' revelation of their expertise and the consideration that their expertise is given. In the following section, we describe the effects of three types of status differences on expertise identification and integration.

Status

The effects of status on contributions of expertise and consideration of member contributions has recently become the subject of numerous studies of knowledge exchange within groups (Phillips & Thomas-Hunt, 2002; Thomas-Hunt et al., 1999; Wittenbaum, 1998, 2000). Status has been defined as the degree of ascribed prestige, power, or competence possessed by an individual (Wittenbaum & Stasser, 1996), and has been shown to have an impact on the relative participation of members (Dovidio, Ellyson, Keating, & Heltman, 1988), the degree to which members are able to influence the group (Kirchler & Davis, 1986), and the level of consideration that members' contributions are given (Alkire, Collum, & Kaswan, 1968). Research on status in groups indicates that lower status members (a) feel pressure to conform to the assertions of higher status members and, therefore, may withhold their novel, controversial perspectives (Kirchmeyer, 1993); (b) obtain less useful information and ask fewer clarifying questions than higher status individuals (Alkire et al., 1968); and (c) are given less consideration by higher status members in group discussions (Propp, 1995).

In recent studies of expertise identification and contribution, three types of status have been studied: (a) relative task experience (Larson et al., 1996; Stasser et al., 1989; Wittenbaum, 1998, 2000) or perceived expertise (Stasser et al., 1995; Stasser, Vaughan, & Stewart, 2000; Stewart & Stasser, 1995; Thomas-Hunt et al., 1999); (b) social connectedness (Phillips, in press; Thomas-Hunt et al., 1999; Williams et al., 1997); and (c) demographic characteristics such as age, gender, or race (Dovidio et al., 1988; Phillips & Thomas-Hunt, 2002). Despite the recent focus of group researchers on how status affects knowledge recognition and communication, there has been little discussion of the differential impact of these various status dimensions on the knowledge-sharing process. Moreover, previous considerations of how status affects expertise recognition and use have been conducted largely within static environments. Within dynamic organizations, team membership and task demands are constantly changing. The potential exists for status hierarchies to be rapidly created and destroyed. Given the lack of experience with members and task, it is possible that team members, while establishing status hierarchies, will rely on readily observable, but potentially less diagnostic, member characteristics. The use of these inappropriate status cues may be quite detrimental to teams that need to utilize the expertise of all of their members.

Task-Relevant Status.   Investigations of the effect of perceived expertise on knowledge sharing within groups have primarily focused on the effects of task experience (Larson et al., 1996; Wittenbaum, 1998, 2000), the prior task performance of similar others (Thomas-Hunt et al., 1999), and ascribed leadership roles (Larson et al., 1996; Larson, Christenson, Franz, & Abbott, 1998). Wittenbaum (1998) found that individuals with no task-related experience pooled and repeated more shared than unshared knowledge. Individuals with task-related experience, however, pooled more unshared than shared knowledge. In a follow-up study, Wittenbaum (2000) found that differences in the relative pooling and repetition of unshared and shared knowledge by group members with task experience and no task experience were accounted for by the increased perceptions of expertise afforded to experienced members. This pattern of findings emerged despite the fact that experience did not necessarily translate into true task expertise. Furthermore, the researcher concluded that high status members reduced their bias toward shared knowledge by limiting their contributions of shared knowledge rather than increasing their contributions of expert knowledge.

Within dynamic organizations, team members may have little firsthand knowledge of other members' task experiences. Consequently, members' self-reports of their experiences and their reputations will have a large impact on the status that members are given. Additionally, the shifting task demands of dynamic organizations promote situations in which status may be afforded based on previous assessments of members' experience and knowledge rather than on members' current experience and knowledge given the new evolved set of task demands.

Proposition 4: Within dynamic organizations, status hierarchies within groups will be more related to prior reputation than to actual task-relevant knowledge.

One way for teams to manage the potential process problems they face is to utilize team leadership. However, leadership roles also act as a status mechanism affording the leader higher status than others in the group. In a series of studies of medical professionals, Larson and colleagues (Larson et al., 1998; Larson et al., 1996) investigated the effects of leadership role and task expertise on the pooling and repetition of shared and expert knowledge. They found that high-status individuals (i.e., those with ascribed leadership status) pooled and repeated more of their unshared knowledge than did low-status members of groups. Within dynamic organizations, the continuous change in membership may affect the emergence of team leaders. Will teams in dynamic organizations have leaders? If not, who will organize the pooling of divergent knowledge? How will teams keep track of their expertise? Perhaps leaders will remain as part of the stable core of team members. If leaders are partially sheltered from exposure to the changing task demands, how will they know how to effectively pool member knowledge? On whom will they rely for information about changing task demands?

Proposition 5: Within dynamic organizations, teams with knowledge managers will be more effective than those without knowledge managers.

Proposition 6: Within dynamic organizations, leaders who establish a mechanism for monitoring changing task demands will be more effective than those who do not.

Further support for the role of task-relevant status on knowledge sharing is derived from Thomas-Hunt et al. (1999). They manipulated the perceived expertise of group members. Using three-person interacting groups consisting of two individuals from one major and one individual from another major, participants were asked to complete a case in which they were required to choose the best candidate for a newly created position at a consulting firm. The correct answer was based on a hidden profile of required qualifications that was distributed across group members. Each group member received two pieces of shared information about required qualifications and one piece of unshared information. Each of the pieces of information was designed to eliminate one of the six candidates. In the study, individuals with perceived expertise participated more than those without perceived expertise. In particular, perceived experts increased their emphasis of shared knowledge and others' expert knowledge, but did not significantly increase emphasis of their own unique knowledge. From this research, the authors concluded that perceived expertise prompts individuals to serve as information managers for the group.

Within dynamic organizations, there will be heightened emphasis on each individual's potential to contribute to a team. In such situations it is likely that each team member will be viewed as an expert of sorts. If expert members are poised to pay attention to others' contributions rather than making their own, will contributions end up being made by the least knowledgeable on the team (i.e., those perceived to be least expert)? Will teams then prematurely commit to a course of action based on the least informed perspective? Will members whose contributions are most heavily weighted increase their status and create reputations as experts?

Additionally, will the continuous change in membership and the shifting relevance of member expertise promote more rapid adjustments in the status hierarchy of dynamic organizations relative to those of more static organizations? Will the contribution of novel ideas improve members' status or diminish it? Research by Sutton and Hargadon (1996) revealed that the brainstorming sessions of design engineers within a product design firm served as status "auctions" in which individuals elevated their status by publicly generating great ideas on which the group could build.

> Proposition 7: Within dynamic organizations, continuous membership changes and changing task demands will make members' status more fluid than it is in more static organizations.

Although it is clear that task-related status has an effect on group members' aggregation and emphasis of member knowledge, other types of status hierarchies also play a pivotal role in expertise identification and use within groups.

Social Connectedness.   Recently, group researchers attempted to study the effects of status derived from the presence of divergent social relations on knowledge sharing and emphasis within groups (Phillips, 2002; Thomas-Hunt et al., 1999; Williams et al., 1997). Unlike task-related status, status derived from social ties seems to limit group members' pooling and emphasis of expert knowledge. Phillips (2002), in a scenario study involving groups in which two of the three individuals were from the same social group (e.g., 2 MBAs and a medical student), found that social status has an impact on individuals' expectations of where unique opinions can be found in a group. Individuals expected their fellow subgroup member to share their same opinion and the "other" to have a distinct perspective. When expectations were violated, individuals reported higher levels of surprise and irritation. Additionally, in an investigation of three-person interacting groups with similar composition, Phillips (2002) and Williams et al. (1997) showed that groups performed better when the social subgroup shared the same information or perspective and the social isolate maintained distinct information or perspectives. Furthermore, status had an effect on minority opinion holders' ability to influence the group outcome (Phillips, 2002). When minority opinion holders were social isolates, they were more influential than when they were socially attached. These findings have implications for contributions of expertise or unique information within groups. Individuals without shared social status may be more willing to contribute their expertise than individuals with shared social status because their need for mutual enhancement, as described by Wittenbaum et al. (1999), may be diminished in that setting. It may be that the presence of a social other makes individuals with socially shared status more concerned with validating their task competence (Tindale & Kameda, 2000; Wittenbaum et al., 1999). Furthermore, group members' expectations that social isolates will hold divergent perspectives may lead them to be more willing to consider the novel information presented by social isolates rather than social insiders in diverse team settings.

Within dynamic organizations, the constant changes in membership may prompt core members to expect divergent perspectives from new members. The contribution of divergent perspectives from core members may actually diminish their status. Their divergence from similar others may be perceived as disloyalty. Research on loyalty indicates that disloyalty is less offensive when it is received from an outsider rather than an insider (Moreland & McMinn, 1999), providing support for the notion that newcomers may be expected to possess and contribute more divergent ideas than oldtimers. These ideas are consistent with the extensive use of outside experts and consultants that is often seen in organizational settings.

Consistent with these findings, Thomas-Hunt et al. (1999) found that members with shared social status exhibited more bias in their contributions of nonexpert information (i.e., shared information) relative to contributions of expert (i.e., unique) information than did social isolates. Additionally, members with shared social status gave greater consideration to the expertise contributions of social isolates than to those of their social other. This series of studies provides evidence that groups may perform best and share more of their expert knowledge (i.e., unique perspective) when those with shared social status also possess similar expertise. Within dynamic organizations, preconceived notions of core members' (i.e., oldtimers) similarity may actually diminish the consideration given to their novel contributions.

Proposition 8: Within dynamic organizations, new members' novel contributions will be given more emphasis than old members' novel contributions.

Diffuse Characteristics.   Thus far we have discussed the effects of status derived from perceived expertise and shared social status. Status differences within groups, however, may also be based on demographic characteristics (e.g., race, ethnicity, gender) that prompt group members to (a) generate performance-related assessments based not on actual performance, but on the preconceived notions that accompany particular demographic characteristics (Berger et al., 1977) and (b) conform to behaviors consistent with social roles established by society (Eagly, 1987). Much research has examined the effects of gender, race, and age diversity on work groups (for review, see Williams & O'Reilly, 1998), so we do not review all of that literature here. However, recent research by Phillips and Thomas-Hunt (2002) focused in on the effects of gender on contributions of expert knowledge. Consistent with other research on gender in groups (Carli, 2001; Eagly, 1987; Ridgeway & Diekema, 1984), the authors found that expertise increased how confident males felt about their opinions, how competent others perceived them to be, and how much influence they had on group outcomes. Conversely, having expertise decreased how confident females felt about their opinions, how competent others perceived them to be, and how much influence they had on group outcomes. Moreover, groups with female experts underperformed groups with male experts. Their findings suggest that demographic characteristics may have a differential impact on the ability of members to contribute their expertise and influence group outcomes. Within dynamic organizations, the diminished availability of firsthand knowledge of competence and rapidly changing task demands may encourage individuals to rely more on preconceived expectations of performance. Within dynamic organizations, a diminished performance expectation may be harder to overcome with demonstrated performance.

Proposition 9: Within dynamic organizations, the lower performance expectations associated with certain demographic characteristics will persist longer than they would in more static organizations.

CONCLUSION

This chapter has only touched the tip of the iceberg regarding the challenges that teams are likely to face in dynamic organizations. Teams are complex entities. Organizations already face many challenges when utilizing teams in static environments. The constant changes that groups face in more dynamic environments are likely to make effective team management even more critical to organizational success. Our e-commerce team is a good example of the type of teams that dynamic organizations are likely to rely on. In some instances, member expertise may be clear. However, even when this information is known, groups may still fail to utilize that information. The use of inappropriate status cues that are pervasive in static groups will persist in dynamic environments and may present an even greater challenge for such groups.

Although we believe that dynamic organizations may be able to garner benefits from their employees by bringing them together in work teams, as discussed throughout this chapter, there are several issues that these organizations must consider and that we as researchers should also consider as we go forward. The changing membership and task demands that groups are likely to face will further complicate the complexities of utilizing expert knowledge and managing status differences in groups. The increasing diversity of the workforce, coupled with more dynamic environments, will open a plethora of issues for researchers and managers to disentangle. We are looking forward to the challenge.

ACKNOWLEDGMENTS

Many of the ideas in this chapter were presented at the Understanding the Dynamic Organization conference held in March 2001 at Cornell University, Ithaca, NY. We thank the conference participants and especially the manuscript reviewers for their helpful suggestions and comments.

REFERENCES

Adams, J. S. (1976). The structure and dynamics of behavior in organizational boundary roles. In M. D. Dunnette (Ed.), *Handbook of industrial and organizational psychology* (pp. 1175–1199). Chicago: Rand McNally.

Alkire, A. A., Collum, M. E., & Kaswan, J. (1968). Information exchange and accuracy of verbal communication under social power conditions. *Journal of Personality & Social Psychology, 9,* 301–308.

Ancona, D. G., & Caldwell, D. F. (1992). Bridging the boundary: External activity and performance in organizational teams. *Administrative Science Quarterly, 37,* 634–665.

Argote, L., Gruenfeld, D. H., & Naquin, C. (2000). Group learning in organizations. In M. Turner (Ed.), *Groups at work: Advances in theory and research.* Mahwah, NJ: Lawrence Erlbaum Associates.

Arrow, H., & McGrath, J. E. (1993). How member change and continuity affects small group structure, process, and performance. *Small Group Research, 24,* 334–361.

Arrow, H., & McGrath, J. E. (1995). Membership dynamics in groups at work: A theoretical framework. *Research in Organizational Behavior, 17,* 373–311.

Bartell, G. D. (1971). *Group Sex: A scientist's eyewitness approach to the American way of swinging.* New York: Wyden.

Berger, J., Fisek, M. H., Norman, R. Z., & Zelditch, M., Jr. (1977). *Status characteristics and social interaction.* New York: Elsevier.

Bloomfield, R., Libby, R., & Nelson, M. W. (1996). Communication of confidence as a determinant of group judgment accuracy. *Organizational Behavior & Human Decision Processes, 68,* 287–300.

Bottger, P. C., & Yetton, P. W. (1988). An integration of process and decision scheme explanations of group problem solving performance. *Organizational Behavior and Human Decision Processes, 42,* 234–249.

Carli, L. L. (2001). Gender and social influence. *Journal of Social Issues, 57,* 725–741.

Davis, F. (1968). Professional socialization as subjective experience: The process of doctrinal conversion among student nurses. In H. S. Becker, B. Geer, D. Reisman, & R. T. Weiss (Eds.), *Institutions and the person* (pp. 235–251). Chicago: Aldine.

Dodge, K. A., Schlundt, D. C., Schocken, I., & Delugach, J. D. (1983). Social competence and children's sociometric status: The role of peer group entry strategies. *Merrill-Palmer Quarterly, 29,* 309–336.

Dovidio, J. F., & Ellyson, S. L. (1982). Decoding visual dominance: Attributions of power based on relative percentages of looking while speaking and looking while listening. *Social Psychology Quarterly, 45,* 106–113.

Dovidio, J. F., Ellyson, S. L., Keating, C. F., & Heltman, K. (1988). The relationship of social power to visual displays of dominance between men and women. *Journal of Personality and Social Psychology, 54,* 233–242.

Dyer, L. (2001). *Some thoughts on dynamic organizations: Lots of stuff we need to know.* Unpublished manuscript, Cornell University.

Eagly, A. H. (1987). *Sex differences in social behavior: A social-role analysis.* Hillsdale, NJ: Lawrence Earlbaum Associates.

Einhorn, H. J., Hogarth, R. M., & Klempner, E. (1977). Quality of group judgment. *Psychological Bulletin, 84,* 158–172.

Fromkin, H. L., & Klimoski, R. J. (1972). Race and competence as determinants of acceptance of newcomers in success and failure work groups. *Organizational Behavior and Human Performance, 7,* 25–42.

Gersick, C. J., & Hackman, J. R. (1990). Habitual routines in task-performing groups. *Organizational Behavior and Human Decision Processes, 47,* 65–97.

Gigone, D., & Hastie, R. (1993). The common knowledge effect: Information sharing and group judgment. *Journal of Personality and Social Psychology, 65,* 959–974.

Gruenfeld, D. H., & Fan, E. T. (1999). What newcomers see and what oldtimers say: Discontinuities in knowledge exchange. In L. L. Thompson, J. M. Levine, & D. M. Messick (Eds.), *Shared cognition in organizations: The management of knowledge* (pp. 3–31). Mahwah, NJ: Lawrence Erlbaum Associates.

Gruenfeld, D. H., Mannix, E. A., Williams, K. Y., & Neale, M. A. (1996). Group composition and decision making: How member familiarity and information distribution affect process and performance. *Organizational Behavior and Human Decision Processes, 67,* 1–15.

Gruenfeld, D. H., Martorana, P. V., & Fan, E. T. (2000). What do groups learn from their worldliest members? Direct and indirect influence in dynamic teams. *Organizational Behavior and Human Decision Processes, 82,* 45–59.

Henry, R. A. (1995). Improving group judgment accuracy: Information sharing and determining the best member. *Organizational Behavior and Human Decision Processes, 62,* 190–197.

Horai, J., Naccari, N., & Fatoullah, E. (1974). The effects of expertise and physical attractiveness on opinion agreement and liking. *Sociometry, 37,* 601–606.

Hovland, C. I., Janis, I. L., & Kelley, H. H. (1953). *Communication and persuasion: Psychological studies of opinion change.* New Haven, CT: Yale University Press.

Katz, D., & Kahn, R. L. (1978). *The social psychology of organizations.* New York: Wiley.

Kim, P. H. (1997). When what you know can hurt you: A study of experiential effects on group discussion and performance. *Organizational Behavior and Human Decision Processes, 69,* 165–177.

Kirchler, E., & Davis, J. H. (1986). The influence of member status differences and task type on group consensus and member position change. *Journal of Personality and Social Psychology, 51,* 83–91.

Kirchmeyer, C. (1993). Multicultural task groups: An account of the low contribution level of minorities. *Small Group Research, 24,* 127–148.

Larson, J. R., Christenson, C., Abbott, A. S., & Franz, T. M. (1996). Diagnosing groups: Charting the flow of information in medical decision making teams. *Journal of Personality and Social Pyschology, 71,* 315–330.

Larson, J. R., Christenson, C., Franz, T. M., & Abbott, A. S. (1998). Diagnosing groups: The pooling, management, and impact of shared and unshared case information in team-based medical decision making. *Journal of Personality and Social Psychology, 75*(1), 93–108.

Laughlin, P. R., & Adamopoulos, J. (1980). Social combination processes and individual learning for six-person cooperative groups on an intellective task. *Journal of Personality and Social Psychology, 38*(6), 941–947.

Liang, D. W., Moreland, R. L., & Argote, L. (1995). Group versus individual training and group performance: The mediating role of transactive memory. *Personality and Social Psychology Bulletin, 21,* 384–393.

Libby, R., Trotman, K. T., & Zimmer, I. (1987). Member variation, recognition of expertise, and group performance. *Journal of Applied Psychology, 72,* 81–87.

Littlepage, G., Robison, W., & Reddington, K. (1997). Effects of task experience and group experience on group performance, member ability, and recognition of expertise. *Organizational Behavior and Human Decision Processes, 69*(2), 133–147.

Littlepage, G. E., Schmidt, G. W., Whisler, E. W., & Frost, A. G. (1995). An input–output analysis of influence and performance in problem-solving groups. *Journal of Personality and Social Psychology, 69,* 877–889.

Mendenhall, M., & Oddou, G. (1985). The dimensions of expatriate acculturation: A review. *Academy of Management Review, 10,* 39–47.

Moreland, R. L. (1999). Transactive memory: Learning who knows what in work groups and organizations. In L. L. Thompson, J. M. Levine, & D. M. Messick (Eds.), *Shared cognition in organizations: The management of knowledge* (pp. 3–31). Mahwah, NJ: Lawrence Erlbaum Associates.

Moreland, R. L., Argote, L., & Krishnan, R. (1998). Training people to work in groups. In R. S. Tindale, L. Heath, J. Edwards, E. J. Posavac, F. B. Bryant, Y. Suarez-Balcazar, E. Henderson-King, & J. Myers (Eds.), *Social psychological applications to social issues: Theory and research on small groups* (Vol. 4, pp. 37–60). New York: Plenum.

Moreland, R. L., & Levine, J. M. (1989). Newcomers and oldtimers in small groups. In P. Paulus (Ed.), *Psychology of group influence* (2nd ed., pp. 143–186). Hillsdale, NJ: Lawrence Erlbaum Associates.

Moreland, R. L., & McMinn, J. G. (1999). Gone but not forgotten: Loyalty and betrayal among ex-members of small groups. *Personality and Social Psychology Bulletin, 25,* 1476–1486.

Moreland, R. L., & Myaskowsky, L. (2000). Exploring the performance benefits of group training: Transactive memory or improved communication? *Organizational Behavior and Human Decision Processes, 82,* 117–133.

Phillips, K. W. (in press). The effects of categorically based expectations on minority influence: The importance of congruence. *Personality and Social Psychology Bulletin.*

Phillips, K. W., & Thomas-Hunt, M. C. (2002). *When what you know is not enough: Expertise and gender dynamics in task groups.* Working paper, Cornell University.

Propp, K. M. (1995). An experimental examination of biological sex as a status cue in decision-making groups and its influence on information use. *Small Group Research, 26,* 451–474.

Ridgeway, C. L., & Diekema, D. (1984). Dominance and collective hierarchy formation in male and female task groups. *American Sociological Review, 54,* 79–93.

Sniezek, J. A., & Henry, R. A. (1989). Accuracy and confidence in group judgement. *Organizational Behavior & Human Decision Processes, 43,* 1–28.

Stasser, G., & Stewart, D. D. (1992). Discovery of hidden profiles by decision-making groups: Solving a problem versus making a judgment. *Journal of Personality & Social Psychology, 63,* 426–434.

Stasser, G., Stewart, D. D., & Wittenbaum, G. M. (1995). Expert roles and information exchange during discussion: The importance of knowing who knows what. *Journal of Experimental Social Psychology, 31,* 244–265.

Stasser, G., Taylor, L. A., & Hanna, C. (1989). Information sampling in structured and unstructured discussions of three to six person groups. *Journal of Personality and Social Psychology, 57,* 67–78.

Stasser, G., & Titus, W. (1985). Pooling unshared information in group decision making: Biased information sampling during discussion. *Journal of Personality & Social Psychology, 48,* 1467–1478.

Stasser, G., Vaughan, S. I., & Stewart, D. D. (2000). Pooling unshared information: The benefits of knowing how access to information is distributed among group members. *Organizational Behavior and Human Decision Processes, 82,* 102–116.

Stewart, D. D., & Stasser, G. (1995). Expert role assignment and information sampling during collective recall and decision making. *Journal of Personality and Social Psychology, 69,* 619–628.

Sundstrom, E. (1999). *Supporting work team effectiveness: Best management practices for fostering high performance.* San Francisco, CA: Jossey-Bass.

Sutton, R. I., & Hargadon, A. B. (1996). The organizational context of brainstorming groups: Lessons from a product design firm. *Administrative Science Quarterly, 41,* 685–718.

Thomas-Hunt, M. C., & Gruenfeld, D. H. (1998). A foot in two worlds: The participation of demographic boundary spanners in work groups. In M. A. Neale, E. A. Mannix, & D. H. Gruenfeld (Eds.), *Research on managing groups and teams* (Vol. 1, pp. 39–57). Greenwich, CT: JAI Press.

Thomas-Hunt, M. C., Ogden, T. Y., & Neale, M. A. (1999). *Who's really sharing? The context dependent effects of social and expert status on knowledge exchange within groups.* Paper presented at the meeting of the Academy of Management, Chicago.

Tindale, R. S., & Kameda, T. (2000). "Social Sharedness" as a unifying theme for information processing in groups. *Group Processes & Intergroup Relations, 3*(20), 123–140.

Trafimow, D., & Sniezek, J. A. (1994). Perceived expertise and its effect on confidence. *Organizational Behavior and Human Decision Processes, 57*(2), 290–302.

Trotman, K. T., Yetton, P. W., & Zimmer, I. R. (1983). Individual and group judgments of internal control systems. *Journal of Accounting Research, 21,* 286–292.

Wegner, D. M. (1986). Transactive memory. In B. Mullen & G. Goethals (Eds.), *Theories of group behavior* (pp. 185–208). New York: Springer-Verlag.

Williams, K., Mannix, E., Neale, M., & Gruenfeld, D. (1997, August). *Sharing unique perspectives: The process of knowledge exchange in social and informational coalitions.* Paper presented at the annual meeting of the Academy of Management, Boston, MA.

Williams, K. Y., & O'Reilly, C. A. (1998). Forty years of diversity research: A review. In B. M. Staw & L. L. Cummings (Eds.), *Research in organizational behavior* (Vol. 20, pp. 77–140). Greenwich, CT: JAI Press.

Wittenbaum, G. M. (1998). Information sampling in decision making groups: The impact of members' task-relevant status. *Small Group Research, 29,* 57–84.

Wittenbaum, G. M. (2000). The bias toward discussing shared information: Why are high-status group members immune? *Communication Research, 27,* 379–401.

Wittenbaum, G. M., Hubbell, A. P., & Zuckerman, C. (1999). Mutual enhancement: Toward an understanding of the collective preference for shared information. *Journal of Personality and Social Psychology, 77,* 967–978.

Wittenbaum, G. M., & Stasser, G. (1996). Management of information in small groups. In J. L. Nye & A. M. Brower (Eds.), *What's social about social cognition? Social cognition research in small groups* (pp. 3–28). Thousand Oaks, CA: Sage.

Yetton, P. W., & Bottger, P. C. (1982). Individual versus group problem solving: An empirical test of a best-member strategy. *Organizational Behavior and Human Decision Processes, 29*(3), 307–321.

Zander, A., & Cohen, A. R. (1955). Atributed social power and group acceptance: A classroom experimental demonstration. *Journal of Abnormal and Social Psychology, 51,* 490–492.

Ziller, R. C. (1965). Toward a theory of open and closed groups. *Psychological Bulletin, 64,* 164–182.

Ziller, R. C., Behringer, R. D., & Goodchilds, J. D. (1960). The minority newcomer in open and closed groups. *Journal of Psychology, 50,* 75–84.

7

Transactive Memory
in Dynamic Organizations

Richard L. Moreland
University of Pittsburgh

Linda Argote
Carnegie Mellon University

In an effort to improve their competitiveness, many organizations have become more dynamic. One feature of such organizations is teamwork, but teams in dynamic organizations differ in certain ways from more traditional work teams. Many of these differences have implications for knowledge management, especially transactive memory. Transactive memory, or a shared awareness of who knows what, can develop in both organizations and work teams. Research shows that stronger transactive memory systems lead to better team performance, and transactive memory is probably valuable for organizations as well. But the special features of teams found in dynamic organizations seem likely to strengthen transactive memory at the organizational level, while weakening it at the team level. Teams in dynamic organizations may also experience other special problems. The challenge, then, is to decide when it is more important to have a strong transactive memory system at each level, and then manage work teams and their members accordingly.

Even a brief tour of organizational Web sites reveals a common theme, namely that many organizations regard themselves as "dynamic." Apparently, it is good for an organization to be dynamic, but what does that term mean, and why is it so positive? Several articles and books have been written about dynamic organizations (e.g., Brown & Eisenhardt, 1997; Chaharbaghi & Nugent, 1994; Mohrman, Galbraith, & Lawler, 1998; Rindova & Kotha, 2001), and that work shows some consensus about the key aspects of such organizations. One important aspect of dynamic organizations, for example, is flexibility. An organization must be capable of changing to meet new demands, take advantage of opportunities, and so on. Flexibility is often achieved through a decentralized organizational structure that features local autonomy. A second aspect of dynamic organizations is speed. Whatever changes an organization makes must be made quickly because delays can often be costly. Finally, learning is another key aspect of dynamic organizations. Acquiring and sharing knowledge related to an organization's mission are valued activities, not only because they can improve the organization's current performance, but also because they foster creativity and thus can improve the future performance of the organization (Argote, 1999). The need for organizations to become dynamic has been attributed to several factors, including globalization, the speed with which business conditions can change, the growing importance of technology, and the need for leaner staffing levels. Given these factors, an organization that is not dynamic will have trouble succeeding and may not even survive.

One way to encourage flexibility, speed, and learning in organizations is to reorganize work around teams. Teamwork is indeed an important feature of many dynamic organizations (Child & McGrath, 2001; Yan & Louis, 1999). Because they are smaller, teams are often more flexible than larger organizational units, and their size allows them to adapt with greater speed as well (see Leavitt, 1996; Lipman-Blumen & Leavitt, 1999). As for learning, teams have more access to knowledge (especially when team members are diverse and have many social network ties) than do individual workers, and because teams tend to be more cohesive than larger units, their members are more likely to share that knowledge with one another. And although there are many doubts about the creativity of teams among social scientists (Paulus, Larey, & Dzindolet, 2001), practitioners are more confident that teams can be creative (Paulus, Dzindolet, Poletes, & Camacho, 1993; Stroebe, Diehl, & Abakoumkin, 1992), and there is indeed some evidence that valuable ideas can arise in teams (Argote, Gruenfeld, & Naquin, 2000; Sutton & Hargadon, 1996).

It is important to note, however, that teams in dynamic organizations differ in certain ways from those found in more traditional organizations. First, in the spirit of local autonomy, teams in dynamic organizations are more likely to be self-managed (Manz & Sims, 1993). Second, these teams often focus on a single project for which there is a deadline and therefore some time pressure. Project teams are thus temporary—once their projects are completed, the teams are disbanded and their members are reassigned (Lacey & Gruenfeld, 1999; Meyerson, Weick, & Kramer, 1996). Third, workers in dynamic organizations tend to belong to more than one team at a time. Fourth, there may be greater diversity among team members, who often are chosen to represent different functional areas in the organization. Some team members might be temporary workers, brought into the organization because they have special knowledge that a team needs to complete its project. As all of this suggests, there is considerable instability in team membership, with people coming and going as they work on other projects, form new teams, or maybe even leave the organization altogether. Finally, team members in dynamic organizations spend more time communicating with each other via e-mail and other electronic media than face-to-face.

INTELLECTUAL CAPITAL
AND TRANSACTIVE MEMORY

As organizations have become more dynamic, a distinct but related trend has taken place, namely a growing concern over intellectual capital (Anand, Manz, & Glick, 1998). Within every organization, there is a great deal of knowledge embodied in workers. If an organization made optimal use of that knowledge, then its performance would benefit enormously. Unfortunately, few organizations enjoy such benefits because they are not fully aware of the knowledge that they possess (Davenport & Prusak, 1998). The knowledge is there, but it cannot be used because too few people (or not the right people) realize that it exists and know how to locate it. Many organizations have tried to solve this problem in recent years, often by developing special software that helps workers to learn "who knows what" (Stewart, 1997, 2001). Such learning allows workers to take part in what psychologists call *transactive memory* (Hollingshead, 1998; Moreland, 1999; Wegner, 1987, 1995).

Wegner (1987) was among the first to analyze transactive memory. Although he focused on dyads and small groups, his ideas are also relevant to organizations. Wegner noted that many people supplement their own memories, which are limited and unreliable, with various external aids. These aids include objects, such as address books, and other people, such as relatives and coworkers. Wegner was intrigued by the use of people as memory aids and believed that transactive memory systems develop in many kinds of groups (from close relationships to large organizations) to ensure that important information is not forgotten. Such systems combine the knowledge of individual group members with a shared awareness of who knows what. When group members need information but cannot remember it themselves or are not sure that their own memories are accurate, they can thus rely on one another for assistance. In this way, transactive memory systems give group members access to more and better information than any one person could remember alone.

Aside from helping everyone to remember more, transactive memory systems may provide groups with other benefits as well. In organizations, for example, a greater awareness of who knows what would probably improve how teams are staffed. Workers with relevant knowledge could be assigned to teams whose projects were expected to require such knowledge. Teams could thus be smaller because redundant knowledge could be minimized, and any problems or delays due to lack of knowledge might be less likely to occur. And what if unexpected problems did occur? A greater awareness of who knows what would probably improve problem solving too. Workers with knowledge relevant to specific problems could be located quickly, then asked or instructed to help. As a result, those problems might be solved more efficiently than if team members tried to solve them on their own or sought outside help without knowing exactly where to locate it. Other possible benefits of transactive memory systems for organizations can readily be imagined.

TRANSACTIVE MEMORY SYSTEMS IN ORGANIZATIONS

Do organizations indeed benefit from transactive memory systems in these and other ways? The answer to that question is not yet clear. Transactive memory systems usually arise through shared experience—as they spend more time together, engaging in a wider variety of activities, group members naturally come to learn more about who knows what. But as we noted earlier, an interest in making better use of their intellectual capital has recently led many organizations to develop special software that helps workers learn who knows what. Such software can be viewed as efforts to build transactive memory systems artificially, without depending on shared experience, which is slower and less likely to reach every worker whose knowledge might prove to be important. Although this software can take several forms, the most common is probably the organizational intranet, on which workers post web pages that summarize their knowledge, skills, and accomplishments. A set of keywords is then generated, so that a search engine can be used to find the web pages of people who seem to possess a specific type of knowledge. In this way, the entire knowledge of the organization, or at least the portion of that knowledge that is referred to on the web pages, becomes available to every worker with access to the intranet and the ability to use the search engine skillfully.

A great deal of time, effort, and money is required to create and maintain such software, but many organizations have made that investment, expecting it to be recovered someday through improvements in organizational performance. So it seems odd that no clear evidence exists for the effectiveness of these intranets, or for other technological attempts by organizations to make better use of their intellectual capital. Although some early claims of success were made, more recent analyses (Moreland, 1999; Prusak, 2002; Stewart, 1997,

2001) are more pessimistic. To illustrate a few of the problems that can occur, consider Context Integration (Koudsi, 2000), a web consulting firm that invested heavily in Intellectual Assets Network, an organizational intranet meant to improve worker productivity. For more than 2 years after the software was ready to use, however, few workers actually used it. One problem was that Intellectual Assets Network was difficult to use at first—the web pages quickly became disorganized because no one was assigned to manage the system. And some workers were reluctant to enter personal information into Intellectual Assets Network, in part because of concerns about privacy, and in part because entering such information was yet another task added to their workloads. This problem was exacerbated by the fact that no initial deadlines were set for entering information, so the task was easily postponed. Another problem was that workers were often reluctant to use Intellectual Assets Network if their information requests were public. They did not want to seem ignorant to their coworkers or managers about matters that they should already understand (see Lee, 1997). Finally, a few workers resented Intellectual Assets Network because it structured help seeking and giving in an artificial way, rather than allowing such activities to occur naturally. The organization's leaders tried in many ways to encourage the use of Intellectual Assets Network. For example, they (a) arranged for public and private demonstrations of the system; (b) trained all new workers to use the system; (c) acknowledged publicly any workers whose system use was extensive; and even (d) paid workers for using the system. Despite these efforts, fully a third of the workers never used Intellectual Assets Network, and few of the other workers were regular users.

This discouraging example is not unusual. Several observers have noted that technological approaches to knowledge management, involving software designed to help workers learn who knows what in an organization, are limited in their effectiveness (Moreland, 1999; Prusak, 2002; Stewart, 1997, 2001). What, then, could organizations do to make better use of their knowledge capital? Perhaps interpersonal approaches would be more effective. Workers appear to enjoy talking about themselves and their activities, and even when such talk is boring, it might still be informative. Why not provide workers with more opportunities to learn about what the people in their organization are like or what they are doing, then allow them to encode, store, and retrieve the information on their own? In other words, simply create more shared experiences, or else circulate more information of the type that shared experience provides. The first goal could be achieved through special events; workplace designs that encourage informal social interaction, especially story telling (Orr, 1996); efforts to identify and reward workers who are well informed (see Gladwell, 2000) about organization members ("connectors") and activities ("mavens"); and work schemes, such as job rotation and cross-functional teams, that allow new relationships to develop among people working in different parts of the organization. The second goal could be achieved through publicity, involving newsletters or other media, that familiarizes workers with people and events related to the organization.

This analysis brings us back to dynamic organizations. Recall that these organizations often contain many small, self-managed teams. Most such teams form to carry out a specific project, then dissolve when that project is completed. Such teams tend to be diverse—members have not worked together before, and they may not work together again, at least not for a long time. Some team members may be outsiders, whose work for the organization is limited to the team's project. Finally, workers are likely to belong to more than one team. There is thus considerable movement by workers from one team to another. How would all of this affect the organization's transactive memory system? In our view, its effects would be similar to those of restructuring schemes, namely providing more chances for shared experiences among workers who might otherwise not meet or interact. In dynamic organizations, workers are thus more likely to learn who knows what than are workers in more traditional organizations. The latter workers might have deeper knowledge about others, because they spend more time working with other team members on a broader variety of projects. But their knowledge is limited to just a few people. In contrast, workers in dynamic organizations might have a shallower knowledge about others, because they have spent less time with each person, working on just a few projects. But their knowledge extends to many people, both in and out of the organization. If someone were asked where a specific piece of knowledge could be found in an organization, a person who worked for a dynamic organization would thus be more likely to know the answer. Of course, that person might be less able to obtain that knowledge if his or her relationships with others were relatively weak (cf. Hansen, 1999), but evidence suggests that even weak relationships between workers can support some knowledge transfer (see Constant, Kiesler, & Sproull, 1996). Thus, it seems likely that as organizations become more dynamic, their transactive memory systems will grow stronger.

TRANSACTIVE MEMORY SYSTEMS IN TEAMS

Now that we have analyzed how organizational transactive memory systems change when organizations become more dynamic, it is time to consider changes in the transactive memory systems of the teams within such organizations. Actually, one could argue that these changes will have the greatest impact on organizational performance, not only because so much of the work in many organizations is now done by teams, but also because teams matter more to workers than do organizations (see Moreland & Levine, 2000; van Knippenberg & van Schie, 2000). Workers are more committed to teams than they are to organizations, and teams have more influence over the behavior of workers than do organizations. All this suggests that team transactive memory systems are especially important.

What is known about transactive memory systems in teams? The potential benefits of these systems for team performance are clear. If workers know more about each other, for example, then they can plan more sensibly, assigning tasks to the people who will perform them best. Coordination should improve as well, because workers can anticipate one another's behavior, rather than reacting to it (Murnighan & Conlon, 1991; Wittenbaum, Vaughan, & Stasser, 1998). Finally, any problems ought to be solved more quickly and easily by workers who know more about one another, because then they can match problems with the people who are most likely to solve them (Moreland & Levine, 1992b). Once those people are identified, they can be asked for help, or the problems can simply be given to them to solve.

Indirect evidence for the beneficial effects of transactive memory on team performance can be found in two research areas, one involving familiarity among team members (see Argote & Kane, in press, for a review), and the other involving the recognition of expertise within decision-making teams. In the first research area, a common (but not universal) finding is that teams tend to perform better when their members have had more experience at working together (e.g., Goodman & Shah, 1992; Kanki & Foushee, 1989; Murnighan & Conlon, 1991; Watson, Kumar, & Michaelsen, 1993). And in the second research area, a common (but again, not universal) finding is that teams make wiser decisions when they can identify which team member has the most expertise on the issues (e.g., Henry, 1993, 1995; Henry, Strickland, Yorges, & Ladd, 1996; Littlepage, Robison, & Reddington, 1997; Littlepage, Schmidt, Whisler, & Frost, 1995; Littlepage & Silbiger, 1992). All of these findings are consistent with the claim that stronger transactive systems are associated with better team performance. As team members gain experience at working together, they should learn more about who knows what on the team, and such learning is obviously a factor in recognizing expertise among team members. It must be noted, however, that transactive memory was not measured in any of the studies just cited, so its exact role in team performance was unclear.

Our Research on Transactive Memory in Teams

Over the past few years, we have carried out a series of laboratory experiments designed to provide more direct evidence about how transactive memory systems affect team performance.

More detailed descriptions of our research can be found elsewhere (Liang, Moreland, & Argote, 1995; Moreland, 1999; Moreland, Argote, & Krishnan, 1996, 1998; Moreland & Myaskovsky, 2000). So in this chapter, we only offer a general description of our methodology and an overview of our findings.

In our research, team transactive memory systems are created through shared experience. We manipulate such experience by training team members in different ways. Everyone learns to perform a rather complex task—building a transistor radio from a kit that contains dozens of parts. Although treatment conditions vary from one experiment to another, we usually train the participants in one condition individually, while the participants in another condition are trained together, in three-person teams. The latter condition creates a shared experience that allows team members to develop a transactive memory system by learning who knows what.

The content of training is the same for all participants, regardless of treatment condition. At the training session, which lasts for about an hour, the experimenter first demonstrates how to build the radio, answering any questions that participants may have as they work. Then, the participants are asked to build a radio themselves. In the individual training condition, each person builds his or her own radio, while in the team training condition, team members build a single radio together. The experimenter answers any questions participants may have as they work on the radios, and once they are done, he or she inspects the radios and provides detailed feedback on any mistakes that were made.

A week later, a second session is held, again lasting for about an hour. At that session, all of the participants are tested in teams to evaluate how well they learned to build the radios. In the individual training condition, each team contains three people who were trained separately, and thus are strangers to one another. In the team training condition, each team contains the three people who were trained together the week before. We first ask the members of each team to recall, working together as a team, as much as they can about building radios, and to record this information on a blank sheet of paper. Then we ask each team to build a radio, working within a time limit and without help from the experimenter. Cash prizes are given to teams that perform best by building radios more quickly and with fewer mistakes. Before the testing session ends, we often ask the participants to complete a brief questionnaire that measures both thoughts and feelings about their teams.

Three measures of team performance are obtained during the testing session: (a) how much the team can recall about building radios; (b) how many mistakes the team makes while building its radio; and (c) how quickly that radio is built. Transactive memory is measured by evaluating videotapes made of the teams as they work on their radios during the testing session. Trained judges carefully examine participants' behavior for three signs that transactive memory systems are operating. The first of these is memory differentiation—the tendency for team members to specialize at remembering different aspects of building a radio. There should be more memory differentiation in teams that have stronger transactive memory systems. A second sign is task coordination—the ability of team members to work together efficiently on the radio. Teams that have stronger transactive memory systems should show greater task coordination. Finally, the third sign is task credibility—the level of trust within the team about whether each person knows what he or she is doing while working on the radio. Task credibility should be higher in teams that have stronger transactive memory systems.

What have our experiments shown? First, team training (shared experience) is indeed one way to create transactive memory systems. When team members are trained together, rather than apart, they behave differently while building their radios—levels of memory differentiation, task coordination, and task credibility, all signs of transactive memory, are significantly higher in such teams. Second, team performance is significantly better when team members are trained together, rather than apart. Team training helps members to recall more about building radios and to make fewer mistakes in the radios they build. These performance benefits can be large, sometimes as much as 40%. Third, statistical analyses and variations in treatment conditions both show that the performance benefits of team training are due to transactive memory and not to other factors that might be associated with team training, such as (a) motivation; (b) team cohesion; (c) social identity; (d) team development; (e) generic learning about building radios in (any) groups; or (f) better communication about radio building. To put it differently, there seems to be nothing about team training, other than the creation of transactive memory systems, that causes team performance to improve.

Along the way, a few other findings that seem worth noting have emerged from our research. First, turnover weakens transactive memory and thus harms the performance of teams whose members are trained together. Second, team training does not seem to produce social loafing (Latane, 1981)—the tendency for people to devote less effort to tasks when they work in groups rather than alone. Some might argue that team training is risky because people are less likely to learn their tasks well. Yet when we test people individually, rather than in teams, we find no difference in the performance of those who received team versus individual training. Finally, the behavioral signs of transactive memory that we look for in our videotapes of team behavior are valid measures—they correlate strongly with other, more direct measures of who knows what (e.g., comparing team members' beliefs about one another's skills with their actual skills, then computing levels of belief accuracy and agreement within teams).

Field Research on Transactive Memory in Teams

Although our findings all come from laboratory experiments, other researchers have recently moved into the field to study the effects of transactive memory systems on the performance of natural (rather than artificial) teams. In all these studies, stronger transactive memory systems are associated with better team performance, just as we find in our laboratory. Austin (1999) studied how "situated expertise" affected the performance of cross-functional teams in a large retail company. Situated expertise included two components, namely the accuracy of the team members' knowledge about one another's skills and their shared knowledge about social ties linking team members to external stakeholders. Team performance was measured as the progress of each team toward achieving its development and financial goals. Austin found that teams with longer tenure had greater situated expertise, which confirms that shared experience is important for transactive memory. Teams with longer tenure, greater situated expertise, and more frequent requests for assistance from outsiders had better performance, but the effects of tenure and requests for assistance on performance were mediated by situated expertise.

Lewis (1999) studied how transactive memory affected the performance of project teams in a graduate business course. These teams contracted with corporate clients to provide consulting services. As in our own research, transactive memory was measured in terms of specialization (similar to memory differentiation), coordination, and credibility. To measure team performance, Lewis obtained team self-evaluations, supervisor (instructor) evaluations, and evaluations from the corporate clients. Transactive memory was stronger in teams whose members had diverse expertise and were more willing to disclose their expertise to one another. Transactive memory grew stronger as time passed, and when team members communicated with one another more often. Both findings confirm again that shared experience is important for transactive memory. Interestingly, only face-to-face communication strengthened transactive memory; neither e-mail nor telephone communication was helpful. Most importantly, stronger transactive memory was associated with better team performance.

Faraj and Sproull (2000) studied how "expertise coordination" affected the performance of software development teams in a large corporation. Expertise coordination included knowing where expertise was located in a team, recognizing when such expertise was needed to solve some problem, and applying that expertise to the problem. Effectiveness and efficiency were used as measures of team performance (performance was evaluated by both the corporation and by client organizations). Teams with more expertise coordination performed better, even when other possible predictors of performance, such as team input characteristics (e.g., team members' age, education, or experience), levels of expertise (e.g., technical expertise, design expertise) in the team, and administrative coordination efforts (e.g., policies/procedures, team meetings) were taken into account. The most important element of situated expertise seemed to be knowing where expertise was located in a team.

Finally, Rau (2001) studied how transactive memory (agreement about expertise) affected the performance of top management teams in banks. Performance was measured as returns on investments by the banks. Rau measured many possible predictors of team performance, including diversity in expertise, the occurrence of task and relationship conflict, organizational size, and several team characteristics (e.g., team size, frequency of meetings, task complexity, leadership style, conflict resolution techniques). Transactive memory was strongly associated with team performance, both directly and through an interaction with task conflict. Teams with stronger transactive memory had better performance, especially when task conflict levels were moderate or high.

How Dynamic Organizations Threaten Team Transactive Memory

Let us return again to dynamic organizations, which often contain many small, self-managed teams that form for specific projects and then dissolve when the projects are completed, and which contain diverse members, many of whom have not worked together before and who may not work together again. Teams may well contain temporary workers, movement into and out of teams is frequent, and much of the communication among team members occurs through e-mail and other electronic media. How would all this affect the transactive memory systems of teams? In our view, the effects are probably negative. Changes in team membership threaten transactive memory because they make it risky for people to rely on each other's knowledge. If someone leaves a team, and other members have relied on that person for valuable knowledge about their team's project, then access to that knowledge becomes much more difficult. At best, team members might try to stay in contact with the person who left, hoping that he or she would still be willing to assist them when necessary; learn what they need to know for themselves; seek help from someone outside the team who has similar knowledge; or bring someone with that knowledge into the team as a new member. Other aspects of dynamic organizations may also threaten transactive memory in teams. For example, shared experience is constrained when a team works on just one project for a limited amount of time. Team members may learn who knows what regarding their project, but they may have few chances to learn much else about one another. And if they do not expect to work together again after the team is disbanded, then team members may not even try to learn much about one another. This lack of interest might be especially problematic when it comes to temporary workers, who will be leaving the organization anyway.

The negative effects of membership changes on transactive memory in teams were clear in one of our early experiments, where teams whose members were trained together were broken apart at the start of the testing session. To the surprise of participants, we asked them to join new teams, each containing three persons who were all trained in teams, but not in the same teams. The purpose of reassigning team members this way was to see whether the benefits of team training were due to generic learning about building radios in (any) groups. We reasoned that if such learning was why team training is beneficial, then it should not matter if participants trained in teams remained in those teams. These new teams showed few signs of transactive memory and performed poorly. In fact, they performed no better than teams whose members were trained individually. Of course, the changes in membership that we made in these teams were dramatic (all members of the original teams were removed) and unexpected. Maybe the negative effects of membership changes are weaker when more team members are left in place and/or teams are warned to expect turnover.

We are currently carrying out two experiments designed to explore these issues. In both of these experiments, all training is being done in teams. In the first experiment, some teams are warned before their training begins that turnover will occur at the start of their testing sessions. They are told that one team member (unidentified) will be removed and replaced by someone who was trained individually. Other teams do not receive this warning. The other factor in our design is whether turnover actually occurs at the start of the testing sessions. For some teams, we indeed remove a team member and replace that person with someone who was individually trained. In other teams, this turnover does not occur. We expect stronger signs of transactive memory, and better performance, when no turnover occurs, whether a warning is given or not. When turnover occurs, we expect weaker signs of transactive memory, but better performance, when a warning is given. Team members who expect turnover, but do not know who is leaving or what that person's replacement may be like, will probably try to learn all that they can about the task themselves, without relying on others.

In the second experiment, all training is again being done in teams. In one condition, teams experience no turnover, whereas in another condition, turnover occurs at the start of the testing session, but without warning. As before, one team member is removed and then replaced with someone who was trained individually. We expect much stronger signs of transactive memory and better team performance in the first condition than in the second. The experiment includes three other conditions as well. In all three cases, teams are warned before their training begins that turnover will occur at the start of their testing sessions. Again, they are told that one team member (unidentified) will be removed and replaced by someone who was trained individually. This, in fact, is what occurs. But in these conditions, we provide either the "oldtimers" (the two team members who remain after turnover occurs), or the "newcomer" (the replacement person), or both the oldtimers and the newcomer, with written information summarizing the newcomer's skills at building radios. This approach reflects research by Moreland and Myaskovsky (2000), who found that written information about team members' skills can produce transactive memory systems that are as helpful as those created through shared experience. Our reasoning is that informing oldtimers about the newcomer's skills might help them to incorporate that person into their team's transactive memory system, thereby limiting the harmful effects of turnover on transactive memory and team performance. We expect to see stronger signs of transactive memory and better team performance when the oldtimers alone, or both the newcomer and the oldtimers, are given information about the newcomer's skills, compared to when the oldtimers are given no such information, or it is given only to the newcomer. In a future experiment, we may try giving a written summary of oldtimers' skills to a newcomer, for similar reasons.

Other experiments on turnover and transactive memory, using our basic research paradigm, can also be imagined. Researchers could vary, for example, the number and/or types of people who enter or leave teams. In general, there should be more damage to transactive memory and performance in teams that experience more turnover. But are these effects linear? As levels of turnover rise, efforts by team members to preserve their transactive memory systems may also increase, but only to a certain point, when people decide that it would be wiser to abandon such efforts and rely instead on their individual memories. What is that point? Do some teams reach it sooner than others? If so, then why? A related issue is whether transactive memory systems are affected equally by the arrival of newcomers and departure of oldtimers. Because oldtimers have been team members longer, they are often more integral than newcomers to the operation of such systems, so their departure could be more disruptive. But for that same reason, it may be easier for teams to adjust their transactive memory systems for the departure of oldtimers, whose knowledge and skills are usually more familiar. As for the types of people who enter or leave teams, researchers could also vary the overlap between what newcomers and oldtimers know in teams that are experiencing turnover. Turnover should be less damaging to transactive memory systems when newcomers bring to teams valuable knowledge that other members do not already possess, but more damaging to transactive memory systems when oldtimers take from teams valuable knowledge that only they possess.

Researchers could also study how teams learn to cope with turnover. Turnover may be less damaging, for example, for teams that are older and more experienced. Over time, such teams often change their practices in ways that make turnover less disruptive (see Moreland & Levine, 1988: Ziller, 1965). These changes might even involve transactive memory systems, which can sometimes serve as tools for their own preservation. When oldtimers leave teams, for example, it is probably easier for those teams to evaluate what knowledge they are losing when they have already developed strong transactive memory systems. Teams with such systems can arrange for oldtimers who are leaving to download their knowledge in some way before they go (e.g., by recording the information or transferring it to other team members), or encourage the oldtimers to maintain future contact with them (e.g., by developing a consulting relationship), so that they retain access to whatever information they need. Strong transactive memory systems can also be useful for recruiting and socializing new team members. Recruitment is improved because current team members agree about what kinds of knowledge their teams need, which helps them to identify who should be encouraged to join their teams. And socialization is improved because current team members know what they want from newcomers, so they communicate their expectations more clearly and consistently. They can also provide newcomers with more and better information about their own knowledge and skills, which should help newcomers to use those resources.

Finally, an intriguing issue that researchers might study is how rotation across teams within an organization affects the transactive memory and performance of those teams. Over time, workers in a dynamic organization may sometimes find themselves in teams containing people with whom they have worked before, in other teams. In other words, team members could be familiar with one another, even though the team to which they now belong is new, and the team(s) to which they once belonged are gone. There is some evidence (see Moreland & McMinn, 1999) that the ex-members of groups that have dissolved may still feel loyal to those groups, which could strengthen their relationships with one another. And prior experience, even in other teams, could help people to build transactive memory systems in new teams, especially if the new and old teams were similar. The damage caused by membership change might thus be minimized when team members are already familiar with one another. But familiarity could also be problematic in some ways. For example, without knowing exactly what has happened to former colleagues since they last worked with them, people may assume that they have not changed (see Greenberg, Saxe, & Bar-Tal, 1978; Swann, Milton, & Polzer,

2000), and thus treat them in ways that do not reflect gains or losses in their knowledge and skills. People may also mistrust their former colleagues, precisely because they have since belonged to other teams (cf. Gruenfeld, Martorana, & Fan, 2000). To study these complex issues, researchers could vary such factors as how often people have worked together before on the same teams, how much time passes between their shared memberships, and how similar the various teams are to one another. Membership change may be less damaging to transactive memory and performance when team members have worked together more often in the past, the intervals between their shared memberships are shorter, and the new and old teams are more similar to one another.

Some may argue that the effects of a dynamic organization on transactive memory systems in teams are much less negative than we have suggested. For example, there is evidence that people who are often newcomers in groups (e.g., children in military families) learn to play that role better as a result (see Moreland & Levine, 1989). They become very efficient at learning what a group is like and then doing whatever is necessary to fit in. Maybe workers in a dynamic organization develop analogous skills, so that as members of teams, they require fewer shared experiences to learn who knows what in those teams. And is the motivation to learn about other team members really so important for the development of transactive memory systems? Maybe not. In another ongoing experiment, we are comparing our typical individual and team training conditions with a team training condition in which team members are told, just before training begins, that it is very important for them to learn as much as possible about who knows what because such information is likely to help them succeed. What effect will that advice have? If motivation is important, then there should be stronger signs of transactive memory, and better performance, in these teams later on, during the testing sessions. But what if it is only natural for people working together in groups to notice who knows what or who is good at what? Such behavior probably has survival value, so it may be an automatic process that does not require much conscious effort. If so, then advising team members to learn who knows what may have little effect on the development of transactive memory, and might even be harmful if it interrupts or otherwise interferes with a natural process. Finally, research by Moreland and Myaskovsky (2000) suggests that some of the problems associated with developing transactive memory systems in dynamic organizational environments could be overcome by giving team members advance information about one another, making shared experience a less important factor.

Although these arguments have some merit, our earlier analysis still leads us to believe that as organizations become more dynamic, team transactive memory systems will probably grow weaker. Moreover, there may well be other negative consequences of dynamic organizations for teams and their members, and these deserve to be considered as well.

Other Harmful Effects of Dynamic Organizations on Teams

One important feature of life in dynamic organizations is the stress it can produce in workers (Mack, Nelson, & Quick, 1998). Although some workers find such stress exciting, its effects on most workers are negative. These effects include higher health care costs, productivity losses, lower job satisfaction, and weaker morale. Lower job satisfaction and weaker morale can also lead, in turn, to increased absenteeism and turnover. Two general sources of stress related to team membership in dynamic organizations can be identified. First, it is often stressful to join a team (Katz, 1988; Keith, 1978; Louis, 1980; Nelson, Quick, & Eakin, 1988)—many newcomers feel self-conscious, are unsure what to expect, lack influence over the team, and may even be mistreated by oldtimers. (These problems are especially likely to be experienced by temporary workers.) And leaving a team is probably stressful as well (Gummer, 1987). Frequent changes in team membership in dynamic organizations may thus create considerable stress for workers, stress that could accumulate over time. Recent research by Kaplan, Manuck, and colleagues (see Kaplan & Manuck, 1999) on heart disease in primates seems relevant to this issue. In both correlational studies and experiments, they have found that instability in the living arrangements (cagemates) of animals is associated with greater disease. Patenaude (1999) found analogous results in a study showing that continually changing work environments can lead to emotional exhaustion in workers, especially those with lower organizational status.

Another source of stress related to team membership in dynamic organizations involves the fact that new teams frequently form and old teams disband in such organizations. A review by Tuckman (1965) of research on group development showed that when a new group forms, all of its members are likely to feel anxious at first because they are unfamiliar with one another and unsure about where the group is headed. Ironically, newcomers often turn to oldtimers for help with their problems (see Louis, 1980; Moreland & Levine, 1989, 2000), but that is impossible, of course, when everyone on a team is new. There is also evidence of anxiety in groups or teams that are about to disband (Greenhalgh, 1983; Krantz, 1988; see also Keyton, 1993; Tuckman & Jensen, 1977). Insofar as workers feel committed to a team, they may be upset by the thought that it will soon be gone, which could produce feelings of sadness or anger that might interfere with their work. The whole issue of temporary groups has been discussed extensively by group psychotherapists, whose groups are not meant to run continuously. And psychotherapists have been forced by managed care to develop creative new methods for achieving group goals more quickly, in less time than once was available to them. Some of their insights (Garvin, 1990) may suggest ways in which the stress associated with membership in temporary, short-term teams in dynamic organizations could be minimized.

Aside from stress, there may be other negative consequences of dynamic organizations for teams and their members. For example, workers probably feel less commitment to teams when they belong to many of them; each of those teams is temporary and focuses on just one project; team members are unfamiliar with one another and diverse; and there is relatively little face-to-face communication. It is possible that workers compensate by developing higher commitment for the organization as a whole, but there is no guarantee that would happen, because there is no clear relationship between commitment to teams and organizations (see Moreland & Levine, 2000). However, Ashforth and Johnson (2001) suggested several tactics for encouraging workers to identify more strongly with (and thus feel more committed to) organizations rather than teams. These tactics include keeping the organization small and focused; creating overarching goals and strategies; picking fights with external "enemies"; socializing newcomers collectively, with an emphasis on higher order identities; linking rewards to higher order goals; minimizing the trappings of rank and hierarchy; creating an organizational logo and a distinctive argot; and invoking such metaphors as "family" to characterize the organization. The same factors that cause workers to feel less committed to their teams may lead to less cohesion in those teams as well (Arrow & McGrath, 1993; Lacey & Gruenfeld, 1999). In "hot" teams, this may not be a serious problem—members are more interested in completing their team projects successfully than they are in developing or maintaining positive relations with one another (see Leavitt, 1996; Lipman-Blumen & Leavitt, 1999). And organizational solidarity could make team cohesion less critical in some settings. (Several of the tactics suggested by Ashforth and Johnson might help to improve organizational solidarity, as well as identification.) For most teams, however, weak cohesion is serious indeed, because it can lead to a variety of other problems, including job dissatisfaction and turnover (Riordan & Griffeth, 1995; see also Jackson et al., 1991; Mueller & Price, 1989; Tsui, Egan, & O'Reilly, 1992) and poor team performance (Mullen & Copper, 1994).

Stereotyping seems more likely to occur in teams operating within dynamic organizations because workers have less time, and perhaps less inclination, to become fully acquainted with the members of their teams. Several studies have shown that when team members first meet, they focus on surface characteristics, such as race, sex, or age, that are readily observable and thus serve as quick guidelines for behavioral expectations (Harrison, Price, & Bell,

1998; Tsui et al., 1992; see also Moreland & Levine, 1992a; Moreland, Levine, & Wingert, 1996; Wegner, 1987). Unfortunately, those expectations often reflect inaccurate social stereotypes, and the effects of those stereotypes on team members and interaction can be quite harmful. Moreover, such effects may be difficult to overcome later on, when team members are able to learn more about one another, discovering more subtle personal characteristics, such as their abilities (intelligence or skills), opinions (beliefs or values), and personalities.

Teams in dynamic organizations may also suffer from miscommunication, misunderstanding (few shared mental models), and conflict (see Cramton, 1997; Elloy, Terpening, & Kohls, 2001; Jehn, Chadwick, & Thatcher, 1997; Keller, 2001; Mueller & Price, 1989; Pelled, Eisenhardt, & Xin, 1999). These problems arise in part from diversity among team members, who often have different backgrounds, diverse areas of expertise, and incongruent values. Team members may also be less motivated to work out such problems if the teams are temporary, workers belong to many other teams, and the teams generate little commitment. The fact that many of the teams in dynamic organizations are self-managed might be a factor as well. Traditionally, a manager's duties included handling problems involving miscommunication, misunderstanding, and conflict among team members. But when a team has no manager, these duties must be performed by the team itself, and team members may lack the knowledge or training to perform those duties effectively (see Laiken, 1994).

Finally, what can be said about the performance of teams in dynamic organizations? On the positive side, there is some evidence that changes in team membership can actually be helpful. Katz (1981), for example, found that if the members of research and development teams remain together too long, they can become isolated from key information sources both in and out of the organization, which limits their performance (see also Berman, Down, & Hill, 2002). And in field experiments by Arrow and McGrath (1993) and by Gruenfeld et al. (2000), classroom teams performed better when students moved briefly from one team to another. In the Arrow and McGrath experiment, this improvement occurred because team members spent more time working on their task and because visitors helped teams to become more aware of their internal processes. In the experiment by Gruenfeld and her colleagues, the performance improvement reflected deeper thinking among team members about task-related issues, although the ideas of the visitors themselves had little impact in this regard, either in their home teams or in the teams that they visited. A laboratory experiment by Argote, Insko, Yovetich, and Romero (1995) showed that although turnover generally harmed team performance, it was less harmful when teams performed complex rather than simple tasks, perhaps because turnover can lead to innovation, which is valuable for performing complex tasks. Some of the other characteristics of teams in dynamic organizations, such as diversity among team members or a reliance on e-mail communication, can also be helpful at times. Nemeth and Staw (1989), for example, reviewed several studies showing that diversity can lead to valuable innovation in teams, and Straus and McGrath (1994) showed that e-mail communication can improve team performance at tasks for which nonverbal feedback is unnecessary or even disadvantageous. Despite all these findings, however, there is still considerable cause for concern about the performance of teams operating in dynamic organizations. As we argued earlier, the transactive memory systems of such teams may be weak, which could limit their performance. And how well can teams perform when they struggle with stress, a lack of commitment and cohesion, stereotyping, miscommunications and misunderstanding, and conflict? Ironically, the changes that dynamic organizations have made to increase performance at the organizational level may actually have decreased performance at the team level.

A SUMMARY AND SOME FINAL THOUGHTS

Increased competitive pressure has led many organizations to become more "dynamic" in recent years. Dynamic organizations emphasize flexibility, speed, and learning in their various activities, and as one means of achieving those goals, they rely heavily on teamwork. Teams in dynamic organizations tend to be self-managed and they are often assigned a single project to carry out. These projects usually have deadlines, creating time pressures, and once teams have completed their projects, they are often disbanded. Thus, teams are constantly forming and dissolving over time. Workers are likely to belong to more than one team in dynamic organizations, and team members can be diverse in many ways. Finally, team members may be geographically dispersed, and often communicate by e-mail or telephone, rather than face-to-face.

Another recent trend among organizations has been a concern over intellectual capital—the optimal use of all the knowledge available to an organization through its workers. Transactive memory, which can operate in both organizations and teams, is one tool for making better use of intellectual capital. A shared awareness among workers of who knows what makes it easier for them to take advantage of that knowledge. Transactive memory is thus valuable because it has the potential for improving the performance of organizations or teams, maybe substantially.

Our own research has repeatedly demonstrated the benefits of transactive memory for the task performance of laboratory teams, and recent research by others has now demonstrated similar benefits for actual work teams of various kinds.

The characteristics of dynamic organizations seem likely to weaken transactive memory at the level of teams. Changes in team membership may be especially problematic in this regard, because the departure of team members removes from transactive memory systems knowledge that others may not possess and to which they might have no other access. The arrival of team members can cause problems as well—their knowledge must be evaluated, others must learn what knowledge they possess, and they must learn what knowledge others possess. Other aspects of life in dynamic organizations may also threaten transactive memory in teams. For example, shared experience is constrained when a team works on a single project for a limited amount of time, which makes it difficult for workers to learn much about who knows what. And if workers do not expect to work together often (or at all) in the future, after their team has been disbanded, then they might not be motivated to learn much about each other anyway.

Dynamic organizations may endanger teams in several other ways, aside from weakening their transactive systems. These dangers include stress, decreased member commitment and team cohesion, increased stereotyping among team members, and greater miscommunication, misunderstandings, and conflict. These effects are likely to produce poorer team performance, just as damage to transactive memory can do.

It may be possible to protect in various ways the transactive memory systems of teams in dynamic organizations. Membership changes might be less damaging if team members knew what to expect, or if special efforts were made to create more shared experiences among team members. And maybe there are ways to make shared experience less critical, say by providing team members with information about one another through other means. We are now testing some of these ideas in our own research.

Clever management might also serve to protect teams against some of the other problems associated with life in dynamic organizations. For example, some workers are less susceptible than others to stress (Bauer & Truxillo, 2000; Saks, 1994), so organizations might try to hire and retain more such persons. Socialization practices could also be changed in ways that help new workers to cope with stress more effectively (Nelson, Quick, Eakin, & Matuszek, 1995). Team-building techniques, especially those that clarify workers' roles, could strengthen team cohesion (Salas, Rozell, Mullen, & Driskell, 1999; Woodman & Sherwood, 1980), and many methods for managing team conflict are now available (see, for example, Ray, 1995). Finally, structuring teams (creating specialized member roles and standardized operating procedures) can buffer them against some of the harmful effects of turnover on their performance (Devadas & Argote, 1995).

Although dynamic organizations may have weaker transactive memory at the team level than do traditional organizations, their transactive memory is probably stronger at the organizational level. Because of the personnel rotation that occurs across teams in dynamic organizations, the workers in those organizations will know more about the knowledge and skills of a larger number of colleagues than will the workers in more traditional organizations. Thus, workers in dynamic organizations are more likely to know whom they can approach, outside of their current teams, for help or advice. Such knowledge may also allow dynamic organizations themselves to make better use of their intellectual capital by assigning the right persons to teams or tasks.

Another benefit of better transactive memory at the organizational level is the facilitation of knowledge transfer across teams in dynamic organizations. Knowledge transfer occurs when one unit of an organization, such as a team, is affected by the experience of another (Argote, Ingram, Levine, & Moreland, 2000). For example, one team in a manufacturing plant might learn about a product innovation from another team, or a team in a consulting firm might learn more effective work processes from other teams. Organizations that are better at knowledge transfer tend to be more productive (Baum & Ingram, 1998; Darr, Argote, & Epple, 1995).

Knowledge transfer across teams probably occurs more often in dynamic than in traditional organizations because levels of personnel rotation and social network connectivity are greater in dynamic organizations. People are effective knowledge conduits (Almeida & Kogut, 1999). As workers move across teams in dynamic organizations, they may share knowledge acquired along the way. And connectivity in the social networks of workers in dynamic organizations may help them to discover where relevant task knowledge can be found outside of their teams. For example, Cummings (2001) found that when the members of teams in a large organization were either more diverse or geographically dispersed, the performance of their teams depended more on knowledge sharing, especially knowledge from external sources. As noted earlier, diversity and dispersal are both common characteristics of teams in dynamic organizations.

All this raises an important issue, namely when organizations should strengthen transactive memory at the organizational level, and when they should try to strengthen transactive memory at the team level. The former practice would foster knowledge transfer across teams, whereas the latter would foster knowledge transfer within teams. The tension between these practices is nicely illustrated by Adler and Cole's (1993) comparison between two automobile manufacturing plants, the Toyota/GM plant at Nummi and the Volvo plant at Uddevalla (see Berggen, 1994, as well). Adler and Cole argued that Nummi was more productive than Uddevalla. This difference was attributed to the kind of learning emphasized at the two plants. Organizational learning was emphasized at Nummi, whereas team learning was emphasized at Uddevalla. Knowledge transfer across teams was thus more common at Nummi. Performance gains made by one team often benefited other teams, so that over time, variability in team performance decreased. But there was a great deal of variability in team performance at Uddevalla, suggesting that knowledge transfer across teams was less common there. Apparently, teams at Uddevalla did not benefit fully from one another's knowledge.

Several factors could tip the balance to favor transactive memory at the organizational level, rather than the level of teams (see Argote, 1999). One such factor is whether the teams in an organization have similar or different tasks. Teams are more likely to benefit from one another's experience when they perform similar tasks (Darr & Kurtzberg, 2000), making an organizational-level transactive memory system especially valuable. Such a system would allow experiences in one team to be leveraged to improve the performance of another.

An organizational-level transactive memory system would also be especially valuable when tasks are "wholistic," and thus cannot be broken down into separate elements to be performed by different teams (see Levinthal & March, 1993). Otherwise, it would be better to foster team-level transactive memory systems, which would help each team improve its own performance without concern for the knowledge that might be found in other teams.

Finally, frequent changes in products or services (reflecting environmental demands) would also make an organization-level transactive memory system especially valuable. When such changes are made, they often require corresponding changes in team composition, so that the expertise of a team's members matches the requirements of its tasks. An organizational-level transactive memory system might well be useful for making optimal assignments of workers to teams.

In closing, we have argued that in dynamic (rather than traditional) organizations, transactive memory systems are probably weaker at the team level, but stronger at the organizational level. How might the performance of dynamic organizations be affected by this difference? We have described some possible advantages and disadvantages of transactive memory systems at the two levels, and identified just a few of the conditions under which systems at either level would be especially valuable. This issue is clearly important and thus merits future research. We are looking forward to that research.

ACKNOWLEDGMENTS

Some of the research described in this chapter was supported by a grant on personnel turnover and team performance from the Army Research Institute (Contract #DASW01-00-K-0018). The views, opinions, and findings described in this chapter are our own and should not be construed as an official Department of the Army position, policy, or decision.

REFERENCES

Adler, P. S., & Cole, R. E. (1993). Designed for learning: A tale of two auto plants. *Sloan Management Review, 34,* 85–94.

Almeida, P., & Kogut, B. (1999). Localization of knowledge and the mobility of engineers in regional networks. *Management Science, 45,* 905–917.

Anand, V., Manz, C. C., & Glick, W. H. (1998). An organizational memory approach to information management. *Academy of Management Review, 23,* 769–809.

Argote, L. (1999). *Organizational learning: Creating, retaining, and transferring knowledge.* Norwell, MA: Kluwer.

Argote, L., Gruenfeld, D., & Naquin, C. (2000). Group learning in organizations. In M. E. Turner (Ed.), *Groups at work: Advances in theory and research* (pp. 369–411). Mahwah, NJ: Lawrence Erlbaum Associates.

Argote, L., Ingram, P., Levine, J. M., & Moreland, R. L. (2000). Knowledge transfer in organizations: Learning from the experience of others. *Organizational Behavior and Human Decision Processes, 82,* 1–8.

Argote, L., Insko, C. A., Yovetich, N., & Romero, A. A. (1995). Group learning curves: The effects of turnover and task complexity on group performance. *Journal of Applied Social Psychology, 25,* 512–529.

Argote, L., & Kane, A. A. (in press). Learning from direct and indirect experience in organizations: The effects of experience content, timing, and distribution. In P. Paulus & B. Nijstad (Eds.), *Group creativity.* New York: Oxford University Press.

Arrow, H., & McGrath, J. E. (1993). How member change and continuity affects small group structure, process, and performance. *Small Group Research, 24,* 334–361.

Ashforth, B. E., & Johnson, S. A. (2001). Which hat to wear? The relative salience of multiple identities in organizational contexts. In M. A. Hogg & D. J. Terry (Eds.), *Social identity processes in organizational contexts* (pp. 31–48). Philadelphia: Psychology Press.

Austin, J. (1999). *Knowing what other people know: Situated expertise and assistance-seeking behavior in cross-functional teams.* Unpublished doctoral dissertation, Boston College, Boston, MA.

Bauer, T. N., & Truxillo, D. M. (2000). Temp-to-permanent employees: A longitudinal study of stress and selection success. *Journal of Occupational Health Psychology, 5,* 337–346.

Baum, J. A. C., & Ingram, P. (1998). Survival-enhancing learning in the Manhattan hotel industry, 1898–1980. *Management Science, 44,* 996–1016.

Berggen, C. (1994). Point/Counterpoint: Nummi vs. Uddevalla. *Sloan Management Review, 35,* 45–49.

Berman, S. L., Down, J., & Hill, C. W. L. (2002). Tacit knowledge and the NBA: An empirical test of the resource-based view of the firm. *Academy of Management Journal, 45*, 13–31.

Brown, S. L., & Eisenhardt, K. M. (1997). The art of continuous change: Linking complexity theory and time-paced evolution in relentlessly shifting organizations. *Administrative Science Quarterly, 42*, 1–34.

Chaharbaghi, K., & Nugent, E. (1994). Towards the dynamic organization. *Management Decision, 32*, 45–48.

Child, J., & McGrath, R. G. (2001). Organizations unfettered: Organizational form in an information-intensive economy. *Academy of Management Journal, 44*, 1135–1148.

Constant, D., Kiesler, S., & Sproull, L. (1996). The kindness of strangers: On the usefulness of weak ties for technological advice. *Organizational Science, 7*, 119–135.

Cramton, C. (1997). Information problems in dispersed teams. *Academy of Management Best Paper Proceedings*, 298–302.

Cummings, J. N. (2001). *Work groups and knowledge sharing in a global organization.* Unpublished doctoral dissertation, Carnegie Mellon University, Pittsburgh, PA.

Darr, E., Argote, L., & Epple, D. (1995). The acquisition, transfer, and depreciation of knowledge in service organizations: Productivity in franchises. *Management Science, 41*, 1750–1762.

Darr, E. D., & Kurzberg, T. R. (2000). An investigation of partner similarity dimensions on knowledge transfer. *Organizational Behavior and Human Decision Processes, 82*, 28–44.

Davenport, T. H., & Prusak, L. (1998). *Working knowledge: How organizations manage what they know.* Boston: Harvard Business School Press.

Devadas, R., & Argote, L. (1995, May). *Collective learning and forgetting: The effects of turnover and group structure.* Paper presented at the annual meeting of the Academy of Management, Chicago.

Elloy, D. F., Terpening, W., & Kohls, J. (2001). Causal model of burnout among self-managed work team members. *Journal of Psychology, 135*, 321–334.

Faraj, S., & Sproull, L. (2000). Coordinating expertise in software development teams. *Management Science, 46*, 1554–1568.

Garvin, C. D. (1990). Short-term group therapy. In R. A. Wells & V. J. Giannetti (Eds.), *Handbook of brief psychotherapies: Applied clinical psychology* (pp. 513–536). New York: Plenum.

Gladwell, M. (2000). *The tipping point: How little things can make a big difference.* London: Abacus.

Goodman, P. S., & Shah, S. (1992). Familiarity and work group outcomes. In S. Worchel, W. Wood, & J. A. Simpson (Eds.), *Group process and productivity* (pp. 276–298). Newbury Park, CA.: Sage.

Greenberg, M. S., Saxe, L., & Bar-Tal, D. (1978). Perceived stability of trait labels. *Personality and Social Psychology Bulletin, 4*, 59–62.

Greenhalgh, L. (1983). Organizational decline. *Research in the Sociology of Organizations, 2*, 231–276.

Gruenfeld, D. H., Martorana, P. V., & Fan, E. T. (2000). What do groups learn from their worldliest members? Direct and indirect influence in dynamic teams. *Organizational Behavior and Human Decision Processes, 82*, 45–59.

Gummer, B. (1987). Organizational puerperium: Employee leavings and heavings. *Administration in Social Work, 11*, 81–94.

Hansen, M. T. (1999). The search-transfer problem: The role of weak ties in sharing knowledge across organizational subunits. *Administrative Science Quarterly, 44*, 82–111.

Harrison, D. A., Price, K. H., & Bell, M. P. (1998). Beyond relational demography: Time and the effects of surface- and deep-level diversity on work group cohesion. *Academy of Management Journal, 41*, 96–107.

Henry, R. A. (1993). Group judgment accuracy: Reliability and validity of post-discussion confidence judgments. *Organizational Behavior and Human Decision Processes, 56,* 11–27.

Henry, R. A. (1995). Improving group judgment accuracy: Information sharing and determining the best member. *Organizational Behavior and Human Decision Processes, 62,* 190–197.

Henry, R. A., Strickland, O. J., Yorges, S. L., & Ladd, D. (1996). Helping groups determine their most accurate member: The role of outcome feedback. *Journal of Applied Social Psychology, 26,* 1153–1170.

Hollingshead, A. B. (1998). Distributed knowledge and transactive processes in decision-making groups. In M. Neale & R. Wageman (Eds.), *Research on managing groups and teams: Composition* (Vol. 1, pp. 103–123). Greenwich, CT.: JAI Press.

Jackson, S. E., Brodt, J. F., Sessa, V. I., Cooper, D. M., Julin, J. A., & Peyronnin, K. (1991). Some differences make a difference: Individual dissimilarity and group heterogeneity as correlates of recruitment, promotions, and turnover. *Journal of Applied Psychology, 76,* 675–689.

Jehn, K. A., Chadwick, C., & Thatcher, S. M. B. (1997). To agree or not to agree: The effects of value congruence, individual demographic dissimilarity, and conflict on workgroup outcomes. *International Journal of Conflict Management, 8,* 287–305.

Kanki, B. G., & Foushee, H. C. (1989). Communication as group process mediator of aircrew performance. *Aviation, Space, and Environmental Medicine, 4,* 402–410.

Kaplan, J. R., & Manuck, S. B. (1999). Status, stress, and atheroclerosis: The role of environment and individual behavior. In N. E. Adler, M. Marmot, B. S. McEwen, & J. Stewart (Eds.), *Socioeconomic status and health in industrial nations: Social, psychological, and biological pathways* (pp. 503–529). New York: New York Academy of Sciences.

Katz, R. (1981). The effects of group longevity on project communication and performance. *Administrative Science Quarterly, 27,* 81–104.

Katz, R. (1988). Organizational socialization. In R. Katz (Ed.), *Managing professionals in innovative organizations: A collection of readings* (pp. 355–369). New York: Ballinger.

Keith, P. M. (1978). Individual and organizational correlates of a temporary system. *Journal of Applied Behavioral Science, 14,* 195–203.

Keller, R. T. (2001). Cross-functional project groups in research and new product development: Diversity, communications, job stress, and outcomes. *Academy of Management Journal, 44,* 547–559.

Keyton, J. (1993). Group termination: Completing the study of group development. *Small Group Research, 24,* 84–100.

Koudsi, S. (2000, March 20). Actually, it is like brain surgery. *Fortune, 141,* 233–234.

Krantz, J. (1988). Group process under conditions of organizational decline. In K. Cameron, R. I. Sutton, & D. H. Whetten (Eds.), *Readings in organizational decline: Frameworks, research, and prescriptions* (pp. 265–278). New York: Ballinger.

Lacey, R., & Gruenfeld, D. (1999). Unwrapping the work group: How extra-organizational context affects group behavior. In M. Neale & R. Wageman (Eds.), *Research on managing groups and teams: Context* (Vol. 2, pp. 157–177). Greenwich, CT.: JAI Press.

Laiken, M. E. (1994). The myth of the self-managing team. *Organizational Development Journal, 12,* 29–34.

Latane, B. (1981). The psychology of social impact. *American Psychologist, 36,* 343–356.

Leavitt, H. J. (1996). The old days, hot groups, and manager's lib. *Administrative Science Quarterly, 41,* 288–300.

Lee, F. (1997). When the going gets tough, do the tough ask for help? Help seeking and power motivation in organizations. *Organizational Behavior and Human Decision Processes, 72,* 336–363.

Levinthal, D. A., & March, J. (1993). The myopia of learning. *Strategic Management Journal, 14,* 95–113.

Lewis, K. (1999). *The impact of interpersonal relationships and knowledge exchange on group performance: A field study of consulting project teams.* Unpublished doctoral dissertation, University of Maryland, College Park, Maryland.

Liang, D. W., Moreland, R. L., & Argote, L. (1995). Group versus individual training and group performance: The mediating role of transactive memory. *Personality and Social Psychology Bulletin, 21,* 384–393.

Lipman-Blumen, J., & Leavitt, H. J. (1999). Hot groups "with attitude": A new organizational state of mind. *Organizational Dynamics, 27,* 63–73.

Littlepage, G. E., Robison, W., & Reddington, K. (1997). Effects of task expertise and group experience on group performance, member ability, and recognition of expertise. *Organizational Behavior and Human Decision Processes, 69,* 133–147.

Littlepage, G. E., Schmidt, G. W., Whisler, E. W., & Frost, A. G. (1995). An input-process-output analysis of influence and performance in problem-solving groups. *Journal of Personality and Social Psychology, 69,* 877–889.

Littlepage, G. E., & Silbiger, H. (1992). Recognition of expertise in decision-making groups: Effects of group size and participation patterns. *Small Group Research, 23,* 344–355.

Louis, M. R. (1980). Surprise and sense-making: What newcomers experience in entering unfamiliar organizational settings. *Administrative Science Quarterly, 25,* 226–251.

Mack, D. A., Nelson, D. L., & Quick, J. C. (1998). The stress of organizational change: A dynamic process model. *Applied Psychology: An International Review, 47,* 219–232.

Manz, C. C., & Sims, H. P. (1993). *Business without bosses.* New York: John Wiley.

Meyerson, D., Weick, K. E., & Kramer, R. M. (1996). Swift trust and temporary groups. In R. M. Kramer & T. R. Tyler (Eds.), *Trust in organizations* (pp. 166–195). Thousand Oaks, CA.: Sage.

Mohrman, S. A., Galbraith, J. R., & Lawler, E. E. (1998). *Tomorrow's organization: Crafting winning capabilities in a dynamic world.* San Francisco: Jossey-Bass.

Moreland, R. L. (1999). Transactive memory: Learning who knows what in work groups and organizations. In L. L. Thompson, J. M. Levine, & D. M. Messick (Eds.), *Shared cognition in organizations: The management of knowledge* (pp. 3–31). Mahwah, NJ: Lawrence Erlbaum Associates.

Moreland, R. L., Argote, L., & Krishnan, R. (1996). Socially shared cognition at work: Transactive memory and group performance. In J. L. Nye & A. M. Brower (Eds.), *What's social about social cognition? Research on social shared cognition in small groups* (pp. 57–84). Thousand Oaks, CA: Sage.

Moreland, R. L., Argote, L., & Krishnan, R. (1998). Training people to work in groups. In R. S. Tindale, L. Heath, J. Edwards, E. J. Posavac, F. B. Bryant, Y. Suarez-Balcazar, E. Henderson-King, & J. Myers (Eds.), *Social psychological applications to social issues: Theory and research on small groups* (Vol. 4, pp. 37–60). New York: Plenum.

Moreland, R. L., & Levine, J. M. (1988) Group dynamics over time: Development and socialization in small groups. In J. McGrath (Ed.), *The social psychology of time: New perspectives* (pp. 151–181). Newbury Park, CA: Sage.

Moreland, R. L., & Levine, J. M. (1989). Newcomers and oldtimers in small groups. In P. Paulus (Ed.), *Psychology of group influence* (2nd ed., pp. 143–186). Hillsdale, NJ: Lawrence Erlbaum Associates.

Moreland, R. L., & Levine, J. M. (1992a). The composition of small groups. In E. Lawler, B. Markovsky, C. Ridgeway, & H. Walker (Eds.), *Advances in group processes* (Vol. 9, pp. 237–280). Greenwich, CT: JAI Press.

Moreland, R. L., & Levine, J. M. (1992b). Problem identification in groups. In S. Worchel, W. Wood, & J. A. Simpson (Eds.), *Group process and productivity* (pp. 17–48). Newbury Park, CA: Sage.

Moreland, R. L., & Levine, J. M. (2000). Socialization in organizations and work groups. In M. Turner (Ed.), *Groups at work: Advances in theory and research* (pp. 69–112). Hillsdale, NJ: Lawrence Erlbaum Associates.

Moreland, R. L., Levine, J. M., & Wingert, M. L. (1996). Creating the ideal group: Composition effects at work. In J. Davis & E. Witte (Eds.), *Understanding group behavior* (Vol. 2, pp. 11–35). Mahwah, NJ: Lawrence Erlbaum Associates.

Moreland, R. L., & McMinn, J. G. (1999). Gone, but not forgotten: Loyalty and betrayal among ex-members of small groups. *Personality and Social Psychology Bulletin, 25,* 1484–1494.

Moreland, R. L., & Myaskovsky, L. (2000). Exploring the performance benefits of group training: Transactive memory or improved communication? *Organizational Behavior and Human Decision Processes, 82,* 117–133.

Mueller, C. W., & Price, J. L. (1989). Some consequences of turnover. *Human Relations, 42,* 389–402.

Mullen, B., & Copper, C. (1994). The relation between group cohesiveness and performance: An integration. *Psychological Bulletin, 115,* 210–227.

Murnighan, J. K., & Conlon, D. E. (1991). The dynamics of intense work groups: A study of British string quartets. *Administrative Science Quarterly, 36,* 165–186.

Nelson, D. L., Quick, J. C., & Eakin, M. E. (1988). A longitudinal study of newcomer role adjustment in US organizations. *Work and Stress, 2,* 239–253.

Nelson, D. L., Quick, J. C., Eakin, M. E., & Matuszek, P. A. C. (1995). Beyond organizational entry and newcomer stress: Building a self-reliant workforce. *International Journal of Stress Management, 2,* 1–14.

Nemeth, C. J., & Staw, B. M. (1989). The tradeoffs of social control and innovation in groups and organizations. In L. Berkowitz (Ed.), *Advances in experimental social psychology* (Vol. 22, pp. 175–210). San Diego, CA: Academic Press.

Orr, J. (1996). *Talking about machines: An ethnography of a modern job.* Ithaca, NY: IRL Press.

Patenaude, J. (1999). *Does a continually changing work environment lead to emotional exhaustion? A test of a theory.* Unpublished doctoral dissertation, Guelph University, Guelph, Ontario, Canada.

Paulus, P. B., Dzindolet, M. T., Poletes, G., & Camacho, L. M. (1993). Perception of performance in group brainstorming: The illusion of group productivity. *Personality and Social Psychology Bulletin, 19,* 78–89.

Paulus, P. B., Larey, T. S., & Dzindolet, M. T. (2001). Creativity in groups and teams. In M. Turner (Ed.), *Groups at work: Advances in theory and research* (pp. 319–338). Hillsdale, NJ: Lawrence Erlbaum Associates.

Pelled, L. H., Eisenhardt, K. M., & Xin, K. R. (1999). Exploring the black box: An analysis of work group diversity, conflict, and performance. *Administrative Science Quarterly, 44,* 1–28.

Prusak, L. (2002, March). *The death and transfiguration of knowledge management.* Invited paper presented at a conference on The Future of Knowledge Management, sponsored by Humboldt University and Fraunhofer IPK, Berlin.

Rau, D. (2001). *Knowing who knows what: The effect of transactive memory on the relationship between diversity of expertise and performance in top management teams.* Unpublished doctoral dissertation, University of Minnesota, Minneapolis, Minnesota.

Ray, R. G. (1995). A training model for implementing self-directed work teams. *Organizational Development Journal, 13,* 51–62.

Rindova, V. P., & Kotha, S. (2001). Continuous "morphing": Competing through dynamic capabilities, form, and function. *Academy of Management Journal, 44,* 1263–1280.

Riordan, C. M., & Griffeth, R. W. (1995). The opportunity for friendship in the workplace: An underexplored construct. *Journal of Business and Psychology, 10,* 141–154.

Saks, A. M. (1994). Moderating effects of self-efficacy for the relationship between training method and anxiety and stress reactions of newcomers. *Journal of Organizational Behavior, 15,* 639–654.

Salas, E., Rozell, D., Mullen, B., & Driskell, J. E. (1999). The effect of team building on performance: An integration. *Small Group Research, 30,* 309–329.

Stewart, T. A. (1997). *Intellectual capital: The new wealth of organizations.* New York: Doubleday.

Stewart, T. A. (2001). *The wealth of knowledge: Intellectual capital and the twenty-first century organization.* New York: Doubleday.

Straus, S. G., & McGrath, J. E. (1994). Does the medium really matter? The interaction of task type and technology on group performance and member reactions. *Journal of Applied Psychology, 79,* 87–97.

Stroebe, W., Diehl, M., & Abakoumkin, G. (1992). The illusion of group effectivity. *Personality and Social Psychology Bulletin, 18,* 643–650.

Sutton, R. I., & Hargadon, A. B. (1996). The organizational context of brainstorming groups: Lessons from a product design firm. *Administrative Science Quarterly, 41,* 685–718.

Swann, W. B., Milton, L. P., & Polzer, J. T. (2000). Should we create a niche or fall in line? Identity negotiation and small group effectiveness. *Journal of Personality and Social Psychology, 79,* 238–250.

Tsui, A. S., Egan, T. D., & O'Reilly, C. A. (1992). Being different: Relational demography and organizational attachment. *Administrative Science Quarterly, 37,* 549–579.

Tuckman, B. (1965). Developmental sequence in small groups. *Psychological Bulletin, 63,* 384–399.

Tuckman, B., & Jensen, M. A. (1977). States of small-group development revisited. *Group and Organization Studies, 2,* 419–427.

Van Knippenberg, D., & van Schie, E. C. M. (2000). Foci and correlates of organizational identification. *Journal of Occupational and Social Psychology, 73,* 137–147.

Watson, W. E., Kumar, K., & Michaelsen, L. K. (1993). Cultural diversity's impact on interaction process and performance: Comparing homogeneous and diverse task groups. *Academy of Management Journal, 36,* 590–602.

Wegner, D. M. (1987). Transactive memory: A contemporary analysis of the group mind. In B. Mullen & G. R. Goethals (Eds.), *Theories of group behavior* (pp. 185–208). New York: Springer-Verlag.

Wegner, D. M. (1995). A computer network model of human transactive memory. *Social Cognition, 13,* 319–339.

Wittenbaum, G. M., Vaughan, S. I., & Stasser, G. (1998). Coordination in task-performing groups. In R. S. Tindale, L. Heath, J. Edwards, E. J. Posavac, F. B. Bryant, Y. Suarez-Balcazar, E. Henderson-King, & J. Myers (Eds.), *Social psychological applications to social issues: Theory and research on small groups* (Vol. 4, pp. 177–204). New York: Plenum.

Woodman, R. W., & Sherwood, J. J. (1980). The role of team development in organizational effectiveness: A critical review. *Psychological Bulletin, 88,* 166–186.

Yan, A., & Louis, M. R. (1999). The migration of organizational functions to the work unit level: Buffering, spanning, and bringing up boundaries. *Human Relations, 52,* 25–47.

Ziller, R. C. (1965). Toward a theory of open and closed groups. *Psychological Bulletin, 64,* 164–182.

8

Integrative Interests? Building a Bridge Between Negotiation Research and the Dynamic Organization

Kathleen M. O'Connor
Wendi L. Adair
Cornell University

In this chapter we explore the potential link between theory and research on negotiation with the concept of dynamic organizations. The drive to constantly reinvent their organizations and reshape their markets requires members of dynamic organizations to innovate, collaborate, redeploy, and take initiative. Coincidentally, these are the kinds of activities that negotiators must be ready to undertake if they are to craft-high value, durable deals. In the first half of the chapter, we draw connections between the demands facing members of dynamic organizations and the skills necessary for effective negotiation. In the second half, we consider whether the existence of agile organizations holds any implications for negotiation scholars. We offer some thoughts on how negotiation research might incorporate the dynamism that distinguishes dynamic organizations from other organizations. Along the way we raise a number of questions for future study.

Maintaining a competitive advantage is every firm's goal. What separates dynamic organizations from the pack, however, is that they pursue their aims by continuously reinventing themselves and their marketplaces (Hamel, 2000). In the first chapter of this volume, Dyer argues that dynamic organizations do not just keep pace with changes in their competitive environments, but they reinvent those marketplaces to maximize their edge. This requires them to continuously change the rules of the competitive game, to aggressively exploit emerging opportunities, and to adapt quickly to unanticipated events in the marketplace (Dyer, chapter 2, this volume). And the people who work in these organizations must have the necessary skills and tools to refine their business processes, product lines, marketing plans, or investment strategies to address the challenges and opportunities the marketplace presents.

As we considered the notion of a dynamic organization, it occurred to us that negotiation research had much to offer and much to learn from these emerging organizational forms. This chapter builds a bridge between negotiation research and the concept of the dynamic organization. We connect these areas in two ways. First, we address whether negotiation theory has any practical advice to offer to members of dynamic organizations who are interested in improving their own as well as their organization's performance. We believe it does, and we offer a few best practices from the negotiation table that could be used by people working in other corners of dynamic organizations. Second, we consider whether the existence of agile organizations holds any implications for those who study negotiation. We offer some thoughts on how negotiation research might incorporate the dynamism that is the very hallmark of agile organizations.

By no means is this chapter meant to be an exhaustive review of any literature. Rather, our goal is to sketch out how each literature can contribute to the other. In the process, we present propositions and research questions that we hope will provide some food for thought for practitioners and scholars alike. We begin by speculating about how negotiation skills might be useful to people who work in today's agile organizations.

TEACHING NEW DOGS OLD TRICKS, OR HOW NEGOTIATION TRAINING CAN IMPROVE PERFORMANCE IN DYNAMIC ORGANIZATIONS

The first question we tackle is whether and in what ways the art and science of negotiation (Raiffa, 1982) can improve individual, team, and organizational performance in dynamic organizations. We begin by highlighting the kinds of tasks and skills that are required of people who work in organizational settings marked by constant change. Then we turn to the negotiation literature to identify the tactics and frameworks that effective negotiators carry in their toolkits. We propose that some of the skills that help negotiators strike high-value, durable deals are the very skills that would help members of dynamic organizations work more productively. Our goal is to show that it is not necessary to create a whole new set of skills to meet the needs of people who work in dynamic organizations. Rather, the requisite skills and training programs already exist and are transferable from the bargaining table to the larger organization.

Broadly speaking, negotiation pertains to the process by which people resolve their conflicts of interests (Pruitt, 1981). The tools and tactics that negotiators use to resolve these conflicts should be applicable to anyone who makes decisions interdependently in situations marked by uncertainty. In chapter 2 of this volume, Dyer outlines a number of key behaviors that members must be willing to enact if the organization is to be successful (Dyer & Shafer, 1999; Shafer, Dyer, Kilty, Amos, & Ericksen, 2000). Many of these correspond to the kind of responsibilities and tasks that negotiators face every day at the bargaining table. In this chapter, we spell out these behaviors and discuss how negotiation training might help members of dynamic organizations improve their firm's performance.

Dyer argues that a responsive workplace demands that members confront a dizzying array of challenges. Members must take initiative, innovate, and educate. This first set of demands corresponds to negotiation skills that include the ability to gather information (even from reluctant counterparts), align interests across the table, craft solutions that meet these interests creatively, and persuade those across the table to accept one's own version of reality. Members of dynamic organizations also must be willing to assume multiple roles and to spontaneously collaborate. These tasks are compatible with negotiators' need to juggle multiple interests (i.e., those of constituents and counterparts, as well as their own), to adopt another side's perspective in their quest for a mutually agreeable settlement, and to develop swift trust with counterparts who have reason to be wary. Finally, members of dynamic organizations must be able to rapidly redeploy as circumstances change and to continuously learn. Negotiation skills such as accessing hidden information and constantly updating assumptions correspond to these tasks.

Next we address in greater detail the match between the demands that people in dynamic organizations face and best practices from the bargaining table. We consider negotiation from two perspectives: negotiation as creative problem solving and negotiation as social interaction.

Negotiation as Creative Problem Solving

When novice negotiators think about negotiation, they imagine two relative strangers who stake out positions and haggle in an effort to narrow the space between these positions (O'Connor & Adams, 1999). Yet, more often than not, negotiators come to the table with multiple interests, in which case negotiations are said to contain integrative potential (Walton & McKersie, 1965). By focusing on finding creative ways to meet their multiple interests, negotiators in these situations are likely to reach more profitable deals than if they had simply haggled over their positions.

Tactically speaking, negotiators who pursue this kind of interest-based strategy must be able to communicate their interests persuasively, educating the other side about their needs, expectations, and alternatives (Pruitt & Lewis, 1975). Sometimes this involves reframing the problem at hand to create a larger set of possible solutions. Negotiators also must be prepared to question the other side about their interests, to pay attention to the other side's answers, and even to watch closely the pattern of offers that come across the table. All of these tactics are aimed at clarifying the other side's interests for the focal negotiator (Thompson, 1991). Then negotiators must be able to assimilate this information quickly to create a more complete picture of both sides' interests. Once interests are out in the open, negotiators must get their creative juices flowing, searching for innovative ways of meeting those interests.

There are number of handy tools that negotiators can use to help each side walk away having some of their interests met. For instance, the parties might consider trading one low-cost concession for another (Pruitt & Rubin, 1986). Alternatively, one side might offer the other an unrelated issue in exchange for a low-cost concession (Pruitt & Rubin, 1986). Or they could break an issue into its component parts, and then repackage them in an imaginative way that would provide each side with gains (Weingart, Thompson, Bazerman, & Carroll, 1990). What is important is that, at its essence, interest-based bargaining requires negotiators to abandon the strategy of haggling over each issue separately, looking to split the difference. Instead, negotiators must be willing to share their underlying interests, needs, and constraints, and then work collaboratively to find creative ways of meeting them.

Another way to meet interests is by making trade-offs over time. Consider the following example. The long-time owner of a pet-grooming business is looking to retire. She has a prospective buyer who is interested in the business as a continuing enterprise. The owner believes that the buyer has what it takes to grow the business, but the buyer is short on capital. Can the parties strike a deal despite the buyer's lack of cash on hand? The answer is yes, if the owner does not need cash immediately and is willing to make a trade over time. A deal is possible, for instance, if the owner makes a loan to the buyer that would enable the buyer to assume the shop and pay the loan with the monies earned from the business. By accounting for differences in parties' time preferences, negotiators are able to strike deals that meet their interests. Parties also might construct a contingent contract based on different expectations of the probability of a future event. For example, a rock band that is confident of its ability to draw a crowd agrees to be paid with a smaller flat fee and a larger proportion of ticket sales when negotiating a venue contract.

Constant innovation is the key to staying ahead of the pack in a fast-moving competitive environment. What does this require of members of dynamic organizations? According to Amabile (1988), innovation demands that people gather existing knowledge, adapt it as necessary, and then use it in ways that challenge current thinking. This approach to solving problems is not new to skilled negotiators. As noted earlier, negotiators need to be vigilant about gathering information and pursuing possible alternatives. Their ability to look at problems from new perspectives, repackage issues in novel ways, and craft proposals that meet multiple interests are the very skills that members of dynamic organizations need to generate creative ideas that will allow their organizations to maintain their competitive edge. Therefore, we propose that training in interest-based bargaining will develop the skills that people who work in dynamic organizations need to meet the innovation demands they face.

Negotiation as Social Interaction

As noted, success in interest-based bargaining hinges on the parties' willingness to divulge information about their interests. This presents a tricky dilemma for negotiators. Openly discussing one's interests can leave one vulnerable to exploitation, especially given that negotiators have incentives to maximize their own gains. Thus, negotiators face temptations to exploit any information they receive from the other side (Murnighan, Babcock, Thompson, & Pillutla, 1999). They also are aware that their counterparts face these same temptations.

Common wisdom tells us that negotiators who share a relationship are likely to bargain differently than dyads composed of strangers. Empirical findings bear this out. Compared to those who do not anticipate working together in the future, negotiators who expect future interaction reach agreements that are more profitable to the dyad, especially when these expectations are coupled with a concern for one's own outcomes (Ben Yoav & Pruitt, 1984a, 1984b). This finding suggests that expectations about future relationships may cause negotiators to think twice before violating trust.

Skilled negotiators recognize the need to develop relationships with their counterparts that encourage the other side to share critical information about interests. Thus, they make an effort to get to know the other side, learning about their needs, intentions, and constraints. They also work to establish a rapport with their counterparts. They know that rapport paves the way to better quality deals (Drolet & Morris, 2000). Moreover, a recent study documents what has long been suspected: Mutual trust leads to higher value deals compared to deals reached by dyads marked by distrust (Oesch, Moore, & Fassina, 2002).

The benefits of trust and rapport to interest-based negotiation cannot be overstated. We also can speculate that when two negotiators share a cooperative relationship, they are more likely to persist in finding a mutually acceptable deal. Finally, looking ahead to the close of a deal, parties who trust each other can count on one another to help sell the deal to constituents. This is likely to be especially crucial when constituents have high expectations and low trust in the other side. Thus, negotiators who are able to forge cooperative relationships are in a better position to strike high-quality deals.

We must be careful to stipulate that, although trust can be beneficial for crafting agreements of high joint value, there are limits to its upsides. A number of empirical studies have found that when negotiators share a social relationship, they lower their aspirations, and, as a consequence, reach deals of lower joint value compared to negotiators who do not share such a relationship (Fry, Firestone, & Williams, 1983; Tenbrunsel, Wade-Benzoni, Moag, & Bazerman, 1999). In other words, negotiators who are motivated to preserve an existing relationship may prize that relationship over the economic gains that might accrue from the negotiation. This is not to say that trust between negotiators is detrimental to achieving gains. Rather, when negotiators emphasize preserving the existing relationship over their performance in the negotiation, suboptimal outcomes follow. However, as Ben-Yoav and Pruitt's (1984a; 1984b) findings show, when negotiators have some social relationship and they also care about their own outcomes, then high-quality deals are possible.

Collaborative working arrangements are another ingredient for innovation. Bringing together people with divergent perspectives and varied skill sets is likely to result in better solutions and products than could be expected if these same people toiled in isolation (Amabile, Conti, Coon, Lazenby, & Herron, 1996; Jehn, Northcraft, & Neale, 1999). Of course, to do this effectively, organizational members must be prepared to work collaboratively. People who have the skills to develop rapport with others and establish "swift trust" (Jarvenpaa & Leidner, 1999) are likely to be able to form productive relationships quickly and get on to the task at hand more efficiently than those who lack these skills.

Teams can be sidetracked by the conflicts that are bound to arise when people with different perspectives put their heads together to solve a problem. A wealth of studies documents the benefits of task conflict and the liabilities of relationship conflict (Amason, 1996; Jehn, 1995). Negotiators' skills at developing swift trust is likely to help them keep conflicts over task-related issues from spilling over and poisoning the relationships among team members (Simons & Peterson, 2000).

On a related point, skilled negotiators are practiced at the art of verbal jujitsu (Fisher, Ury, & Patton, 1991). They have learned to sidestep angry invectives and keep the negotiation focused on interests (Ury, 1991). This skill is likely to be especially useful to teammates in dynamic organizations who find themselves locked in a battle over perspectives in their project teams.

Taken together, negotiators' skills in developing rapport and creating trusting, productive relationships are likely to be useful to members of dynamic organizations who must be able to collaborate quickly to produce innovation.

We reviewed a number of skills that have proven to benefit negotiators as they try to forge lasting, mutually beneficial agreements. We argue that these same skills can help people in dynamic organizations to improve their own, their teams', and their organization's performance. Given the efficiencies to be gained from training that serves multiple goals, we believe that it would behoove dynamic organizations to provide their members training in interest-based negotiating. They are likely to see a payoff not only at the negotiating table, but also in other corners of the organization.

TEACHING OLD DOGS NEW TRICKS, OR ADAPTING NEGOTIATION THEORY TO FIT THE REALITY OF LIFE IN DYNAMIC ORGANIZATIONS

The demands of an ever-changing environment mean that dynamic organizations must be flexible about meeting their strategic goals, and their goals are likely to be revised as the firm enters new competitive markets or responds to unanticipated opportunities. The reality of a constantly changing workplace stands in stark contrast to the bulk of research on negotiation, which presumes a fairly static environment and little fluctuation in bargainers' preferences, interests, and alternatives once the negotiation is underway. Given a fixed set of issues, for example, we know that negotiators can maximize the overall value of the deal by identifying differences in preferences among the issues and exchanging concessions on these differently valued issues (Pruitt & Lewis, 1975). But how can parties increase the value of the agreement when shifts in parties' interests affect how much value is available? Similarly, we know that the advantage goes to negotiators whose alternatives are better than their counterpart's outside options (White & Neale, 1991). However, we have little empirical evidence about how one should negotiate if one's alternative partner declares bankruptcy during negotiations. How does losing power during negotiation compare to entering negotiation with little power? These are just a handful of questions that occurred to us, but they speak to the need to account for more dynamic business realities in negotiation research.

Negotiations are commonplace in firms. Given the need to collaborate in dynamic organizations, we believe that negotiations are likely to be even more prevalent in these organizations. Thus, negotiation theory has much to offer practitioners in these firms. However, we believe that this literature would be even more useful if it could account for changing interests, actors, and alternatives. Next we explore ways of doing this.

Negotiation Theory and the Dynamic Organization at the Crossroads

To respond nimbly to emergent threats, challenges, and opportunities, members of dynamic organizations must try to hammer out deals while keeping an eye out for changes in the fast-paced competitive environments in which they bargain. This means that bargainers must enter negotiations aware that both sides' interests, constraints, aspirations, reservation prices, and alternatives are likely to shift over the course of negotiation. An example might be a manufacturer that implements a new business process or unveils a new product line. These updates are likely to affect the ongoing negotiations across the firm. For instance, a newly streamlined supply chain may make a manufacturer more appealing to a very large discount chain with which the manufacturer currently has no relationship. Imagine that the manufacturer is engaged in talks with a smaller retailer. Having caught the eye of the larger chain, how would a shift in the power dynamics affect the process and outcomes of the current negotiation? How could a negotiator most effectively introduce and leverage this new and powerful alternative, while at the same time making a deal with the smaller retailer? How does a negotiator go about discussing changes in his or her firm's interests without alienating the other party? As one can see, there are many ways in which a change in the marketplace reverberates throughout the negotiation process.

Yet, few studies have examined this. Perhaps it is not surprising. In other literatures, too, the effects of change on social interaction have been given short shrift. With few exceptions (see Arrow, 1997, for an example of an exception), change has been considered an "externality that disrupt(s) the ideal path of development" (Arrow, 1997, p. 75; Hill & Gruner, 1973). But negotiation scholars have begun to account for the fact that bargainers' interests and strategies might change over the course of a negotiation. Brett, Northcraft, and Pinkley (1999) articulated an interaction-based model of negotiation that captures the kind of changes and shifts that are likely to occur when members of dynamic organizations sit down to negotiate. They made a case for thinking about negotiation as a dual process—the external negotiation that takes place with another party, and the internal negotiation that occurs within the bargainer. In a departure from the traditional negotiation paradigm (Pruitt & Carnevale, 1993), they posited that negotiators are likely to revise, clarify, and even discover their interests and goals as the negotiation process unfolds. They suggested that the fruits of this discovery process should influence the negotiation that takes place across the table. They proposed an interlocking model of self-regulation in which the negotiation process causes each negotiator to adjust his or her interests and positions (i.e., intrapersonal negotiation), which, in turn, affects the interparty negotiation (i.e., the explicit negotiation).

We believe that this model nicely illustrates the way negotiations are likely to unfold for people who operate in dynamic organizations. Members of dynamic organizations must manage a complex intrapersonal negotiation in which their interests and needs will change not only as they are clarified over the course of their external negotiation, but also in response to shifts in their organization's strategy and the marketplace. Therefore, these negotiators may need to be highly skilled Bayesians, constantly updating their beliefs in the face of new information. While negotiations progress, they may need to work to identify new BATNAs in different markets, adjust their goals in the wake of a poor earnings report, or change the mix of issues under consideration in response to a new product launch. These external changes, and the accompanying strategic adjustments, make the negotiation process that much harder for members of dynamic organizations.

Next we identify five aspects of negotiation—planning, parties and preferences, power, process, and presentation. For each aspect, we discuss how the need for agility that defines dynamic organizations would raise new empirical questions for negotiation scholars. We believe that these are the kinds of questions that researchers might address if they consider how negotiation theory could be adapted to take into account life in dynamic organizations.

Planning

Systematic planning is a key step along the road to getting good deals. Practical guides typically advise negotiators to set firm limits, identify their goals, and establish their priorities among the issues to be negotiated before the negotiation (Lewicki, Saunders, & Minton, 1997). Typically, such planning presumes that negotiators' interests, alternatives, and the bargainers themselves will remain constant over the course of negotiation.

Negotiations that take place in dynamic organizations are not likely to be affected by the pressures of the larger organization and its embedding environment. Establishing fixed goals and reservation prices may not be helpful when negotiators must rapidly update their initial plan to take advantage of new developments. A more flexible approach would include contingencies, or more than one way to reach a goal. Flexible planning has several advantages over more traditional kinds of planning. First, because it provides negotiators with tactical options that take newly discovered information into account, negotiators are better able to consider and help meet the other party's interests, which is likely to improve their chances of reaching mutually beneficial deals (Bazerman, Magliozzi, & Neale, 1985). Second, by encouraging negotiators to think about different routes to achieving their goals, flexible planning reminds negotiators that their strategy might need to change over the course of negotiation. This may leave them better prepared to consider such a change once the negotiation is underway. This kind of thinking is likely to be particularly useful in contexts marked by change.

Life in dynamic organizations implies a number of questions for negotiation researchers to pursue. Are there particular aspects of planning that should remain fixed if planning is going to pay off at all for negotiators? For instance, should reservation prices always be fixed, lest negotiators be tempted to revise these inappropriately in the heat of the moment? Are there aspects of planning—for instance, one's preestablished list of issues—that are most likely to change over the course of negotiation as interests are clarified, and, thus, should be considered contingent?

Parties and Preferences

As negotiators rapidly redeploy, the configuration of parties at the table may change as well. For instance, a negotiator may be called in on another deal and may have to leave one team and join another midstream. Although the effectiveness of negotiation teams has received some empirical attention over the years (O'Connor, 1997; Thompson, Peterson, & Brodt, 1996), questions about how changes in teams affect the team's functioning have not been asked. For example, although comparisons of teams and solos show an advantage going to teams, is this still the case if the team experiences an abrupt change in membership during the negotiation? One can imagine that a disruption might be costly to the team's smooth functioning and, thus, might undermine its outcomes. Alternatively, bringing in reinforcements with fresh ideas and new perspectives might help the team (Gruenfeld, Matorama, & Fan, 2000), and increase its flexibility and responsiveness compared to more stable teams.

It is possible that a dynamic organization might respond to changes in its competitive landscape by forging an alliance with another firm. What if this new partner joins a negotiation in progress, and enters with some interests that overlap with the dynamic organization and some that diverge? How might the introduction of an alliance partner affect the power dynamics in a negotiation? How might this affect the rapport and trust that has been established by the two original negotiation counterparts?

Power

Part of any negotiation planning process includes identifying alternatives to the current deal. And the relatively stronger a negotiator's alternative to agreement (BATNA) is, the greater that negotiator's power (e.g., Pinkley, 1995; White & Neale, 1991). BATNAs also provide a point of comparison for negotiators. If a negotiator knows the details of the alternative deal, this can provide a guide to help determine his or her limits, goals, and strategies (Fisher et al., 1991).

If the power of an alternative is only as strong as the quality of the alternative, as a negotiation progresses and as interests change, negotiators must work to keep the quality of their alternatives high if the alternative is to continue to be a source of leverage. Certainly, negotiators in dynamic organizations need to be adept at monitoring and managing their BATNAs during negotiations. This requires them to manage two negotiations simultaneously—the current negotiation and the outside option. Such a complicated task may pose a significant challenge to negotiators. How can negotiators best manage two ongoing negotiations? Would it behoove negotiators to organize in teams with some members who focus on the current deal and others who focus on negotiating the BATNA?

Particularly troubling is the idea that a BATNA actually could damage a negotiator's position. Specifically, once established, a clear BATNA presents negotiators with a specific package of options that creates a standard for evaluating the quality of other deals. Might this package prevent negotiators from considering issues that deviate from the BATNA? The empirical question is whether BATNAs anchor negotiators to a particular set of issues, thereby limiting their creativity and flexibility.

Process

As noted, through systematic planning, negotiators come to the table with a particular understanding of the task at hand. However, their understanding of the conflict may change as new interests and issues unfold at the table (Putnam & Holmer, 1992; Putnam & Jones, 1982). As a function of social interaction, the expectations that people bring with them to the situation are likely to shift (Bettenhausen & Murnighan, 1985, 1991). As they work together, people develop shared understandings of the task at hand (Gruenfeld & Hollingshead, 1993) that are considered beneficial to team performance. However, members of dynamic organizations face challenges to developing shared understandings because each party's perception is subject to change in response to what is happening in the environment. This leads us to ask whether it is possible for negotiators in dynamic organizations to develop a common understanding of their task and approach when each party's goals and strategies are changing. If it is possible, then one could raise questions about the kinds of strategies that would facilitate the emergence of a socially shared understanding in negotiations marked by high levels of uncertainty. One strategy might be for members to initiate deliberate interruptions (Okhuysen, 2001) that would give them an opportunity to evaluate their progress and to correct any drift away from a common understanding of the parties' interests.

Negotiators can develop synchrony not only in their cognitive representations of conflict, but also in their behaviors. In work group situations, people's behavior becomes entrained when they unconsciously adjust and modify their behavior to synchronize with another person's behavior (McGrath & Kelly, 1986), with smooth coordination leading to more positive interactions (Kelly & Barsade, 2001). In negotiation research, scholars found that negotiators regularly reciprocate strategies (Brett, Shapiro, & Lytle, 1998; Weingart, Prietula, Hyder, & Genovese, 1999), matching distributive and integrative behaviors (Olekalns & Smith, 2000; Putnam & Jones, 1982). Even in intercultural negotiations—for example, United States–Japan negotiations—bargainers exhibit patterns of tactical synchrony, even though parties enter negotiation with very different norms for sharing information and making persuasive arguments (Adair, 2001; Adair, Okumura, & Brett, 2001). Can negotiators who operate in dynamic organizations reap the benefits of reciprocity when each party's motivations and strategies are subject to change?

Adaptation in dynamic organizations requires that people learn from their experiences, continuously honing their skills. Negotiators are likely to bargain with unfamiliar partners as conditions warrant. Studies show that negotiators have great difficulty transferring lessons learned in one context to another (Loewenstein, Thompson, & Gentner, 1999). This is especially true if the superficial characteristics of a bargaining situation do not resemble former situations. What does this mean for members of dynamic organizations? Do negotiators who operate in a constantly changing negotiation face even greater challenges to learning from their past experiences?

The challenges of intercultural negotiation have yielded insights that might be particularly relevant to scholars interested in studying negotiation in dynamic organizations. For instance, in response to the uncertainty inherent in intercultural exchanges, individuals are advised to establish commonalities and adopt similar behavior patterns to reduce uncertainty (Gudykunst, 1985). In other words, it is presumed that one can learn tactics for building quick rapport and avoiding friction, which is likely to be important for negotiations in dynamic organizations. On a related note, studies show that because collectivist cultures value group harmony, negotiators from these cultures are especially adept at detecting differences across parties, and then avoiding conflict by promoting harmony between parties (Ting-Toomey, 1985; Triandis, 1995). This leads us to wonder whether training aimed at cultivating these kinds of collectivist values might help individualist negotiators in dynamic organizations develop more harmonious relationships that will allow them to strike better deals more efficiently.

The fast pace of adaptation and change in dynamic organizations has significant implications for the role of trust and relationships in negotiation. As noted, trust and rapport pave the way for integrative agreements, yet negotiators have trouble establishing trust. Oftentimes, they assume that parties have opposing interests, making it difficult to reach a deal (Neale & Bazerman, 1991). This problem should be even more vexing for members of dynamic organizations. In their pursuit of a competitive advantage, will these firms prize short-term gains over longer term success? If this is the case, then nurturing relationships that are likely to pay dividends in the longer run might move further down the list of priorities for negotiators. The irony is that, given the importance of networks of relationships for access to critical information and for collaboration (Burt, 2000), nurturing one's relationships should be even more critical for members of dynamic organizations than for static organizations of the past. However, one wonders whether the need for quick action might distract negotiators from relationship-building activities and, instead, cause them to focus on the gains they can extract immediately. We believe this empirical question deserves attention.

Moreover, will they find it increasingly difficult to build lasting trust? Pressure to seek out new collaborations and to forge new partnerships that will give them a leg up in the marketplace should increase negotiator mobility, which has been found to lead to relatively low-value deals (Mannix, Tinsley, & Bazerman, 1995). In general, uncertainty is unlikely to foster trust and rapport. One question is, what kinds of ties should negotiators in dynamic organizations cultivate in order to be ready to collaborate and create profitable arrangements? How can negotiators in dynamic organizations build the kind of swift trust necessary to reach high quality deals? Are there heuristics that might be helpful? Perhaps the big question is, how can negotiators manage trust and rapport in their relationship, which requires stability, while simultaneously managing their embedding environment, which is constantly changing?

Presentation

Dynamic organizations are likely to take advantage of the latest technologies to help their members gather information in real time and communicate across the organization as rapidly as possible. Dynamic organizations with access to such technologies afford a wealth of choices for negotiators—including e-mail, customized synchronous electronic communication programs, and video conferencing. Which medium should negotiators choose to present themselves and their offers in the best possible light? Negotiation researchers are just beginning to explore the comparative advantages of communication media, examining how they affect choice of strategy, perception of counterparts, quality of communication, and quality of outcomes.

Much of the research on negotiation and technology has compared face-to-face negotiations with either telephone or e-mail negotiations, asking which medium is most beneficial to negotiators in a given context (Bazerman, Curhan, Moore, & Valley, 2000; Purdy, Nye, & Balakrishnan, 2000). For instance, comparisons of face-to-face versus e-mail negotiations show that the use of e-mail inflates misperceptions of the other side's interests, which, in turn, leads to lower quality deals and more uneven distribution of resources (Arunachalam & Dilla, 1995). In part, this result might be traced to the difficulty negotiators have in establishing rapport and cooperation when they use e-mail (Drolet & Morris, 1995; 2000). Comparing telephone, video conference and face-to-face negotiations, Valley and her colleagues found that less truth telling and lower quality deals mark negotiations that are conducted at a distance (Valley, Moag, & Bazerman, 1998).

When choosing one medium over another, negotiators must also consider that e-mail evens out participation due to status differences in groups (Sproull & Kiesler, 1991). Thus, one could speculate that lower status negotiators may be more likely to make the kinds of persuasive arguments necessary to higher status counterparts. Moreover, some of the difficulties that negotiators experience when working over e-mail are attenuated when they have a chance to build rapport through a get-to-know-you conversation before beginning to negotiate (Moore, Kurtzberg, Thompson, & Morris, 1999).

What kinds of communication media make sense for negotiators who operate in dynamic organizations? As noted, dynamic organizations require people to make quick decisions about how to divide resources in a new enterprise or strike an alliance with a new partner. Negotiators might not have the luxury of booking flights ahead and then spending several days at an off-site, bargaining face-to-face. In the interest of time, they might have to choose between telephone and e-mail, for instance. Which is more effective, and for what types of negotiations?

More typically, negotiators use a mix of media to get their deals done. One can imagine a negotiator picking up the phone to get a transaction off the ground. As it progresses, the parties would decide to meet face-to-face to work through the thornier parts of the deal. This suggests that research needs to move beyond the simple effects of one medium versus another and investigate the best blend of technologies for particular kinds of deals. A question to consider is whether the best sequence is to launch negotiations with a face-to-face meeting in which parties are able to develop rapport, then rely on e-mail to do most of the bargaining, and finally meet face-to-face to nail down the more difficult concluding aspects of the deal.

Similarly, might there be strategic implications for moving from one medium to another? In other words, might certain media be better suited to particular strategies? For example, if negotiators choose to pursue a black hat/white hat strategy (Hilty & Carnevale, 1993), is it best to enact the less cooperative (black hat) strategy over e-mail and the more cooperative (white hat) strategy face-to-face? One can imagine that in the relative anonymity of e-mail, negotiators might be more comfortable using a tougher strategy. However, when the time comes to adopt a more concessionary tone, a face-to-face meeting may be the more effective medium.

Thompson (2000) recommended that negotiators using e-mail send concise and clear messages and explicitly discuss the procedures they plan to follow. What are the implications for particular tactics across media? In the absence of social and audio cues, would it behoove negotiators who bargain over e-mail to use more logical persuasion tactics than affective persuasion tactics? If negotiators' interests change over the course of negotiation, as might happen for people in dynamic organizations, is it better to avoid e-mail where behavior is more likely to be misinterpreted?

The need to rapidly redeploy may mean that negotiators experience abrupt and unplanned changes in communication media. What would the effects of these changes be on negotiation process and outcomes? Changes from one medium to another have been found to lead to immediate performance decreases for teams, even when the switch is from e-mail communication to face-to-face meetings (Hollingshead, McGrath, & O'Connor, 1993). Would the same performance slowdowns mark negotiations that change media midstream? Might an abrupt change in medium have different effects on the process and outcomes of negotiation than an anticipated change in medium?

CONCLUSION

Our goal was to build a bridge between negotiation research and the emerging literature on dynamic organizations. We did this from two different starting points. First, we considered what negotiation theory could offer to help members of dynamic organizations improve their own, their teams', and their organization's performance. We argued that members of dynamic organizations stand to gain from the efficiencies that come from interest-based negotiation skills training. Not only do these skills improve performance at the negotiation table, but they also help people improve their ability to spontaneously collaborate and innovate in pursuit of competitive advantage. We sum up our ideas in two broad propositions:

Proposition 1: Training in interest-based negotiation will help members of dynamic organizations to share knowledge more effectively, integrate divergent viewpoints, and generate innovative solutions.

Proposition 2: Training in interest-based negotiation will help members of dynamic organizations to develop more productive working relationships, even in situations marked by uncertainty. This will help people to collaborate more effectively.

Second, we considered the link from the perspective of the dynamic organization: What do these organizations imply for negotiation theory? Throughout the chapter, we sprinkled a number of research questions that we hope might strike a chord with negotiation scholars. We believe that if scholars choose to investigate questions like these, they will contribute to a more realistic view of negotiations in fast-paced firms. We conclude by summarizing our ideas in two broad research questions:

Research Question 1: How might changes in any aspect of negotiation—for example, parties, communication medium, preferences—affect the progress of talks, and inevitably, the quality of deals?

Research Question 2: What factors ought to be considered fixed and which should best be considered variable to ensure the highest quality deals in dynamic organizations?

We cannot end this chapter without acknowledging that our tone is rather optimistic; we believe that the concept of the dynamic organization can be integrated with negotiation research, with benefits for each. However, we also must consider that there are some negative implications to the integration we suggest. For example, might the change that marks dynamic organizations actually serve to undermine interest-based negotiation? Will negotiators in agile organizations no longer find it useful to build and manage long-term relationships, look for mutually beneficial agreements that deepen and strengthen relationships, and make trade-offs across time that depend on an ongoing relationship? Questions like this lead us to end this chapter with two rather sober dilemmas:

Dilemma 1: The pace of change that marks dynamic organizations might keep these firms focused on short-term gains. Will this emphasis preclude them from investing in the kind of training programs we believe will have longer term benefits for dynamic organizations?

Dilemma 2: Can interest-based bargaining strategies be effective in contexts marked by constant and often unanticipated change?

ACKNOWLEDGMENTS

Many of the ideas in this chapter were presented at the Leading Organizations conference held in Ithaca, NY, March 2001. We thank two anonymous reviewers, Randall Peterson, and Chris Anderson for their very helpful suggestions. We also thank the conference participants for their presentations, which gave us food for thought.

REFERENCES

Adair, W. L. (2001). *Reciprocal information sharing and negotiation outcome in East/West negotiations.* Manuscript under review.

Adair, W. L., Okumura, T., & Brett, J. M. (2001). Negotiation behavior when cultures collide: the U.S. and Japan. *Journal of Applied Psychology, 86,* 371–385.

Amabile, T. M. (1988). A model of creativity and innovation in organizations. In B. M. Staw & L. L. Cummings (Eds.), *Research in organizational behavior* (Vol. 10, pp. 123–167). Greenwich, CT: JAI.

Amabile, T. M., Conti, R., Coon, H., Lazenby, J., & Herron, M. (1996). Assessing the work environment for creativity. *Academy of Management Journal, 39,* 1154–1184.

Amason, A. C. (1996). Distinguishing the effects of functional and dysfunctional conflict on strategic decision-making: Resolving a paradox for top management teams. *Academy of Management Journal, 39,* 123–148.

Arrow, H. (1997). Stability, bistability, and instability in small group influence patterns. *Journal of Personality and Social Psychology, 72,* 75–85.

Arunachalam, V., & Dilla, W. N. (1995). Judgment accuracy and outcomes in negotiation: A causal-modeling analysis of decision-aiding effects. *Organizational Behavior And Human Decision Processes, 61,* 289–304.

Bazerman, M. H., Curhan, J. R., Moore, D. A., & Valley, K. L., (2000). Negotiation. *Annual Review Psychology, 51,* 279–314.

Bazerman, M. H., Magliozzi, T., & Neale, M. A., (1985). Integrative bargaining in a competitive market. *Organizational Behavior and Human Decision Processes, 35,* 284–313.

Ben Yoav, O., & Pruitt, D. G. (1984a). Accountability to constituents: A two-edged sword. *Organizational Behavior and Human Decision Processes, 34,* 283–295.

Ben Yoav, O., & Pruitt, D. G. (1984b). Resistance to yielding and the expectation of cooperative future interaction in negotiation. *Journal of Experimental Social Psychology, 20,* 323–335.

Bettenhausen, K. L., & Murnighan, J. K. (1985). The emergence of norms in competitive decision-making groups. *Administrative Science Quarterly, 30,* 350–372.

Bettenhausen, K. L., & Murnighan, J. K. (1991). The development of an intragroup norm and the effects of interpersonal and structural challenges. *Administrative Science Quarterly, 36,* 20–35.

Brett, J. F., Northcraft, G. B., & Pinkley, R. L. (1999). Stairways to heaven: An interlocking self-regulation model of negotiation. *Academy of Management Review, 24,* 435–451.

Brett, J. M., Shapiro, D. L., & Lytle, A. L. (1998). Refocusing rights- and power-oriented negotiators toward integrative negations: Process and outcomes effects. *Academy of Management Journal, 41,* 410–424.

Burt, R. S. (2000). The network structure of social capital. *Research in Organizational Behavior, 22,* 345–423.

Drolet, A. L., & Morris, M. W. (1995). *Communication media and interpersonal trust in conflicts: The role of rapport and synchrony of nonverbal behavior.* Unpublished manuscript, Stanford University, Palo Alto, CA.

Drolet, A. L., & Morris M. W. (2000). Rapport in conflict resolution: Accounting for how face-to-face contact fosters mutual cooperation in mixed-motive conflicts. *Journal of Experimental Social Psychology, 36,* 26–50.

Dyer, L., & Shafer, R. A. (1999). From human resource strategy to organizational effectiveness: Lessons from research on organizational agility. In P. Wright, L. Dyer, J. Boudreau, & G. Milkovich (Eds.), *Strategic human resources management in the twenty-first century* (pp. 145–174). Stamford, CT: JAI Press.

Fisher, R., Ury, W., & Patton, B. (1991). *Getting to yes* (2nd ed.). New York: Penguin.

Fry, W. R., Firestone, I. J., & Williams, D. L. (1983). Negotiation process and outcome of stranger dyads and dating couples: Do lovers lose? *Basic and Applied Social Psychology, 4,* 1–16.

Gruenfeld, D. H, & Hollingshead, A. B. (1993). Sociocognition in work groups: The evolution of group integrative complexity and its relation to task performance. *Small Group Research, 24,* 383–405.

Gruenfeld, D. H, Matorama, P. V., & Fan, E. T. (2000). What do groups learn from their worldliest members? Direct and indirect influence in dynamic teams. *Organizational Behavior and Human Decision Processes, 82,* 45–59.

Gudykunst, W. B. (1985). The influence of cultural similarity, type of relationship, and self-monitoring on uncertainty reduction processes. *Communication Monographs, 52,* 203–217.

Hamel, G. (2000). *Leading the revolution.* Boston: Harvard Business School Press.

Hill, W. F., & Gruner, L. (1973). A study of development in open and closed groups. *Small Group Behavior, 4,* 355–381.

Hilty, J. A., & Carnevale, P. J. (1993). Black-hat white-hat strategy in bilateral negotiation. *Organizational Behavior and Human Decision Processes, 55,* 444–469.

Hollingshead, A. B., McGrath, J. E., & O'Connor, K. M. (1993). Group task performance and communication technology: A longitudinal study of computer-mediated versus face-to-face work groups. *Small Group Research, 24,* 307–333.

Jarvenpaa, S. L., & Leidner, D. E. (1999). Communication and trust in global virtual teams. *Organization Science, 10,* 791–815.

Jehn, K. A. (1995). Multimethod examination of the benefits and detriments of intragroup conflict. *Administrative Science Quarterly, 40,* 256–282.

Jehn, K. A., Northcraft, G. B., & Neale, M. A. (1999). Why differences make a difference: A field study of diversity, conflict, and performance in workgroups. *Administrative Science Quarterly, 44,* 741–763.

Kelly, J. R., & Barsade, S. G. (2001). Mood and emotions in small groups and work teams. *Organizational Behavior and Human Decision Processes, 86,* 99–130.

Lewicki, R. J., Saunders, D. M., & Minton, J. W. (1997). *Essentials of negotiation.* Boston: Irwin McGraw-Hill.

Loewenstein, J., Thompson, L., & Gentner, D. (1999). Analogical encoding facilitates knowledge transfer in negotiations. *Psychonomic Bulletin & Review, 6,* 586–597.

Mannix, E. A., Tinsley, C. H., & Bazerman, M. H. (1995). Negotiating over time: Impediments to integrative solutions. *Organizational Behavior and Human Decision Processes, 62,* 241–251.

McGrath, J. E., & Kelly, J. R. (1986). *Time and human interaction: Toward a social psychology of time.* New York: The Guilford Press.

Moore, D. A., Kurtzberg, T. R., Thompson, L. L., & Morris, M. W. (1999). The long and short routes to success in electronically mediated negotiations: Group affiliations and good vibrations. *Organizational Behavior and Human Decision Processes, 77,* 22–43.

Murnighan, J. K., Babcock, L., Thompson, L., & Pillutla, M. (1999). The information dilemma in negotiations: Effects of experience, incentives, and integrative potential. *International Journal of Conflict Management, 10,* 313–339.

Neale, M. A., & Bazerman, M. H. (1991). *Cognition and rationality in negotiation.* New York: Free Press.

O'Connor, K. M. (1997). Groups and solos in context: The effects of accountability on team negotiation. *Organizational Behavior and Human Decision Processes, 72,* 384–407.

O'Connor, K. M., & Adams, A. A. (1999). What novices think about negotiation: A content analysis of scripts. *Negotiation Journal, 15,* 135–147.

Oesch, J. A., Moore, D. M., & Fassina, N. E. (2002). *The effects of trust and distrust on negotiations: Evidence from an online experiment.* Manuscript under review.

Okhuysen, G. A. (2001). Structuring change: Familiarity and formal interventions in problem-solving groups. *Academy of Management Journal, 44,* 794–808.

Olekalns, M., & Smith, P. L. (2000). Understanding optimal outcomes: The role of strategy sequences in competitive negotiations. *Human Communication Research, 26,* 527–557.

Pinkley, R. L. (1995). Impact of knowledge regarding alternatives to settlement in dyadic negotiations—whose knowledge counts. *Journal of Applied Psychology, 80,* 403–417.

Pruitt, D. G. (1981). *Negotiation behavior.* New York: Academic Press.

Pruitt, D. G., & Carnevale, P. J. (1993). *Negotiation in social conflict.* Buckingham: Open University Press.

Pruitt, D. G., & Lewis, S. A. (1975). Development of integrative solutions in bilateral negotiation. *Journal of Personality and Social Psychology, 31,* 621–633.

Pruitt, D. G., & Rubin, J. Z. (1986). *Social conflict: Escalation, stalemate, and settlement.* New York: Random House.

Purdy, J. M., Nye, P., & Balakrishnan, P. V. (2000). The impact of communication media on negotiation outcomes. *International Journal of Conflict Management, 11,* 162–187.

Putnam, L. L., & Holmer, M. (1992). Framing and reframing in negotiations. In L. L. Putnam & M. E. Roloff (Eds.), *Communications and negotiation.* Newbury Park, CA: Sage.

Putnam, L. L., & Jones, T. S. (1982). Reciprocity in negotiations: An analysis of bargaining interaction. *Communication Monographs, 49,* 171–191.

Raiffa, H. (1982). *The art and science of negotiation.* Cambridge: Harvard University Press.

Shafer, R. A., Dyer, L., Kilty, J., Amos, J., & Ericksen, J. (2000). Crafting a human resource strategy to foster organizational agility: A case study. *Human Resource Management, 40,* 197–211.

Simons, T. L., & Peterson, R. S. (2000). Task conflict and relationship conflict in top management teams: The pivotal role of intragroup trust. *Journal of Applied Psychology, 85,* 102–111.

Sproull, L., & Kiesler, S. B. (1991). *Connections: New ways of working in the networked organization.* Cambridge, MA: MIT Press.

Tenbrunsel, A. E., Wade-Benzoni, K. A., Moag, J., & Bazerman, M. H. (1999). The negotiation matching process: Relationships and partner selection. *Organizational Behavior and Human Decision Processes, 80,* 252–283.

Thompson, L. L. (1991). Information exchange in negotiation. *Journal of Experimental Social Psychology, 27,* 161–179.

Thompson, L. L. (2000). *The mind and heart of the negotiator.* Upper Saddle River, NJ: Prentice Hall.

Thompson, L., Peterson, E., & Brodt, S. E. (1996). Team negotiation: An examination of integrative and distributive bargaining. *Journal of Personality and Social Psychology, 70,* 66–78.

Ting-Toomey, S. (1985). Toward a theory of conflict and culture. In W. B. Gudykunst, L. P. Stewart, & S. Ting-Toomey (Eds.), *Communication, culture, and organizational processes* (Vol. 9, pp. 71–86). Newbury Park, CA: Sage.

Triandis, H. C. (1995). *Individualism and collectivism.* Boulder, CO: Westview Press.

Ury, W. (1991). *Getting past no: Negotiating with difficult people.* New York: Bantam Books.

Valley, K. L., Moag, J., & Bazerman, M. H. (1998). A matter of trust: Effects of communication on the efficiency and distribution of outcomes. *Journal of Economic Behavior in Organizations, 34,* 211–238.

Walton, R. E., & McKersie, R. B. (1965). *A behavioral theory of labor negotiations: An analysis of a social interaction system.* Ithaca, NY: ILR Press.

Weingart L. R., Prietula, M. J., Hyder, E. B., & Genovese, C. (1999). Knowledge and the sequential processes of negotiation: A Markov chain analysis of response-in-kind. *Journal of Experimental Social Psychology, 35,* 266–393.

Weingart, L. R., Thompson, L. L., Bazerman, M. H., & Carroll, J. (1990). Tactical behavior and negotiation outcomes. *International Journal of Conflict Management, 1,* 7–31.

White, S. B., & Neale, M. A. (1991). Reservation prices, resistance points, and BATNAs—Determining the parameters of acceptable negotiated outcomes. *Negotiation Journal, 7,* 379–388.

IV

LEADERSHIP IN THE DYNAMIC ORGANIZATION

9

Leadership, Learning, Ambiguity, and Uncertainty and Their Significance to Dynamic Organizations

Philip V. Hodgson
Ashridge Management College

Randall P. White
Executive Development Group

This chapter reports on the research that Phil Hodgson and Randy White have been doing on leadership, learning, ambiguity, and uncertainty. We argue that people in organizations are facing unprecedented levels of ambiguity and uncertainty, and that their previous experience as leaders and managers has often left them unprepared to cope. We suggest that some of the key skills needed for people to operate effectively in a dynamic organization derive from the essential capability to handle ambiguity and face uncertainty. We propose that particular kinds of learning contain the keys to understanding behaviors that help people cope with ambiguity and that these behaviors taken together may represent a new development of leadership style. We describe the results of our research, which identifies five behavioral areas that are significant in handling ambiguity, and we propose further areas for research in organizations.

This research initiative started in the early 1990s when our two separate research interests coincided around one question: What new skills and behaviors would turn-of-the-century leaders need?

Previously the second author was investigating how leaders learned (McCall, Lombardo, & Morrison, 1988; Morrison, White, & Van Velsor, 1987) and the first was trying to understand how leaders had formulated strategies for change (Hodgson & Crainer, 1993; Wille & Hodgson, 1991). Our previous work, although completely independent, pointed to similar conclusions about a possible gap in what was known about the skills that would be significant for leaders in the future.

Much was known about how leaders developed strategies, vision, and a sense of strategic direction. Equally well researched was how managers executed these strategies through teams and the use of interpersonal skills. The area that had not received much attention was how leaders handled ambiguity and uncertainty. Yet it appeared from our previous research to be an area of importance. What skills and behaviors are evident and how significant is this area in dynamic organizations?

THE FIELD OF AMBIGUITY AND UNCERTAINTY

The concepts of ambiguity and uncertainty were widely used. In the areas of economics and financial forecasting, huge amounts of statistical and model-building work had been done.

In the area of chaos and complexity, there was much talk of uncertainty (Lewin, 1993; Wheatley, 1992). Although the field has given rise to a rich crop of metaphors that have been useful in describing the dilemmas that leaders face, it does not seem to have shed much light on the new skills that leaders would need. What should they do, and how should they do it? As far as we could discover, our original question about skills and behavior had not been answered. We realized that an intriguing gap had emerged. What were the new skills and behaviors that leaders of the future would need?

As all our previous work had focused on managers and executives in organizations, we decided to continue this research in the same area. Thus, our results do not include subjects from the military, the emergency services, the law, or government. There are many research possibilities to compare business leaders and, say, military leaders in their handling of ambiguity and uncertainty.

Our research concentrated on five questions:

1. How much does the modern executive face uncertainty and ambiguity in her or his everyday working life?
2. Is this kind of ambiguity increasing or decreasing?
3. How does ambiguity affect strategic decision making?
4. What behavior do executives use when faced with high levels of ambiguity and uncertainty?
5. What development opportunities exist?. How could executives and others develop their skills in this area? (We do not report on this aspect of our work in this chapter.)

We decided from the outset that we wanted to research behavior, not personality, and we say more on this subject later in this chapter.

THE BUSINESS SITUATION

Popular literature (Welch & Byrne, 2001) suggests that the business world seems to work on an ever faster clock cycle, as speed becomes not just a sales differentiator but a key aspect of organizational strategy, so we hypothesize that the rules by which decisions get made and the skills needed to manage and lead effectively are likely to change. This has a direct effect on business; for instance, at Hewlett-Packard, a significant proportion (estimates vary from 30% to 50%) of revenues come from products that did not exist a year ago (based on a private conversation with a Hewlett-Packard employee in 2001).

Speed and change are on many leaders' agendas. To illustrate the point, take just three quotes from quite different people who have all held the highest leadership roles:

- "The key to competitiveness is education and re-education." —Percy Barnevik speaking at ABB about speed of response (Barham & Heimer, 1999)
- "We live in the post modern world where everything is possible and almost nothing is certain." —Václav Havel
- "We are always 18 months away from failure." —Bill Gates

The natural consequence of the continuing desire for speed and faster decision making is the reduction of preparation and planning time and with it the confidence people feel for the outcome of a decision they have made. In addition, most of the markets in which organizations operate have increased their pace of operation.

Mergers, acquisitions, and alliances mean constant shifts in culture and continually revised business goals. Cisco acquired 51 companies in just over 6 years, which includes 21 companies acquired in a 12-month period.

But sometimes an organization determines to bring about huge levels of change for itself in order to develop its product range and enter new markets. For instance, Corning sold its major cookware division after 145 years in order to concentrate on glass fiber communication technologies.

Organizations are changing to face pressures from speed, a more fluid marketplace, and an inability to forecast very far out front. To survive and stay effective, organizations need to become more dynamic (Brown & Eisenhardt, 1998b).

So in a dynamic organization, what do people need to do to handle their responsibilities effectively? And how can they help their organizations be more effective? We propose that at least some of the answers to these questions can be found through an investigation of how people cope with ambiguity and uncertainty. In short, our proposition is that dynamic organizations are staffed by people who are comfortable coping with ambiguity and uncertainty.

REDUCE OR EMBRACE AMBIGUITY?

We need to make an important distinction at this stage. In our research, we have not tried to answer the question of how to reduce ambiguity and uncertainty. We see that as an issue of decision making and strategy formulation. We are interested in how people cope with ambiguity when they are not yet in a position to make a decision that will reduce it.

In the original research we did for *The Future of Leadership* (White, Hodgson, & Crainer, 1996), we received many anecdotal reports from managers who told us that they frequently felt unable to make a decision because it would reduce their flexibility for further actions. So our research has been to look at how executives cope in situations of continual and continuing ambiguity, where the only option is to embrace the ambiguity (Brown & Eisenhardt, 1998a).

WHAT IS THE DIFFERENCE
BETWEEN AMBIGUITY AND UNCERTAINTY?

Until now in this chapter, we have used ambiguity and uncertainty interchangeably. However, we found it useful to make a distinction between the two words. *Ambiguity* is a physical reality. It is a lack of clarity and unpredictability that exists in the world and is thus, theoretically at least, objectively measurable in some way. *Uncertainty* is a psychological state. It is the effect that ambiguity has on the individual, and is a feeling and a perception. Thus, the same level of absolute ambiguity can produce different levels of uncertainty in different people.

In addition, it is useful to distinguish between two kinds of "perceived" uncertainty: One kind is where you do not know something, but somewhere in the world the knowledge does exist—imagine a person trying to find a street in a city they did not know well—someone else will know that street, and there will probably be a map. This is the kind of uncertainty that can be reduced by the hiring of experts and consultants. However, we do caution that when the uncertainty involves a lack of skill, then not all consultants can convey the skills as well as the knowledge. Imagine hiring a consultant to teach you to juggle—the knowledge may be there and is easy to demonstrate, but skill acquisition on the part of the learner may take much longer.

The second kind of uncertainty is where not only do you not know something, but no one else knows it either. Consider a manager putting together a business plan for an entirely new product where the market size is unknown. Although many people have ideas of what the market size will turn out to be, no one in fact knows. In our view, hiring an expert in this situation may even be counterproductive. Experts can only know what has happened in the past. If the product is completely new, there is *no* expertise to forecast what needs to be done. As everybody's view is a guess, then anybody's view may turn out to be correct—expert or not.

IS AMBIGUITY INCREASING?

Executives in leadership roles complain that they have to cope with higher levels of ambiguity, which makes taking effective decisions harder. Ambiguity seems to be on the increase. Many people at all levels in organizations of every kind complain that they feel less certain than they used to about how to do their jobs.

There seem to be two main processes that lead to an increase in ambiguity. First, the widespread use of digital technology and information networks has increased the options offered to managers. They now have many more choices about where they source materials, where they manufacture, where they sell, and where they and their workforce are based. The vast increase in choice, coupled with an equivalent increase in speed (or maybe it is better to call it a reduction in discretionary decision time), means that people experience the range of opportunities that more options gives them as a feeling of uncertainty. This range of options permeates every aspect of people's lives. Even asking a mundane question such as, "what will you be doing 1 day from now, 1 week from now, 1 month from now, 1 year from now?" demonstrates to most people the unforcastable nature of their lives.

Second, in most organizations of whatever design, people moving into leadership roles take on greater levels of responsibility. When a problem is experienced by people with lower levels of responsibility (further down the hierarchy if it is that kind of organization), then they tend to push the problem further up the organization to people with higher levels of authority.

The overall process acts almost like a pump, and it is a pump of ambiguity. The ambiguity in the problem is pumped toward people with higher levels of responsibility. This is all well and good if the ones who take on the roles of highest responsibility are prepared for the daily deluge of ambiguity that comes pouring across their desks, but all too often these same people have harbored a dream that "Once I get to the top job, then I'll have better information and have the ability to control things and therefore reduce the uncertainty I feel." Sadly, they are almost always disappointed.

WHAT IS THE LINK BETWEEN STRATEGY, LEADERSHIP, AND UNCERTAINTY?

Our premise is that if there is more ambiguity in the world, then managers may have to learn to live with it rather than try to reduce it. Uncertainty is reduced by taking decisions, which normally involves reference to a public (or sometimes undeclared) strategy. But the link to leadership is usually strong. Is the leadership taking the organization toward or away from uncertainty?

Consider Fig. 9.1, where difficult learning is the y axis. Difficult learning is what people find hard to do and to learn to do. It represents the second type of uncertainty previously described. Value to the organization is the x axis—how much value does this activity bring to the organization? Now, looking at the chart, where would be the area representing highest competitive advantage?

Assuming that an organization is trying to be first or second in a market, then the top right of the graph is likely to be the preferred area of operation. (If the strategy is to be a rapid follower, then the organization could live comfortably in the bottom right box, but only as long as competitors do not change too much too often).

To live at the top right of the chart is continually to be doing difficult learning. It is tough, testing, always changing and, for many, exhilarating. But it is tiring too, and there is probably a limit to how much difficult learning an organization or a team in that organization can do. We have met people in organizations who say they have too many new and challenging projects on the go at the same time. The likely result is that none of the projects gets the attention and the energy that it needs.

There is also the possibility that the organization keeps doing things, but forgets why, so that over time the value that the actions bring tends to diminish. We know of an informal survey of companies that were using total quality initiatives, where the managing directors in more than 70% of companies surveyed were finding "no discernable value" after just 18 months of the quality initiative (Binney & Williams, 1995). To be quite clear, the authors are not putting forward an argument against quality initiatives, but an argument saying that if your organization is tying up its resources by doing something difficult, then it would do well to inquire frequently just what benefit is coming from that investment.

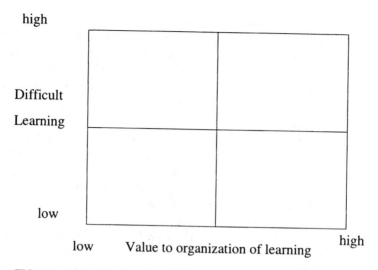

Difficult

Learning

low

low   Value to organization of learning   high

FIG. 9.1.   Difficult learning and competitive strategy. Adapted from White, Hodgson, and Crainer (1996).

The other feature of the top right box (or as one "Trekkie" colleague of ours calls it, the Star Trek strategy—boldly going where no one has gone before) is that over time, what was hard for almost any organization gets easier. In terms of the diagram, the action slips down toward the bottom right. For the pioneer, it was hard; for those that follow, it will usually be easier.

But what is the link with ambiguity and uncertainty? In order to be competitive, organizations have to do things that demand difficult learning, and where, hopefully, their competitors are discouraged by the difficulty of the learning. Where do organizations go to find things that are difficult to learn? They head for areas of uncertainty and ambiguity rather than head for the things that they know already. So via the link of difficult learning, tolerance for ambiguity is linked to competitive strategy.

SKILLS OF HANDLING AMBIGUITY AND THE FEELINGS OF UNCERTAINTY

When we decided to research this area, we made a decision not to explore personality and skills related to ambiguity and uncertainty. We felt that understanding behavior would be of more immediate help to the people we worked with. In making this decision, we are not denying that personality may play a part in the way a person handles ambiguity; it is simply that we wanted to study behavior first before we could get very far in understanding any underlying personality traits. We believe that there is a huge area of potential research in mapping personality characteristics against competence in handling uncertainty.

Our research was based on interviews and structured conversations we were able to have with managers in the United States, Europe, Asia, Australia, and New Zealand. The period during which we collected data lasted about 18 months, and we collected transcripts with approximately 80 people. In all of these conversations, we asked people about how they handled ambiguity and uncertainty. The process of analyzing the interviews was not without its low moments. When we collected all the tape transcripts, at first we could not see anything new or useful in the mass of data. It seemed that people's answers had largely been made up of current management and business clichés.

We were seriously thinking of abandoning the entire project when we decided to look in a new direction. We put aside our thoughts of managers and organizations, and instead asked ourselves a different question: What kind of person, irrespective of whether he or she was a manager or not, was good at handling ambiguity? One answer we considered were people who travel and explore; they must surely be able to handle the uncertainty of exploration. We also considered people who work in the emergency services who have to deal with the unexpected. But for us, our most fruitful source of ideas came from the behavior of children.

Young children, almost by definition, face huge amounts of ambiguity and uncertainty simply because they do not know how the world works. Sometimes we see our role as parents as helping our children move from uncertainty to certainty in the process of growing up.

The more we studied the behavior of the children we knew, the more we were stimulated to identify a number of behavioral sets that could be used to classify and understand our original managerial interview data. It could be reinterpreted in the light of the behavior sets that we had seen children use, and did indeed show useful skill sets concerned with handling ambiguity. It was not the interview data that contained the clichés, it was our way of interpreting it. As we changed our method of analysis, a rich source of material unfolded. Incidentally, we are not suggesting that all children handle ambiguity and uncertainty well, although it would be fascinating to research how far or under what conditions that generalization could be made.

KEY SKILL SETS

In *The Future of Leadership* (White, Hodgson, & Crainer, 1996), we identified five skill sets. Our subsequent book (Hodgson & White, 2001) was based on interviews and questionnaire data from nearly 1,000 subjects across three continents. The spread was approximately 40% from North America, 40% from Europe, and 20% from Asia. From the data we identified 14 specific behaviors linked to the skill sets. In this chapter there is not sufficient space to describe all 14 behaviors; we describe the five underlying skills sets from which the 14 are derived.

Overcoming Fear of Failure

In modern organizations, managers and leaders face high levels of uncertainty, and therefore need to experiment and take risks. Unfortunately, for many their background education and experience has trained them that public risk taking eventually leads to public failure. And public failure is not seen as attractive, either at the time or as a way of improving one's future prospects.

We believe the stimulus for avoiding risk is embedded early for many people. Imagine a scene at school with, say, a class of 6- or 7-year-olds. The teacher asks a question such as, "Who was the first president of the USA?" The behavior that now occurs is reasonably forecastable. The kids that know put up their hands or indicate in some way. The kids who do not know find something terribly attractive about the desk surface in front of them. Typically, the teacher chooses someone who knows and in various ways the people who put their hands up feel rewarded for doing so. Occasionally, the teacher picks on someone with his or her hand up who does not know, but all the while, the "don't knows" usually feel safer by not putting up their hands. The lesson learned: It's safer not to expose your ignorance.

Now move the timescale forward a few decades. Those same kids, now grown, are sitting in executive meetings debating the future of their company and its products. The CEO asks a question analogous to that asked by their teacher so many years ago. What is the likely response? Typically, it is of the same basic kind we found in school, but with more sophisticated behavior thrown in. There are computers and flip charts and digital presentations. But the essence is the same: If you know, you show, and if you do not, it is safer to keep quiet.

But the behavior the CEO really wants to see (and we have asked many senior managers about this and they all agree) is if someone does not know, he or she says something like, "I don't know but I want to find out." It is almost as if they are being encouraged to revel in their lack of knowledge. And this behavior was indicated in the difficult learning diagram in Fig. 9.1. Only by acknowledging that the manager or their organization does not know something can they get on the learning curve to find out about it.

Now return to the school classroom. We estimated that the average child who experiences 10 to 15 years of schooling will be exposed to the situation we described between 5,000 and 15,000 times. These are heavyweight levels of conditioning and therefore hard to shrug off. No wonder that in our most recent research (Hodgson & White, 2001), the majority of senior managers we interviewed say that it is still hard for them to admit making mistakes. And they all recognize that it takes a major effort for most people to overcome that old school conditioning and publicly announce that they "don't know, but want to find out." It would be useful to do a survey of kinds of organization, perhaps linked to age or education level, to explore who finds this hardest and who easiest. Our tentative observation would be that the longer a person spent in school, the more they were exposed to that conditioning, and therefore the harder it would be for them to learn the new behavior of admitting publicly to not knowing.

Energy and Fun

It has been known for a long time that effective leaders have lots of energy (Bennis & Nanus, 1985). What our findings show is that effective leaders in situations of ambiguity are good at helping others find energy, too. It is analogous to another "skill" that we frequently observed in children, which is to make fun of boring things.

The manager facing high levels of ambiguity will almost certainly have to experiment in order to find out which approach is most likely to work. Imagine people looking for a road in a city without a map and there are no taxis. They have to walk a lot and do a lot of trial and error behavior in order to achieve their objective.

For a short time at least, children seem to do trial and error very well. They experiment with their food (often to a parent's consternation); they play with the wrapping on the box as well as the contents of the box. It seems quite natural for children to find experimental learning and trial and error learning fun.

In the workplace, the notion of fun has only recently become a widespread concept. Dress-down days, barbecues, and all manner of informal workplace behavior have become popular. The aim, assuming it is not just a fad, should be to make trial and error learning more attractive and more fun.

The authors have challenged organizations with the following question: "If you took money out of the compensation equation, would your people still come to work for your organization? Would you?" In other words, they found working in the organization the most interesting and exciting thing they could do with their time. The first few times the authors asked that question, the response from senior executive audiences was laughter. But we know of many high net worth individuals who really do not come to work for the money any more. It is the "fun" that keeps them with a particular organization. The authors invite managers to perform a thought experiment. Imagine two organizations in competition with each other that in most respects were very similar. If one could answer yes to our question whereas the other could not, which is more likely to get the most value for its employees in the long term? The authors' hypothesis is that the organization where people want to come to work irrespective of the money is likely to have a long-term advantage over a similar competitor. There are a number of possible research opportunities here.

Simple Questions, Simple Answers

Our original concept for the dynamic organization and how it was different from conventional organizations was to compare a steamship with a white-water raft. In the "good old days," companies were run with a lot of certainty about where they were going and how they should be managed. Much like the steamship, the organization moved steadily and predictably along its course. Steering corrections were made well in advance, and apart from stormy weather, progress was almost inevitable.

Compare the steamship to a rubber raft used for white-water rafting. For someone brought up on steamships, the whole construction of the raft would seem flimsy and insubstantial. The bow looks the same as the stern, the floor is not solid, and the walls bend and twist. Yet the moment the mariner sets out on white water in the raft, then the need for flexible walls becomes obvious. Instead of being dashed to pieces on the first set of rocks, the raft simply flexes around them and keeps floating. Given that the swirls of water are difficult to read, sometimes the raft is going forwards, sometimes backwards, sometimes sideways. This flexibility of movement would never be tolerated on the steamship but is essential on white water.

Finally, compare the way messages are sent and received on the steamship to the way they need to be handled on the raft. On the steamship there is time for the captain to tell a member of the watch to alter speed, for the watch to call down to the engine room, and for the speed to finally be altered. On a raft the paddlers need be very coordinated and together to respond very quickly to the demands of the river. A good raft crew will spend some time practicing to work well together quickly; their leader must give signals that are short (one or two words only) and easily understood. On the tougher stretches, lives may indeed depend on messages being understood and implemented effectively.

Simple and clear communication is essential in the dynamic white-water environment that many organizations find themselves in. Children expect it, too. They ask deep and penetrating questions and do not like being fobbed off with trivial answers.

We ask managers if they can summarize the strategy of their organization in 25 words or less. It should be easy, but a surprisingly large number find it hard to do. The contrast is between the ease of sending a 3-page e-mail about something, or compressing the essence of a message into a single sentence. One organization the authors know has a red star day. On just one day in the month, if anyone gets a communication that he or she feels is too long or too complex to easily understand, then he or she is allowed to mark it and send it back. They are encouraged to ask the writer to rework it to make it easier and quicker to understand.

Our observations of organizational life suggest that the rise in the number of e-mails has correlated with a decrease in the simplicity of messages sent around companies (Sellen & Harper, 2002). It is hard to be precise, but it would be an interesting piece of research to see if the number, length, and clarity of messages was changing. Certainly the anecdotal evidence we collected suggests that many managers feel close to being overwhelmed by the quantity of the messages they receive. In addition, the quality of writing contained in an e-mail is often so poor that the receiver may miss an important point.

The overall result of all this lack of simplicity is poor implementation and execution, and longer working hours for many people. We want organizations to realize the benefits that simple, clear communication would bring. Of course, simple communication takes time and effort and the payback may not be immediate or obvious. It would be interesting to conduct some experiments comparing execution times and success rates between two matched groups of executives where one group had made the effort to simplify communications and the other group had not.

Achieving Focus

In a complex world, knowing what to do first is a problem. We found that some people seemed to have the ability of keeping just a few key tasks in mind. In the confusion of the white-water existence, understanding which were those few key tasks made life much easier and simpler. In Corning Glass, executives talk about "the vital few"; it is their constantly reviewed list of four or five key issues, the key strategic tasks and initiatives that everyone in the organization must be aware of and must in some way subscribe to.

Sometimes that focus lasts for a long time. Trevor Bayliss, the English inventor and entrepreneur, spent 12 years perfecting a clockwork radio. Why clockwork? Because in many parts of the developing world, where electricity supplies were unreliable or nonexistent, the ability for people and villages to receive broadcast messages concerning health, education, weather warnings, and so on, was of great importance. The price of batteries for a conventional radio is often seen as too high in these countries, so a radio that has no running costs is of enormous value. But Bayliss found that most of the backers he approached to help develop his product could not see the possibilities for the radio. It shows considerable focus on his part that he persevered to make the clockwork radio a reality.

Of course, being very focused can have disadvantages. The person who is too focused can be accused of being narrow and blind to other possibilities, even obsessive in pursuing a goal that is now irrelevant. So part of the skill of being effectively focused is to know when to stop.

Mastering Inner Sense

Leading is not just about the rational and the factual. Instinct, experience, and intuition all have a part to play. But in our increasingly open, transparent world, observers of leaders demand reasons and rationale. But how does the leader operate if the hard facts are not available, yet decisions still have to be made? We suggest that the most effective people in these situations have access to what we called an "Inner Sense."

This is more than intuition; it includes experience, and also instinct. In the Western world, the concept of proceeding without factual data seems odd, even incompetent. But in some parts of the world, it may not be so unusual. Nonaka and Takeuchi (1995) argued that Western companies remain caught up in "explicit" knowledge, whereas the Japanese thrive on what they call "tacit" knowledge. Tacit knowledge is more elusive than explicit knowledge and is based on idealism, skills, and a gut feeling.

Our research discovered that Western managers were not keen, perhaps not able to talk easily, about inner sense. They knew that shareholders and institutional investors would be unimpressed by decisions made on intuition rather than demonstrable facts.

Yet there is a paradox buried here. We asked many executives whether they used their inner sense, and approximately 80% said they did, but fewer than 30% said they would admit to it in public—the boardroom, for example.

One of the clearest uses of inner sense is in spotting ideas, trends, possible patterns in the market, or the industry—to be able to read faint signals. It seems to be something that some managers do almost unconsciously. They just seem to be aware of developments that might affect them or their business one day. Consequently, they are that little bit less surprised when the unlikely happens.

This concept of inner sense and particularly the sensitivity for faint signals was well described by Jack Welch, former CEO of GE. He said, "Our job is capital allocation—intellectual and financial. Smell, feel, touch, listen, and then allocate. Make bets, with people and dollars. And make mistakes" (Jackson & Gowers, 1995).

The same notion of inner sense was described more charmingly by Arthur C. Clarke, who commented: "When a distinguished but elderly scientist states that something is possible, he is almost certainly right. When he states that something is impossible, he is almost certainly wrong" (quoted in Nampoori, 2001, p. 8).

CONCLUSION AND SUGGESTIONS FOR FURTHER RESEARCH

We see our work as the start of an approach to leadership that we hope is original but nonetheless relevant. In our publications, we have gone to some pains to argue that our approach to leadership does not carry with it the implication that "all the others must be wrong." We want to build on what is already known and understood about the subject. Our stance is that handling ambiguity is a set of skills that until recently most people did not need. But now they do, and thus research into these skills is now relevant and appropriate.

We have three broad suggestions for future research.

• We deliberately did not get into the issue of personality and the skills we described. But it seems to us in reviewing the interviews and questionnaire results that there is likely to be a connection between how easily a person learns and develops his or her behaviors in the skill sets we have described and his or her personality. For instance, are some personality types (take the Myers Briggs typology as an example) more likely to be comfortable with high levels of uncertainty?

• Similarly, although we researched managers and executives around the world, we did not try to look for national or geographic cultural differences. The work of Hofstede (1980) and Trompenaars and Hampden-Turener (1997) has gone some way in exploring national characteristics, but there is still much more to discover. For instance, how does a person from one country adapt to the assumptions about ambiguity when working in or with nationals from another country?

• Finally, throughout our work the importance of effective communication has been apparent. How much difference does it make in practice? A series of structured observations or comparisons between matched work groups could throw enormous light on this vital and fascinating area. Does, for instance, the number of e-mails received per day correlate with the feeling of perceived uncertainty? Does effort put into creating "simpler" communication pay off if there are fewer requests for clarification, fewer errors among direct reports?

REFERENCES

Barham, K. & Heimer, C. (1999, March). ABB: The dancing giant. *Financial Times*. London: Prentice Hall.

Bennis, W., & Nanus, B. (1985). *Leaders: The strategies for taking charge*. New York: Harper & Row.

Binney, G., & Williams, C. (1995). *Leaning into the future*. London: Nicholas Brealey.

Brown, S., & Eisenhardt, K. M. (1998a). *Competing on the edge*. Boston: Harvard Business School Press.

Brown, S., & Eisenhardt, K. M. (1998b, March-April). Time pacing: Competing in markets that won't stand still. *Harvard Business Review*, pp. 59–69.

Hodgson, P., & Crainer, S. (1993). *What high performance managers really do*. London: Pitman London.

Hodgson P., & White R. (2001). Relax, it's only uncertainty. *Financial Times*. London: Prentice Hall.

Hofstede, G. (1980). *Cultures' consequences*. Beverly Hills, CA: Sage.

Jackson, T., & Gowers, A. (1995, December 21). Big enough to make mistakes. *Financial Times*. London.

Lewin, R. (1993). *Complexity, life on the edge of chaos*. London: Orion Books.

McCall, M. W., Lombardo, M. M., & Morrison, A. M. (1988). *Lessons of experience*. Lexington, MA: Lexington Books.

Morrison, A. M., White, R. P., & Van Velsor, E. (1987). *Breaking the glass ceiling*. Reading, MA: Addison-Wesley.

Nampoori, V. P. N. (Ed.) (2001, February). *Photonics News* [online bulletin from the International School of Photonics], *Vol. 3*(01), p. 8. Available: http://www.photonics.cusat.edu/Photonics News.html

Nonaka, I., & Takeuchi, H. (1995). *The knowledge-creating company: How Japanese companies create the dynamics of innovation*. New York: Oxford University Press.

Sellen, A. J., & Harper, H. R. (2002). *The myth of the paperless office*. Cambridge, MA: MIT Press.

Trompenaars, F., & Hampden-Turner, C. M. (1997). *Riding the waves of culture*. London: Nicholas Brealey.

Welch, J., & Byrne, J. A. (2001). *Jack: What I've learned leading a great company and great people*. New York: Warner Books.

Wheatley, M. J. (1992). *Leadership and the new science*. San Francisco: Berrett-Koehler.

White, R., Hodgson, P., & Crainer, S. (1996). *The future of leadership*. London: Pitman London.

Wille, E., & Hodgson, P. (1991). *Making change work*. London: Mercury Books.

10

Real Options Reasoning and the Dynamic Organization: Strategic Insights From the Biological Analogy

Rita Gunther McGrath
Columbia University

Max Boisot
Universitat Oberta de Catalunya

Those biological analogies that have been imported to apply to the study of the dynamic organization are incomplete because they have emphasized a gene frequency approach rather than a gene complex approach. The "gene frequency" approach implies a massive investment to create requisite variety. The gene complex approach allows requisite variety to be achieved parsimoniously by leveraging the combinatorial potential within an organization. We believe that real options reasoning, in which firms can create dynamic potential that conveys the right to make choices at some future point, is a useful analogue to gene complexes in biology. We introduce the idea of real options acting in the organizational equivalent of "gene complexes" to expand the range of contingencies to which an organization can respond.

Biological metaphors abound in the quest to understand dynamic, changing organizations and populations of organizations. Useful though these metaphors are, organizations are not like living organisms in many important respects (Penrose, 1952). One of the most critical differences between organizations and organisms is that managerial discretion and strategic intelligence influence adaptation in organizations.

This chapter suggests an emerging theory of the dynamic organization that extends the biological metaphor, yet incorporates a useful role for managerial discretion. We make three essential points: (a) new developments in biology shed significant light on the workings of adaptive mechanisms; (b) the emergence of real options reasoning in strategy offers a conceptual vehicle with which to apply these insights to organizations; and (c) an options-oriented theory of the dynamic organization centers on the parsimonious creation of requisite variety.

ADAPTIVE MECHANISMS IN BIOLOGY

The Ecological Metaphor

The familiar processes of ecological change are variation, selection, and retention (Aldrich, 1999; Campbell, 1965). In biology, variation is created as the result of genetic crossovers and random mutations occurring within an interbreeding population. The population evolves by selecting from this variety, endowing the fittest organisms with a reproductive advantage (Mayr, 1978). Competition for scarce resources is one selection process, in that better adapted organisms will triumph over less well adapted ones, within a given context. Those characteristics that are "selected in" are retained, or preserved in the population, by being passed on to future generations.

Note that in biology, an organism may be short-lived but still play an important evolutionary role, provided that it has survived long enough to pass on its genetic traits to the next generation. It is the genetic profile, not the organism's fate, that is of interest. Biologists are thus careful to distinguish between the genotype of an organism and its phenotype. The *genotype* constitutes the total genetic endowment that a given organism can potentially draw on. One can think of this as a built-in capacity to handle a range of environmental contingencies. As a result of the interaction between the organism and its environment, there emerges the phenotype of the individual organism. The *phenotype* represents its physical, observable characteristics.

In biological systems, selection does not operate directly on genes, but on the phenotype (Mayr, 1978). For selection processes to result in evolutionary change, variations in phenotypic traits across individual members must be stabilized (made consistent) across a sufficiently large number of individual organisms that they then affect the reproductive success of their underlying genotypes. One implication is that chance mutations seldom lead to meaningful changes in the genetic composition of a population because they are either fatal to the organism that generated them, or because they have insufficient impact at the phenotypic level to create differential reproductive success. Furthermore, learned behaviors exhibited at the level of the phenotype do not affect subsequent generations unless they likewise alter reproductive success.

How then do *some* mutations create a lasting change in a biological population? A necessary first step is that a given mutation must become stabilized via the chromosomes of the population, which constitute its genotype. Until a characteristic is stable, it does not create the potential for population level variation. Two kinds of genes influence the effects of a mutation in response to an environmental signal. These two kinds of genes, harbored in the chromosomes, are called *structural* and *regulatory* genes. Signals from the environment put regulatory genes to work to either repress or induce production of a particular gene product by the structural genes (Jacob & Monod, 1961). This creates a mutation. If the trait that the structural genes code for fits the environmental signal, it is selected in. If not, it is selected out.

As recently as the 1950s, genetic evolution was treated as a purely additive phenomenon, in which specific phenotypic characteristics depended on possession of a specific set of genes from which they were derived on a one-to-one basis (Fisher, 1930). Genetic evolution was characterized as the replacement of one gene by another in a frequency distribution of characteristics. Thus Fisher (1930) echoed Mendel's famous idea of transmission genetics. In its simplest form, the concept is that for any given phenotypic property (such as eye color), an organism inherits half of the relevant genotype from its maternal parent and half from its paternal parent. In reproducing, the organism would pass along half its inheritance, and its mate would supply the other half. The genotypes within a population would, over time, come to reflect differential advantage given to offspring advantaged by phenotypic characteristics. Thus, if blue-eyed people (for whatever reason) reproduced at twice the rate as all other eye colors, the population would constitute an ever-growing proportion of people with blue eyes.

ORGANIZATIONS
AND THE BIOLOGICAL METAPHOR

With this brief overview of adaptation in biology in mind, let us consider how the biological metaphor has been transferred to organization studies. Evolutionary models are present in several theoretical traditions (see Aldrich, 1999, for an excellent overview). Perhaps the most clearly articulated and rigorously tested are models from organizational ecology, with the advantage that its underlying assumptions regarding change and adaptation are explicitly articulated (Baum, 1996). In the ecological tradition, organizations obtain resources from their environments by achieving efficiency. In response to pressures for reliable performance and accountability, organizations create highly reproducible, bounded structures, with orderly internal processes.

Because they are fixed in routines and competencies, ordered structures are difficult to change.

The initial life period of a new organization is therefore crucially important because it establishes the parameters for organizational functioning thereafter (Hannan & Freeman, 1977). Such thinking of the way in which organizations function is consistent with the contemporaneous biological thinking of the 1960s and 1970s. Scholars such as Von Bertalanffy (1962) placed emphasis on stability in interdependent systems. Selection was viewed as the primary way in which order was imposed on natural variation.

An important premise of the ecological tradition is structural inertia (Hannan & Freeman, 1984). Structural inertia draws attention to the downside risk of change. Changing processes destroys the efficiency of established routines, which can alienate resource providers. Changes can cause so much disruption that, in the short run, the organization's performance drops sharply. Before a change has time to produce desired long-term effects, short-run pressures can lead to organizational collapse. Hannan and Freeman (1984) summed up the argument in this way: "In a world of high uncertainty, adaptive efforts . . . turn out to be essentially random with respect to future value" (p. 150). Structural inertia suggests that organizational change is disruptive at best, and deadly at worst, and that there is little utility in managerial discretion.

Scholars have made many attempts to test the structural inertia hypothesis empirically. Little support has been found for it in its strongest form. Indeed, as Baum (1996) noted, "Organizations change frequently in response to environmental changes, and often without any harmful effects" (p. 106). On the other hand, neither is there strong support for the effectiveness of managerial discretion in creating organizations that can dynamically adapt.

The ecological framework treats the boundaries of a firm as relatively fixed, and the routines and competencies contained within those boundaries as inseparable from the organizational whole. The amount of variety that a given organization can face and survive is established in its formative period, by its choice of initial strategy. Two possibilities were specified in Hannan and Freeman's initial (1977) formulation: specialist organizations, who survive by focusing on a narrow set of customers; and generalist organizations, who attempt to appeal more broadly to wider customer groups. Even though later studies elaborated on the basic distinction, with some exceptions (e.g., Haveman, 1992) strategies are usually operationalized as fixed. Firms are seen as not being able to change strategies quickly enough to meet the needs of dynamic environments, meaning that change in a population is primarily a consequence of entries and exits of individual firms.

Enter the New Biology

Starting in the 1960s, a few developmental biologists articulated an alternative to the additive-gene view of evolution (see Dobzhansky, 1962). One of the more influential ideas was Sewall-Wright and Provine's (1986) view that genes are tied together into adaptive bundles or complexes. In contrast to the additive view, in which the genotype's ability to produce phenotypic characteristics is limited by its initial endowment, Sewall-Wright maintained that the same basic genetic material could be used to produce phenotypic characteristics of considerable diversity because of interconnections between genes. Interlinked gene complexes permit more population level diversity than a one-to-one correspondence between a fixed allotment of genes and their expression in a population—the gene frequency view—might suggest.

To understand this better, consider Edelman's (1992) description of clonal selection theory at work in the immune system. The job of the immune system is to combat foreign molecules (antigens) that might represent a threat. It does this by making proteins called antibodies that bind to the antigens and destroy them. Any individual has the capacity to produce a huge variety of antibody molecules, each of which has a different shape at its binding site. When a foreign molecule enters the immune system, it encounters a population of antigen bearing cells (or lymphocytes), each with different antibodies on their surfaces. It is bound to those cells whose shape at the combining site is complementary to some portion of the antibody. Figure 10.1 illustrates this process—the foreign body F is bound to the appropriate lymphocytic cells (in this case 702, 735, and 886) and is destroyed by the combination of antigens produced.

This stimulates each lymphocyte cell, which bears the antibody, to divide repeatedly. This clones the relevant lymphocyte cells (hence clonal selection), and results in many more cells with a good fit to the invading molecule. As a result of the selection in of cells with the right fit and their subsequent multiplication, the population of lymphocytes in the host body is changed.

There are two major points to be made from this example. First, more than one antibody cell is involved in fending off the invader—they work in teams. So in Fig. 10.1, instead of there being only 12 possible responses, one for each lymphocyte, there are actually a vast number of responses from the same basic genetic material. Second, instead of the organism being at the mercy of whatever phenotypical structure it inherited from its "parents," it is able *itself* to develop and elaborate its immune capabilities. The immune system in effect evolves in order to combat the specific contingencies a particular organism faces. Consequently, no two organisms have the identical set of antibodies. Figure 10.2 provides a conceptual illustration.

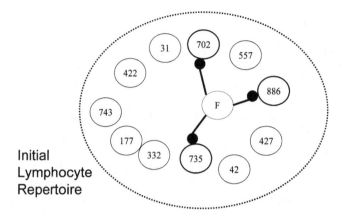

Initial
Lymphocyte
Repertoire

FIG. 10.1. Foreign molecule F bound to antibodies on lymphocytes that fit parts of its shape (small black dots represent antigens with a binding site that fits the antibody surface). Adapted from *Bright Air, Brilliant Fire* by Gerald M. Edelman. Copyright © 1992 by Basic Books, Inc. Adapted by permission of Basic Books, a member of Perseus Books, L.L.C.

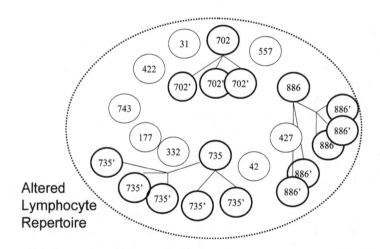

Altered
Lymphocyte
Repertoire

FIG. 10.2. Affected lymphocytes (702, 886 and 735) are stimulated to make clones and increase their numbers in the population of cells in an individual's immune system. These clones also all have the potential to mutate to, say, 702', 735', 886'. Adapted from *Bright Air, Brilliant Fire* by Gerald M. Edelman. Copyright © 1992 by Basic Books, Inc. Adapted by permission of Basic Books, a member of Perseus Books, L.L.C.

Genes coding for the antibody secreted in response to a specific antigen accumulate successive replications and mutations that progressively increase the affinity of antibody for antigen (Kauffman, 1993). The ability to carry over nonselected alternatives for possible future use mitigates to some extent the cost of generating variety on this scale. In the case of genes that code for antibody proteins, for example, a few hundred genes can be recombined to produce antibodies for over 10 million possible antigens, any of which can be manufactured when needed (Depew & Weber, 1995; Kauffman, 1994). This means that the variety of responses the system may summon is substantial, for a cost, in the form of genes, that is far more parsimonious than would be the case in the additive, gene frequency model.

Ashby (1956) suggested that adaptive entities must be able to summon responses to environmental contingencies that are as varied as the demands placed on them. In other words, a dynamically adaptive entity needs to be able to generate "requisite variety." In the gene frequency model, requisite variety was thought to mandate substantial investment in genetic potential because a gene was needed to respond to each of all possible environmental contingencies. In the combinatorial model, variety is achieved by leveraging the combinatorial power of the genes in the genotype, thus increasing the adaptive capacity of any set of genes exponentially.

The requisite variety appropriate for any living system is a function of its own internal capacity to generate and recognize variety as well as of how much complexity and variety it actually encounters in its environment. The current thinking in evolutionary biology is that the two mechanisms, both additive accumulation of genes and genes working in combinatorial complexes, operate in tandem. Evidence is accumulating that because of the combinatorial capability of the genotype, the chromosome is capable of dealing with far more variety than had originally been supposed.

In biology, adaptability in the face of environmental novelty depends on what Edelman (1992) called *recognition systems*. By recognition, Edelman meant "the continual adaptive matching or fitting of elements in one physical domain to novelty occurring in elements of another, more or less independent physical domain, a matching that occurs *without prior instruction*" (p. 74, emphasis added). In other words, even though the form and function of the response is unknown prior to the emergence of environmental novelty, the response viewed ex post facto appears to be adaptive. The immune system is characteristic of a recognition system, in that it can take corrective action across a wide range of possible bacterial assaults, without knowing in advance what these will consist of. Because lymphocytes can combine together to repel invasion, they can respond to a much wider range of potential threats than if the antibody-to-antigen relationship were one-to-one.

The Combinatorial Model from Biology
and the Dynamic Organization

The "new" biology, we believe, offers interesting insight into the design of adaptive mechanisms for dynamic organizations. Just as biological recognition systems allow an organism to summon an adaptive response without being prepared for the challenge in advance, could there be an organizational analogue? Perhaps, in emphasizing selection, organizational scholars have transposed only one adaptive mechanism from modern biological theory into their discipline, leaving it an incomplete representation.

If we allow for the operation of an adaptive system that is internal to the organization, the new biological metaphor comes into its own, with the parallel metaphors of interactive gene complexes. The organizational analogy to a gene complex is a combination of attributes at a level of analysis below that of the firm. Nelson and Winter (1982) argued for the term *routine* as a way to describe this combination. In their view, "Routines play the role that genes play in biological evolutionary theory" (p. 14). Strategy scholars have adopted this idea of routines as the core building blocks of organizational functioning, although there are definitional differences in the various points of view, with terms such as *resources, capabilities,* or *competencies* used (see Amit & Schoemaker, 1993; Barney, 1991; Wernerfelt, 1984). Evolutionary theorists such as Aldrich (1999) use the terms in a complementary way, defining organizations as "viable carriers of routines and competencies" (p. 113). We follow suit and use the term "routines and competencies" to imply both patterned behaviors (routines) and the skills, competencies, and assets (resource endowments) with which they interact (see also Teece, Pisano, & Shuen, 1997).

In the world of organizations, the genotype might thus be exemplified by its total resource endowment of routines, competencies, and assets. The equivalent of the phenotype constitutes the implementation of a subset of these in economic activities, what Penrose (1959) called the "services" it currently provides. The idiosyncrasy of the organization–environment interaction creates a population of routines and competencies that are a consequence of past challenges the organization has faced and that contain the potential to address future challenges. Clearly, this distinction implies a role for managerial discretion to the extent that particular routines and competencies are mobilized in response to organizational challenges (see Eisenhardt & Martin, 2000). We think it is important to capitalize on Baum's (1996) suggestion that organizational polymorphism needs to be incorporated in ecological views of organizations.

We suggest that the current ecological metaphor that has been imported to organization studies has not incorporated two ideas that are central to current understanding of biological development. The first is that in addition to gene frequencies, gene complexes act to produce adaptive behavior. For organizations scholars, the gene complex approach suggests that we would be well advised to question the assumptions of structural inertia that are consistent with a gene frequency approach. If internal routines and competencies can be mobilized in such a way that they work in teams, a wide range of adaptive behavior is possible, without inevitably dooming the organization to performance declines, because the cost of change given combinatorial possibilities is not fatally high.

The second key idea suggested by the new biology is that selection processes can operate at a level below that of the firm. Diversity in a population may be influenced by internal actions that enhance or diminish sets of routines and competencies within a firm, as well as through behavior that transfers routines and competencies across organizational boundaries. Such transfers might consist of an entire unit that is separated from its parent organization (as in a spinoff or joint venture) or through processes such as population-level learning and isomorphic imitation. The key point is that management activities influencing the growth and decline of complexes of routines and competencies can have the effect of generating population-level change that is not derived from the entries and exits of fixed-strategy firms.

Management discretion influences, although it does not determine, how the competencies in a company evolve. We make no claim that senior managers are necessarily insightful. The point is that as they try to create dynamic, adaptive organizations, they influence resource flows to different routines and competencies, which then affects which evolved routines and competencies are observed to have emerged, ex post at both the level of the firm and the level of the population. Let us next suggest a theory of strategy in a dynamic organization that might take these two points into account. We begin with the idea that real options are the organizational analogue of an endowment of genetic potential and that they can be activated to create dynamic adaptation in much the same way as biological systems are activated.

REAL OPTIONS
AND THE DYNAMIC ORGANIZATION

Options as Part of an Adaptive System

Bowman and Hurry (1993) were influential in suggesting that the options lens is useful for understanding both incremental choice processes in organizations and for providing an analytical structure with which to comprehend emergent strategies (Mintzberg & Waters, 1985; Quinn, 1980). Options represent contingent investment commitments that secure decision-making rights in the future. When the investment is made in an asset, rather than in a financial contract, it is termed an investment in a real option (Dixit & Pindyck, 1994; Trigeorgis, 1993). Making toehold investments, investing in R&D, taking out patents, founding new businesses, and entering into joint ventures have all been classified as real options for organizations (Kester, 1981; Kogut, 1991; McGrath, 1997, 1999; McGrath & Nerkar, 2001; Mitchell & Hamilton, 1988). Options are thus combinations of routines and competencies as are other organizational components.

Although any management decision potentially creates some option value (see Dixit & Pindyck, 1994), real options are usually described in terms of a characteristic sequence of events. The initial event is the creation of an option—either through the deliberate decision to invest or through the "recognition" of a potentially valuable combination of routines and competencies that was randomly accumulated (Bowman & Hurry, 1993). After the passage of time, in which more information becomes available, the organization might choose to exercise the option, which usually implies a significant investment to capitalize on the emergent opportunity, or to take some other action. In the case of real options (as opposed to financial ones), the underlying asset in question is typically a strategically valuable asset (such as a commercialized technology or an ongoing business).

There is a good deal of similarity in the pattern of creating and exercising real options and the functioning of adaptive biological systems. By investing in an option (say, a new product division), a firm creates the organizational equivalent of a gene. Depending on signals from the environment, it may exercise the option or not. Making the larger investments required to exercise the option is analogous to mobilizing antibodies to combat a foreign molecule, in that such investments cause the routines and competencies associated with the option to increase. Absent a signal that exercise is warranted, the organization can simply hold the option or permit it to "expire."

To qualify as a real option, a particular investment must also meet three conditions: (a) the investment must be small, relative to the investment required to capture control of the underlying asset; (b) the initial investment must not imply the later one (in other words, the organization preserves the option to abandon); and (c) there must exist the possibility that more information at some future point will improve the outcomes of the investment than were it to be made outright at an earlier point.

Possessing options allows an organization to operate at a higher level of uncertainty than it might otherwise be able to handle. This is because rather than investing today in the capacity for dealing with an unknowable degree of future variety, decision-makers can instead invest smaller amounts in latent dynamic capacity. Options, such as those to defer, expand, contract, abandon, postpone, or alter patterns of investment, enhance the potential value of investment streams (Trigeorgis, 1997). The presence of options decreases the investment required to deal with a given level of variety while increasing the range of possible future states to which an organization can effectively respond.

As in biological recognition systems, to deploy options effectively requires that organizations likewise develop recognition systems. Managers have a key role to play in this activity. It is managers, and other participants in the sense-making behavior of organizations, who create cognitive representations of the challenges facing the organization. These cognitive representations facilitate (or not) organization members' interpretation of the meaning of patterns occurring in the organization's environment (Weick, 1995). Although subsequent discoveries may reveal the choice of representation to be wrong, until some choice of representation is actually made, there can be no selection process in the internal ecology of the organization. In other words, until a given environmental stimulus is given an interpretive meaning, it will not provoke activation of routines and competencies.

We now come to the crux of our argument regarding the biological analogy to real options. Real options constitute an organizational analogue of the biological mechanisms for the working of a recognition system. Like the lymphocytes in the immune system, they carry latent potential to produce a variety of routines and competencies in the organization in response to the stabilization of external variety in the organization's cognitive repertoire. They thus have the potential to increase the range of environmental variations that an intelligent organization can adapt to. Through judicious deployment of options, socioeconomic organizations can meet two adaptive challenges: securing the right to be selected into more appropriate environments for themselves, and gaining enough time in which to adapt.

Many forces can interfere with the ability of an organization's members to represent the challenges it faces. The political nature of organizational decision making, bounded rationality, difficulty in distinguishing cause and effect in noisy environments, and reorganization costs all are likely to inhibit change (Hannan & Freeman, 1984). The presence of these conditions suggests a role for strategy and leadership in creating the dynamic organization. To the extent that leaders can put forth cognitive representations that are legitimate, simple, specific, clear, and urgent, the more likely the organization is to be able to take action (Brown & Eisenhardt, 1998). To the extent that causal relationships are articulated in these representations, the more likely the organization is to mobilize coordinated "teams" of routines and competencies. And the smaller and less complex the organizing unit required to make a change occur, the more quickly a representation is likely to be acted on. We can articulate testable propositions based on this argument:

Proposition 1: The more specific strategists' cognitive representation of an environmental challenge is, the faster organization members will be able to identify a set of routines and competencies to address it.

Proposition 2: The more specific strategists' cognitive representation of an environmental challenge is, the more coordinated the response is likely to be.

Proposition 3: The more competencies and routines contained within a given intraorganizational boundary (e.g., the larger the units responsible for creating the adaptive response), the slower an adaptive response will be.

Note that we deliberately have not specified that the adaptive response will be successful. Many things can go wrong, even with a clear cognitive representation of the challenge. Managers may not correctly perceive the nature of the challenge. They may not be able to design an appropriate response. The threat may yet overwhelm the organization before it can react.

THE ROLE OF VISION (OR "BALLPARKING")

Our discussion so far suggests that the adaptive potential of a gene complex approach can only be realized if a mechanism exists to create a patterned response to uncertainty and that an important role is thus created for managerial discretion. Those involved with an organization's strategizing are faced with the task of extracting signals of emerging patterns from a background high with noise and articulating specific exigencies to which organization members can then respond. Extracting weak signals from a noisy background requires scanning skills. Interpreting and making sense of such signals calls for recognition skills. Both are facilitated to the extent that a cognitive process takes place in which organization members agree on the most salient features of the adaptive landscape.

In scanning, organization members recognize meaningful patterns, most often by comparing expectations regarding states of nature with perceptions of actual states of nature. Resulting gaps suggest the need for a contingent response and provoke a learning process. The scanning process is vulnerable to a seemingly endless set of cognitive and emotional biases. Thus, a prerequisite for effective scanning is the creation of enough cognitive variety to comprehend the implications of a gap between things as they were expected to be and things as they are.

If there is too much variety, however, organization members simply cannot keep track of all the intersecting possibilities. Something between the infinitely possible and the more computationally tractable probable is needed. This is the world of the plausible, in which scenarios are used as part of the organization's recognition system (Schwartz, 1991; Van der Heijden, 1996). In well-constructed scenarios, plausible variations are built up out of correlated possibilities, which is another way of saying that each scenario reflects a cohesion among correlated variables. Correlated possibilities have the effect of reducing the size of the problem space that a strategist need either recognize or attend to. The world of the plausible is still likely to encompass more contingencies than the organization can currently respond to, yet it will be smaller than the possibility space produced by an uncontrolled proliferation of intersecting contingencies.

For an organization to respond to meaningful patterns, their key features must be cognitively stabilized and stored so that meaningful choice over them may be exercised. This is directly analogous to the observation that selection processes in biology can only act if variety is first stabilized and fixed. This explains why various forms of scenario analysis have become a popular way of developing scanning skills. The essence of scenario analysis is to envision a set of plausible futures that will facilitate the recognition of events that foreshadow them, should these come to pass (Van der Heijden, 1996). Meaningful variety can then be selectively stabilized by making investments in configurations of real options on the basis of scenarios. These configurations of options secure the right to take action, but only if the particular scenario occurs. For those scenarios that do occur, the options are exercised. For those that do not, the options can be allowed to expire, or can remain in the organization's inventory for use at a later time (see Garud & Nayyar, 1994). The firm then proceeds to extract value from those options that are exercised, and uses the most recent learning to prepare scenarios for the next round of options. Dynamic adaptation is accomplished through successive cycles of option creation, option exercise, and option expiration.

Options thinking, of course, has always been implicit in scenario analysis. Why else would an organization invest scarce time and effort conjuring up possible futures if not to invest in low-cost measures ahead of time to deal with them? What our forays into biological thinking highlight is that, in addressing multiple scenarios, a firm can deploy two options strategies—adopt either a gene frequency or a gene complex approach. This has implications for the way that scenarios are created and portfolios of routines and competencies are constructed.

There are two ways in which managers developing scenarios in an attempt to achieve requisite variety can go astray. First, an organization might fail to invest in the capacity to think in terms of scenarios at all. Or its members might engage in very rudimentary scenario design that exhibits low variance relative to the environmental variance the organization is facing. Such situations are likely to constrain the organization to the analysis of relatively few variables. Furthermore, if the organization is mainly concerned with extracting near-term value from its existing resource and capability configuration, it can fail to generate any options at all. Scenarios based on optimization or business process reengineering, for example, are sometimes thought to prevent organizations from allocating resources to experimental probes and playfully imagined futures. Such constrained situations are described in terms of excessive "simplicity" (Miller, 1993) or even "rigidity" (Staw, Sandelands, & Dutton, 1981) and are consistent with structural inertia. This suggests the following proposition:

Proposition 4: Low variety in possibilities contained in an organization's planning scenarios will be associated with low variety of options it is likely to take out and low overall investment in options.

The second way in which scenarios can generate errors is when they generate a random rather than patterned set of possibilities, offering little guidance for how the organization should respond. Too many scenarios chasing too many variables over too varied a set of timeframes is likely to overload the organization's cognitive capacity. This brings us to the discretionary role of managers within the organization as articulating the nature of the key contingencies that it faces and specifying which environmental signals its members should address. Many have termed this a process of creating a vision or sense of purpose for the organization that specifies critical contingencies and how the organization should respond (Collins & Porras, 1994).

McGrath and MacMillan (2000) termed this *ballparking*. They borrowed the idiom from the world of playing fields. The construct has to do with establishing the arenas in which the organization must be prepared to meet environmental contingencies and in general how these contingencies are to be met. A clearly specific ballpark (or vision, or set of "simple rules"—see Eisenhardt & Sull, 2001) has enormous power in terms of reducing the complexity to which organizational members must attend, and offers guidance as to which specific projects merit inclusion in the options portfolio. As Brown and Eisenhardt (1998) observed, "In businesses whose people are faced with rapid and unpredictable change, a simple perspective that captures the heart of their activity can be critical to keeping the activity together" (p. 237).

In terms of our biological analogy, managerial discretion manifest in articulating such a simplifying perspective acts as an ordering force. It allows for discretion at the level of operating parts of the organization, but also provides guidance as to how coherent wholes are to be constructed. We submit that this activity on the part of senior executives can quite appropriately be classified as the sentient, intentional equivalent of emergent natural orders. Thus, the new biology offers an interesting way to consider the value of a traditional leadership process, namely the role of leaders in setting overall direction and focusing attention. We can articulate the following propositions:

Proposition 5: The more clear and simple a "ballpark statement" is, the more consistent discrete acts at an operating level will be.

Proposition 6: The more clear and simple a "ballpark statement" is, the more quickly and consistently choices involving tradeoffs among alternatives will be made at an operating level.

It is important to note that we have not, either in our theory or in our propositions, posited that managerial discretion will lead to successful adaptation. In highly uncertain and changing environments, selection out is always a possibility. What we have tried to do instead is articulate a role for managerial discretion within a broad ecological framework, at the level of intraorganizational routines and competencies.

TOWARD THE DESIGN
OF DYNAMIC ORGANIZATIONS

Gene Frequency and Gene Complex Analogues in Real Options

As we have already seen, in biological systems, two approaches are used to generate requisite variety. The first, the gene frequency approach, absorbs variety by generating one gene for each of every conceivable contingency. The second uses the combinatorial potential of genes operating in cohesive complexes to generate patterns of adaptive responses when needed. This second approach dramatically reduces the variety that needs to be mobilized (i.e., that is requisite) to deal with the complexities of the environment.

The two approaches to the creation of adaptive capacity in genetic systems correspond conceptually to two distinctly different ways of using options that are available to strategists. Under some conditions, the only way of absorbing variety is to create a position in an uncertain context and prepare to exercise or exit when critical uncertainties are resolved. This is analogous to the gene frequency approach. For instance, if real option "a" can help an organization adapt to environmental context "A," real option "b" to environmental context B, and so on, the pattern of investment would look something like this:[1]

Real Option		Ex Post Environmental Context
a	→	A
b	→	B
c	→	C
?	→	D

Taking a position and waiting for time to resolve uncertainty presumes that the assets and the contingencies covered by the options are clearly identifiable, and secondly, that the signals that would imply that the time has come to exercise or exit are clear. The critical contingencies, moreover, are likely to be outside the control of the firm. Under these conditions, a gene frequency approach makes sense because the complexity present is sufficiently manageable that it can be absorbed. Absent these conditions, attempts to deploy enough positioning options to cover all possible contingencies could lead an organization to exhaust its resources. A mechanism for narrowing the range of contingent responses is therefore essential.

As used in finance, the current approach to the evaluation of real options corresponds to this idea, similar to the gene frequency approach in biology. Options tend to be viewed as discrete, linear, and additive. In effect, they are treated as members of a portfolio to which they can be added or subtracted with little or no effect on the other members of the portfolio. Yet suppose that we were to take the more recent model that recognizes complexes of genes as our point of departure for real options reasoning? It could be that options are at their most effective when they confront uncertainty coordinated into meaningful combinations—they benefit from "teamwork." Thus the firm may be able to leverage the combinatorial potential of its options, in much the same way that occurs in the gene complex approach.

To continue the previous example, if we assume that in addition to possessing a particular option, an organization also possesses a greater or lesser skill for combining options. This might help it to combine two real options, say a and b, designed to deal with contingencies A and B to fit a different environmental context than anticipated, for instance an environment C that was not envisioned when the options investment was made.

---

[1]We are indebted to an anonymous reviewer of this chapter who offered this extremely insightful set of examples on the nonteleological use of real options investments and combinatorial capacity.

The possible situations that might result look something like this:

Ex ante real option	Can adapt to ex post environmental context
(a)	A
(b)	B
(a + b)	C

Let us consider a hypothetical pharmaceutical industry scenario. Real option "a" could be a geriatric drug and the appropriate environmental context (A) could be a global aging population that makes the geriatric drug relevant. There needs to be an appropriate sensing mechanism (Lant, Milliken, & Batra, 1992) than can activate option "a" to cope with context "A." This is a view of options as more or less linear, discrete, and additive. Organizations might acquire both "a" and "c" more or less randomly, or its acquisition might be probabilistic.

Leveraging the potential for combinations of options in complexes is somewhat more complex, but still consistent with the biological analogy. Let us say that option "b" is a treatment for cancer that is mildly less invasive than chemotherapy, but results in hair loss as a side effect. Option "b" could be useful in context "B," which is all markets where lung cancer is on the rise. This replicates the first condition, a simple option to environment match. Suppose, however, that our firm was also pursuing option "c," a drug that stimulates hair follicles to grow hair. Looked at simply, option "c" can be activated to serve the market for hair regrowth (context "C"). Imagine, however, that there is a heretofore unknown context D, a new market for chemotherapy that does not have hair loss as a side effect. This market may or may not have been "discovered" yet (Daft & Weick, 1984). Suppose the combinatorial skills of the drug company allows it to pool options "b" and "c" to create a chemotherapy treatment where the hair-loss side effect does not occur. Then the statement:

$$(b, c) \rightarrow D$$

means that the company has extended the range of contingencies to which it can adapt to encompass D. This provides an example of how real options can be deployed in a manner that is not simply linear, additive, and discrete, largely by hypothesizing the existence of combinatorial skills that can exploit unpredictable yet recognizable opportunities.

Patterned Investments in Options. Even with a combinatorial approach, of course, organizations face limits on their adaptive capacity. Resource and other constraints limit their ability to recognize and mobilize options for the full range of external and internal variety that they need to confront. Cognitive and coordination constraints are also present. This suggests that to design an adaptive system, the strategist first must find a way to narrow the range of contingencies to which the organization must prepare to respond.

In dynamic environments, the design goal is to create an entity with sufficient stability to maintain adequate performance in ongoing operations, while creating sufficient requisite variety through investment in options that permit adaptive evolution. Clearly, many routines and competencies within the organization are dedicated to its ongoing operations, and these need continuous enhancement simply to cope with changing demands from the current environment. March (1991) called this the challenge of balancing exploitation and exploration in organizational learning.

A useful framework to begin considering the design challenge can be found in Teece, Rumelt, Dosi, and Winter (1994). They argued that the greater the distance from existing products and markets in which a firm operates, the more difficult learning becomes because such distance introduces noise that confounds the effort to draw cause and effect conclusions. They characterize distance in terms of increasing technological distance and increasing market distance. When firms are most distant from their existing base, uncertainty is greatest and learning is most difficult.

By adopting Teece et al.'s (1994) framework, we can begin to visualize the relationship between the nature of the uncertainty facing a firm and design choices it might make with respect to its array of routines, competencies, and options (see also McGrath & MacMillan, 2000). This is found in Fig. 10.3.

A firm's existing products and services can be thought of as located on the lower left-hand side of this figure, at a point where organization members

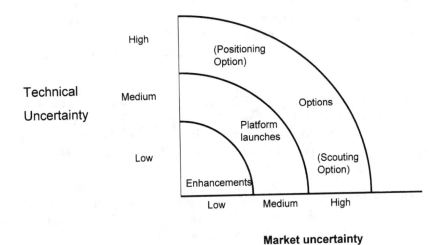

FIG. 10.3.   An uncertainty landscape.

experience the least uncertainty. As one moves to a greater distance in either new technological directions or new market directions, uncertainty becomes greater. On the outer perimeter of this chart, uncertainty is substantial and opportunities for experiential learning are constrained. At the same time, dynamic organizations must be able to operate in such high-uncertainty spaces given substantial change in their products and markets over time. We believe this outer space is best addressed by the creation and utilization of options, in which uncertainty is too great to be able to anticipate the distribution of outcomes with confidence (see Knight, 1971). As before, we suggest that options come in two forms: those that position the organization for anticipated future states and those that might offer the potential for combinatorial discovery in an unanticipated future state. We term the first type of option a *positioning* option and the second type a *scouting* option or probe.

Positioning options are those undertaken by an organization facing significant uncertainty, but for which some kind of scenario can be articulated. An example of a positioning option might be investments in assets and alliances in mobile telecommunications in the United States, where the most critical uncertainty has to do with the future standards in the industry. As of this writing, there are at least four viable mobile communications technologies. Should one of them emerge as a standard, any firm aspiring to compete in this arena will need to participate in the standard or be locked out. Firms are thus taking positions in technology options based on scenarios for the future development of the technology that will allow them to rapidly adopt the standard (or even help create it). When the standard does emerge, obviously some of the options will be worthless because they will represent investment in a standard that will not dominate.

Scouting options, in contrast, are relatively low-cost forays into arenas new to the firm (McGrath & MacMillan, 2000; see also Brown & Eisenhardt's 1998 discussion of probes). They may be experimental products or prototypes that will be used to convince important potential customers of the value of a firm's offering. When properly managed, a scouting option is a limited downside investment in learning. It is not intended to result in a huge business. Rather, it is intended to discover if there is a huge business. As a consequence, downside exposure should be known and limited. In effect, the firm deploying a scouting option is offering a complex variation from existing offerings for selection by the environment. Scouting options also imply the existence of a combinatorial ability, which might allow a firm to discover, experientially, what the true future market is.

Deploying scouting options is often the only way a firm with an interesting new technology can gain sufficient exposure to new markets to determine the form of an offering that customers will adopt. Customers find it notoriously difficult to articulate their needs in the abstract. Von Hippel's (1988) research suggested that asking them to articulate needs for a product or service they have never experienced is doomed to disappointment because most customers must interact with an offering before they can evaluate it. Scouting options enact a new reality in which the technology and the market are brought together.

In contrast to options, a platform launch represents the exercise of a given option or complex of options with the intention of creating an entirely new business or transforming an existing one. Such launches are only appropriate if sufficient investments in scouting and/or positioning options have reduced uncertainty so that a manager can place a coordinated bet. Indeed, some of the great corporate disasters of recent times can be traced to firms' launching new businesses before using options to reduce uncertainty (a recent example is the Iridium Satellite business, which lost over $5 billion on the basis of mistaken assumptions about both technological progress and market demand). This suggests the following proposition:

Proposition 7: Organizations that invest in options prior to launches will experience results that are closer to their launch expectations than organizations that do not precede launches with options

An Example

The story of the transformation of Springfield Remanufacturing Company is an interesting illustration of the utility of using options to create a dynamic organization (Stack, 2002). The company originated as a spin-off from International Harvester in the early 1980s as an employee-owned, independent organization that remanufactured diesel engines. Since then, it has created 39 spin-off subsidiary organizations of its own, 22 of which are still viable. The example of one of these, a company called Engines Plus, is interesting. Managers in the parent organization identified a potential problem in chronically leaky oil coolers that had to be replaced with expensive new ones. Although the parent company had the potential capability to figure out a process for remanufacturing the coolers, there was little interest in so doing. The company thus decided to form a separate entity with the sole goal of addressing the cooler issue.

In essence, the company created an option on this opportunity in the form of a separate business to tackle the oil cooler problem. Investment was kept low, leverage was kept high, and the initial application was to solve the problem for the parent. The option was, at that stage, of the positioning variety—a calculated bet that the problem could be solved at a profit. The bet turned out to be correct. Selling remanufactured oil coolers generated some cash flow. Next, the company invested in the equivalent of scouting options, namely the decision to go for additional business by combining different routines and competencies it had learned in the oil cooler business to go after other, different businesses. Today, the company has three major lines of business and is worth a substantial sum per employee. The parent, now called SRC International, used Engines Plus and other ventures to continue to grow, even as the two divisions that formed the core of its business when Engines Plus was founded have since gone into decline. SRC implicitly, we believe, took advantage of the power of options to sustain itself as a dynamic organization, even in an industry widely regarded as hopelessly mature.

CONCLUSION AND IMPLICATIONS

In this chapter, we sought to build bridges between new ideas on the workings of biological systems on the one hand, and the design of dynamic organizations on the other. We argued that real options can be seen as the organizational analogue of raw genetic potential, and particularly that the capacity to combine and reconfigure routines and competencies by opening and exercising options allows organizations to develop requisite variety parsimoniously.

Of particular interest to us is that elements of the biological analogy have received insufficient attention in the organizations literature. Even if their tools for prediction and forecasting are imperfect, we suggest that strategists can, and do, help organizations develop, learn, and change in ways that can be adaptive. In effect, strategists become the custodians of a firm's representation systems taken as generators of hypotheses that, as Popper (1972) suggested, "can die in our place." In short, managerial discretion has a larger role to play than it is often given credit for.

We have extended the biological analogy by suggesting several ways in which strategy and the active management of options can increase the range of uncertainty to which an organization can fruitfully respond. Specifically, under uncertainty, we suggest that key tasks of the strategist are to:

1. Develop a set of scenarios appropriate to the level of uncertainty the organization is facing.

2. Use these scenarios to guide investments in an interrelated network of options, deploying fixed (frequency) type options where primary uncertainties can be bounded, and combinatorial patterns of options where they cannot.

3. Consciously manage the learning that emerges when assumptions diverge from experience.

4. Aggressively leverage the exercise of options so as to fully exploit their ability to operate jointly when the scenarios that gave rise to them have been validated.

In strategy, many scholars interested in the application of real options draw heavily on financial options thinking for their inspiration. It is an approach that is intuitively appealing to managers and furthermore has the alluring promise of rendering complex, uncertain situations amenable to computational modeling. The distinction that we have been at pains to draw between options deployed discretely and those deployed in options complexes highlights the fact that the latter are considerably more complex than the former and, indeed, may not yield to a computational approach at all. This is one reason why students of real options have tended to keep away from interacting options (Amran & Kulatilaka, 1999).

What we are concerned with here is a particular way of thinking about options, not a particular way of valuing them. The contribution of biological thinking is to help us to realize that real options are potentially important building blocks of the design of dynamic organizations and that they have their counterpart in natural systems.

In theorizing about the dynamic organization, a balance needs to be struck between what Lewontin (1983) called transformational and variational theories, or what Sober (1985) labelled developmental and selectionist theories. By enriching the scope of an organization's recognition and response systems, options underpin a developmentalist view of organizations. The danger of an evolutionary "selecting out," of course, does not disappear, but it is more easily kept at bay. The implication of our perspective is that ecological analysis may only examine part of the story, the part that applies fully only to organizations that fail to deploy adequate recognition systems. Biologists realize that genes acting in complexes can complement and enhance adaptive capacity relative to an approach based purely on gene frequency. Strategists can likewise see that carefully designed and managed options complexes can enhance and magnify the benefit to be gained from traditional choices in strategy, such as positioning.

Just as a developmental perspective on recognition systems challenges conventional views of biological adaptation as being entirely reducible to selective processes, so too does options theory challenge those who disregard the potential for an organization's adaptation and change to shift the population of competencies and routines in a population. Options reasoning can provide a traceable mechanism for how deep changes in industry structure can be triggered by a single firm's exploitation of the options at its disposal. Genetic material at the level of a firm, for instance, can be reblended in such a way that it provokes major shifts in populations, as has long been argued by those who study technology cycles and architectural innovation (Henderson & Clark, 1990; Tushman & Anderson, 1986). Conclusion: a mechanism for the creation of diversity exists independent of firm level entries and exits. It further does not require the assumption of sentient, planned change.

Effective dynamic organizations must be able to act in the absence of the ability to preplan these actions. This suggests important new roles for the strategist. Rather than running a variety-reducing planning process that commits the organization prematurely to a single invariant concept of the future, strategists become promoters of conceptual diversity. When used as part of a recognition system, strategic use of scenarios and real options provides the organizational tools needed to achieve requisite variety.

It is, of course, difficult for the strategist to establish how much variety is actually requisite. One possibility is to deliberately decentralize option generation activity. This can foster a "bottom up" process consistent with Baldwin and Clark's (2000) ideas of how modularity might be managed and with Mintzberg and Waters' (1985) concept of emergent strategy. In such a process, the strategist can add considerable value by configuring options into "options complexes," leaving it to top management to act as a selection device on the resulting configurations (what Burgelman, 1991, referred to as the autonomous strategic process).

Organizations are simplifying systems that seek out an ordered regime so as to reduce their rate of entropy production (March & Simon, 1993). They are being placed in a state of permanent tension by the need to generate ever greater variety in their attempts to cope with a growing multitude of unforeseen contingencies. They thus find themselves constantly being pulled toward a chaotic regime. Options offer a way of handling proliferating variety without having to succumb to it organizationally. Under the limited uncertainty of the ordered regime, real options reasoning turns out to have little purchase other than in the serial, additive, and linear forms in which it finds application in finance. Here, the gene frequency model applies. In either a complex or a chaotic regime, by contrast, options constitute a relatively low-cost device for recognizing and stabilizing evanescent patterns. Where they draw on the gene complex model, such options, properly configured, facilitate the learning that can allow organizations to manage and survive in a truly dynamic fashion.

ACKNOWLEDGMENTS

We appreciate comments from Randall Peterson, Ian MacMillan, Charles Baden-Fuller, Howard Aldrich, Karen Belanger, Gökçe Sargut, the late Ned Bowman, N. Anand, and Lee Dyer. This research was partially funded by the

ECLIPSE (Entrepreneurial Careers, Learning and Investment Patterns) project at the Columbia Business School.

REFERENCES

Aldrich, H. (1999). *Organizations evolving*. Thousand Oaks, CA: Sage.

Amit, R., & Schoemaker, P. (1993). Strategic assets and organizational rent. *Strategic Management Journal, 14*(1), 33–46.

Amran, M. M., & Kulatilaka, N. (1999). *Real options*. Boston: Harvard Business School Press.

Ashby, W. R. (1956). *An introduction to cybernetics*. London: Chapman and Hall, Ltd.

Baldwin, C., & Clark, K. B. (2000). *Design rules: The power of modularity*. Cambridge, MA: MIT Press.

Barney, J. B. (1991). Firm resources and sustained competitive advantage. *Journal of Management, 17*(1), 99–120.

Baum, J. A. C. (1996). Organizational ecology. In S. R. Clegg, C. Hardy, & W. R. Nord (Eds.), *Handbook of organization studies* (pp. 77–114). Thousand Oaks, CA: Sage.

Bowman, E. H., & Hurry, D. (1993). Strategy through the option lens: An integrated view of resource investments and the incremental-choice process. *Academy of Management Review, 18*(4), 760–782.

Brown, S. L., & Eisenhardt, K. M. (1998). *Competing on the edge: Strategy as structured chaos*. Boston, MA: Harvard Business School Press.

Burgelman, R. A. (1991). Intra-organizational ecology of strategy making and organizational adaptation: Theory and field research. *Organization Science, 2*, 239–262.

Campbell, D. T. (1965). Variation and selective retention in socio-cultural evolution. In H. R. Barringer, G. I. Blanksten, & R. Mack (Eds), *Social change in developing areas*. Cambridge, MA: Schenkman.

Collins, J. C., & Porras, J. (1994). *Built to last: Successful habits of visionary companies*. New York: HarperCollins.

Daft, R. L., & Weick, K. (1984). Toward a model of organizations as interpretation systems. *Academy of Management Review, 9*(2), 284–295.

Depew, D., & Weber, B. (1995). *Darwinism evolving: Systems dynamics and the genealogy of natural selection*. Cambridge, MA: MIT Press.

Dixit, A. K., & Pindyck, R. S. (1994). *Investment under uncertainty*. Princeton, NJ: Princeton University Press.

Dobzhansky, T. (1962). *Mankind evolving*. New Haven, CT: Yale University Press.

Edelman, G. (1992). *Brilliant air, brilliant fire*. Middlesex: Penguin Books.

Eisenhardt, K., & Sull, D. (2001, January). *Strategy as simple rules*. Harvard Business Review, pp. 107–116.

Eisenhardt, K. M., & Martin, J. A. (2000). Dynamic capabilities: What are they? *Strategic Management Journal, 21*, 1105–1122.

Fisher, R. (1930). *The genetical theory of natural selection*. Oxford: Oxford University Press.

Garud, R., & Nayyar, P. (1994). Transformative capacity: Continual structuring by intertemporal technology transfer. *Strategic Management Journal, 15*, 365–385.

Hannan, M., & Freeman, J. (1984). Structural inertia and organizational change. *American Sociological Review, 49*, 149–164.

Hannan, M. T., & Freeman, J. (1977). The population ecology of organizations. *American Journal of Sociology. 82*, 929–964.

Haveman, H. (1992). Between a rock and a hard place: Organizational change and performance under conditions of fundamental environmental transformation. *Administrative Science Quarterly, 37*, 48–75.

Henderson, R. M., & Clark, K. (1990). Architectural innovation: The reconfiguration of existing product technologies and the failure of established firms. *Administrative Science Quarterly, 35*, 9–30.

Jacob, F., & Monod, J. (1961). Genetic regulatory mechanisms in the synthesis of proteins. *Journal of Molecular Biology, 3*, 318–356.

Kauffman, S. (1993). *The origins of order.* Oxford: Oxford University Press.

Kauffman, S. (1994). *At home in the universe.* New York: Viking.

Kester, W. C. (1981). *Growth options and investment: A dynamic perspective on the firm's allocation of resources.* Unpublished Ph.D. dissertation, Harvard University, Cambridge, MA.

Knight, F. H. (1971). *Risk, uncertainty and profit.* Chicago: University of Chicago Press. (Original work published 1921)

Kogut, B. (1991). Joint ventures and the option to expand and acquire. *Management Science, 37*, 19–33.

Lant, T. K., Milliken, F., & Batra, B. (1992). The role of managerial learning and interpretation in strategic persistence and reorientation: An empirical exploration. *Strategic Management Journal, 13*, 585–608.

Lewontin, R. (1983). Gene, organism and environment. In D. Bendall (Ed.), *Evolution from molecules to men.* Cambridge: Cambridge University Press.

March, J. G. (1991). Exploration and exploitation in organizational learning. *Organization Science, 2*, 71–87.

March, J. G., & Simon, H. (1993). *Organizations.* New York: Wiley.

Mayr, E. (1978). Evolution. *Scientific American, 239*, 46–55.

McGrath, R. G. (1997). A real options logic for initiating technology positioning investments. *Academy of Management Review, 22*, 974–996.

McGrath, R. G. (1999). Falling forward: Real options reasoning and entrepreneurial failure. *Academy of Management Review, 24*, 13–30.

McGrath, R. G., & MacMillan, I. C. (2000). *The entrepreneurial mindset: Strategies for continuously creating opportunity in an age of uncertainty.* Boston, MA: Harvard Business School Press.

McGrath, R. G., & Nerkar, A. (2001, October). *Real options reasoning and a new look at the R&D investment strategy of pharmaceutical firms.* Paper presented at the 2001 Strategic Management Society Meetings in San Francisco, California.

Miller, D. (1993). The architecture of simplicity. *Academy of Management Review, 18*(1), 116–138.

Mintzberg, H., & Waters, J. A. (1985). Of strategies, deliberate and emergent. *Strategic Management Journal, 6*, 257–272.

Mitchell, G. R., & Hamilton, W. F. (1988, May/June). Managing R&D as a strategic option. *Research-Technology Management, 27*, 15–22.

Nelson, R. R., & Winter, S. J. (1982). *An evolutionary theory of economic change.* Cambridge, MA: Harvard University Press.

Penrose, E. (1952). Biological analogies in the theory of the firm. *American Economic Review, 52*, 804–819.

Penrose, E. (1959). *The theory of the growth of the firm.* New York, NY: Wiley.

Popper, K. R. (1972). *Objective knowledge: An evolutionary approach.* Oxford, UK: The Clarendon Press.

Quinn, J. B. (1980). *Strategies for change: Logical incrementalism.* Homewood, IL: Irwin.

Schwartz, P. (1991). *The art of the long view.* New York: Doubleday.

Sewall-Wright, S., & Provine, W. B. (1986). *Evolution: Selected papers.* Chicago: University of Chicago Press.

Sober, E. (1985). Darwin on natural selection: A philosophical perspective. In D. Kohn (Ed.), *The Darwinian heritage.* Princeton, NJ: Princeton University Press.

Stack, J. (2002, April). The Innovator's Rule Book. *Inc Magazine.* Available: http://www.inc.com/magazine/20020401/24045.html

Staw, B. M., Sandelands, L., & Dutton, J. (1981). Threat-rigidity effects in organizational behavior: A multilevel analysis. *Administrative Science Quarterly, 26,* 501–524.

Teece, D., Rumelt, R., Dosi, G., & Winter, S. (1994). Understanding corporate coherence: Theory and evidence. *Journal of Economic Behavior and Organization, 23,* 1–30.

Teece, D. J., Pisano, G., & Shuen, A. (1997). Dynamic capabilities and strategic management. *Strategic Management Journal, 18*(7), 509–533.

Trigeorgis, L. (1993). Real options and interactions with financial flexibility. *Financial Management, 22,* 202–224.

Trigeorgis, L. (1997). *Real options: Managerial flexibility and strategy in resource allocation.* Cambridge, MA: MIT Press.

Tushman, M., & Anderson, P. (1986). Technological discontinuities and organizational environments. *Administrative Science Quarterly, 31,* 439–465.

Van der Heijden, K. (1996). *Scenarios: The art of strategic conversations.* Chichester, UK: John Wiley.

Von Bertalanffy, L. (1962). General system theory—A critical review. *General Systems, VII,* 11–30.

Von Hippel, E. (1988). *The sources of innovation.* New York: Oxford University Press.

Weick, K. E. (1995). What theory is not, theorizing is. *Administrative Science Quarterly, 40,* 385–390.

Wernerfelt, B. (1984). A resource-based view of the firm. *Strategic Management Journal, 5,* 171–180.

11

Organization Design:
A Network View

N. Anand
Brittany C. Jones
London Business School

Organization design aims to better align an organization's capabilities with the demands made by its environment. We start with the assumption that in order to best thrive in dynamic environments, an organization should have distinctive design criteria that help it cope. In this chapter, we use insights from recent development in network theory to propose a set of three criteria for assessing the appropriateness of an organizational design: relationships, redundancy, and representation (the "three Rs"). By *relationships,* we mean the internal social architecture of an organization—that is, the way in which people are predisposed to interact—and we use Goffee and Jones' (1998) organizational culture model to demonstrate how distinctive social architectures create unique capabilities. By *redundancy,* we mean an organization's ability to create slack capacity from ongoing activity. Organizations constantly trade flexibility for reliability, and redundancy helps optimize this trade-off. By *representation,* we mean the manner in which the external environment is interpreted and conveyed internally. Since design's role is to harmonize an organization with its environment, it matters how the environment is socially constructed within an organization. In this chapter we show how each of these three Rs is important to a network view of organization design. Our approach is distinctive in focusing on the organizational level, and our theorizing has important implications for future research in both organization design and network theory.

In recent years the network perspective has emerged as one of the most fertile and interesting areas of organizational research. Most of the attention in network analysis has thus far been directed at elaborating the role played by ties among groups of individuals or among organizational groupings (Podolny & Page, 1998; Powell, 1990). The individual perspective highlights the role social capital plays in individual outcomes such as job performance reputation (Kilduff & Krackhardt, 1994), career success (Seibert, Kraimer, & Liden, 2001), and ability to cope with adverse circumstances (Shah, 2000). The extraorganizational perspective highlights the network relations that help an organization cope with its environment, focusing on selected issues including corporate governance (Mizruchi, 1992), competitive market interaction (Burt, 1992; Podolny, Stuart, & Hannan, 1996; Uzzi, 1997), interorganizational learning (Powell, Koput, & Smith-Doerr, 1996; Tsai, 2001), and strategic alliance formation (Gulati & Garguilo, 1999; Stuart, 1998).

As Krackhardt and Brass (1994) noted, one item that has been relatively neglected in the literature to date is research on networks at the organizational level of analysis. Although a number of studies informed by networking theory have investigated, inter alia, organizational issues such as power (e.g., Brass, 1992; Krackhardt, 1990), job-related perceptions (Ibarra & Andrews, 1993), and knowledge-sharing (e.g., Cross, Borgatti, & Parker, 2002), we lack anything resembling an integrated network-based theory of organization design.

We take seriously the view of organization as a network of social relations and try to develop a set of design criteria that might inform such a view. Consequently, the distinctive contribution of this chapter is to develop a network view of organization design. We intend to apply recent insights developed by network theory on the nature and function of relationships for organizational activity, and to go beyond them by integrating work in other areas of organizational research. This approach complements the individual—as well as extra-organizational—perspectives that have dominated recent research on network theory.

Organization design is the attempt to shape an organization to better align its capabilities with the demands made by its environment. Dynamic environments make a number of distinctive demands on organizations: the need to sense markets accurately and mobilize adequate response, the ability to exploit temporary advantage, and the capacity to embed learning continually (see chapter 2 by Dyer and Shafer in this volume). We start with the assumption that in order to best thrive in dynamic environments, an organization should have distinctive design criteria that help it cope. In this chapter we focus on three criteria of importance, which we call the "three Rs": relationships, redundancy, and representation. By *relationships*, we mean the internal social architecture of an organization, that is, the way in which people are predisposed to interact; by *redundancy*, an organization's ability to create slack capacity from ongoing activity; and by *representation*, the manner in which the external environment is interpreted and conveyed internally. In this chapter we demonstrate the importance of each of these "three Rs" to a network view of organization design.

RELATIONSHIPS

Network researchers study relationships in two distinct ways, first, in terms of the nature of ties (symmetry, direction, intensity, or frequency) and second, in terms of the types of network (workflow, friendship, authority, communication, or multiplex). In this section we use the latter approach, particularly focusing on workflow and friendship networks because these have a long tradition of use in both organizational design and network research (see Lincoln & Miller, 1979).

The Social Architecture of Relationships: Sociability and Solidarity

We use a model of corporate culture developed by Goffee and Jones (1998) as a framework for understanding the architecture of social relationships—that is, internal networks—within organizations. Underlying the model are two dimensions: *sociability* and *solidarity*. Goffee and Jones followed Simmel (1949) in defining sociability as the measure of sincere friendliness among members of an organization, and Durkheim (1947) in defining solidarity as the measure of an organization's ability to pursue shared objectives quickly and effectively, regardless of personal ties.

The structure of sociability is likely to comprise tight ties and dense interaction, as networks of sociable ties tend to be used frequently given the self-rewarding nature of such interactions. According to Simmel (1949), sociability is association that is valued for its own sake. Because sociability provides the joy of pure association, highly sociable organizational networks are likely to be characterized by positive social attributes such as inclusion of colleagues, a supportive context for creativity, and empathy. Constant interaction within a sociable group is also likely to lead members to develop shared interpretive schemes that shape their abilities to make sense of the world around them. Simmel (1949) noted that sociability is contingent on social location: sociability simply does not happen by chance among individuals. Therefore, highly sociable networks are also likely to be shaded by particularism evidenced by strong "in-group" cliques, compromise for the sake of friends, and indulgence of poor performers.

Solidarity is an instrumental association between individuals deriving from the division of labor (Durkheim, 1947). In contrast to sociability, networks of solidarity tend to be used only as needed, that is, as demanded by the task at hand. In periods when task demands are low, the structure of solidarity is likely to comprise loose ties and sparse interaction. In contrast, when task demands are high, ties of solidarity are constantly invoked. Organizational networks characterized by high solidarity are likely to be associated with positive attributes such as a sharp focus on the task at hand, rapid response to task developments, and optimum sharing of the information and resources necessary to get tasks completed. However, excessive solidarity can lead to hyperrationality and obsessive task orientation. Some negative attributes associated with high solidarity include instrumentality, an unhealthy bias for action (as opposed to reflection), and overbearing rationality.

Goffee and Jones (1998) defined four architectures or prototypical organizational cultures that result from varying high and low values on dimensions of sociability and solidarity: communal, cliqued, mercenary, and fragmented (see Fig. 11.1). Here we present a brief review of the model and its propositions on corporate culture, before building on it by arguing that each type of architecture might fit a different type of dynamic environment. We believe that this, in turn, has important implications for organizational design. We then draw out the role of social architecture in constituting redundancy and creating representation in organizations.

Communal Architecture.   A communal architecture arises from a network that is high in both sociability and solidarity (see Fig. 11.1, area no. 1). Relationships among organizational members are characterized by high task as well as friendship ties. Communal-type architectures are likely to be associated with the following organizational values: a great sense of belonging among members of the organization; clear mission; and equitable sharing of the labor as well as the rewards. Symbolism within the organization is likely to be highly developed in forms such as social rituals. According to Goffee and Jones (1998), communal networks are likely to have been founded and nurtured by highly charismatic leaders. On the bright side, communal architectures can be passionate, creative, intensive, loyal, fair, and equitable; working within such organizations is more than fun—it can be an obsession. In communal architectures, espoused practices and manifest behaviors are consistent. Goffee and Jones speculated that communal architectures tinged with negative sociability and solidarity can suffer serious problems. They may foster a sense of moral superiority, where beliefs are confused with objective performance, an excessive reliance on leaders, and an unwillingness to change with the circumstances around them. The Macintosh team led by Steve Jobs at Apple Computer in the early 1980s provides a good example of the positive and negative aspects of communal architectures (see Levy, 1994).

Cliqued Architecture.   A cliqued architecture is a network that is high in terms of sociability but low in solidarity (see Fig. 11.1, area no. 2).

1: COMMUNAL

Values: Sense of belonging, clear mission, equitable sharing; intense social rituals; charismatic leaders

Positive aspects: Passionate environment which is perceived as intense, loyal, fair, and equitable.

Negative aspects: Sense of moral superiority and infallibility; excessive dependence on leaders.

Redundancy supported: Duplicative (strong)

Representation: Restricted external cues; rich, unitary interpretations

Business environment: Complex and unstable, requiring synergistic innovation

2: CLIQUED

Values: Many cliques; bargaining and jockeying; use of informal authority; highly political leaders

Positive aspects: Informal atmosphere, with trusting, flexible, relaxed people.

Negative aspects: Gossip, rumor and enduring conflicts; tolerance of underperformance.

Redundancy supported: Duplicative (moderate)

Representation: Restricted external cues and sophisticated but differentiated interpretations contingent on fault-lines in coalitions.

Business environment: Differentiated local markets, where technology is critical; strategy is an aggregation of sub-unit performance.

4: FRAGMENTED

Values: Professional pride among individual specialists, personal autonomy, calculative commitment and dissent around goals.

Positive aspects: Individual producers thrive free from bureaucracy.

Negative aspects: Selfish, secretive, secluded individuals working in isolation.

Redundancy supported: Regenerative (strong)

Representation: Multiple external cues and rich, fragmented interpretations.

Business environment: Requiring little interdependence and rapid innovation e.g. to survive in faddish business cycles.

3: MERCENARY

Values: Clear mission and enemy; co-operation as a necessary evil; leaders as "winners"

Positive aspects: Swift, energetic focused; shared interests are quickly recognized; conflict and dissent constructive.

Negative aspects: Instrumentalism, ruthlessness and strife.

Redundancy supported: Regenerative (moderate)

Representation: Rich, diverse external cues and multiple, simplistic interpretations.

Business environment: Intensely competitive, with no tolerance of laggards.

HIGH   **LEVEL OF SOLIDARITY**   LOW

FIG. 11.1.   Social architecture of relationships, redundancy, and representation.

Relationships among organizational members are characterized by intense friendship ties and less intense task-related ties. A cliqued architecture is likely to be associated with the following organizational values: presence of a number of different cliques or coalitions vying for limited resources, and frequent bargaining, negotiation, or displays of power to influence resource allocation. Formal authority is less effective than informal influence in making and implementing decisions. Effective leaders in such a context are likely to need a great deal of political acumen. Cliqued architectures can be informal, trusting, flexible, relaxed, and spontaneous. Subunits and individuals that are relatively weak are likely to be tolerated and accommodated. Cliqued architectures can also suffer from enduring, destructive coalitions that color the internal environment with gossip, rumor, and negative politics. Goffee and Jones (1998) have found that many long-established large multinational organizations, such as Unilever and Philips, are particularly good examples of the cliqued type.

Mercenary Architecture. A mercenary architecture is a network characterized by low sociability and high solidarity (see Fig. 11.1, area no. 3). Relationships among organizational members are characterized by intense task-related ties and less intense friendship ties. Mercenary architectures are likely to be associated with a clear mission and a clearly identified organizational "enemy," high levels of achievement motivation among organizational members, and a view of cooperation as a necessary evil. Effective leaders in such a context are likely to be those with a proven, winning track record. On the positive side, mercenary architectures can be swift, energetic, and focused; shared interests among individuals may be quickly recognized and acknowledged; conflicts may be addressed positively and openly; and there is likely to be a shared goal of relentless improvement. However, mercenary architectures can suffer from too much instrumentalism, with plenty of suspicion, ruthlessness, and strife. Auletta's (1986) description of the House of Lehman provides great insight into an organization with a mercenary architecture.

Fragmented Architecture. A fragmented architecture is a network that is low in both in sociability and solidarity (see Fig. 11.1, area no. 4). Relationships among organizational members are few, and even those few lack intensity, whether task- or friendship-related. Fragmented architectures are likely to be associated with organizational values such as professional pride among individual specialists, high levels of personal autonomy, calculative commitment of individuals toward organizational citizenship, and dissent around organizational goals. At their best, fragmented architectures can provide appropriate individuals with freedom from bureaucracy and other organizational impediments, give them the liberty to work with whomever they chose, and direct resources toward "star" producers. Effective leaders in such a context are likely to be of the "diva" or "star" type—someone with a well-developed reputation and acknowledged expertise. On the other hand, fragmented architectures can be selfish, secretive, and secluded; they can create an atmosphere of overbearing expectation and harsh criticism; and they may lack the ability to manage or even organize collective activity. Fragmented architectures often exist in university research departments, creative organizations, and elite professional service and consulting firms that thrive on the productive genius of individual researchers, artistes, or consultants.

Dynamic Business Environments and the Social Architecture of Relationships

Although Goffee and Jones' (1998) model is a simple one, it communicates a number of sophisticated insights for thinking about the design of social relationships within organizations. The model explicitly acknowledges that there is no "one best way" in terms of social architecture. Previous research on corporate culture generally assumed that there was "one best culture" that organizations needed to adopt in order to adapt to their environment—a unitary, integrative, "strong," or communal culture (e.g., Kotter & Heskett, 1992). Current research is beginning to reveal that although strong cultures are beneficial under certain types of environmental conditions, they are less so in others (Sorensen, 2002). Indeed, research on organization design has emphasized the role of the external environment as the most important influence on the structure of organizations. We would therefore expect external business demands made by an organization's environment to shape internal networking relationships so as to foster adaptation.

The business environment that supports communal architecture is likely to be complex, dynamic, and unstable, requiring synergistic innovation arising out of teamwork among a number of organizational members. The Apple Macintosh project brought together highly talented individuals from diverse backgrounds such as computer science, graphic design, musical composition, and history, who enjoyed working together on the design of an easy-to-use personal computer.

The business environment that supports cliqued architectures is likely to be highly differentiated: complex and unstable in some sectors, simple and stable in others. In large multinational organizations that are characterized by a cliqued culture, knowledge of local markets and access to local technology is critical to the success of the organization. Strategy is likely to be a "long game," requiring the aggregation of performance outcomes over a period of time from a number of differentiated subunits, some mature and developed, others emerging and less well developed.

The business environment that supports mercenary architectures is likely to be highly competitive and intolerant of slow-moving or laggard organizations. An exercise of collective will and a bias for action are paramount. In his analysis of desertion among Confederate army units toward the end of the American Civil War, Bearman (1991) noted that soldiers from companies with high solidarity quit and deserted at higher rates than did those from companies with low solidarity because once the more competitive soldiers had decided the war was not winnable they acted on the belief that it was better to return home to pursue civilian life. Such quick thinking and rapid acting can similarly be found in financial services firms that compete for reputation and deal-making (Auletta, 1986).

The business environment that supports fragmented architectures is likely to be one that values innovations that tend to come out of the work of individuals, requires low levels of interdependence among producers, and experiences faddish business cycles. Peters' (2001) description of the researching and writing of his renowned work *In Search of Excellence* describes just such an environment. Peters and his colleague Waterman were assigned to a low-priority project in the marginal San Francisco office of McKinsey & Company to investigate the "people" side of organizational change. The insights they gathered during the course of the project rather unexpectedly resulted in a best-selling business book and a profitable consulting practice for McKinsey.

Organization Design Implications

To conclude, a key implication of the preceding discussion is that one should not take for granted the existing patterns of network relationships within an organization—there may be an issue of whether or not certain types of architectures fit a given environment. This insight, in turn, underscores the futility of designing roles and structures in organizations independent of the expected pattern of relationships, although social relationships within organizations can be reshaped by accident or design.

REDUNDANCY

The concept of redundancy is an important, but often neglected, aspect of organizational design. Redundancy is an important constraint on the reliability of an organization, and hence determines how flexible it can be. We argue that redundancy deserves attention for the benefits it can bring to the study of design. In this section we examine how social architecture interacts with redundancy in the design of organizations. We propose that there are two forms of redundancy—regenerative and duplicative—contingent on internal organizational networks and that each form may be suited to different types of business environment.

Felsenthal and Fuchs (1976) noted that the concept of redundancy was first used in the area of technical design to describe the reasoning behind elements such as spare tires in cars and emergency generators in operating rooms and elevators. The term was extended to the context of organizational design in the 1960s. Felsenthal (1980) cited as examples of redundancy the practice of requiring two or more referees to concur in the acceptance of an academic article for publication and the strategy pursued by some nations of maintaining several state intelligence agencies in parallel. This, however, still carries the connotation of a backup measure designed to insure against the failure of an organizational component and prevent adverse outcomes.

Although the term is used similarly in both of these contexts, there are two important ways in which technical and organizational redundancy differ in practice (Felsenthal & Fuchs, 1976). First, redundant technical components can be made identical and can be designed to a predictable level of reliability, but redundant people are not identical and therefore their reliability is hard to predict. Second, redundant technical components are designed to operate sequentially, so that a backup component is activated only when the main one has failed, but redundant people generally operate in parallel in such a manner that the backup individuals may not always be idling.

It is also interesting to note that the usual connotation of the term redundancy is negative. Traditionally, redundant elements of a system are the superfluous parts that can be eliminated without sacrificing functionality. In technical systems, the value of building in redundancy is recognized—for example, when it is used to insure against the risk of failure—but it is still seen as a cost to be borne. Conventional wisdom holds that organizational redundancy is a waste of resources that should be eliminated by shedding any units that duplicate the activities of others (Lerner, 1986). This kind of thinking is especially evident during periods where there is pressure to cut costs. Why, then, should we advocate designing in redundancy as a key organizational feature?

The answer is that the conventional view of redundancy is narrow and even misleading. As Landau (1969) pointed out, redundancy should have a positive connotation, inasmuch as the most robust social organizations have redundancies built in to ensure reliable performance. His list of examples, drawn from political governance mechanisms in the United States, includes the separation of powers, federalism, checks and balances, and partially concurrent terms of office. It shows how redundancy can create partial, supporting duplication and overlap.

Nonaka and Takeuchi (1995) followed Landau's lead by highlighting redundancy as an enabling condition for the knowledge-creating company. They defined redundancy as "the existence of information that goes beyond the immediate operational requirements of organizational members" (p. 80). In their view, redundancy in the form of excess information promotes the sharing of tacit knowledge and the dissolution of hierarchical barriers that impede organizational learning. Redundancy creates a strong context for combining existing knowledge in various parts of the organization, which leads to innovation.

Nonaka and Takeuchi (1995) described two methods for creating redundancy. One is to create overlap in the initial stages of developing a new concept by having competing teams work in parallel. At a subsequent stage, competing ideas are thrashed out in order to synthesize the best approach. The second way of building redundancy into the organization is the rotation of personnel between jobs in vastly different parts of the business. Such rotation is intended to help individuals gain a more rounded view of the business that can be beneficial in sharing knowledge and supporting innovation.

A review of recent literature on knowledge creation and sharing in terms of Nonaka and Takeuchi's model leads us to conceptualize redundancy in two related but distinctly different forms. We call these two forms of redundancy *regenerative* and *duplicative*. Regenerative redundancy is the ability of an organization to combine internal and external ingredients in order to create new and innovative knowledge. Duplicative redundancy is the ability of an organization to replicate exactly what it created before.

The two forms of redundancy are both present in the plural form observed in the management of fast-food outlets (Bradach, 1997). Bradach reported that maintaining two "parallel" chains of outlets within a system enhances effectiveness in restaurant chains. Company-owned units (replicated and tightly controlled from the center) and franchised units (operated in collaboration with groups of individual entrepreneurs) serve two very different purposes. The former concentrate on developing capabilities in replication, maintaining uniformity, and constraining variety. The latter help achieve system-wide adaptation to changing markets by introducing requisite variety. Personnel are regularly moved around the system, ensuring that innovations are brought to the center and uniformity is enhanced at the periphery. Likewise, Sorenson and Sorensen (2001) found that chain-owned and franchised units provide fundamentally different organizational learning capabilities.

Regenerative Redundancy

Current scholarly writing on organizational learning has pointed out the need for organizations to be able to exploit external knowledge as well as internal capabilities. Cohen and Levinthal (1990) argued forcefully that the ability of an organization to evaluate and utilize external knowledge productively is a function of the prior level of related internal knowledge. In other words, organizations have to create redundancy internally in order to absorb external knowledge.

Absorptive capacity has been shown to be critical for interfirm knowledge transfer and successful new product development within strategic alliances (e.g., Mowery, Oxley, & Silverman, 1996; Sivadas & Dwyer, 2000). More recent research suggests that the absorptive capacity of an organization is not a general propensity to acquire external knowledge indiscriminately. It is a quality that resides within the context of specific relationships that members within an organization are able to create. Lane and Lubatkin (1998) argued that absorptive capacity should be conceptualized in terms of specific dyadic relationships that organizations are able to enter into in order to acquire knowledge, whereas Kumar and Nti (1998) viewed the concept in terms of collaborative strategies adopted among a broad set of partnering firms.

In our view, absorptive capacity is a type of redundancy that we call *regenerative*. Redundant knowledge, that is, knowledge that exceeds the current working requirements of an organization, creates a partial template on which external knowledge can be grafted to create new knowledge. We see regenerative redundancy not as an indiscriminate capacity to create new knowledge, but as a specific design capability that resides within the network relationships of individuals within organizations. Cohen and Levinthal (1990) proposed that an organization's absorptive capacity "will depend on the absorptive capacities of its individual members" (p. 131). In a case study describing how Hyundai Motor Company of Korea caught up with rival global automotive manufacturers, Kim (1998) described the organization's acquisition of specific migratory knowledge through hiring a small network of knowledgeable personnel from competing firms such as British Leyland. Likewise, Cockburn and Henderson (1998) demonstrated that the cornerstone of absorptive capacity of firms in the pharmaceutical industry resides in a group of scientists that network actively with the wider scientific community in order to research and publish their findings on new drug discoveries. These studies suggest that the capacity for regenerative redundancy resides in, and is accomplished through, individuals. However, it is equally important to understand that knowledge that can be replicated through recombination does not reside in individuals alone. It is present in a set of embedding relationships that help people cooperate (Kogut & Zander, 1992) and in the contents and characteristics of the type of knowledge that is being transferred (Zander & Kogut, 1995).

Regenerative redundancy need not be confined to an organization's external domain alone. In some firms that suffer coordination loss (inter alia) due to size, this form of redundancy may help internal units collaborate with one another to help the organization innovate. Organizational units that excel at innovating tend to occupy central network positions and have high absorptive capacity (Tsai, 2001). This finding leads us to argue that regenerative redundancy is not just absorptive capacity alone, but also comprises a specific configuration of network relationships. Because regenerative redundancy requires at least some (if not significant amounts of) attention directed externally, there is a cost to pay in terms of relationships that can be cultivated internally (Burt, 1992). Therefore, we might conclude that, in terms of the Goffee & Jones model, mercenary or fragmented architectures might be the best atmosphere for creating regenerative redundancy.

It may be that sociability entails a high cost in terms of the cultivation of internal relationships. Such a cost may prove to be onerous while dealing with the "search" problem in innovation. High levels of sociability may be poorly matched with elements designed for their regenerative redundancy. The goal-directed cohesion provided by solidarity may be enough, and better suited to the task of holding groups together when tasks are somewhat interdependent. Where there is little task interdependence, not even this source of cohesion is required. However, the opposite is true in the case of replication: Dense social relations are critical to the transfer of organizational capabilities.

Duplicative Redundancy

We defined duplicative redundancy as the ability of an organization to replicate exactly what it was able to create before. This form of redundancy is clearly quite different from regenerative, and on the face of it, seems a simpler organizational problem. However, recent research has uncovered some interesting as well as surprising findings about the ability of organizations to reproduce processes and outputs.

Von Hippel (1994) noted that knowledge within organizations tends to be "sticky" in that it does not always transfer smoothly to the locus of problem solving as required. Szulanski (1996) framed this problem in terms of the transfer of best practices within organizations. He found that a number of knowledge-related factors, such as casual ambiguity and difficult relationships between the source and target, could impede internal knowledge transfer. One insight from this important line of research is that the right kind of context—or in our parlance, the right form of redundancy—needs to exist in order to help organizations reproduce forms they were capable of producing in the past. In fact, this problem has been stated in the popular business press as *If Only We Knew What We Know* (O'Dell, Grayson, & Essaides, 1998). The intuition conveyed is that organizations, by and large, lack a network of relationships that can help them leverage and recombine useful knowledge that resides internally.

According to Szulanski and Winter (2002), the ability to replicate is essential for an organization to grow and expand geographically and exploit new markets and resources. A number of large and prominent firms, such as Intel, have recognized that replicating past routines is extremely difficult. They note a number of barriers that can hinder duplicating efforts: sources that are uncooperative, strained personal relationships, internal competition, an obsession for perfectionism, and individual "copiers" who are not very mindful. This list leads us to argue that the social relations element of networks is essential for duplicative redundancy. We posit that a modicum of sociability is required to create duplicative redundancy within organizations because a threshold level of trust (as opposed to mere cooperation) is necessary for successful intrafirm knowledge transfer (Tsai & Ghoshal, 1998).

Dynamic Business Environments and Redundancy

Different types of environments require different types of redundancy. Relatively homogeneous environments might require stability and consistency provided by duplicative redundancy, whereas heterogeneous environments might benefit from regenerative redundancy (see Sorenson & Sorensen, 2001).

We propose that the social architecture that creates duplicative redundancy is fundamentally different from the one that creates regenerative redundancy. Network relationships—those that are densely and tightly connected, overlapping, and thick with social glue—might be better suited to duplicative redundancy. Such a network, found in communal or cliqued architectures, can help an organization replicate structures and processes in stable, unchanging environments.

The dense connections of sociability and solidarity in a communal architecture may be best suited to duplicative redundancy, especially in the context of "replicating exactly" when there is causal ambiguity and unclear understanding about why a certain organizational form worked well in the past under similar circumstances. Descriptions provided by Szulanski and Winter (2002) about replication teams at Intel and Bank One hint at an architecture that can be characterized as communal because the preconditions for successful replication are both positive sociability and solidarity.

The informal politicking and fluid influence structures of cliqued architectures may well work to identify and remove "sticky" barriers to internal knowledge transfer. In fact, a number of multinational organizations, such as Unilever and Philips, rely on such loose and less formal mechanisms to transfer technology and practice from one country and division to another (Bartlett & Ghoshal, 1998).

On the other hand, network relationships that have multiple and sparsely connected weak external ties (such as mercenary or fragmented architectures) might be better suited to regenerative redundancy. Such networks are rich in structural holes and are efficient at scanning for and acquiring relevant new knowledge. This can help an organization adapt to changing environments because of its reach and sensing capability.

Mercenary architectures tend to have sharp, goal-focused solidarity. Such a network might bring innovations to fruition in a relatively efficient manner as there is not much distraction in terms of energy required to support sociable relations. Deal-writing units at investment banks offer a good example of mercenary architecture with cognate regenerative redundancy. Such units produce and reproduce syndicates of partnering banks that come together rapidly to underwrite investment deals. Investment bankers are well aware of the status of all of their competitor banks and strive to develop complementary external linkages that can allow them to respond quickly to opportunities that appear in their environment (Podolny, 1994).

Fragmented architectures tend to be characterized by weak internal and strong external ties. Such architecture might be well suited to the issue of locating external information and resources. Research departments at private and public sector pharmaceutical institutions are a good example of fragmented architecture with cognate regenerative redundancy. Staff in such organizations typically tend to have external collaborators with whom they work to tackle novel theoretical and practical problems and with whom they co-author research publications (Cockburn & Henderson, 1998).

Organization Design Implications

A summary of networks' impact on redundancy is provided in Fig. 11.1. Communal and cliqued architectures constitute duplicative redundancy, whereas mercenary and fragmented architectures constitute regenerative redundancy. The relationship between social architecture and redundancy type is not quite so straightforward. Goffee and Jones (1998) clearly stated that sociability and solidarity have both positive and negative incarnations. Our discussion so far has sanguinely assumed the presence of the positive form. We believe that negative sociability and solidarity would weaken, or even destroy, an organization's capacity for regenerative or duplicative redundancy. Vitiated network relationships would significantly compromise redundancy, inasmuch as we define redundancy as a quality of relationships in the first place. The task of organization designers who take a network view is doubly complex. First, they have to discern the appropriate social architecture. Second, they have to ensure that the relationship creates, rather than hinders, the development of the type of redundancy that is required. Our propositions regarding the suitability of particular types of social architecture to the different kinds of redundancy carry important implications for current thinking in network theory. The usual view is that dense, interconnected, and close networks are redundant. As we have shown here, there are two very different kinds of redundancy. Business environments that are complex and dynamic impose a need for regenerative redundancy, whereas environments that require stable and reliable performance impose a need for duplicative redundancy.

REPRESENTATION

A central requirement for any organization is the need to process information (March & Simon, 1958). Social architectures also have an important effect on the way that organizations process information and shape individual and organizational action. We consider these vital functions to be part of the process of representation, or how the organization as a system creates common understandings for its members.

Daft and Weick (1984) proposed a model of organizations as "interpretation systems" using a few plausible assumptions concerning the ways in which organizations and environments interact. We restate three of their assumptions slightly in order to fit our perspective. First, organizations are a network of relations embedded in an open social system. This means that networking activity among organizational members occurs both within and outside of organizational boundaries. Because organizational environments are uncertain, individual boundary spanners seek out information about the environment and use that information to base their decisions and actions. Second, within organizations there is some process of cognitive aggregation that at once consolidates and blurs individual interpretation of ongoing activity: Organizational interpretations are continual, social, informed by past experience and the identity of the group, and fleshed out from a small set of salient cues (Weick, 1995). Third, organizations differ systematically in terms of the processes they use to interpret the environment, as well as in the resulting interpretations they form of their external environment. Because individuals differ in terms of what they notice in the external environment (e.g., Milliken, 1990; Sutcliffe, 1994) and organizations differ in the way in which they assemble interpretations (e.g., Isabella, 1990; Lant, Milliken, & Batra, 1992), it is plausible to assume that there is a difference in the way various organizations interpret the environment.

We use these three assumptions to try to elaborate how network relations might be used in the vital function of organizational representation. We have two kinds of representation in mind. The first we call *environmental representation*, which is the task of representing the external environment internally within the organization. As Daft and Weick (1984) theorized, organizations may have different interpretation modes that they use to understand and act on their environment. The second type of representation, which we call *identity representation*, concerns the manner in which an organization articulates its identity self-reflexively in order to shape decision and action (Dutton & Dukerich, 1991).

We contend that environmental representation makes an organization aware of demands made on it by external constituents. Organizational members' perception of the dynamism of their environment is contingent on the manner in which their networks represent it accurately. Poorly connected external networks may not be as effective in sensing dynamic and changing environments; well-connected external networks might be able to detect the tenor and quality of environmental change in good time for the organization to adapt. Organizational responses to environmental demands in turn are conditioned by identity representation—internal networks that make sense of issues that need to be attended, and then guide and coordinate appropriate action (Dutton & Dukerich, 1991). The two types of representation are intertwined as organizations largely enact their worlds through social and cognitive sensemaking devices (Weick, 1995). We contend that organizational networks, both internal and external, are the substance of organizational sense-making mechanisms.

Environmental Representation

Requisite variety is a fundamental criterion of organizational design. The complexity of an organization's scanning system must match that of its environment. Contingency theory holds that organizations in complex, dynamic environments need to have more sophisticated interpretation modes than those in simple, stable environments (e.g., Daft, Sormunen, & Parks, 1988). Interpretation of environments occurs through a number of different mechanisms (Daft & Weick, 1984; Weick, 1987): personal sources, such as individuals both internal and external to the organization; impersonal sources, such as news agencies, research reports, and the like; trial and error learning; and substitutes for trial and error learning, such as imagination, vicarious experience, stories, simulations, and other symbolic representations.

Information that leads to an organization's representation of its external environment is received and processed ultimately by individuals who are part of a social network. Individuals with far-reaching, sparse networks that span structural holes will collect a large amount of novel information, whereas individuals with closed-in and dense networks will have little information that is new or unique (Burt, 1992). In other words, whatever the quality of a piece of information, it is largely individuals who receive that information and provide the potential to render it useful. Daft and Weick's (1984) model suggests that there is an added level in the form of an organizational process that generates interpretations. Network theory predicts that the character of relationships between people in an organization fundamentally affects both the diversity of information and the quality of interpretations that are generated. A well-observed finding in organizational research is that cognitively diverse groups are very good at picking up a large variety of environmental cues, but are notoriously imperfect at pooling together coherent, usable interpretations of them (e.g., Miller, Burke, & Glick, 1998).

Orr (1996) provided a good example of the trade-off between network relationships and external representations in his ethnographic account of workers in Xerox's repair division. When Orr began observing the repair personnel, the company policy was to design them into fragmented units where they operated on their own, consulting machine-generated data about the nature of each error. Service personnel were advised to rely on the company's repair manual, a comprehensive compendium covering most contingencies that might be encountered. However, a solitary repair person working with machine-error data and manual alone was generally unable to generate a plausible interpretation of what had gone wrong and how it might be set right. In defiance of company policy, repair personnel began to seek more rich data from various users of the machine and also began informally networking with each other in order to share information and resources. The Xerox staff regularly shared "coffee mornings," trading war stories that created a repertoire of handy interpretations when confronted with a faulty machine. In other words, the repair personnel went around the fragmented architecture that was imposed on them and self-organized into a communal architecture in order to cope with the complexity of their work.

Identity Representation

Organizations create not only external representations but also internal structures that are self-consistent with a sense of identity (e.g., Meyer, 1982; Ranson, Hinings, & Greenwood, 1980). The literature on corporate culture also often makes a distinction between "strong" and "integrated" cultures as opposed to "weak" and "fragmented" ones (e.g., Deal & Kennedy, 1982; Martin, 1992), where the former are those with a self-consistent and dominant internal identity. From the perspective of network theory, we argue that the extent to which the identity of an organization is "strong" and internally consistent or "weak" and internally fragmented, and also the extent to which it is controlled externally (Pfeffer & Salancik, 1978), might depend on the character of social relations between individuals within the organization.

According to Clemens (1996), an organization's identity serves as a backdrop against which members relate to each other and to external groups and institutions. As Weick (1993) noted in his analysis of the Mann Gulch disaster, identity both enables and constrains organizational action: When faced with a rapidly advancing blaze, firefighters sometimes find it very hard to "drop their tools" and run because the tools of their trade define who they are and what they do.

In their study of the Port Authority of New York, Dutton and Dukerich (1991) articulated the role that identity plays in response to environmental change. They showed that the Port Authority initially interpreted the problem of homeless people using their facilities as an annoyance. Subsequently, when a sufficient number of employees were convinced, largely through contact with views external to the Authority, that homelessness was a major social issue and not a minor irritant, the organization changed its official stance to become more proactive, forming special project teams and funding fellowships to help solve the problem. When internal representations are no longer congruent with the demands of the environment, the resulting loss of faith in its validity/identity triggers a process of adaptation. Identity representation as a process, however, iterates organizational representation: Without accurate representations of the environment and its demands, the internal representations may be strong and consistent, but ultimately maladaptive. In the case of the Port Authority, it was encounters with people outside the organization that triggered a crisis of identity and from that came the realization that existing routines were no longer adequate for dealing with the new issue of homelessness. Thus external control of the organization may be related not only to how accurately the environment is represented, but also by how much the organization can summon itself to collective adaptation.

Dynamic Business Environments and Representation

If we assume that networks with high levels of sociability tend to focus on internal networking at the expense of external, we can hypothesize that communal and cliqued architectures might be somewhat circumscribed in the variety of environmental cues that are picked up. Conversely, fragmented and mercenary architectures might be better at collecting diverse and complex environmental data.

In addition, if we assume that a modicum of sociability and solidarity is required to form sophisticated representations of the environment, then communal architectures are likely to enact the most complex representation of their environment. Cliqued architectures might form sophisticated representations of the environment based on few cues. We can predict that mercenary architectures, given their intense goal-oriented focus, might form somewhat simple and rapid representations of the environment in relation to the data to which they have access in order to provide a justification for action. Fragmented architectures may actually be quite poor at integrating all the richness of the environmental information that they are able to collect.

The implications of architecture for identity representation are somewhat similar to those that we hypothesize for environmental representation. As noted, communal and cliqued architectures may have difficulties in obtaining the variety and richness of information that comes from a large number of distinct external sources, but any information that is received is likely to be widely and quickly shared. A common interpretation is likely to be quickly arrived at and, if the situation is routine, a reliable response will emerge. However, their relatively strong sense of identity may further restrict the information available for environmental representation. A set of shared beliefs might further restrict requisite variety by providing a "filter" that excludes potentially important information.

Communal organizations are likely to have a unitary or integrated identity. Cliqued architectures, on the other hand, are likely to feature a more differentiated sense of identity depending on the number of internal coalitions that comprise the organization. Coalitions are likely to process information about the external information consistently in terms of the various organizational fault-lines that comprise them (Lau & Murnighan, 1998). So although the amount of cues collected about the external environment might be limited, their internal representation is likely to be richly diverse.

As suggested, mercenary and fragmented architectures are better at collecting diverse cues from the environment. Mercenary architectures, although good at collecting diverse information and formulating a rapid response, may lack the ability to create strong internal structures that lead to consistent, reliable action. It may be difficult to imbed routines as established when rapid action generates appropriate responses to changing environments. In "quick or dead" environments, where "good enough is good enough" and any response is better than a late one, this economical restriction of structure may serve an organization well. Mercenary organizations are likely to have a limited set of issues around which there is a shared organizational identity, such as defeating a common enemy. Thus internal representation is likely to be differentiated, but somewhat simple.

It is hard to see how a sense of internal identity would develop in a fragmented organization and how these representations could be related to a common set of values that support action. It is interesting to note that in many
fragmented organizations, such as professional service firms, identity seems to
come from strong professional identification rather than from personal interactions within the organization. This may give a clue as to how individuals in
fragmented organizations can have a common identity without any internal
means for constructing one. We conclude that fragmented architectures would
likely have trouble agreeing on creating usable interpretations of the environment without these "borrowed" cultural norms and values.

Hansen's (1999) study of network ties required for successful knowledge
sharing across organizational subunits illustrates well the role of representation in organization design. In the context of new product development that
requires the acquisition of complex and noncodified new knowledge, the
search for new information, resources, and ideas is best done through the
medium of weak ties such as those found in fragmented architectures. As weak
ties are not expensive to maintain (when compared with strong ties), they
prove to be efficient in environmental scanning and search. However, the
transfer of complex knowledge required to actually create and market new
products requires strong (and by implication, expensive) ties such as those
found in communal architectures. Hence, according to Hansen, the problem
of knowledge sharing is a two-stage issue, with search—conveyed by weak
ties—followed by transfer—conveyed by strong ties. His research suggests
that organization designers need to carefully assess the networks implicated in
both external representation as well as internal mobilization.

Implications for Organization Design

A summary of networks' impact on representation is provided in Fig. 11.1.
Communal and cliqued organizations are likely to have somewhat restricted
access to external cues due to their strong internal focus; hence their external
representation of the environment around them might be somewhat compro-
mised. On the other hand, internal sensemaking mechanisms are likely to be
rich due to strong internal identity; interpretations of ongoing activity are
likely be unitary in communal architectures and rich and differentiated in
cliqued ones. Fragmented and mercenary architectures are likely to be biased
toward external cues but may trade that off for somewhat simplistic and fragmented internal interpretation routines. Traditional research on organization design frequently emphasized the importance of representation both in
terms of required roles (e.g., boundary spanners) and processes (e.g., scanning). What emerging research on networks can help illuminate is the man-

ner in which environmental issues are sensed and organizational action is mobilized.

CONCLUSION

In this chapter we drew on diverse areas of organization theory to develop a network view of organization design. We argued that network research can help us better understand the design of organizations in dynamic environments. To this end, we identified and elaborated on three network-related criteria that organization designers need pay attention to: relationships, redundancy, and representation. We briefly described the Goffee and Jones (1998) model of corporate culture and then moved on to situate this in the context of network and organization design research. We argued that business environments favor or select networks that respond to their demands appropriately. We then showed that organizational networks constitute designed-in redundancy and that different network ties might result in either the duplicative or the regenerative form of redundancy, hypothesizing that each form of redundancy might best fit a different environment. We concluded by proposing that networks are central to the manner in which the external environment is represented within organizations, and to the ways in which organizational action is mobilized.

Although our theorizing here is somewhat exploratory, we believe that it has radical implications for future research in both organization design and network theory. Conventional organization theory presents undersocialized accounts of actors within organizations. Current network theory, on the other hand, tends to be too "micro" in terms of focusing on the individual, or too "macro" in terms of emphasizing the extraorganizational level of analysis. The challenge is to develop a theory of design that can adequately describe the collective capabilities created by networked actors bounded within the envelope that we call "organization."

REFERENCES

Auletta, K. (1986). *Greed and glory on Wall Street: The fall of the House of Lehman*. New York: Random House.

Bartlett, C. A., & Ghoshal, S. (1998). *Managing across borders: The transnational solution.* (2nd ed.). Boston: Harvard Business School Press.

Bearman, P. S. (1991). Desertion as localism: Army unit solidarity and group norms in the U.S. civil war. *Social Forces, 70,* 321–342.

Bradach, J. L. (1997). Using the plural form in the management of restaurant chains. *Administrative Science Quarterly, 42,* 276–303.

Brass, D. (1992). Power in organizations: A social networks perspective. *Research in Politics and Society, 4,* 295–323.

Burt, R. S. (1992). *Structural holes: The social structure of competition.* Cambridge, MA: Harvard University Press.

Clemens, E. (1996). Organizational form as frame: Collective identity and political strategy in the American labor movement, 1880–1920. In D. McAdam, J. D. McCarthy, & M. N. Zald (Eds.), *Comparative perspectives on social movements: Political opportunities, mobilizing structures, and cultural framings* (pp. 205–226). Cambridge, UK: Cambridge University Press.

Cockburn, I. M., & Henderson, R. M. (1998). Absorptive capacity, co-authoring behavior, and the organization of research in drug discovery. *Journal of Industrial Economics, 46,* 157–182.

Cohen, W., & Levinthal, D. (1990). Absorptive capacity: A new perspective on learning and innovation. *Administrative Science Quarterly, 35,* 128–152.

Cross, R., Borgatti, S. P., & Parker, A. (2002). Making invisible work visible: Using social network analysis to support strategic collaboration. *California Management Review, 44,* 2, 25–46.

Daft, R. L., Sormunen, J., & Parks, D. (1988). Chief executive scanning, environmental characteristics, and company performance: An empirical study. *Strategic Management Journal, 9,* 123–139.

Daft, R. L., & Weick, K. E. (1984). Toward a model of organizations as interpretation systems. *Academy of Management Review, 9,* 284–295.

Deal, T. E., & Kennedy, A. A. (1982). *Corporate cultures: The rites and rituals of corporate life.* Reading, MA: Addison-Wesley.

Durkheim, E. (1947). *The division of labor in society.* New York: Free Press.

Dutton, J. E., & Dukerich, J. M. (1991). Keeping an eye on the mirror: Image and identity in organizational adaptation. *Academy of Management Journal, 34,* 517–554.

Felsenthal, D. S. (1980). Applying the redundancy concept to administrative organizations. *Public Administration Review, 40,* 247–252.

Felsenthal, D. S., & Fuchs, E. (1976). Experimental evaluation of five designs of redundant organizational systems. *Administrative Science Quarterly, 21,* 474–488.

Goffee, R., & Jones, G. (1998). *The character of a corporation.* New York: HarperBusiness.

Gulati, R., & Garguilo, M. (1999). Where do inter-organizational networks come from? *American Journal of Sociology, 104,* 1439–1493.

Hansen, M. T. (1999). The search-transfer problem: The role of weak ties in sharing knowledge across organizational sub-units. *Administrative Science Quarterly, 44,* 82–111.

Ibarra, H., & Andrews, S. B. (1993). Power, social influence, and sense making: Effects of network centrality and proximity on employee perceptions. *Administrative Science Quarterly, 38,* 277–303.

Isabella, L. A. (1990). Evolving interpretation as change unfolds: How managers construe key organizational events. *Academy of Management Journal, 33,* 7–41.

Kilduff, M., & Krackhardt, D. (1994). Bringing the individual back in: A structural analysis of the internal market for reputation in organizations. *Academy of Management Journal, 37,* 87–108.

Kim, L. (1998). Crisis construction and organizational learning: Capability building in catching up at Hyundai Motor. *Organization Science, 9,* 506–521.

Kogut, B., & Zander, U. (1992). Knowledge of the firm, combinative capabilities, and the replication of technology. *Organization Science, 3,* 383–397.

Kotter, J. P., & Heskett, J. L. (1992). *Corporate culture and performance.* New York: Free Press.

Krackhardt, D. (1990). Assessing the political landscape: Structure, cognition, and power in organizations. *Administrative Science Quarterly, 35,* 342–369.

Krackhardt, D., & Brass, D. J. (1994). Intra-organizational networks: The micro side. In S. Wasserman & J. Galskiewicz (Eds.), *Advances in social network analysis* (pp. 207–229). Thousand Oaks, CA: Sage.

Kumar, R., & Nti, K. O. (1998). Differential learning and interaction in alliance dynamics: A process and outcome discrepancy model. *Organization Science, 9*, 356–367.

Landau, M. (1969). Redundancy, rationality, and the problem of duplication and overlap. *Public Administration Quarterly, 29*, 346–358.

Lane, P. J., & Lubatkin, M. (1998). Relative absorptive capacity and inter-organizational learning. *Strategic Management Journal, 19*, 461–477.

Lant, T. K., Milliken, F. J., & Batra, B. (1992). The role of managerial learning and interpretation in strategic persistence and reorientation: An empirical exploration. *Strategic Management Journal, 13*, 585–608.

Lau, D. C., & Murnighan, J. K. (1998). Demographic diversity and fault-lines: The compositional demography of organizational groups. *Academy of Management Review, 23*, 325–340.

Lerner, A. W. (1986). There is more than one way to be redundant: A comparison of alternatives for the design and use of redundancy in organizations. *Administration and Society, 18*, 334–359.

Levy, S. (1994). *Insanely great: The life and times of Macintosh, the computer that changed everything.* New York: Viking.

Lincoln, J. R., & Miller, J. (1979). Work and friendship ties in organizations: A comparative analysis of relational networks. *Administrative Science Quarterly, 24*, 181–199.

March, J. G., & Simon, H. A. (1958). *Organizations.* New York: John Wiley.

Martin, J. (1992). *Cultures in organizations: Three perspectives.* New York: Oxford University Press.

Meyer, A. D. (1982). How ideologies supplant formal structures and shape response to environment. *Journal of Management Studies, 19*, 45–61.

Miller, C. C., Burke, L. M., & Glick, W. H. (1998). Cognitive diversity among upper-echelon executives: Implications for strategic decision processes. *Strategic Management Journal, 19*, 39–58.

Milliken, F. J. (1990). Perceiving and interpreting environmental change: An examination of college administrators' interpretation of changing demographics. *Academy of Management Journal, 33*, 42–63.

Mizruchi, M. S. (1992). *The structure of corporate political action: Interfirm relations and their consequences.* Cambridge: Harvard University Press.

Mowery, D. C., Oxley, J. E., & Silverman, B. S. (1996). Strategic alliances and inter-firm knowledge transfer. *Strategic Management Journal, 17* (Winter Special Issue), 77–91.

Nonaka, I., & Takeuchi, H. (1995). *The knowledge creating company: How Japanese companies create the dynamics of innovation.* New York: Oxford University Press.

O'Dell, C., Grayson, C., & Essaides, N. (1998). *If only we knew what we know: The transfer of internal knowledge and best practice.* New York: Free Press.

Orr, J. E. (1996). *Talking about machines: An ethnography of a modern job.* Ithaca, NY: Cornell University Press.

Peters, T. (2001, December). Tom Peters' true confession. *Fast Company,* pp. 78–94.

Pfeffer, J., & Salancik, G. R. (1978). *The external control of organizations: A resource dependence perspective.* New York: Harper & Row.

Podolny, J. M. (1994). Market uncertainty and the social character of economic exchange. *Administrative Science Quarterly, 39*, 458–483.

Podolny, J. M., & Page, K. L. (1998). Network forms of organization. *Annual Review of Sociology, 24*, 57–76.

Podolny, J. M., Stuart, T. E., & Hannan, M. T. (1996). Networks, knowledge, and niches: Competition in the worldwide semiconductor industry, 1984–1991. *American Journal of Sociology, 102,* 659–689.

Powell, W. W. (1990). Neither market nor hierarchy: Network forms of organization. *Research in Organizational Behavior, 12,* 295–336.

Powell, W. W., Koput, K. W., & Smith-Doerr, L. (1996). Inter-organizational collaboration and the locus of innovation: Networks of learning in biotechnology. *Administrative Science Quarterly, 41,* 116–145.

Ranson, S., Hinings, C. R., & Greenwood, R. (1980). The structuring of organizational structures. *Administrative Science Quarterly, 25,* 1–17.

Seibert, S. E., Kraimer, M. L., & Liden, R. C. (2001). A social capital theory of career success. *Academy of Management Journal, 44,* 219–237.

Shah, P. P. (2000). Network destruction: The structural implications of downsizing. *Academy of Management Journal, 43,* 101–112.

Simmel, G. (1949). The sociology of sociability. *American Journal of Sociology, 55,* 254–261.

Sivadas, E., & Dwyer, F. R. (2000). An examination of organizational factors influencing new product success in internal and alliance-based processes. *Journal of Marketing, 64,* 31–49.

Sorensen, J. (2002). The strength of corporate culture and reliability of firm performance. *Administrative Science Quarterly, 47,* 70–91.

Sorenson, O., & Sorensen, J. (2001). Finding the right mix: Organizational learning, plural forms, and franchise performance. *Strategic Management Journal, 22,* 713–724.

Stuart, T. E. (1998). Network positions and propensities to collaborate: An investigation of strategic alliance formation in a high-technology industry. *Administrative Science Quarterly, 43,* 668–698.

Sutcliffe, K. M. (1994). What executives notice: Accurate perception in top management teams. *Academy of Management Journal, 37,* 1360–1378.

Szulanski, G. (1996). Exploring internal stickiness: Impediments to the transfer of best practice within the firm. *Strategic Management Journal, 17,* 27–44.

Szulanski, G., & Winter, S. (2002, January). Getting it right the second time. *Harvard Business Review,* 62–69.

Tsai, W. (2001). Knowledge transfer in intra-organizational networks: Effects of network position and absorptive capacity on business unit innovation and performance. *Academy of Management Journal, 44,* 996–1004.

Tsai, W., & Ghoshal, S. (1998). Social capital and value creation: The role of intra-firm networks. *Academy of Management Journal, 41,* 464–476.

Uzzi, B. (1997). Social structure and competition in inter-firm networks: The paradox of embeddedness. *Administrative Science Quarterly, 42,* 35–67.

Von Hippel, E. (1994). "Sticky information" and locus of problem solving: Implications for innovation. *Management Science, 40,* 429–439.

Weick, K. E. (1987). Organizational culture as a source of high reliability. *California Management Review, 29*(2), 112–127.

Weick, K. E. (1993). The collapse of sensemaking in organizations: The Mann Gulch disaster. *Administrative Science Quarterly, 38,* 628–652.

Weick, K. E. (1995). *Sensemaking in organizations.* Thousand Oaks, CA: Sage.

Zander, U., & Kogut, B. (1995). Knowledge and speed of the transfer and imitation of organizational capabilities: An empirical test. *Organization Science, 6,* 76–92.

V

CONCLUSIONS

12

Emerging Themes From a New Paradigm

Randall S. Peterson
London Business School

Ana C. Sancovich
Cornell University

In this chapter we identify themes struck across the chapters in this volume. In doing so, we hope to provide general direction for scholars interested in pursuing the leadership and managerial implications of an increasingly dynamic business marketplace. The themes that emerge from a reading of this volume include: (a) the need to embrace paradox (i.e., even in fast-paced environments, some things need to remain stable); (b) dynamic organizations are better suited to some individuals than others (e.g., people who are more open to change are more likely to adapt to this environment successfully); (c) all managers need to be able to deal with ambiguity (i.e., ambiguity is pushed lower in the organization here as managers are more empowered to make decisions); (d) speed and experimentation are more important than flawless implementation (i.e., it is almost impossible to succeed by watching from the sidelines); and (e) knowledge is a flow more than a fixed asset (i.e., most organizations are overflowing with information—success comes in knowing which of it is timely and important).

When we brought a diverse group of organizations scholars together in March of 2001 and challenged them to "think outside their usual box" on how scholarship might change as organizations find themselves in increasingly unpredictable and dynamic business environments, we were, to be perfectly honest, wholly unsure of what would happen. One possibility was that we would all come together and talk past each other as each person thought differently about the leadership and managerial implications for his or her own research area. What actually happened, however, was something very different and exciting. We found a number of deep and fundamental themes among this diverse group of scholars. Even where scholars approached the question from completely different theoretical and historical perspectives (e.g., McGrath and Boisot coming from organizational strategy, compared with Smith and Dickson coming from an interest in individual personality), we found common ideas about the implications of the changing macroenvironment of business on the microbehavioral processes of leading and managing people. What follows are the major themes that emerged during the conference. We hope that drawing them together will provide overall direction to other scholars interested in the problem of how to manage in a dynamic organization. Thus, we hope this chapter provides direction even for those areas of management where we did not provide a chapter on a specific topic (e.g., justice, social influence, etc.).

THE NEED TO EMBRACE PARADOX

The strongest and most consistent theme across the chapters in this book is the need to accommodate what appear, in many ways, to be contradictory ideas. Much of this comes in the form of direct recognition of the need to embrace paradox. For example, one of the basic assumptions of the notion of managing in a dynamic organization is the need for flexibility and constant reconfiguration of the human resources of the organization (e.g., Dyer & Shafer; O'Connor & Adair; Smith & Dickson). And yet, there is also the acknowledged need for stability and commitment to the organization in the form of shared values (Dyer & Shafer), team cohesion (Thomas-Hunt & Phillips), and worker commitment (Dyer & Shafer; Smith & Dickson). This theme suggests that managers are not likely to succeed by simply throwing everything up in the air and preaching the need for continuous change. Employees need some kind of guiding beacon in order to remain committed to the organization.

This message is consistent with recent work suggesting two apparently contradicting ideas. The first idea is that values, culture, and subcultures in any organization need to be relatively stable and in alignment with each other to motivate employees (e.g., O'Reilly & Pfeffer, 2000). Michaels, Handfield, and Axelrod (2001), for example, focused on the need for careful recruitment, development, mentoring, and coaching of employees. This stands in contrast to others who argued that prescribed methods of leadership are not possible in fast-changing environments (e.g., Fullan, 2001). Taken at face value, these two ideas appear to contradict each other. However, the chapters in this volume point to a single reality in dynamic organizations that reconciles these two views—the need for stability at the level of firm strategy and values in tandem with the need for extreme flexibility in methods of day-to-day operation.

One of the more provocative paradoxes suggested by the authors in this volume is the need for swift trust (O'Connor & Adair) and to work simultaneously with several teams of people that any one individual barely knows

(Moreland & Argote; Smith & Dickson; Thomas-Hunt & Phillips; Wageman). The temptation of such constantly "new" teams is to weight team member contributions by irrelevant cues, especially visible demographic stereotypes such as race and gender (Littlepage, Robison, & Reddington, 1997; Littlepage & Silbiger, 1992; also see Thomas-Hunt & Phillips; Wageman). On the other hand, the more people know each other and their task, the less likely the team is to make this error (Gruenfeld, Mannix, Williams, & Neale, 1996; Kim, 1997). Many of the authors in this volume suggest that one effective way to help resolve this dilemma is by encouraging a general relationship-building culture. O'Connor and Adair and Anand and Jones, for example, suggest that successful dynamic organizations should encourage a sociable and collegial climate to encourage people to talk with each other and work together, thereby encouraging quick trust.

A second and closely related dilemma presents itself through the increasingly common work strategy of circumventing the need for face-to-face working environments. Virtual teamwork (over e-mail and other electronic media) is often touted as the future of teamwork because virtual teams are less likely to misweight team member talents based on nonskill-related characteristics (Thomas-Hunt & Phillips; Wageman; McGrath & Hollingshead, 1994; McGuire, Kiesler, & Siegel, 1987). However, this can also go too far, as virtual teams may have the tendency to treat everyone completely equally, even when they should not. Teams err when they treat people equally without regard to underlying knowledge, expertise, or skill (Boisnier & Chatman; Moreland & Argote; Thomas-Hunt & Phillips; Wageman). Thus, virtual teams are both an essential strategy for success in the dynamic organization, but also potentially a major source of danger for them. This is why Wageman specifically suggests in her chapter that virtual teams need some face-to-face time in order to build the affective side of their relationships and engage in intense interactions around task deadlines.

In addition to the direct references to paradox, there are a number of places where different authors discuss the benefits and drawbacks to particular kinds of management, implying the possibility of paradox. One such example is over the issue of uncertainty or ambiguity. McGrath and Boisot take a basically negative view of uncertainty. They suggest that because there is a great deal of uncertainty about the future in a dynamic business environment, organizations should invest in a number of small capacity change schemes so that the destabilizing effects of uncertainty can be minimized. Hodgson and White, on the other hand, take a much more positive view. They argue that managers should embrace uncertainty and then engage in the difficult learning that results in an effort to gain competitive advantage. Both authors agree that ambiguity is increased in dynamic organizations, but make separate and compelling arguments about why this is good or bad. Thus, there is a paradox to be resolved here. Uncertainty presents both a threat to the status quo as McGrath and Boisot suggest, but is also an opportunity for advancement and advantage as Hodgson and White argue.

Another example of this is found in the issue of subcultures. Boisnier and Chatman see strong culture as a necessary stabilizing force in the dynamic organization, but do not believe it needs to be organization-wide. In other words, subcultures can develop without weakening the overall culture of the organization. Others in this volume (e.g., Moreland & Argote, Wageman) see the establishment of strong subcultures as potentially disruptive and divisive. These differences reflect a basic division among those who study organizational culture between those who believe that strong subcultures can play the role of "faithful dissenter" and encourage necessary change from within, versus those who see the danger in this kind of task-related conflict turning into something more personal and disruptive (see Nemeth & Staw, 1989, for a discussion of this issue). Again, this is a paradox to be resolved. Subcultures have both negative and positive potential for dynamic organizations.

DYNAMIC ORGANIZATIONS ARE BETTER SUITED TO SOME INDIVIDUALS THAN OTHERS

The notion that some people will thrive in the dynamic organization whereas others will struggle is a common theme. The reasons backing this conclusion vary to some degree by author, but the conclusion is often repeated. Smith and Dickson, for example, take a trait approach to dynamic organizations. They argue that dynamic organizations are stressful places to work because of the unpredictability in the environment. Therefore, this should benefit people who are both low on neuroticism and high on openness to experience. In other words, people who are tolerant of stress and who thrive on change are best suited to dynamic organizations. Similar stress resistance arguments are made by Moreland and Argote.

Hodgson and White also make a related argument about people's ability to handle uncertainty. They have found that some people are much more able to deal with uncertainty than others. As a result, Hodgson and White are optimistic about the capacity of some people to develop what they call more "child-like" capabilities of having lots of energy, focusing on fun at work, and generating simple answers to simple questions. Moreland and Argote, on the other hand, are pessimistic about whether most people are prepared to handle very much ambiguity. Similarly, taking this idea up two levels of analysis, both of these chapters also asked about the role of national culture. Are some cultures more attuned to uncertainty and stress than others? This is an important question for knowing how generalizable the dynamic organization is beyond the United States and other Anglo-American national cultures that tend to embrace the idea of constant change. Indeed, Smith and Dickson build on the work of House et al. (2003) to propose that societies that prefer less ambiguity (e.g., Germany and China) will provide less suitable locations for successful dynamic organizations.

Despite their differences in relative optimism or pessimism about the long-term sustainability of dynamic organizations, however, the authors in this book who talk about individual differences all draw two strongly related conclusions. The first is the notion that some people are better suited to dynamic organizations than others. Some people will struggle with the stress and constant demand for change placed on workers by dynamic organizations. The second and related conclusion is that selection, motivation, and retention of people who are well suited to the environment is crucial to maintaining competitive advantage in a constantly changing environment.

ALL MANAGERS NEED TO BE ABLE
TO DEAL WITH AMBIGUITY

Top management team scholars have historically argued that making decisions without full information and dealing with ambiguity is a distinctive feature of the upper echelons of management (e.g., Eisenhardt, 1989; Hambrick, 1994). The authors in this volume argue, however, that this is changing in dynamic organizations. Hodgson and White's chapter, for example, suggests two interrelated ideas on ambiguity. First, they suggest that because decision making needs to be fast and decisions are being pushed further down organizations, this implies that ambiguity is being experienced at lower and lower levels in organizations as they become more dynamic. They even go one step further to suggest that this can be good for organizations as this prepares managers for senior roles earlier in their careers.

A parallel argument is also made by a number of the other authors in this volume who suggest that dynamic businesses require changing team membership (Moreland & Argote; Dyer & Shafer; Smith & Dickson; Thomas-Hunt & Phillips); task demands (Smith & Dickson; Thomas-Hunt & Phillips); and job descriptions (Dyer & Shafer; Smith & Dickson). This means that people who work in dynamic organizations play more roles than ever before—being peer, leader, and follower all at the same time (i.e., Smith & Dickson; O'Connor & Adair). They are also likely to be expected to work on multiple projects simultaneously (Dyer & Shafer; Hodgson & White). In short, the basic assumption that the business environment is becoming more fast-paced, unpredictable, and dynamic implies rather directly that the staffing in a dynamic organization needs to be reconfigurable, fluid, and flexible.

SPEED AND EXPERIMENTATION
ARE MORE IMPORTANT
THAN FLAWLESS IMPLEMENTATION

A basic tenet of the research in high velocity environments is the notion that decision speed is paramount (e.g., Eisenhardt, 1989, 1990). The authors in this volume have fleshed out the specific leadership and management implications of this idea. The most consistent way in which this idea was expressed was reconfigurability—the notion that much of the work gets done with short-term teams that are formed and reformed as environmental circumstances demand (Dyer & Shafer; Moreland & Argote; Thomas-Hunt & Phillips; Smith & Dickson; and Wageman all make this point). From this, quite a number of implications flow. Some of these implications have already been mentioned (e.g., multiple roles, multiple teams, etc.). But there are some additional implications we have not discussed. First is the need to be able to read people quickly and accurately (Boisnier & Chatman; O'Connor & Adair; Smith & Dickson) and to read faint signals from others (Hodgson & White). If work teams and configurations change often, then "new group" situations will happen often. Hence, faster trust and reading of others will result in teams performing better, quicker. If this does not happen, then there is a strong risk of miscommunication and interpersonal conflict (Moreland & Argote).

A second closely related behavioral implication of reconfigurable teams is the need to bring in expertise from outside the organization as information needs change. Teams are not just reconfiguring with existing internal people; outside experts need to be brought in on, at least, a temporary basis. This has many important implications for socialization and training into the organizational culture, the degree to which outsiders' judgments will be trusted, and (if they are temporary) what happens to the knowledge they accumulate (Moreland & Argote; Smith & Dickson; Thomas-Hunt & Phillips). In short, dynamic organizations need strong socialization or orientation programs and clear plans for knowledge management. If these are absent, the new people who do enter the organization can be wasted talent if they are not comfortable fully sharing their information quickly (i.e., a failure to socialize), are not trusted by others (i.e., a failure of the culture), or take everything with them when their temporary assignment is complete (i.e., a failure in information management).

The third behavioral implication of reconfigurable teams is the focus on the future and the need to be ready for virtually anything. The exact language used to describe this readiness for anything is different across the chapters, ranging from being preemptive to new situations (O'Connor & Adair), to being proactive in general (Dyer & Shafer), to developing real options (McGrath & Boisot). But the importance of being ahead of actual and would-be competitors (Dyer & Shafer) and continuous learning (Smith & Dyer) is consistent across this entire volume. In short, a future focus helps members to anticipate changes and respond as effectively as possible (O'Connor & Adair; McGrath & Boisot). This includes behaviors such as collaborating spontaneously (O'Connor & Adair), personal experimenting and risk taking (Hodgson & White; McGrath & Boisot), and a variety of generative behaviors (Dyer & Shafer; O'Connor & Adair).

Finally, the fourth implication of reconfigurable teams is the challenge managers have in creating organizational culture and structures that promote, rather than inhibit, requisite variety. Boisnier and Chatman, for example, specifically argue that allowing strong subcultures to develop is the answer to the requisite variety that organizations need. By allowing subcultures to grow, this provides the seeds of variety that may be needed one day by the entire organization as the environment shifts. Anand and Jones also address this issue in their network perspective on organizational design. They argue that organizational design needs to focus on (a) relationships (i.e., create a culture and structure that encourages relationships), (b) redundancy (i.e., similar to Boisnier and Chatman, they argue that different ways of working should be allowed), and (c) representation (i.e., creating a consistent story explaining how the dynamic environment relates to organizational structure). Indeed, this issue of variety is also at the very heart of McGrath and Boisot's arguments about how to create combinations of people and teams for maximum variety and best chance of survival in a constantly changing business environment.

KNOWLEDGE IS A FLOW
MORE THAN A FIXED ASSET

The importance of organizational learning has been well noted in a variety of outlets (i.e., Senge, 1990), and our authors confirm this here in noting the importance of things like continuous learning (Smith & Dickson), learning through experience (Hodgson & White; McGrath & Boisot), and learning through shared experience (Hodgson & White; Moreland & Argote). Our authors did not question this assumption. However, they did delve into what kind of learning and information flow might be unique to the dynamic organization. What many of them independently suggested is that learning in the traditional sense does not fully explain what happens in the dynamic organization. If we think of learning as acquiring, holding, and applying information, the part that fails in the dynamic organization is the holding part. Proprietary information, whether proprietary to the organization or senior compared with lower levels of management, is an increasingly difficult barrier to maintain. Information is increasingly like a flow of liquid rather than a solid that can be put on a shelf or in a file. The implications of this are multiplex. We have already mentioned some of the most important implications of this observation such as the need for continuous learning. However, there are other important behavioral implications of the idea that information is a flow rather than a commodity. Recognition and rewards, for example, need to be rethought to recognize rapid learning and quick application (Dyer & Shafer). The use of transactive memory systems (knowing who is a specialist in what subject) is probably a critical strategy in any information system where information flows quickly (see Moreland & Argote). People also need skills in framing problems and repackaging issues in creative ways in order to generate a constant stream of ideas for gaining competitive advantage (O'Connor & Adair). In other words, one brilliant strategic idea is not likely to persist as a long-term advantage.

CONCLUSION

The conference from which all of these chapters come was viewed as a learning experience, and also as a "stretch assignment." Authors were asked to do a fair amount of speculation. As such, this book is filled with many testable (but largely not empirically tested) ideas, research propositions, agendas, hypotheses, and even full models that might be explored. We believe that scholars urgently need to understand the implications of this new business environment for supporting dynamic and agile organizations. The area is ripe for exploration. Our hope is that this volume has stretched your mind and filled you with ideas for proceeding with new and stimulating research on how to lead and manage people in the dynamic organization.

REFERENCES

Eisenhardt, K. M. (1989). Making fast strategic management decisions in high-velocity environments. *Academy of Management Journal, 32,* 543–576.

Eisenhardt, K. M. (1990). Speed and strategic choice: How managers accelerate decision making. *California Managmenet Review, 32*(3), 1–16.

Fullan, M. (2001). *Leading in a culture of change.* New York: Wiley.

Gruenfeld, D. H., Mannix, E. A., Williams, K. Y., & Neale, M. A. (1996). Group composition and decision making: How member familiarity and information distribution affect process and performance. *Organizational Behavior and Human Decision Processes, 67,* 1–15.

Hambrick, D. (1994). Top management groups: A conceptual integration and reconsideration of the "team" label. *Research in Organizational Behavior, 16,* 171–213.

House, R. J., Hanges, P. J., Javidan, M., Dorfman, P. W., Gupta, V., & GLOBE Associates. (2003). *Cultures, leadership, and organizations: GLOBE, a 62 nation study* (Vol. 1). Thousand Oaks, CA: Sage.

Kim, P. H. (1997). When what you know can hurt you: A study of experiential effects on group discussion and performance. *Organizational Behavior and Human Decision Processes, 69,* 165–177.

Littlepage, G., Robison, W., & Reddington, K. (1997). Effects of task experience and group experience on group performance, member ability, and recognition of expertise. *Organizational Behavior and Human Decision Processes, 69*(2), 133–147.

Littlepage, G. E., & Silbiger, H. (1992). Recognition of expertise in decision-making groups: Effects of group size and participation patterns. *Small Group Research, 23,* 344–355.

McGrath, J. E., & Hollingshead, A. B. (1994). *Groups interacting with technology.* Thousand Oaks, CA: Sage.

McGuire, T., Kiesler, S., & Siegel, J. (1987). Group and computer-mediated discussion effects in risk decision-making. *Journal of Personality and Social Psychology, 52,* 917–930.

Michaels, E., Handfield, H., & Axelrod, B. (2001). *The war for talent.* Boston: Harvard Business School Press.

Nemeth, C. J., & Staw, B. M. (1989). The tradeoffs of social control and innovation in groups and organizations. *Advances in Experimental Social Psychology, 22,* 175–210.

O'Reilly, C. A., & Pfeffer, J. (2000). *Hidden value: How great companies achieve extraordinary results with ordinary people.* Boston: Harvard Business School Press.

Senge, P. M. (1990). *The fifth discipline.* New York: Currency Doubleday.

Author Index

A

Abakoumkin, G., 136, *162*
Abbott, A. S., 121, 123, 124, 125, *131*
Abraham, L., 101, *108*
Abrahamson, E., 66, *84*
Adair, W. L., 174, 175, 176, *179, 181*
Adamopoulos, J., 121, *131*
Adams, J. S., 118, *129*
Adler, P. S., 155, *157*
Aiken, M., 98, *110*
Aldrich, H., 202, 203, 208, *224*
Alkire, A. A., 123, *129*
Allen, N., 102, *111*
Almeida, P., 155, *157*
Amabile, T. M., 166, 168, *179*
Amason, A C., 168, *179*
Ambrenas, M., 49
Ambrose, M. L., 49, *61*
Amit, R., 208, *224*
Amos, J., 11, 16, 18, 20, 21, 23, 26, 27, 28, 30,
    31, 32, 34, *37*, 165, *181*
Amran, M. M., 222, *224*
Anand, V., 137, *157*
Ancona, D., 76, *84*, 120, *129*
Anderson, P., 222, *226*
Andrews, S. B., 228, *248*
Argote, L., 116, 118, 120, 121, *129, 131*, 136,
    141, 142, 148, 149, 150, 152, 155, 156,
    157, 158, 160
Argyris, C., 15, *35*, 69, *84*
Aronson, E., 102, *108*
Arrow, H., 116, 117, 118, *129, 130*, 151, 152,
    157, 170, *179*
Arunachalam, V., 176, *179*
Arvey, R., 101, *108*
Ashby, W. R., 106, *108*, 207, *224*

Ashforth, B. E., 94, *108*, 151, *157*
Ashkenas, R., 4, *6*, 21, *35*, 42, *61*
Auletta, K., 232, 234, *247*
Austin, J., 144, *157*
Axelrod, B., 254, *261*

B

Babcock, L., 167, *181*
Balakrishnan, P. V., 176, *181*
Baldwin, C., 223, *224*
Barham, K., 187, *199*
Barley, S. R., 91, 92, 97, 98, 99, 102, 105, *112*
Barney, J. B., 8, 14, 34, *36*, 208, 223, *224*
Baron, R. S., 71, *85*
Barrick, M. R., 52, *61*
Barsade, S. G., 174, *180*
Bar-Tal, D., 148, *158*
Bartell, G., 118, *130*
Bartlett, C. A., 240, *247*
Batra, B., 217, *225*, 241, *249*
Bauer, T. N, 154, *157*
Baum, J. A. C, 155, *157*, 203, 204, 208, *224*
Bazerman, M. H., 166, 168, 172, 175, 176,
    179, 181, 182
Bearman, P. S., 234, *247*
Becker, F., 22, *36*
Beehr, T. A., 54, *62*
Behringer, R. D., 117, 118, *133*
Bell, M. P., 151, *158*
Bell, N. E., 101, *112*
Ben Yoav, O., 167, 168, *179*
Benimov, N., 73, *84*
Benner, M., 87, 100, *108*
Bennis, W., 194, *199*
Berger, J., 122, 128, *130*

Berggen, C., 156, *157*
Berman, S. L., 152, *158*
Berscheid, E., 100, *108*
Bettenhausen, K. L., 69, *84,* 172, 173, *180*
Beyer, J., 88, 91, 92, 97, 98, 99, 102, *112*
Binney, G., 190, *199*
Bloomfield, R., 122, *130*
Bloor, G., 91, 93, 98, 99, *108*
Bojean, C. M., 103, *108*
Bono, J., 53, *62*
Boone, C., 98, 99, *110*
Borgatti, S. P., 228, *248*
Bottger, P. C., 121, *130, 133*
Bouchard, T., 101, *108*
Boudreau, J., 25, 34, *36*
Bourdieu, P., 95, *108*
Bowen, D., 52, *61*
Bowman, E. H., 209, 210, *224*
Boxall, P., 12, 10, 34, *36*
Bradach, J. L., 236, *247*
Brandt, D., 31, *36*
Brass, D. J., 228, *248*
Braver, S., 100, *108*
Brehm, J., 95, 101, *108*
Brett, J. F., 170, *180*
Brett, J. M., 174, *179, 180*
Brewer, M., 96, *109*
Bridges, W., 29, *36*
Brodt, J. F., 151, *159*
Brodt, S. E., 172, *182*
Brosseau, K. R., 74, *84*
Brown, B. J., 103, *108*
Brown, S. L., 4, 5, 6, 9, 15, 14, 33, 34, *36,* 81,
    84, 135, 152, *158,* 187, 188, *199,* 211,
    214, 219, *224*
Budner, S., 54, *61*
Burgelman, R. A., 223, *224*
Burke, L. M., 243, *249*
Burns, T., 4, 6, 99, *109*
Burt, R. S., 175, *180,* 228, 238, 243, *248*
Byrne, J. A., 187, *199*

C

Caldwell, D., 56, *63,* 102, 105, *109,* 120, *129*
Camacho, L. M., 136, *161*
Campbell, D. T., 16, *36,* 202, *224*
Campbell, R. J., 50, *62*

Cannon-Bowers, J. A., 75, *85*
Cappelli, P., 12, 24, *36*
Carli, L., 128, *130*
Carnevale, P. J., 170, 177, *180, 181*
Carroll, J., 166, *182*
Cha, S., 89, 95, 101, *109*
Chadwick, C., 152, *159*
Chaharbaghi, K., 135, *158*
Chatman, J., 56, *63, 87,* 89, 92, 95, 96, 99,
    101, 102, *109, 111*
Child, J., 8, 33, *36,* 87, *109,* 136, *158*
Chong, C. L., 76, *84*
Christenson, C., 121, 123, 124, 125, *131*
Clark, K. B., 222, 223, *224, 225*
Clausen, J. A., 101, *112*
Clemens, E., 244, *248*
Cockburn, I. M., 237, 239, 240, *248*
Cohen, A. K., 93, 99, 101, *109*
Cohen, A. R., 93, 98, 99, 100, 101, 118, *133*
Cohen, D., 30, 31, *36*
Cohen, W., 237, *248*
Cole, R. E., 155, *157*
Collins, J., 89
Collins, J. C., 21, *36,* 214, *224*
Collum, M. E., 123, *129*
Conlon, D. E., 141, *161*
Connolly, T., 71, *85*
Constant, D., 140, *158*
Conti, R., 168, *179*
Coon, H., 168, *179*
Cooper, D. M., 151, *159*
Copper, C., 151, *161*
Costa, P. T., 53, *61*
Cotton, J. L., 54, *63*
Crainer, S., 185, 191, 192, *199*
Cramton, C., 152, *158*
Cropanzano, R., 102
Cross, R., 228, *248*
Cummings, J. N, 155, *158*
Curhan, J. R., 176, *179*

D

Daft, R. L., 73, *84,* 217, *224,* 241, 242, 243, *248*
Dalzell, F., Jr., 90, *111*
Darr, E. D., 155, 156, *158*
D'Aveni, R., 4, 6
Davenport, T. H., 137, *158*

Davis, F., 118, *130*
Davis, J. H., 123, *130*
Davis, T., 28, *36*
Dawson, P., 91, 93, 98, 99, *108*
Deal, T. E., 87, 89, *109*, 243, *248*
Deci, E. L., 51, *61*
Delery, J., 10, 34, 35, *36*
Delugach, J. D., 118, *130*
DeMarie, S. M., 66, *85*
Denison, D. R., 89, *109*
Depew, D., 207, *224*
Dess, G. G., 65, 66, *84*
Devadas, R., 155, *158*
Dickson, M. W., 44, 50, 47, *61, 62*
Diehl, M., 136, *162*
Diekema, D., 128, *132*
Dilla, W. N., 176, *179*
DiTomaso, N., 89, *110*
Dixit, A K., 210, *224*
Dobzhansky, T., 205, *224*
Dodge, K. A., 118, *130*
Dorfman, P. W., 59, *62*, 257, *261*
Dosi, G., 218, *226*
Dove, R., 21, 22, 23, 27, *36*
Dovidio, J., 122, 123, 124, 125, *130*
Dowd, T. E., 101, *109*
Down, J., 152, *158*
Driskell, J. E., 154, *162*
Drolet, A L., 167, 176, *180*
Duarte, D., 66, 69, 70, 73, 77, 79, *84*
Dubrovsky, V. J., 71, *84*
Dukerich, J. M., 94, *109, 242, 244, *248*
Dunford, B., 8, *38*
Dunham, K., 31, *36*
Durkheim, E., 229, *248*
Dutton, J. E., 90, 94, 96, *109, 112*, 214, *226*, 242, 244, *248*
Dwyer, D., 90, *111*
Dwyer, F. R., 237, *250*
Dyer, L., 5, *6*, 11, 12, 14, 16, 18, 21, 23, 26, 27, 28, 29, 30, 31, 32, 34, *36, 37, 38*, 42, *61*, 87, *109*, 115, *130*, 165, *180, 181*
Dzindolet, M. T., 136, *161*

E

Eagly, A., 128, *130*
Eakin, M. E., 150, 154, *161*

Edelman, G., 205, 206, 207, *224*
Edmondson, A., 101, *109*
Egan, T. D., 151, 152, *162*
Egri, C., 103, *110*
Ehrhart, M., 47, *61*
Eibl-Eibesfeldt, E., 54, *61*
Einborn, H., 121, *130*
Eisenhardt, K. M., 4, 5, *6, 9*, 15, 14, 25, 33, 34, *36, 37*, 81, *84*, 95, 105, *110*, 135, 152, *158, 161*, 187, 188, *199*, 208, 211, 214, 219, *224*, 257, 258, *261*
Elloy, D. F., 152, *158*
Ellyson, S. L., 123, 124, *130*
Epple, D., 155, *158*
Ericksen, J., 11, 16, 18, 20, 21, 23, 26, 27, 28, 30, 31, 32, 34, *37*, 165, *181*
Essaides, N., 238, *249*

F

Fan, E. T., 118, 119, *130*, 149, 152, *158*, 172, *180*
Faraj, S., 144, *158*
Fassina, N. E., 167, *181*
Fattoullah, E., 122, *131*
Felsenthal, D. S., 235, *248*
Ferracuti, F., 93, *112*
Ferry, D., 91, *110*
Firestone, I. J., 51, *61*, 168, *180*
Fisek, M. H., 122, 128, *130*
Fisher, C. D., 54, *61*
Fisher, R., 168, 173, *180*, 203, *224*
Fishman, C., 21, *36*
Flatt, A., 105, *111*
Flynn, F., 89, 92, *109*
Foster, R., 8, 14, 21, 32, *37*
Foushee, H. C., 141, *159*
Fradette, M., 4, *6*, 14, 27, *37*
Franz, T. M., 121, 123, 124, 125, *131*
Freeman, J., 204, 211, *224*
Friedberg, J., 89, *110*
Friedberg, K., 89, *110*
Fromkin, H., 118, *130*
Frost, A. G., 121, *131*, 141, *160*
Frost, P., 103, *110*
Fry, L. W., 91, 93, 97, *110*
Fry, W. R., 168, *180*
Fuchs, E., 235, *248*

Fullan, M., 254, *261*
Fulmer, W. E., 4, *6*, 42, 43, *61*
Fussel, S., 73, *84*

G

Gagliardi, P., 90, 94, *110*
Gaines, J., 91, 93, 97, *110*
Galbraith, J. R., 105, *110*, 135, *160*
Galegher, J., 71, *85*
Gallupe, B., 78, *86*
Galunic, C., 25, *37*
Galunic, D. C., 95, 105, *110*
Gardner, T., 10, 12, 18, 34, *38*
Garguilo, M., 228, *248*
Garud, R., 213, *224*
Garvin, C. D., 151, *158*
Genovese, C., 174, *182*
Gentner, D., 174, *181*
Gersick, C. J. G., 72, 76, 78, *84*, 118, *130*
Gevers, J. M. P., 50, *61*
Ghoshal, S., 238, 239, 240, *247*
Gigone, D., 121, *130*
Ginnet, R. C., 76, 78, *84*
Gioja, L., 9, 23, 25, 27, 29, 30, 33, *37*
Gitelson, R., 54, *61*
Gladwell, M., 139, *158*
Glick, W. H., 137, *157*, 243, *249*
Glomb, T. M., 45, 60, *62*
Godin, S., 24, *37*
Goffee, R., 229, 230, 232, 233, 240, *247*, *248*
Golberg, B., 42, *63*
Golberg, L., 53, *61*
Goleman, D., 58, *61*
Goodchilds, J. D., 117, 118, *133*
Goodman, P. S., 141, *158*
Gordon, F., 72, *85*
Gordon, G. G., 89, *110*
Gowers, A., 198, *199*
Graham, J. W., 102, *110*
Grandjean, B. D., 103, *108*
Grant, R., 15, *37*
Grayson, C., 238, *249*
Greenberg, M. S., 148, *158*
Greenhalgh, L., 150, *158*
Greenwood, R., 243, *250*

Gregory, K. L., 97, 105, *110*
Grenier, R., 65, 70, 76, 78, *84*
Griffeth, R. W., 151, *162*
Grojean, M. W., 47, *61*
Gruenfeld, D. H., 116, 117, 118, 119, 121,
    124, 126, 127, *129*, *130*, *132*, *133*, 136,
    149, 151, 152, *157*, *158*, *159*, 172, 173,
    180, 255, *261*
Gruner, L., 170, *180*
Gudykunst, W. B., 174, *180*
Gulati, R., 228, *248*
Gully, S. M., 75, *85*
Gummer, B., 150, *158*
Gupta, N., 54, 59, *62*, 257, *261*
Guzzo, R. A., 44, 50, *62*

H

Hackman, J. R., 66, 67, 74, 75, 76, 78, *84*, *85*,
    118, *130*
Haeckel, S. H., 4, *6*, 27, 29, 30, *37*, 42, *62*
Hage, J., 98, *110*
Hall, D. T., 103, *110*
Hambrick, D., 257, *261*
Hamel, G., 9, 14, 15, 17, 21, 23, 27, 29, *37*,
    163, *180*
Hamilton, W. F., 210, *225*
Hampden-Turner, C. M., 198, *199*
Handfield, H., 254, *261*
Hanges, P. J., 59, *62*, 257, *261*
Hanna, C., 121, 123, *132*
Hannan, M. T., 204, 211, *224*, 228, *249*
Hansen, M. T., 140, *158*, 246, *248*
Hargadon, A. B., 89, 92, *112*, 126, *132*, 136,
    162
Harper, H. R., 196, *199*
Harrison, D. A., 151, *158*
Hastie, R., 121, *130*
Haveman, H., 204, *225*
Haywood, M., 69, 70, 77, 79, 81, 82, *84*, *85*
Hebdige, R., 93, 95, *110*
Hecksher, C., 9, 21, 25, 32, *37*
Heimer, C., 187, *199*
Heltman, K., 123, 124, *130*
Henderson, R. M., 222, *225*, 237, 239, *248*
Hendrickson, A. R., 66, *85*
Henry, R. A., 121, 122, *131*, *132*, 141, *159*

Herron, M., 168, *179*
Hertel, G., 75, *85*
Hesketh, B., 46, *62*
Heskett, J. L., 87, 90, 91, *110,* 233, *248*
Hill, C. W. L., 152, *158*
Hill, W. F., 170, *180*
Hilty, J. A., 177, *180*
Hinings, C. R., 243, *250*
Hirschman, A. O., 102, *110*
Hock, D., 9, 33, *37*
Hodgson, P., 185, 188, 191, 192, 194, *199*
Hofstede, G., 59, *62,* 91, 105, *110,* 198, *199*
Hogan, R., 52, *62*
Hogarth, R. M., 121, *130*
Hollenbeck, J. R., 45, *62*
Hollingshead, A. B., 70, *85,* 137, *159,* 173,
    177, *180,* 255, *261*
Holmer, M., 173, *181*
Horai, J., 122, *131*
House, R. J., 50, 59, *62,* 257, *261*
Hovland, C. I., 122, *131*
Hubbell, A.. P., 121, 127, *133*
Hulin, C. E., 45, 60, *62*
Hurry, D., 209, 210, *224*
Hyder, E. B., 174, *182*

I

Ibarra, H., 228, *248*
Ilgen, D., 44, 45, *62*
Illies, R., 53, *62*
Ingram, P., 155, *157*
Insko, C. A., 152, *157*
Isabella, L. A., 241, *248*

J

Jackson, D. N., 52, *63*
Jackson, J., 89, *110*
Jackson, S. E., 12, *37,* 46, 47, 50, 54, 60, *62,*
    63, 151, *159*
Jackson, T., 198, *199*
Jacob, F., 203, *225*
Janis, I. L., 122, *131*
Jarvenpaa, S. L., 73, *85,* 168, *180*
Javidan, M., 59, *62,* 257, *261*

Jehn, K. A., 152, *159,* 168, *180*
Jennings, K. R., 54, *63*
Jensen, M. A., 150, *162*
Jermier, J. M., 91, 93, 97, *110*
Jessup, L. M., 71, *85*
Jick, T., 4, *6,* 21, *35,* 42, *61*
John, O. P., 53, *62*
Johnson, S. A., 151, *157*
Jones, G., 229, 230, 232, 233, 240, 247, *248*
Jones, O., 104, *110*
Jones, T. S., 173, 174, *181*
Judge, T. A., 53, 54, *62,* 101, *110*
Julin, J. A., 151, *159*

K

Kahn, R. L., 118, *131*
Kahneman, D., 96, *110*
Kameda, T., 126, 127, *132*
Kane, A. A., 141, *157*
Kanki, B. G., 141, *159*
Kanter, R. M., 106, *110*
Kaplan, J. R., 150, *159*
Kaplan, K. J., 51, *61*
Kaplan, S., 8, 14, 21, 32, *37*
Kaswan, J., 123, *129*
Katz, D., 118, *131*
Katz, R., 150, 152, *159*
Kauffman, S., 207, *225*
Keating, C. F., 123, 124, *130*
Keith, P. M., 150, *159*
Keller, R. T., 152, *159*
Kelley, H. H., 122, *131*
Kelly, J. R., 76, *85,* 174, *180, 181*
Kennedy, A. A., 87, 89, *109,* 243, *248*
Kerr, S., 4, *6,* 21, *35,* 42, *61*
Kester, W. C., 210, *225*
Keyton, J., 150, *159*
Khan, R., 118
Kiesler, S. B., 71, 73, 74, *84, 85,* 140, *158,*
    176, *181,* 255, *261*
Kilduff, M., 228, *248*
Kilty, J., 11, 16, 18, 20, 21, 23, 26, 27, 28, 30,
    31, 32, 34, *37,* 165, *181*
Kim, L., 237, *248*
Kim, P. H., 119, *131,* 255, *261*
Kirchler, E., 123, *131*

Kirchmeyer, C., 123, *131*
Klempner, E., 121, *130*
Klimoski, R. J., 118, *130*
Knight, F. H., 219, *225*
Knoll, K., 73, *85*
Koene, B., 98, 99, *110*
Kogut, B., 155, *157*, 210, *225*, 237, *248*, *250*
Kohls, J., 152, *158*
Konradt, U., 75, *85*
Koput, K. W., 228, *250*
Koslowski, S. W. J., 75, *85*
Kotha, S., 135, *162*
Kotter, J. P., 87, 90, 91, *110*, 233, *248*
Koudsi, S., 139, *159*
Krackhardt, D., 228, *248*
Kraimer, M. L., 228, *250*
Kramer, R. M., 136, *160*
Krantz, J., 150, *159*
Kriegel, R., 31, *36*
Krishnan, R., 118, *131*, 142, *160*
Kristof, A. L., 56, *62*
Kulatilaka, N., 222, *224*
Kulik, C. T., 49, *61*
Kumar, K., 141, *162*
Kumar, R., 237, *249*
Kurzberg, T. R., 156, *158*, 176, *181*

L

Lacey, R., 136, 151, *159*
Ladd, D., 141, *159*
Laiken, M. E., 152, *159*
Lake, D., 16, 18, 34, *37*
Landau, M., 235, *249*
Lane, P. J., 237, *249*
Lant, T. K., 217, *225*, 241, *249*
Larey, T. S., 136, *161*
Larsen, R., 101, *110*
Larson, J. R., 121, 123, 124, 125, *131*
Latane, B., 143, *159*
Latham, G. P., 48, *63*
Lau, D. C., 245, *249*
Laughlin, P. R.., 121, *131*
Lawler, E. E., 31, *37*, 49, *63*, 135, *160*
Lawrence, P. R., 88, 91, *110*
Lazenby, J., 168, *179*
Leavitt, H. J., 136, 151, *159*
Ledford, G. E., Jr., 52, *61*

Lee, F., 139, *159*
Leidner, D. E., 73, *85*, 168, *180*
Lengerl, R. H., 73, *84*
Lepak, D., 34, *37*
Lepper, M., 96, *110*
Lerner, A. W., 235, *249*
Levine, E. L., 46, *63*
Levine, J. M., 15, *37*, 76, *85*, 118, *131*, 141, 148, 149, 150, 151, 152, 155, *157*, *160*, *161*
Levinthal, D. A., 156, *160*, 237, *248*
Levy, S., 230, *249*
Lewicki, R. J., 171, *181*
Lewin, K., 18, *37*
Lewin, R., 186, *199*
Lewis, K., 144, *160*
Lewis, S. A., 166, 169, *181*
Lewontin, R., 222, *225*
Liang, D. W., 121, *131*, 142, *160*
Libby, R., 121, 122, *130*, *131*
Liden, R. C., 228, *250*
Lincoln, J. R., 229, *249*
Lipman-Blumen, J., 136, 151, *160*
Lipnack, J., 69, 79, 82, *85*
Littlepage, G. E., 119, 121, *131*, 141, *160*, 255, *261*
Locke, E. A., 48, *63*
Loewenstein, J., 174, *181*
Lombardo, M. M., 185, *199*
London, M., 44, *63*
Lord, C., 96, *110*
Lorsch, J. W., 91, *110*
Louis, M. R., 96, *112*, 136, 150, *160*, *162*
Lubatkin, M., 237, *249*
Lytle, A L., 174, *180*

M

Mack, D. A., 150, *160*
Macken, P. O., 103, *108*
MacMillan, I. C., 214, 218, 219, *225*
Mael, F., 94, *108*
Magliozzi, T., 172, *179*
Maguire, S., 4, *6*
Malekzadeh, 100, *111*
Mannix, E. A., 121, 124, 126, 127, *130*, *133*, 175, *181*, 255, *261*
Mansfield, R., 103, *110*

Mantovani, G., 70,
Manuck, S. B., 150, *159*
Manz, C. C., 136, 137, *157, 160*
Mara, A., 14, *37*
March, J. G., 156, *160,* 218, 223, *225,* 241, *249*
Marks, M., 96, *111*
Marti, M. W., 71, *85*
Martin, J. A., 88, 91, 93, 94, 96, 97, 98, 101, 105, 107, *111,* 208, *224,* 243, *249*
Martorana, P. V., 119, *130,* 149, 152, *158,* 172, *180*
Matuszek, P. A. C., 154, *161*
Mayr, E., 202, *225*
McCall, M. W., 185, *199*
McCormick, B., 10, *38*
McCrae, R. R., 53, *61*
McGrath, J. E., 70, 76, *85,* 116, 118, 117, *129, 130,* 151, 152, 153, *157, 162,* 174, 177, *180, 181,* 255, *261*
McGrath, R. G., 8, 33, *36,* 136, *158,* 210, 214, 218, 219, *225*
McGuire, T., 71, *85,* 255, *261*
McKelvey, B., 4, *6*
McKersie, R. B., 165, *182*
McLaughlin, K. J., 65, 66, *84*
McLeod, P. L., 71, *85*
McMahan, G., 10, *38*
McMinn, J. G., 127, 137, *132,* 138, 148, *161*
McQueen, R., 78, *86*
Meek, P. M., 54, *63*
Mendenhall, M., 118, *131*
Metes, M., 65, 70, *84*
Meyer, A. D., 105, *111, 243, 249*
Meyer, J., 102, *111*
Meyerson, D., 136, *160*
Michaels, E., 254, *261*
Michaelsen, L. K., 141, *162*
Michaud, S., 4, *6,* 14, 27, *37*
Milgrom, P., 32, *37*
Milleman, M., 9, 23, 25, 27, 29, 30, 33, *37*
Miller, C. C., 243, *249*
Miller, D., 96, *110,* 214, *225*
Miller, J., 229, *249*
Milliken, F. J., 217, *225,* 241, *249*
Milne, C. R., 101, *109*
Milton, L. P., 148, *162*
Minton, J. W., 171, *181*
Mintzberg, H., 210, 223, *225*

Mirvis, P., 96, *111*
Mishra, A. K., 89, *109*
Mitchell, G. R., 210, *225*
Mitchell, T. R., 45, *63*
Mizruchi, M. S., 228, *249*
Moag, J., 168, 176, *182*
Mohrman, S. A., 135, *160*
Mone, E. M., 44, *63*
Monod, J., 203, *225*
Moore, D. A., 176, *179, 181*
Moore, D. M., 167, 176, *181*
Moreland, R. L., 76, *85,* 118, 121, 127, *131, 132,* 137, 138, 139, 141, 142, 147, 148, 149, 150, 151, 152, 155, *157, 160, 161*
Morgan, G., 5, *6,* 15, 21, *37*
Morris, C. G., 67, *84*
Morris, M. W., 167, 176, *180, 181*
Morrison, A. M., 185, *199*
Mount, M. K., 52, *61*
Mowery, D. C., 237, *249*
Mueller, C. W., 151, 152, *161*
Mullen, B., 151, 154, *161, 162*
Murnighan, J. K., 69, *84,* 141, *161,* 167, 172, 173, 176, *180, 181,* 245, *249*
Murphy, K. E., 43, 50, *63*
Murphy, P. R., 46, 47, 50, 54, 60, *63*
Myaskovsky, L., 121, *131,* 142, 147, 149, *161*

N

Naccari, N., 122, *131*
Nahavandi, A.., 100, *111*
Nampoori, V. P., 198, *199*
Nanus, B., 194, *199*
Naquin, C., 116, *129,* 136, *157*
Nathan, B. R., 52, *61*
Nayyar, P., 213, *224*
Neale, M. A., 121, 123, 124, 125, 126, 127, *130, 132, 133,* 168, 169, 172, 173, 175, *179, 180, 181, 182,* 255, *261*
Nelson, D. L., 150, 154, *160, 161*
Nelson, M., 122, *130*
Nelson, R. R., 208, *225*
Nemeth, C. J., 87, 90, 105, *111,* 153, *161,* 256, *261*
Nerkar, A., 210, *225*
Nohria, N., 90, *111*
Nonaka, I., 15, *37,* 197, *199,* 236, *249*

Norman, R. Z., 122, 128, *130*
Northcraft, G. B., 168, *180*
Nti, K. O., 237, *249*
Nugent, E., 135, *158*

O

O'Connor, K. M., 165, 172, 177, *180, 181*
Oddou, G., 118, *131*
O'Dell, C., 238, *249*
Oesch, J. A., 167, *181*
Ogden, T. Y., 121, 123, 124, 125, 126, 127, *132*
Okhuysen, G. A., 174, *181*
Okumura, T., 174, *179*
Olekalns, M., 174, *181*
O'Reilly, C. A., 56, *63,* 87, 88, 89, 91, 92, 93, 95, 96, 98, 101, 102, 105, 106, *109, 111, 112,* 128, *133,* 151, 152, *162,* 254, *261*
Orlikowski, B., 75, *85*
Orr, J. E., 139, *161,* 243, *249*
Ouchi, W. G., 90, *112*
Oxley, J. E., 237, *249*

P

Page, K. L., 227, *249*
Parker, A., 228, *248*
Parks, D., 242, *248*
Pascale, R., 9, 23, 25, 27, 29, 30, 33, *37*
Patenaude, J., 150, *161*
Patton, B., 168, 173, *180*
Paulus, P. B., 136, *161*
Pearce, T., 89, *111*
Pelled, L. H., 152, *161*
Penrose, E., 201, 208, *225*
Peters, T., 234, *249*
Peterson, E., 172, *182*
Peterson, R. S., 168, *181*
Peyronnin, K., 151, *159*
Pfeffer, J., 12, *37,* 45, *63,* 89, *111,* 244, *249,* 254, *261*
Phillips, K. W., 122, 123, 124, 126, 127, *132*
Pillutla, M., 167, *181*
Pindyck, R. S., 210, *224*
Pinkley, R. L., 170, 173, *180, 181*
Pisano, G., 14, *37,* 208, *226*

Podolny, J. M., 227, 228, 240, *249*
Poletes, G., 136, *161*
Polzer, J. T., 148, *162*
Popper, K. R., 221, *225*
Porras, J. I., 21, *36,* 89, *109,* 214, *224*
Porter, L. W., 49, *63*
Pottruck, D., 89, *111*
Powell, W. W., 227, 228, *250*
Prahalad, C., 14, *37*
Pratt, M. G., 92, *111*
Price, J. L., 151, 152, *161*
Price, K. H., 151, *158*
Priem, R. L., 65, 66, *84*
Prietula, M. J., 174, *182*
Propp, K. M., 123, *132*
Provine, W. B., 205, *226*
Pruitt, D. G., 164, 166, 167, 168, 169, 170, *179, 181*
Prusak, L., 30, 31, *36,* 138, 139, *158, 161*
Pucik, V., 54, *62*
Puffer, S., 92, *111*
Pulakos, E., 44, *62*
Purcell, J., 10, 34, *36*
Purdy, J. M., 176, *181*
Putnam, L. L., 173, 174, *181*

Q

Quick, J. C., 150, 154, *160, 161*
Quinn, J. B., 210, *226*
Quinn, M., 96, *111*
Quinn, R., 17, *38*

R

Rafaeli, A., 92, *111*
Raiffa, H., 164, *181*
Ramstad, P., 25, 34, *36*
Ranson, S., 243, *250*
Rasheed, A. M. A., 65, 66, *84*
Rau, D., 145, *161*
Ray, C. R., 78, *85*
Ray, R. G., 154, *161*
Reddington, K., 119, 121, *131,* 141, *160,* 255, *261*
Ridgeway, C. L., 128, *132*
Rindova, V. P., 135, *162*

Riordan, C. M., 151, *162*
Roberts, J., 32, *37*
Robison, W., 119, 121, *131,* 141, *160,* 255, *261*
Romero, A. A., 152, *157*
Rose, R., 91, 97, 98, 99, 101, 102, *111*
Ross, J., 101, *112*
Ross, L., 96, *110*
Rothstein, H., 58, *63*
Rothstein, M., 52, *63*
Rozell, D., 154, *162*
Rubin, J. Z., 166, *181*
Ruddy, T. M., 78, *85*
Rumelt, R., 218, *226*
Russell, J. C., 51, *61*
Rutte, C. G., 50, *61*
Ryan, R. M., 51, *61*

S

Sackmann, S., 91, 93, *111*
Saffold, G. S., 88, 89, *111*
Saks, A. M., 154, *162*
Salancik, G. R., 45, *63,* 244, *249*
Salas, A. M., 154
Salas, E., 75, *85,* 154, *162*
Salgado, J. F., 52, *63*
Salvaggio, A. N., 47, *63*
Sanchez, J. I., 46, *63*
Sandelands, L. E., 90, 96, *112,* 214, *226*
Saunders, D. M., 171, *181*
Saxe, L., 148, *158*
Schachter, S., 51, *63*
Schaubroeck, J., 54, *63*
Schein, E., 61, *63,* 75, 83, *85,* 92, 107, *111*
Schlundt, D. C., 118, *130*
Schocken, I., 118, *130*
Schoemaker, P., 208, *224*
Schmidt, G. W., 121, *131,* 141, *160*
Schneider, B., 43, 47, 56, 57, 61, *63*
Schuler, R. S., 12, *37,* 45, 54, *62*
Schwartz, P., 213, *226*
Schwarz, R. M., 69, *85*
Scott-Morgan, P., 14, *37*
Seibert, S. E., 228, *250*
Sellen, A. J., 196, *199*
Senge, P. M., 4, *6,* 257, *261*
Serwer, A., 15, *37*

Sessa, V. I., 151, *159*
Sethna, B. N., 71, *84*
Sewall-Wright, S., 205, *226*
Shafer, R. A., 5, *6,* 11, 14, 16, 18, 20, 21, 23, 26, 27, 28, 30, 31, 32, 34, *36, 37,* 42, *61,* 165, *180, 181*
Shah, P. P., 228, *250*
Shah, S., 141, *158*
Shapiro, D. L., 174, *180*
Shaw, J., 10, 34, 35, *36*
Shea, G. P., 50, *62*
Sherman, W., 10, 12, 25, 32, *38*
Sherman, S., 12, 25, 32, *38*
Sherwood, J. J., 154, *162*
Shoemaker, P., 208
Shuen, A., 14, *37,* 208, *226*
Siegel, J., 71, *85,* 255, *261*
Siehl, C., 91, 93, 94, 96, 97, 98, 101, 105, 107, *111*
Sifonis, J. G., 42, *63*
Silbiger, H., 141, *160,* 255, *261*
Silverman, B. S., 237, *249*
Simmel, G., 229, *250*
Simon, H. A., 223, *225,* 241, *249*
Simons, T. L., 168, *181*
Sims, H. P., 136, *160*
Sims, W., 22, *36*
Singh, S., 12, *36*
Sivadas, E., 237, *250*
Slocum, J. W., 91, 93, 97, *110*
Smith, D. B., 47, *61*
Smith, P. L., 174, *181*
Smith, W., 88, *112*
Smith-Doer, L., 228, *250*
Snell, S., 8, 34, *37, 38*
Sniezek, J. A., 122, *132*
Snyder, N. T., 66, 69, 70, 73, 77, 79, *84*
Sober, E., 222, *226*
Soeters, J., 98, 99, *110*
Sorensen, J. B., 90, 100, *112,* 233, 236, 239, *250*
Sorenson, O., 236, 239, *250*
Sormunen, J., 242, *248*
Spataro, S. A., 99, *109*
Sproull, L., 71, 73, 74, *85,* 140, 144, *158,* 176, *181*
Stack, J., 27, 28, *37,* 220, *226*
Stalker, G. M., 4, *6,* 99, *109*
Stamps, J., 69, 79, 82, *85*

Stasser, G., 121, 123, 124, *132, 133,* 141, *162*
Staw, B. M., 87, 90, 96, 101, 102, 105, *111,112,* 153, *161,* 214, *226,* 256, *261*
Steiner, I. D., 67, *85*
Stewart, D. D, 121, 124, *132*
Stewart, T. A., 137, 138, 139, *162*
Straus, S. G., 153, *162*
Strickland, O. J., 141, *159*
Stroebe, W., 136, *162*
Stuart, T. E., 228, *250*
Subirats, M., 47, *63*
Sull, D., 214, *224*
Sundstrom, E., 116, *132*
Sutcliffe, K. M., 241, *250*
Sutton, R. I., 89, 92, 96, *112,* 126, *132,* 136, *157, 162*
Swann, W. B., 148, *162*
Szilagyi, A. D., Jr., 48, *63*
Szulanski, G., 238, 239, *250*

T

Takeuchi, H., 197, *199, 236, 249*
Takla, M., 24, *38*
Taylor, L. A., 121, 123, *132*
Teece, D. J., 14, *37,* 208, 218, *226*
Tenbrunsel, A. E., 168, *182*
Terpening, W., 152, *158*
Tett, R. P.., 52, *63*
Thatcher, S. M., 152, *159*
Thierry, H., 49, *64*
Thomas-Hunt, M. C., 117, 121, 123, 124, 125, 126, 127, *132*
Thompson, L. L., 166, 167, 172, 174, 176, 177, *181, 182*
Thoreson, C. J., 54, *62*
Tindale, R. S., 126, 127, *132*
Ting-Toomey, S., 175, *182*
Tinsley, C. H., 175, *181*
Titus, W., 121, *132*
Townsend, A. M., 66, *85*
Trafimow, D., 122, *132*
Trevino, L. K., 73, *84*
Triandis, H. C., 175, *182*
Trice, H., 88, 91, 92, 97, 98, 99, 102, *112*
Trigeorgis, L., 210, 211, *226*
Trompenaars, F., 198, *199*

Trotman, K. T., 121, *132*
Truxillo, D. M., 154, *157*
Tsai, W., 228, 238, 239, *250*
Tsui, A S., 151, 152, *162*
Tuckman, B., 75, 76, *85,* 150, *162*
Tushman, M. L., 87, 88, 89, 91, 93, 95, 98, 100, 105, 106, *108, 112,* 222, *226*

U

Ulrich, D., 4, *6,* 16, 18, 21, 34, *35, 37,* 42, *61*
Ury, W., 168, 173, *180, 182*
Useem, J., 31, *37*
Uzzi, B., 228, *250*

V

Valley, K. L., 176, *179, 182*
Van der Heijden, K., 213, *226*
Van de Ven, A., 91, *110*
van Eerde, W., 49, *61, 64*
Van Knippenberg, D., 141, *162*
Van Maanen, J., 91, 92, 97, 98, 99, 102, 105, *112*
van Schie, E. C., 141, *162*
Van Velsor, E., 185
Vaughan, S. I., 124, *132,* 141, *162*
Venkatachalam, M., 55, *64*
Volberda, H., 4, *6,* 42, 49, *64*
Von Bertalanffy, L., 204, *226*
Von Hippel, E., 220, *226,* 238, *250*
von Oudenhowen, J., 59, *64*
Vroom, V., 42, 49, *64*

W

Wade-Benzoni, K. A., 168, *182*
Wageman, R., 67, 72, 74, 76, 78, 79, *85*
Wallace, M. J., Jr., 48, *63*
Walther, J. B., 78, *86*
Walton, R. E., 165, *182*
Waters, J. A., 210, 223, *225*
Watson, W. E., 141, *162*
Weber, B., 207, *224*
Webster, C., 93, *112*

Wegner, D. M., 121, *133,* 137, 152, *160, 162*
Weick, K. E., 17, *37, 38,* 136, *160,* 211, 217, *224, 226,* 241, 242, 243, 244, *248, 249, 250*
Weingart, L. R., 166, 174, *182*
Weiss, J. A., 74, *84*
Welch, J., 187, *199*
Wellbourne, T. M., 54, *62*
Wernerfeldt, B., 208, *226*
Wheatley, M. J., 186, *199*
Whisler, E. W., 121, *131,* 141, *160*
White, R. P., 185, 188, 191, 192, 194, *199*
White, S. B., 169, 173, *182*
Whitworth, B., 78, *86*
Wilkins, A. L., 90, *112*
Wille, E., 185, *199*
Williams, C., 190, *199*
Williams, D. L., 168, *180*
Williams, K. Y., 121, 124, 126, 127, 128, *130, 133,* 255, *261*
Willis, P., 93, *112*
Wilson, L., 100, *108*
Wingert, M. L., 152, *161*
Winter, S. J., 208, *225, 226,* 239, *250*
Wise, S. L., 101, *109*
Wittenbaum, G. M., 121, 123, 124, 127, *132, 133,* 141, *162*
Wolfgang, M. E., 93, *112*
Woodman, R. W., 154, *162*

Woolley, A., 80, *86*
Wright, P., 8, 12, 23, 25, 32, 35, *38*

X

Xin, K. R., 152, *161*

Y

Yan, A., 136, *162*
Yetton, P. W., 121, *130, 132, 133*
Yinger, J., 93, *112*
Yoon, K., 71, *85*
Yorges, S. L., 141, *159*
Yost, P. R., 50, *62*
Youngblood, M., 21, *38*
Yovetich, N., 152, *157*

Z

Zander, A., 118, *133*
Zander, U., 237, *248, 250*
Zelditch, M., Jr., 122, 128, *130*
Zellner, W. W., 93, *112*
Ziller, R. C., 117, 118, *133,* 148, *162*
Zimmer, I., 121, *131, 132*
Zuckerman, C., 121, 127, *133*

Subject Index

A

Accountability, 24–27, 29–30, 33, *see also*
  Human resources strategy
Adaptability, 44, 46, 174, 217–218
  myth of infinite human adaptability, 53–54
Adaptation, 203, 208, 213, 236
Agile organizations, *see* Dynamic organiza-
  tions
Agreeableness, *see* Five-factor model of
  personality
Albert Einstein Healthcare Network, 28
Ambiguity, 45, 54, 188–192, 238, 255–257
  definition, 188
  pump of, 189–190
  tolerance of, 54–56
Apple Computer, 230
Attrition, strategic, 57–58
Autonomy, 24–29, 33, *see also* Human
  resources strategy

B

Ballparking, 212–215
Bank One, 239
Biological metaphor, 203–209
Black box, 11, 34–35
Boundary-spanning, *see* Teams
British Leyland, 237

C

Capital One, 29
Center for Leadership in Dynamic Organi-
  zations, 3
Chaordic organizations, 9, 33
Charles Schwab, 31

Children, behavior of, 192–195
Cisco Systems, 15, 187
Climate strength, 47–48
Coaching,
  role of coach, 75, 77
  team coaching, 74–76
  as team leadership, 74–75
  timing of, 75–76, 78–80
  virtual teams, 76–80, 82–83, *see also* Virtual
    teams
Cohesion, 50–52, 151, 154, 254, *see also*
  Teams
Commitment, 27, 29–30, 33, 154, 254, *see also*
  Teams
Communication
  asynchronous communication, 68–70,
    see also Virtual teams
  media, 176–177, *see also* E-mail
  miscommunication, 152–154
  simplicity, 195–196, 198, 256
  surround communication, 27–28, 30, 33
Communities of practice, 27, 30
Competitive strategy, 191
Conflict, 152–154, 168, 255, 258, *see also* Role
  conflict
Conscientiousness, *see* Five-factor model of
  personality
Contingency theory, 242
Contingent workers, 45, 52, 60, 145, *see also*
  Staffing
Continuity, 24–27, 31, 33, *see* also Human
  resources strategy
Corning Glass, 187, 196
Counterculture, *see* Subculture
Creativity, 105–106, 136, 165–167, 229
Culture, 59–60, 198, 254, 255–256
  change, 61, 88, 90
  cultural fit, 56–57

Culture *(continued)*
  and negotiation, 174–175
  organizational culture, 87–89, 227, 258–
  259, *see also* Social architectures
  content vs. strength, 91–93
  strong, 87–97, 243–244
  subculture, *See* Subculture

D

Demographic characteristics, 128
Diffuse characteristics, *see* Demographic
  characteristics
Discipline, 23, 25–28, 33, *see also* Human
  resources strategy
Diversity, 136, 140, 145, 152–153, 155, 209
Drive, 23, 25–27, 33, *see also* Human
  resources strategy
Dynamic environment, 7–8, 41–42, 87, 228,
  see also Marketplace agility
  factors that create a, 4
Dynamic organizations, 9, 10, 41–42, 115,
  135–137, 163, 254
  characteristics of, 44–45, 140
  effects on transactive memory, 149–156, *see*
  also Transactive memory
  external pressures that produce, 65
  model, 5, 11–12
  stability and flexibility in, 53–54
  strategic capabilities for, 5

E

E-mail, 137, 144, 153, 176–177, 196
Employee behaviors, agility-oriented, *see*
  Marketplace agility
Employee mindset, agility-oriented, *see*
  Marketplace agility
Empowerment, 29–30, 66
Engines Plus, 220–221
Enhancing subculture, *see* Subculture
Environmental representation, *see* Organiza-
  tional design criteria
Expectancy theory, 49–50
Experiential learning, *see* Learning, trial and
  error

Expertise, 120–123, 144–145
  communication of, 122
  in dynamic organizations, 123–124
  recognition of, 121
Extroversion, *see* Five-factor model of
  personality

F

Failure, fear of, 193–194
Five-factor model of personality, 53, 256
  and dynamic organizations, 54–56
Focus, 196–197

G

Gene complex, 215–217, 223
Gene frequency, 215–217, 222–223
Genotype, 202, 207–208
Goals
  in a dynamic context, 48
  and expectancy theory, *see* Expectancy
  theory
  goal-setting, 48–49
  management by objectives, 48
Group cohesion, *see* Cohesion
Group instrumentality, *see* Group potency
Group potency, 50–51
Groups, *see* Teams
Growth, 24–27, 30, 33, *see also* Human
  resources strategy

H

Hewlett-Packard, 187
House of Lehman, 232
Human resources management, 8, 9, 18–19
Human resources strategy, 8, 9
  agility-oriented , 18, 23–26
  guiding principles, 23–25, 26, 27, 33
  policies, programs, and practices, 26–32,
  47–48
  horizontal fit, 12, 32–33
  vertical fit, 12, 26
Hyundai Motor Company of Korea, 237

I

IBM, 30
Identity representation, *see* Organizational design criteria
Incentives, *see* Rewards
Information sharing, *see* Knowledge
Inner sense, 197–198
Innovation, 166–167, 236
Instinct, Experience and intuition, *see* Inner sense
Instrumentality, 49–50, 230, 232
Intel, 239
Intellectual capital, 137, 153–154
Intelligence
  generalized, 58
  emotional, 58
International Harvester, 220
Intranet, 138–139

J

Job rotation, 140

K

Knowledge
  exchange, 121, 123, 125–126, 155–156, 230, 236–239, 245
  explicit and implicit, 197
  management, 138–139, 236, 241

L

Layoffs, 27, 31
Leadership
  and ambiguity, 189–191, 192–193
  ascribed leadership status, 124–125
  in coaching, *see* Coaching
  implications of dynamic environments, 257
  inner sense, 197–198
  Path-Goal Theory of, 50
  role for, 211, 215

Learning, 193–194, 259, *see* also Organizational competencies
  adaptive, 15, 17, 174
  continuous, 44, 259
  difficult, 190–191, 218, 255
  double-loop, *see* generative learning
  generative, 15, 17–18
  organizational, 15, 236
  single-loop, *see* adaptive learning
  in teams, 136, 143, 156
  trial and error, 194, 219, 242, 259

M

Management by objectives, *see* Goals
Marketplace agility, 11, 13, *see also* Dynamic environment
  required behaviors, 13, 16–18, 25–26
  required mindset, 13, 16, 25–26
Minority opinion, 127
Motivation, 42–43, 60–61, 254
  and expectancy theory, *see* Expectancy theory
  from group cohesion, 50–52
  motivational strategies in a dynamic context, 45–52
  and organizational justice, 47
  in virtual teams, 68–69, 78–79
Mutual enhancement, 121

N

Negotiation, 164–165
  alternatives, *see* Negotiations, BATNA
  BATNA, 169, 171, 173
  as creative problem solving, 165–167
  interest-based, 165–169, 178
  parties and preferences, 172
  planning for, 171–172
  power in, 173
  presentation, 175–177
  process of, 173–175
  reciprocity in, 174
  as social interaction, 167–169
  trust in, 167–168, 175, *see also* Trust
Network theory, 243–244, 247

Neuroticism, *see* Five-factor model of
      personality

O

Openness to experience, *see* Five-factor model
      of personality
Options, 209–215, 216–220, 221–223
Organization design, 21, 228, 259, *see also*
      Social architectures
Organization design criteria, *see also* Social
      architectures
   redundancy, 227, 234–241
      and business environments, 239–240
      duplicative, 235, 236, 238–239
      regenerative, 235, 236–238
   relationships, 227, 229–234
   representation, 227, 241–247
      and dynamic business environments,
         244–246
      environmental, 242–243
      identity, 242, 243–244
Organizational agility, 11, 19, 87
Organizational capabilities, *see* Organiza-
      tional competencies
Organizational competencies, 14–16
   exploiting temporary advantage, 15
   mobilizing rapid response, 14–15
   organizational learning, 15, 236, *see also*
      Learning
   sensing the market, 14
Organizational infrastructure, 18–23
   adaptable workplace design, *see* Workplace
      design
   flexible core business processes, 21
   fluid organization design, *see* Organization
      design
   information systems, 21–22
   performance metrics, 21, 27–28, 44
   reconfigurable outer ring, 21–23
   stable inner core, 20–21, 27–28
   values, 21, 27–28, *see also* Values
   vision, 21, 27–28
Organizational justice, 47
Organizational learning, *see* Learning
Orthogonal subculture, *see* Subculture

P

Paradox, embracing, 253–256
Performance, 44, 50
Personality characteristics, *see* Personality
      traits
Personality traits, 52–53, 198, 256
   competencies for dynamic organizations,
      55
Person-organization fit, 43, 56–57, *see also*
      Human resources strategy
Phenotype, 202, 208
Philips, 232, 239
Pooling information, 124
Port Authority of New York, 244
Process gains in virtual teams, 72, 74
   effort, 73
   knowledge and skill, 73
   strategy, 73–74, 80
Process losses in virtual teams, 68–72, 74
   effort, 68–70
   member knowledge and skill, 70–71
   task strategy, 71–72
Psychological contract, 43
Psychological reactance, 101–103

R

Real options, 209–215, 216–220, 221–223
Reconfiguration, *see* Teams, membership
      changes
Redundancy, *see* Organization design criteria
Reinforcement, *see* Rewards
Representation, *see* Organization design crite-
      ria
Requisite variety, 106, 207, 221, 236, 242, 259
Resource based view of the firm, 8
Retention, 202
Rewards, 31–32, 45–48, 259, *see also* Human
      resources strategy
   individual-based, team-based, or organiza-
      tion-based, 47
   rewarding behaviors vs. outcomes, 46–47
   short-term vs. long-term, 46
Role conflict, 45, 54, 118, *See also* Conflict
Routines, 204, 208, 210, 221–223

S

Scenarios, 213–214, 221
Selection, 31–32, 46, 60–61, 154, 202–203, 208, *see also* Human resources strategy
Serial incompetents, 24
Sociability, 229–233, 238, 245
Social architectures, 227
  cliqued architecture, 230–232, 239, 245–246
  communal architecture, 230–231, 239, 245–246
  fragmented architecture, 231–233, 238, 240, 245–246
  mercenary architecture, 231–232, 238, 240, 245–246
  of relationships, 229–233, 254
  and dynamic business environments, 233–234
Social loafing, 70, 75, 143, *see also* Process losses in virtual teams
Solidarity, 229–233, 238, 245
Springfield Remanufacturing Company, 220
SRC International, 221
Staffing, 43, 52–56
  contingent workers, 60, *see also* Contingent workers
  hiring for the organization vs. the job, 52, 154
Status, 123–128
  and negotiation, 176
  definition, 123
  diffuse characteristics, 128
  social ties, 126–128, 144
  status hierarchy, 118, 123–124, 126
  task relevant, 124–126
Stress, 45, 54, 150, 153–154
Structural inertia, 204
Subculture, 254, 255–256, 259
  consequences for strong cultures, 104–106
  counterculture, 93–94, 95–97
  definition, 91
  emergence, 93–95, 97–104
    group processes, 99–100
    individual bases, 100–104
    structural bases, 98–99

  and organizational agility, 87–88, 90, 105–106
  as a source of creativity, 105–106
  types, 94–95, 102–103

T

Talent
  open market for, 27, 29–30
  in teams, 67
  in virtual teams, 66, 70, 255
Task demands, *see also* Teams
  task familiarity, 119–120
Teams, 136
  boundaries, 79
  bounday-spanning, 116, 119
  challenges in dynamic organizations, 117–120
  membership changes, 117–119, 122–123, 145–149, 152–154, 172, 254, 257–259, *see also* Turnover
  task demands, 119–120, 122–123, *see also* Task demands
  coaching, *see* Coaching
  cohesion, 151, 153–154, *see also* Cohesion
  commitment, 151, 153–154, *see also* Commitment
  cross-functional, 140, 144
  habitual routines, *see* Virtual teams
  member knowledge, 68, 70–71, 120, *see also* Knowledge
  process and performance, 67–68, *see also* Process losses and gains in virtual teams
  temporary membership, 66
  training, *see* Training
  transactive memory in, *see* Transactive memory
  virtual, *see* Virtual teams
Temporary advantage, *see* Organizational competencies
Temporary employees, *see* Contingent workers
Training
  teams, 142–143, 146–147, 149
  on the fly, 27, 30
Transactive memory, 135, 137–138, 153–156, 259
  in teams, 140–150, 153–156

Trust, 167–168, 172, 175, 239, 254, 258, *see
    also* Negotiation, trust in
Turnover, 54, 143, 145–148, 152–153, *see also*
    Teams, membership changes
    voluntary, 31

U

Uncertainty, 188–192, 210, 212, 215–220,
    221, 255–257
    definition, 188
    in negotiation, 174–175
    perceived, 188
Unilever, 232, 239

V

Valence, 49–50
Values, 56–57, 254, *see also* Organizational
    infrastructure
    pivotal and peripheral, 91–93, 94–95
    societal values and culture, 58, 88, 89

and subculture formation, 102
Variation, 202, 204
Variety, 204, 207, 211, 213, 236
Virtual teams, 255, *see also* Teams
    asynchronous communication, 68–70
    benefits as task performing units, 66
    boundaries, 79
    coaching, *see* Coaching
    definition, 65–66
    habitual routines, 71–72, 81–82
    physical distance, 68–70

W

Westinghouse, 90
Work design
    discretionary-based, 27, 29–30, 33
Workplace design, 22

X

Xerox, 243